The Play of God

The Play of God

Visions of the Life of Krishna

by

Vanamali

Preface by
Eknath Easwaran

Foreword by
Swami Krishnananda

BLUE DOVE PRESS
SAN DIEGO, CALIFORNIA · 1996

Blue Dove Press publishes books by and about sages and saints of all
religions, as well as other spiritually and inspirationally oriented works.
Blue Dove also distributes similar books by other publishers, including various
versions of the two original and ancient works that relate the life of Krishna:
the *Shrimad Bhagavata* and the *Mahabharata*. Catalog sent free upon request.

Contact:

BLUE DOVE PRESS
Post Office Box 261611
San Diego, CA 92196
Phone: 800 691-1008
    or 619-271-0490

Special thanks to Dr. Lance Nelson
Department of Religious Studies, University of San Diego,
for inspired and unstinting help

Cover and text design: Brian Moucka,
Poppy Graphics, Santa Barbara, California

Cover art: detail from devotional Gujarati painting, courtesy of Shyamdas
Back cover photo courtesy of Bruce Burger

Thanks for help in the production of this edition to: Carlene Faucher, Mary Kowit,
Cynthia Henderson, Ellen Paul, Swami Atmarupananda, Lawrence Grinnell,
Deepak Trikannad, and Sara Pattee.

Eternal gratitude to Swami Satchidananda of Anandashram, Kanhangad, Kerala,
India, by whose grace Blue Dove Press exists.

Eternal gratitude to John Panama, without whose grace this editon would not have
come to be.

ISBN: 1-884997-07-4

Library of Congress Cataloging in Publication Data:
Vanamali
     The Play of God: Visions of the Life of Krishna / by Vanamali
                p.   cm.
     ISBN 1-884997-07-4 (pbk.)
     1. Krishna (Hindu deity)   I. Title
BL1220.V36 1995
294.5'2113--dc20   95-35071
                                                    CIP

ॐ O Vanamali![1]
Wilt Thou dance with me?
Wilt Thou walk beside me on the shore of Infinity?

Wilt Thou be my partner in the dance of Eternity?

O Vanamali!
Wilt Thou hold my hand on stony paths and thorns?

Wilt Thou teach me to play the game of the soul?

O Vanamali!
In the *Rasalila*[2] of life, wilt Thou dance with me?
     My forever-partner!
     My sole support, my only friend.

O Vanamali!
Wilt Thou guide me thru the tragedy of life?

Thru the comedy of Death?
Into the deathless realm,
Where game and players merge into One,
     in Thee,

O Vanamali!
     My only love!
Wilt Thou dance with me?

---

[1] *Vanamali* — a name of Krishna, meaning "wearer of the wildflower garland."
[2] *Rasalila* — the eternal cosmic dance between God and God's lovers.

ॐ **DEDICATION**

Thy Divine Lilas, Lord,
for my niece Lila

TABLE OF CONTENTS

BOOK THREE THE GAME SUPREME

Hari Aum Tat Sat

PREFACE
BY EKNATH EASWARAN

WHENEVER HUMANITY FACES a terrible crisis which deprives us of our direction in life, the *Bhagavad Gita* declares that God will rescue us by being born on earth as a human being. This is called *avatara* or descent of the Divine, in which the Supreme Spirit participates in the joys and sorrows of human beings and reestablishes dharma in their hearts. This has happened a number of times in the history of mankind, and I share the faith of practicing Hindus that if we long with all our hearts, a divine incarnation will appear to rescue us from this age of materialism that has tempted us to lose our way on our long march to the goal supreme.

Among all the divine incarnations we look upon Shri Krishna as *purna avatara* or the Complete One, who led the life of a cowherd whose magic flute stole the hearts of all the *gopis* and *gopas* in Brindavan. When I visited Brindavan thirty years ago, my host, who was a Vaishnava monk, showed me a garden at night in which he said, "If you have faith, you can still see Shri Krishna dancing with Radha under the tropical full moon."

This is the kind of faith and devotion that Shrimati Vanamali shows in describing the life of Shri Krishna, not only among the cowherds in Brindavan, but later on among the royal princes in Hastinapura. To me, Shri Krishna is the central figure not only in the *Bhagavatam*, but also in the *Mahabharata*, where he guides the destiny of a great country like ancient India. His is the inspiring spirit that leads the Pandavas to victory and brings about the downfall of the Kauravas. In my commentary on the *Bhagavad Gita* I have walked in the footsteps of Mahatma Gandhi to interpret the war as an internal conflict that goes on in the human heart between the forces of light and darkness. I hope that the readers of Shrimati Vanamali's *The Play of God* will find the motivation to join the forces of light in their long-drawn-out war against the forces of darkness.

FOREWORD

BY HIS HOLINESS SWAMI KRISHNANANDA

Sri Anandaya namaha

Homage to the One who is pure bliss

IT PLEASES ME IMMENSELY to know that Devi Vanamali, the author of this admirable book on the life of Bhagavan (Lord) Shri Krishna, wants me to write a few words by way of an introductory appreciation and suggestion. I have gone through this book carefully and my first impression after reading it was that this is the first attempt perhaps ever made by a scholar-devotee to present in one compact volume the multifaceted and majestic life of the Great Incarnation. What charmed me especially was the perspicacious and deeply touching style and expression in which the whole story is told so beautifully and so comprehensively.

Usually, devotees of Lord Shri Krishna confine their attention to the childhood and boyhood days of Krishna in Gokula, Vrindavan, and Mathura and even if they are a little more extended, the writings generally add only the events in Dwaraka, of Shri Krishna's regime and His social greatness as delineated in the *Shrimad Bhagavata Mahapurana.*

Very few pay sufficient attention to the wonderful deeds of the towering Krishna of the *Mahabharata*, without which facet of His life the great story would remain incomplete. It is delightful to observe that Devi Vanamali has not omitted any salient feature and has managed to press into her book the essentials of the story as we have it both in the *Shrimad Bhagavata* and the *Mahabharata.*

The divine play of the child in Vrindavan, the serious posture of a mature potentate in Dwaraka, and the transcendent power exhibited in the *Mahabharata* constitute the three chapters in the book of Shri Krishna's life. The author of this book is not merely a devotee in

xii · *The Play of God – Visions of the Life of Krishna*

the ordinary sense of the term, but one who has endeavored to saturate her very life with Krishna *bhakti*, due to which speciality in her the work glows with a fervor of spirit and a radiance of clarity in presentation. A book written by a seeker who veritably lives in the presence of the Lord will no doubt have the magnetic influence it will obviously exert on every reader of this divine saga, this chronicle of God come fully in visible form.

A reading of the life of Shri Krishna will not only be a rewarding treat as an enchanting vision of the deeds of the Divine Superman but also charge the reader's personality with an energy and vigor not to be had on this earth.

May works of this kind see the light of day in more and more numbers, for the blessing of all humankind.

Swami Krishnananda
General Secretary
Divine Life Society
Rishikesh, India
June 25th, 1989

AUTHOR'S
INTRODUCTION

ॐ

Sri Krishnaya
Paramatmane
namaha

Homage to
Krishna, the
Supreme soul

*I know of no Reality other than Lord Krishna, whose face is as
radiant as the full moon, whose color is that of the fully laden rain
cloud, whose eyes are as large and lustrous as the petals of a lotus,
whose lips are red as the bimba berry, whose hands are adorned
with the flute, and who is clad in resplendent yellow garments.*
—MADHUSUDANA SARASVATI

THE STORY OF THE LORD'S manifestation in the world
as Krishna, scion of the Yadava clan, is one which
has thrilled the hearts of all those who have been
fortunate enough to have heard it. It is the glorious tale
of how the One who is *aja*, or unborn, and *arupa*, without form, was born in this world of dualities with a form
that has delighted the hearts of people for over five thousand years. It is the story of that Infinite, Eternal One,
Who was born as Krishna, the son of the Yadava chief
Vasudeva and his wife Devaki, Who was the nephew of
Kamsa, the King of the Bhojas; Krishna, a prince Who
was born in a dungeon and brought up as a common
cowherd boy by their chieftain Nanda and his wife
Yashoda in the village of Gokula. It is the story of a man
Who was also God and of God Who was born as a man.
There is no tale comparable to it in all times.

The main facts of His life can be gathered from the
Shrimad Bhagavata and the *Mahabharata*—the first half
of the story from the former and the second from the latter. He was born in captivity in the prison of the tyrant
king Kamsa of Mathura as the son of Vasudeva and thus
was known as Vaasudeva. Immediately after birth, He
was transferred from Mathura to the cowherd settlement
of Gokula, where He grew up as the foster son of their
chief Nanda and his wife Yashoda. As a child He was

mischievous and willful, charming all with His precocious acts. At the age of twelve He went to Mathura, where He killed His uncle Kamsa, thus freeing the Yadavas from the rule of the tyrant. He grew up to be a hero, valiant and invincible, and gradually assumed leadership of the Yadava and Vrishni clans, even though He did not accept the title of "King." He defeated many of the tyrant kings and made the Yadavas into one of the most powerful forces of His time. He founded His new capital on the island of Dwaraka on the western seacoast of India, which was then known as Bharatavarsha, and played an important part in shaping the cultural and political life of His times. Though He did not take up arms, He played a decisive part in the great war of the *Mahabharata*.

As a man He was a *mahayogi*, the greatest of all *yogis*, totally unattached, having complete mastery over Himself and nature, capable of controlling the very elements, if need be. His miracles were only an outflow of His perfect unity with God and therefore with nature. The spiritual gospel which He taught is known as the *Bhagavata Dharma* and is chiefly expounded in the *Bhagavad Gita*, the *Uddhava Gita*, and the *Anu Gita*. The simplicity of His teaching was such that it could be followed by any man, woman, or child, unlike the *Vedic*[1] teachings, which were meant only for the elite. The *Vedic* religion had become elaborated into a vast system of complicated sacrificial rituals, which could be deciphered and performed only by the brahmins[2] and conducted only by the *kshatriyas*.[3] Out of the *Vedic* religion had developed the glorious philosophy of the *Upanishads*,[4] which required high intellectual ability, moral competence, and training under a qualified spiritual preceptor, or *guru*, before it could be comprehended. The advent of Lord Krishna came at a time when the common man in Bharatavarsha was without a simple religion that would satisfy his emotional wants and elevate him spiritually without taxing him too much intellectually. The *Bhagavata Dharma* provided a devotional gospel in which action, emotion, and intellect played equal parts and proclaimed Krishna as Ishvara (God), Who had incarnated Himself for the sake of humanity, Who could be communed with through love and service, and Who responded to the earnest prayers and

---

[1] *Vedic*—pertaining to the most ancient Hindu religion, based on the *Vedas*, the four scriptural books of Hinduism.
[2] *brahmin*—the traditional highest caste, comprising priests and scholars.
[3] *kshatriya*—the caste of warriors and rulers.
[4] *Upanishads*—concluding portions of the *Vedas*, dealing with the Supreme Reality.

deepest yearnings of the ordinary person. Thus, Lord Krishna was not only a precocious child, an invincible hero, and a *mahayogi*, but He was the very God Whose contact transforms even sinners into saints, ignorant men into sages, sense-bound beings into spiritual ecstatics, and even animals into devotees. Krishna is the human version of the metaphysical Satchidananda Brahman (existence-consciousness-bliss) of the *Upanishads* Who took on a human form to help the ordinary mortal who cannot rise to union with the formless *Brahman* (the Indivisible Absolute) through the path of meditation and *samadhi* (super-conscious state), as advocated in the *Upanishads*. All His human actions during the span of His earthly life are meant not only to bless His contemporaries and establish righteousness on earth, but to provide a spiritually potent account of His earthly deeds for the contemplation of posterity. By meditating on them they could establish with Him a devotional relationship like that which His great devotees had with Krishna during His lifetime. He is the expression of the redeeming love of God for man which manifests itself in different ages and in different lands, bringing spiritual enlightenment and bliss into the otherwise dreary life of humanity.

The theory of the *avatar*, or the descent of God into the human form, is one of the established beliefs of *Vaishnava*[5] theism and is very difficult for the modern mind to conceive. If we believe in the unborn, impersonal godhead of *Brahman*, how can we accept the fact that it can be born as a human personality? The *Vedantic*[6] view postulates that everything is divine. Every particle in the universe is imbued with the divine spirit. Far from the "Unborn" being unable to assume a form, *Vedanta* declares that all forms are the endless reflections of that One, Unborn Spirit Who is without beginning and without end. The assumption of imperfection by the perfect is the whole phenomenon of this mysterious universe and can only be attributed to the divine *lila*, or play. "*Avatar*" means "descent," and this descent is a direct manifestation in humanity by the divine in order to aid the human soul in its ascent to divine status. It is a manifestation from above of that which we have to develop from below. It is to give the outer religion of humanity an inner meaning which will enable it

---

5 *Vaishnava*—devotees of God as Lord Vishnu. Vaishnava's consider Krishna to be Lord Vishnu incarnate.
6 *Vedantic*—pertaining to *Vedanta*, a general term for the *Upanishads*. The philosophy based on the *Upanishads* that in ultimate reality only God exists.

to grow into divine status that the *avatar* comes. The ordinary person has to evolve and ascend into godhead, but the *avatar* is a direct descent into the human form. The one is a birth from ignorance into ignorance under the shroud of *maya*, or the cosmic veil of illusion, and the other is a birth from knowledge into knowledge, with all powers intact and a full awareness and consciousness of His supreme status. He is thus a dual phenomenon, for He appears human and is yet divine. This has to be, for the object of the *avatar* is to show that a human birth with all its limitations can still be made the means for a divine birth. If the *avatar* were to act in a superhuman way all the time, this purpose would be nullified. He might even assume human sorrow and suffering, like Christ or Shri Rama, in order to show that suffering itself may be the cause of redemption. The *Krishnavatar* is unique because even in hours of sorrow and travail, He showed Himself a complete master of the situation, thus exemplifying how one established in unity with the divine can remain unaffected in the midst of pain and sorrow. Hence, this *avatar* in the form of Krishna is known as *purnavatar*, or the complete descent of the entire divinity into the form of humanity. The *Bhagavad Purana* declares, "*Krishnasthu Bhagavan Svayam*," Krishna is the Supreme Lord in His completeness.

Even during His lifetime, He became canonized among those of His own clan, as well as among many others. He was looked upon as the incarnation of Vishnu, the godhead of *Vaishnava* theology and the Preserver in the trinity made up of Brahma, Vishnu, and Shiva. Vishnu later came to be identified with the solar deity of the *Vedas*, who is invoked in the great *Gayatri* hymn. In the course of time, Vishnu became the most dominant among the *Vedic* deities and came to be accepted as the Supreme Being. By worshipping Krishna as an incarnation of Vishnu one can gain the status achieved by striving *yogis* through the difficult forms of various *yogic* practices.[7]

The charm of His *avatar* is the perfection with which He played every role He was called upon to play. He was a staunch friend, a dutiful son, an exciting lover, and a model husband not to just one, but to all women who desired Him. There was none who called to Him with intensity to whom He did not go with all speed!

"However a man approaches Me, in that same manner do I go to Him," was His creed. In whatever guise people looked upon Him—as

---

[7] *yogic practices*—practices aimed toward achieving oneness with the Supreme.

son, lover, friend, or husband—He went to them in that very form in which they visualized Him and satisfied their desires in that way. At the same time, He sublimated their desires and thus fulfilled their earthly lives and led them to eternal bliss. There was no one who approached Him, whether saint or sinner, in hatred or fear or love who did not attain liberation. The difference between a Kamsa, who tried to kill Him, and a Kuchela, who worshipped Him, is slight indeed. One approached Him with hatred and the other with love, but both thought of Him constantly and were thus rewarded with *moksha*, or liberation. An object of mortal dread and antagonism can produce as much absorption in the mind as an object of love. If this object of dread happens to be God, concentration on Him, though motivated by antagonism, must purify the person, just as potent but unpleasant medicine still effects a cure. This is what the *Bhagavad Purana* declares.

Thus Lord Krishna is not only the *Sat-chid-ananda*, the existence-knowledge-bliss, of the Absolute without any diminution or contamination of His perfection, He is also the *Uttama Purusha*, the perfect person, amidst all imperfect situations. He is the eternal boy, the paragon of masculine beauty, Who always retains His spiritual nobility, absolutely unaffected and unperturbed in every situation, be it amidst the poverty and hardships of the cowherd settlement, the rigors of a hermitage, the seductive charms of dancing beauties, the gory scenes of the battlefield, in the self-destructive holocaust of His own kith and kin, or in peaceful interludes with His friends. As He Himself teaches, Krishna lived in this world of dualities as the lotus leaf in water, absolutely untouched and unaffected by the environment, a witness of situations, never a victim.

The river of time collects much flotsam and jetsam on its way, and the story of the Lord's life has been embellished with a wealth of detail, perhaps true, perhaps imaginary. Fact and fiction, truth and fantasy are entwined. But the final test of truth is Time itself. It is the true touchstone. It deletes the dross and retains the gold. The story of a divine manifestation is always filled with mystery and defies all attempts at human analysis. But it has the quality of being *svayamprakasha*, or self-illuminating, and therefore the person who narrates it will find illumination coming from within, for Krishna is the charioteer seated in the heart of everyone, the supreme *guru*. In and through the seemingly redundant detail that has woven itself around the story through the centuries, it retains its breathtaking beauty, for it is dominated by the powerful influence of Krishna's enchanting personality, in which the wisdom of the seer is mingled with the charm and simplicity of a child and the glory of God gushes forth in an inexhaustible fountain of divine love and wisdom.

The story of such a life can only be written by His grace and can only be understood by His grace. May that grace flow into us, inspire and enlighten us, and lead us to eternal bliss!

> Though I'm totally incapable of grasping
> Even the fringes of Thine infinite majesty,
> Yet due to Thy supreme grace alone
> I have dared to compile these lines
> Containing the story of
>   Thy playful incarnation.

> For this I ask Thy forgiveness.

> May Thy choice blessings of long life, good health,
>   and supreme beatitude
> Be showered on all those who listen
> To this account of Lord Narayana,
> Narrated by Narayana Himself
> In the form of my beloved Lord—
>   Vanamali.

Glory to Lord Krishna—Vanamali—the wearer of the garland of wildflowers.

Devi Vanamali
Vanamali Ashram
Lakshmanjhula, Rishikesh
India

Hari Aum Tat Sat

Publisher's
INTRODUCTION

Readers may wonder why Devi Vanamali's name on the cover appears to be abbreviated, appearing as "Vanamali" only. The reason is significant. Though outwardly speaking she is the author of this volume, she herself insists that it is not her work, but that it was given to her by Krishna. Understanding herself to be an instrument, not the author, she therefore insisted that her name not be on the front cover at all. Still, it happens that her favorite among the traditional epithets of Krishna is "Vanamali" (Wearer of the Wildflower Garland) and that, following Indian custom, she has adopted this name as her own for religious purposes. This circumstance made it possible for us to preserve a certain meaningful ambiguity in the cover copy by listing the author simply as Vanamali. Still, Devi Vanamali's name and photo does appear on the back cover, but only at our repeated insistence, to which she acquiesced only with great reluctance.

The Play of God is a kind of spiritual literature that has no exact analogy in the West. It is designed as a device to inspire and deepen one's loving devotion (*bhakti*) to God. The essence of its message is that only unconditional love of the Divine and a life of service of God in our fellow beings will in the end provide a solution to the dilemmas of existence.

I first met Devi Vanamali in Rishikesh, India, where I visited her small but attractively appointed ashram overlooking the Ganges. Later, during her first and only visit to America, I arranged for some speaking engagements for her in San Diego, where many people fell in love with her. Although she is in her late fifties, she has in both appearance and actions the aura of a woman perhaps in her early thirties. She is simple, childlike, and humble, yet where spiritual principles are involved she can be diamond hard. When people would project hostility or confusion in her direction she had a way of cutting through it, directly and lovingly striking the core. I felt very privileged to spend time with her.

At one of her talks, someone asked about whether Krishna is an actual historical figure. Her answer was interesting. Devi, whose whole life is lived in devotion to her Lord Krishna, said that if it was proved that Jesus Christ was not an actual historical figure, many Christians would feel that the underpinnings of their faith had been destroyed. But if it was proved that Krishna was not an actual historical figure, Hindus would hardly care! The message of this book is of a reality that transcends cultural and historical particularities.

We hope you are inspired by this delightful work as much as we have been.

Jeff Blom,
for Blue Dove Press

ॐ

BENEDICTION

THE INCARNATION OF SHRI KRISHNA is the complete manifestation of the supreme Brahman, whose very nature is Consciousness. Hiding His real form behind the veil of His own *maya*, He played out many *lilas* or divine games. The *Shrimad Bhagavata*, which is a jewel among scriptures, contains an account of His supernatural powers and invokes that pure devotion which is the best way to attain Him.

These topics have been very beautifully brought out in a lucid and erudite style in the book about the Supreme Person, to which Devi Vanamali has given the title *The Play of God*.

I hope by reading this immensely beneficial book, English-speaking readers will get a proper understanding of the meaning and significance of Truth, which will enable them to make their own lives purposeful and blessed.

In remembrance of God,

Swami Jayendra Sarasvati
Reigning Shankaracharya
Kanchipuram
April 14th, 1989

ॐ TILL MY ADVENT, O UDDHAVA, a dip in
the Ganges was supposed to eradicate
all sins, but now a dip in the holy story of
My life is enough to cleanse the sins of a
thousand lifetimes.

He who listens to the story of My life
sanctifies himself.

—Lord Krishna,
in the *Shrimad Bhagavata*

The
Play
of
God

BOOK ONE

BALA LILA

THE PLAY
OF THE CHILD

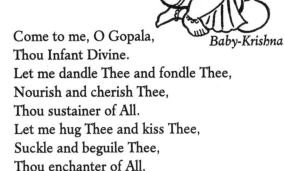

Baby-Krishna

Come to me, O Gopala,
Thou Infant Divine.
Let me dandle Thee and fondle Thee,
Nourish and cherish Thee,
Thou sustainer of All.
Let me hug Thee and kiss Thee,
Suckle and beguile Thee,
Thou enchanter of All.

What need have I for anything,
When Thou art nestling in my heart?
Exalted am I, enriched, divine,
When Thou art dancing in my mind.
Come to me then, O Gopala,
Thou Infant divine.
Nourish me and cherish me,
For I am Thy child.

ॐ INVOCATION

Sri Krishna Dwaipayanaya namaha

Homage to sage Vyasa

I bow to Lord Ganesha.
May He remove all obstacles and grant
The highest spiritual perfection.

Adorations to Thee,
O Krishna Vanamali!
At Thy lotus feet is offered
This immortal garland of
Unfading blossoms, depicting
Thy divine *lilas*.

Salutations to Thee, O Vyasa of keen intellect,
Whose eyes are like the petals of a fully blossomed lotus,
By whom was lit the lamp of wisdom
Filled with the oil of the *Mahabharata*.

Humble prostrations to Shri Vyasa,
From whose nectar-like writings, the *Shrimad Bhagavata*
    and the *Mahabharata*,
The salient features of Lord Krishna's *lilas* have been
    gathered.

Salutations to Shri Shuka, the son of Vyasa,
Who was born enlightened,
Who wandered forth alone from the time of his birth,
Renouncing home and relations,
Having realized the Vedantic truth of nonduality,
He is one with the Self of all things,

Grateful prostrations to thee, O Shuka,
Thou eternally enlightened boy-sage, from whose
    immortal words
Narrated in the *Shrimad Bhagavata*,
The stories of the early life of the Lord's *lilas*
    have been gleaned.

Prostrations to all the sages and saints
Through whose grace this humble storyteller
Has been emboldened to undertake the stupendous task
Of narrating the *lilas* of the greatest incarnation, the Purna Avatar.

Prostrations to Thee, O Mother Bharatavarsha (India),
The Holy Land, birthplace of countless sages,
In whose immaculate womb the Lord was born,
On whose bosom He acted His cosmic drama,
And on whose dust the footprints of His lotus feet are still imprinted.

May Lord Narayana, who took on the auspicious form of Krishna,
Adorned with the wildflower garland,
Grant me protection on all sides with His divine accouterments—
The mace, the conch, the discus, the bow Saranga, and the sword Nandaka.

I offer humble prostrations at the lotus feet of my beloved preceptor,
Shri Jayendra Sarasvati,
Who has blessed me in countless ways.

I bow to the *guru*, who is Brahma, Vishnu, and Maheshvara (Shiva),
Who is the supreme, transcendental Brahman.

I bow to the *guru*,
Who has removed the blindness of ignorance
By applying the collyrium of wisdom.

The focus of meditation is the form of the *guru*.
The objects of worship are the feet of the *guru*.
The *mantra* is the holy word given by the *guru*,
Liberation is due to the grace of the *guru* alone.

I meditate on the form of my most illumined preceptor,
Shri Jayendra Sarasvati,
The glorious successor in the line of the brilliant Shri Shankaracharya,
Who removed the ignorance of the world.

Hari Aum Tat Sat

ONE

THE ADVENT

Vishnave namaha

Homage to Vishnu, the all–pervading One

Whenever virtue declines and unrighteousness prevails, I manifest Myself as an embodied being in order to protect the good, to destroy evil, and to establish dharma (righteousness). For this I am born in every age.
—*SHRIMAD BHAGAVAD GITA*

This was the solemn promise made by the Lord and for this He incarnated Himself in the city of Mathura as the son of Devaki and Vasudeva.

Five thousand years ago the city of Mathura was ruled by the tyrant King Kamsa. He was the chief of the tribe of the Yadavas, who were made up of many different clans such as the Bhojas, Vrishnis, Dasharhas, and Andhakas. He was reputed to be the incarnation of the wicked demon Kalanemi, and his actions proved the truth of it. None of the Yadava chiefs dared to say a word against him, since Kamsa was known for his atrocities.

In other parts of Bharatavarsha (the ancient name of India) also there seemed to be an upsurge of wicked rulers and a consequent upsurge of unrighteous behavior, for as the king is, so are the subjects. The earth was groaning under the weight of their iniquities, and unable to bear the load of wickedness any longer, she is said to have taken on the form of a cow and approached the Lord Vishnu in His divine abode of Vaikuntha. She reminded Him of His promise that He would incarnate Himself whenever righteousness declined.

"So be it," He said. "I shall incarnate Myself in the city of Mathura in the clan of the Yadavas as the son of Devaki and Vasudeva, to whom I made a promise in another age that I would be born as their son."

3

Pleased by this assurance, the earth goddess began to prepare herself for the advent of the Lord. The stage was being set for the mighty drama. All the lesser gods and celestial beings took birth in the Yadava clan to be ready to welcome the Lord and to participate in His *lila*, or play. For what reason would that unmanifest Being want to manifest Himself except to delight in His own playful exploits? The celestials knew that this was to be the supreme culmination of all His incarnations—a tremendous play of the divine clothed in human form, inexplicable and mysterious as nature herself, yet simple and easy to love as a flower, which can be appreciated even by a child, but still is full of a deep and inner meaning to the scientist, the seer, and the sage. So also the Lord's life, when looked at with the eyes of wisdom, will reveal to us not only the nature of the universe but our own nature, for He is none other than the Self within us.

Kamsa had a sister called Devaki, who was as pure as he was depraved. Her beauty rivaled that of the celestials and could be outshone only by the radiance of her mind, which was as perfect as any mortal woman's could be. She was a fitting recipient of the signal honor of being the mother of God. In her previous births she had practiced many austerities in order to get the Lord as her son. This was her last birth, and for the third time she would carry the Lord in her womb. Vasudeva, too, was a noble soul and belonged to the Yadava clan.

When the curtain rose for the first act, the scene was one of revelry and joy, for Devaki, the only sister of Kamsa, was being given in marriage to Vasudeva. The bridal couple came out of the palace preceded by Kamsa and followed by a throng of relatives and royal guests. The fanfare of bugles and the sound of melodious songs filled the air, which was drenched with the perfumes rising from hundreds of incense burners and the jasmine flowers scattered in profusion. Devaki herself was just sixteen years of age, shining with happiness and beauty and laden with jewels, and her head was bent with modesty as well as the weight of the flowers decorating it. She clung to her brother's arms as he lifted her into the flower-bedecked bridal chariot. Vasudeva jumped in beside her and prepared to start the journey to their palace. Then, to everyone's surprise, Kamsa ordered the charioteer to step down and he himself took the reins, as if to show the extent of his love for his cherished sister. This act did not pass unremarked. That the King of the Bhojas would stoop to be a mere charioteer for the sake of his sister was news indeed! The populace cheered wildly; though they hated him, they could not but appreciate this particular deed, for Devaki was a great favorite. Moreover, it was always expedient to cheer the king, for who knew what spies were around and whose head would roll on the morrow?

Devaki, however, was supremely content. Her cup of happiness was full to the brim and she cast a tremulous look of gratitude at this stern brother who had so far shown her nothing but kindness. It was her wedding day and she was marrying the man of her choice. What more could she want? But her happiness was to be short-lived, as all human happiness is. The minds of the wicked are unpredictable. They know not the meaning of true love, and they can love only so long as it benefits them. They are incapable of a love that transcends the self. This was soon to be proved.

As the procession set out, the auspicious sounds of the conch and kettledrums were heard. The four mettlesome horses sprang forward and were whipped by Kamsa so they went forward at a spanking pace. But hardly had they gone a few yards when the sky became overcast, thunder rumbled, and lightning flashed and a mighty voice split the clouds and froze the entire wedding party to immobility.

"O Kamsa, beware! The hour of your death draws nigh! The eighth son of Devaki will kill you and deliver this land from your wickedness," thundered the voice in the sky.

For one startled second none spoke and Kamsa stared at the heavens, while from his nerveless fingers the reins fell unheeded and there rose in his heart a fear so great that he trembled from the very force of the emotion, so awe-inspiring had the voice been. Devaki clung to her husband's arm and hid her face in terror. In a trice the sky cleared, the sun appeared, the rumbling died away, and the excited people started to babble. But Kamsa wasted not a moment. Jumping out of the chariot, he caught hold of Devaki's jasmine-laden hair and pulled her down to the ground beside him. Drawing his sword from its scabbard, he hoisted it aloft to bring it down upon her defenceless and jewel-laden neck. At that moment, Vasudeva sprang down between them and catching hold of Kamsa's hand said, "O Kamsa! Where has your honor gone? Where has your code of *kshatriya* (warrior) chivalry fled that you can think of killing your own sister and that, too, at the time of her wedding, before her desires have been fulfilled? O hero! You have enhanced the fame of the Bhojas (Yadava clan) by your heroic deeds and do you now stoop to such a heinous act? Death is certain for everyone. It may come today or a hundred years hence, but it is certain. Those who do such things will suffer both here and in the hereafter. This girl is your own sister and helpless as a doll. It is most unbecoming of you to think of killing this innocent creature!"

Kamsa shook off his restraining hand as if to say, "Woman or girl or sister, what do I care? From today she is my enemy. For me, my own life is much more important than that of a sister!" Again he lifted his arm and again Vasudeva restrained him and tried another argument to restrain him from his evil resolve.

"O dear Brother-in-law! Why do you have to kill Devaki? What has she done? According to the ethereal voice it is only her child, and her eighth child at that, who is fated to kill you. Spare her therefore and I give you my word as a man of honor to bring to you every child of ours, be it boy or girl, for you to do with as you wish."

This logic seemed to work. At last the threatening arm was lowered and the cruel hold on Devaki's hair was loosened. Kamsa turned and looked piercingly at Vasudeva. "What you say is true. I know you for a man of honor and I shall believe your word. Moreover, I have ways and means of seeing that you do not forget your promise. Go! And take her with you. I can no longer bear to look at her face."

A moment ago there was none so dear to him as his sister and now there was none so hated. Without a backward glance, Kamsa left the couple stranded on the streets and drove off as the people, trembling with fear, made way for him. Outwardly they stilled their joy, but inwardly their hearts rejoiced when they thought of his approaching end, and they blessed Devaki to have a child every year so that the time would pass quickly and the eighth child, their deliverer, would be born in eight years. Sadly Vasudeva escorted his bride to his own house unaccompanied by music and dancing. An hour ago they were the most envied couple in the whole kingdom; now no one dared to look at them.

The people's prayers were answered and within a year Devaki gave birth to a lovely baby boy. The umbilical cord had hardly been cut when Vasudeva hurried with the child to Kamsa's palace, disregarding Devaki's pleas that she should be allowed to nurse the child at least once. For a man of wisdom there is no object that cannot be given up and no sorrow that cannot be borne.

Impressed by Vasudeva's adherence to truth and his extreme equanimity Kamsa said, "Let this child be taken back. He poses no threat to me. It is only from your eighth child that I am destined to die. Take the infant back to my sister and tell her that her brother is not as cruel as she thinks."

Far from being happy at this show of leniency, Vasudeva was perturbed at this unexpected turn of events, for he well knew how vacillating are the minds of the wicked. One day he would speak thus and the next he would change his mind; by then they would have become attached to the infant. It would have been easier to have parted with it now, when it lay quiescent and unresisting in his arms, than later, when it would start to smile and talk and wind its little arms round his neck and his heart, thus making the parting more heartbreaking.

So Vasudeva left the palace with bent head, clutching the child and trying not to look at him, trying not to love him too much, for as a wise man he knew it was better not to become too attached to something from which he would soon have to be parted.

Thus, six years flew by on wings and every year saw the birth of another baby boy to the couple. Vasudeva would faithfully take each child to Kamsa, who would return it as a gift. By all rights, the couple should have been blissfully happy. They had each other, they had six lovely boys, each more beautiful than the last, and they kept to themselves without mixing in court life and intrigue. They said their prayers and purified themselves by vows and fasts in order to prepare themselves for the advent of their eighth child, who would be the Lord Himself. But all the time they felt as if they were balanced on the edge of a precipice. No one could tell when the delicate balance would be upset and they would be plunged into the swirling waters below.

It was at this time that the celestial sage Narada went to the court of Kamsa in order to play his small part in hastening the advent. If Kamsa started showing signs of leniency, the Lord would take longer to incarnate Himself, for it is only when wickedness reaches its zenith than an incarnation is called for. So armed with his *vina* (stringed instrument) he entered the audience chamber of the king. Kamsa hardly glanced at him, for he did not consider a mendicant like him, who went about singing the Lord's praises, to be worthy of respect. Narada, however, was unperturbed.

Strumming his *vina* he said softly, "I hear, O King, that you are not keeping too well these days, not so much at the peak of your powers of observation as you were before."

"What!" Kamsa said, rising up in anger. "What makes you speak such arrant nonsense! I never felt better in my life!"

Now that the king had taken notice, Narada quietly took his seat, uninvited, and continued amicably, "I hear that you had your sworn enemy within your grasp and yet you let him slip away like a wily fish from the hook of an inexpert angler."

"You heard wrong," shouted the enraged king. "There's no enemy either big or small who has ever come within my grasp and lived to tell the tale. But what can you, a mere singer of ballads, know of deeds of valor?"

"I think your memory is getting poor, O Kamsa!" Narada taunted. "Have you forgotten the prophecy at the time of Devaki's marriage that you have allowed six of her children to slip from your grasp? Is this the action of a shrewd man?"

"And why not?" shouted the irate king. "Since you seem to know so much about it, you should also know that it was the eighth child who was denounced in the prophecy and not the first or sixth or any other!"

"Poor Kamsa," Narada commiserated in his gentle voice. "There's so much you don't know. But don't make the mistake of underestimating your enemy. He is Vishnu, the master magician who can delude the entire world into believing anything. He can make eight into one and one into eight. If you count from the top downward, the last is the eighth, but if you count from the bottom upward, what happens? The first becomes the eighth, and if you put them in a circle and count, what happens? Any one of them could be the eighth! You're living in a fool's paradise, my poor man, lulled into a feeling of false security, which is exactly what He wants you to feel. Moreover, you should realize that this is all a master plot on the part of the *devas* (gods) to kill the *asuras* (demons). You, O Kamsa, are the great *asura* of old called Kalanemi. The rest of your clan, with a few exceptions, are all *devas* involved in the mighty plot to annihilate you and your kind. Of this you are ignorant, poor Kamsa, and that is why, at long last, even though I know you despise me, I came to warn you, for I am a true well-wisher of the world. I want nothing but the well-being of the universe."

So saying Narada quietly left strumming his *vina*, just as he had come, unannounced and unescorted. He left behind a stunned Kamsa, aghast at his stupidity in having let six children go free. There was not a moment to be lost. Six years of folly had to be retrieved in a day. He summoned all his evil counselors, Kesi, Putana, and others, and started a regular campaign of suppression of the Yadavas with the backing of his father-in-law, Jarasandha, the powerful king of Magadha. A campaign of terror followed in which he mercilessly murdered all those whom he suspected of being *devas*, so that there was a panic among all the good people and a general exodus out of the city into the outlying districts, where they went into hiding. Vasudeva sent his first wife, Rohini, to the house of Nanda, the cowherd chief of Gokula, who was a friend of his. Kamsa's father, Ugrasena, remonstrated with him and warned him of the consequences of his atrocious deeds. Kamsa spoke not a word, but quietly had his father removed and clapped into jail. Then he turned the full force of his fury on his sister and her husband. One by one their children were taken up and smashed to death on a rock before their horrified eyes! What is it that the wicked will not resort to in order to save their own skins? Vasudeva's worst fears were realized. Devaki saw but one child being killed, and then mercifully fell into a deep swoon. Dry-eyed and stony-hearted, Vasudeva watched until the bitter end. As his children were savaged, one thought alone sustained him: he and his wife were still alive and capable of bearing children. Whatever happened, however much they suffered, theirs would be the fortune to be the instruments by which the divine purpose would be fulfilled. Only two more years, he exulted, and then the prophecy would come true. Their work on earth would be done and the reason for their birth accomplished. So great was his faith and devotion that not even the ghastly scene before him had the power to move him. But even this hope was soon dashed, for Kamsa decided that the best place for this traitorous couple would be the dungeon, next to his father, where he would be able to keep an eye on their doings. So he clapped them in jail, with guards on duty night and day.

Soon Devaki conceived for the seventh time. The land was groaning under the weight of Kamsa's iniquities and the prayers of the people were rising in a constant stream, so, it is said, that the Lord Vishnu decided that He could not wait for another year before incarnating Himself. Such is the force of mass prayer, as Narada had foreseen. The Lord commanded His *yogamaya*, or *shakti* (feminine force of action), as follows, "O Devi (goddess), you must go to Vraja, the cowherd settlement, to the house of Nanda, where Rohini, the wife of Vasudeva, has taken refuge. My spiritual power known as Shesha has already entered the womb of Devaki. Transplant the fetus from her womb into Rohini's. Soon after, I shall incarnate Myself in Devaki's womb, and you, O Devi, will be born as

Yashoda's daughter. You will be the bestower of boons to all and will be worshipped on earth under many names."

Being thus ordered by the Lord, the goddess transferred herself to the earth and accomplished all that she was expected to do. The news was bruited abroad that Devaki's seventh pregnancy had been aborted. Hearing the news, Kamsa suspected a trick and went himself to the dungeon to find out the truth.

"Is it true that you conceived for the seventh time?" he thundered.

"Yes," replied Devaki meekly.

"Then what happened to the child?" he enquired suspiciously.

"I don't know," she whispered, and in truth she did not, for who can know the ways of God? She had been pregnant until a few days ago and then suddenly she had felt her womb to be empty.

Kamsa ruminated for a while. Trick or no, the next child would surely be the eighth. Since prevention was better than cure, he decided to prevent the couple from conceiving at all and gave instructions for heavy chains to be brought. With his own hands he bound Vasudeva to one pillar and Devaki to the opposite, thus ensuring that there was no possibility of any physical contact between them. Strict orders were given that they were not to be let out together. Satisfied with his handiwork, he left, banging the dungeon doors together and shutting out the last ray of hope.

"O God! What about your promise?" groaned Vasudeva. "Are you going to desert us now in the hour of our darkness? We have none but you to aid us." So saying, he bowed his head and was plunged in grief. At that moment, the Supreme Lord, protector of the universe, entered into the mind of Vasudeva, so that he began to shine in splendor like the sun. Such bliss transformed his face and aspect that his unhappy wife felt bound to exclaim,

"O Husband!" she cried. "What is that secret thought that is drenching you with happiness? What have we unfortunate creatures to be happy about? O unlucky parents! We have been forced to see our children murdered before our own eyes. Our only hope was to see the birth of our eighth infant and now even that hope has been dashed to the ground. What have we to rejoice about?"

"There is a form shining within my heart, O Beloved," Vasudeva exclaimed in rapture, "that thrills me to the very core of my being, so that I no longer feel the hardness of the pillar to which I am bound nor the weight of the chains that bite my flesh."

"O Husband!" she cried, "pray describe this vision in detail to me so that I too can share your rapture."

So Vasudeva transmitted to his wife through the medium of the mind that world-redeeming aspect of the Supreme Divine, who is the all-comprehensive Being present in all, including herself, and she received the mental transmission even as the eastern horizon receives the glory of the full moon. Thus did she conceive the Lord mentally through her husband Vasudeva.

When the jailer opened the dungeon doors the next day, he saw the cell bathed in a divine radiance and Devaki transformed and shining as if within her she carried a living fire, a fire which would consume all the evil in the world and leave it pure and shining. Hurriedly closing the doors, he ran as fast as he could to the king to give the news that something strange and wondrous had happened to Devaki. Kamsa went posthaste to investigate for himself. It was just as the jailer had described. When he opened the doors, his eyes were dazzled by such a blinding flash of burning blue brilliance that he staggered back, unable to bear it.

He thought to himself, "Surely the Lord Hari (Vishnu), who is to be the cause of my death, must be within her. Never before have I seen her with such divine lustre. What shall I do now? If I kill her outright, I shall surely be condemned by all, so I shall wait for the child to be born and then kill him."

He gave orders that the guards were to be doubled, the chains strengthened, and every precaution taken so that none entered or left the dungeon. All his instructions were carried out faithfully, but neither Devaki nor Vasudeva cared or even noticed what was happening around them. They were bathed in a sea of bliss and as the child within her womb grew bigger, Devaki's joy knew no bounds. She did not feel the discomforts of her position, nor was she worried as to the ways and means of protecting the child when it was born and caring for it until it grew old enough to kill her brother. Such mundane considerations worried her not a whit, for she had time only to meditate continuously on that wondrous form which filled her being and suffused her with delight.

Kamsa, too, was in a very similar state. His mind sharpened in single-pointed concentration on Lord Vishnu through intense fear, his entire world was filled with Vishnu, even though it was of Vishnu as avenger and killer. Waking, sleeping, eating, or talking, he quaked in fear, constantly wondering how his killer would appear. He had heard of His previous incarnation, who had jumped out of a pillar as *Narasimha* (the man-lion) to kill the *asura* Hiranyakashipu. Thinking thus, he would suddenly jump off the throne on which he had been sitting and inspect his bed and mattress very carefully before sleeping. He would scrutinize every ball of rice to see if Vishnu was lurking within. Thus, waking and sleeping, Kamsa's world was peopled by Vishnu alone. This was truly an enviable state, one which meditating *yogis* strive in vain to achieve. Thus did Kamsa pass the ten months preceding the advent of the Lord in constant contemplation.

Thus ends the first chapter of The Play of God, *named "The Advent."*

Hari Aum Tat Sat

We pray to and worship the Supreme Lord Vishnu for the welfare of all. May all miseries and shortcomings leave us forever so that we may always be able to sing His glories. May medicinal herbs grow in potency so that diseases may be cured effectively. May the gods rain peace on us. May both bipeds and quadrupeds be happy. Peace, peace, peace.
—PURUSHA SUKTAM OF THE RIG VEDA

TWO

THE BIRTH OF THE UNBORN

Janardanaya namaha

Homage to the One who removes the evils of birth and death

At this auspicious time, in the pitch darkness of midnight, Lord Vishnu, who is the resident within the hearts of all creatures, was born of the divinely beautiful Devaki, like the full moon rising in the eastern horizon.
—SHRIMAD BHAGAVATA

With the approach of the most auspicious time when the star Rohini was in the ascendant and all the other stars and planets were in favorable positions, Janardana, the Lord who takes away the pangs of birth and death, the eternal, the immortal, and the birthless, chose to be born as the son of Devaki and Vasudeva.

Peaceful silence reigned in all the quarters. The stars shone clear in the sky. The rivers flowed with pellucid waters. The ponds were full of lotus blossoms. The woods were resonant with the chirping of birds and the buzzing of bees fluttering between the trees and creepers laden with flowers. Softly blew the breeze, dust-free and fragrant, and gently glowed the fires in the sacrificial hearths of the holy. An ineffable peace stole into the minds of all men. The time was approaching midnight and many jewels sprouted in the bowels of the earth, and all the birds woke up and started crooning softly. The sun and moon both peeped out with their full complement of stars, among which the star Rohini was the brightest. This special conjunction of the eighth-day moon with the constellation Rohini heralded the birth of the Lord. Muddy waters became clear, springs gushed forth, and the waves of the sea came rushing in to try to present themselves at the place where the mighty drama was

13

about to commence. Little breezes carrying the sweet perfume of a million newly opened blossoms thrust their way into the dungeon and played with the curls around Devaki's head as she lay in labor. Noble people everywhere were wide awake, for they felt as if something momentous was about to take place. The wicked slept the sleep of the dead. In fact, Kamsa had never slept so soundly since the day of the prophecy and, as for the guards, they were snoring so loudly that nothing short of an earthquake would have awakened them.

The creator Brahma and the other celestials entered the labor room and hymned the Lord, whom they could see shining within Devaki's womb. The sages and gods showered flowers from above. The clouds lowed gently in tune with the ocean.

At such a time, in the pitch darkness of midnight, Vishnu, the resident in the hearts of all, was born of the divinely beautiful Devaki. At the moment of His birth, the prison was filled with a soft light emanating from the babe Himself. In that one brief instant when she held Him in her arms, Devaki forgot the ordeal of the morrow, forgot the cruel death that awaited her child, and knew only the bliss of the mother as she holds her newborn in her arms. Vasudeva was in a trance of delight, for he saw before him that divine form which had shone in his heart ten months ago and which had throbbed in Devaki's womb ever since.

O lucky parents! What tortures would one not go through to have a sight like this? Lotus-eyed, four-armed, sporting the conch, mace, and other weapons, with the luminous *Shrivatsa* mark on the chest and the shining jewel *Kaustubha*, wearing a yellow garment, possessed of the majesty and grace of a rain cloud, with locks gleaming with the lustre of the diadem, earrings studded with precious gems, and bedecked with splendid ornaments—such was the wondrous form of the divine child that appeared before them. Realizing the child to be none other than Hari, the Supreme Being, Vasudeva prostrated himself before Him and sang a hymn of praise. He gazed into those glorious eyes, which were overflowing with love, and felt such waves of bliss washing over him that he could no longer keep his balance. Again and again he prostrated before this vision, knowing Him to be indeed that formless Brahman extolled in the *Vedas*, which had taken on the form of his son.

Then Devaki exclaimed, "You are verily Vishnu, the light spiritual, the unmanifest, the vast, the luminous. I take shelter in You, the Supreme Shelter. That You, who bear the whole universe within Yourself should have taken birth in my small womb is part of Your divine *lila*, Your incomprehensible play by which You beguile the entire creation."

The Lord now spoke, "O Great Lady! Having controlled your mind and meditated on Me in your two previous births, you had repeatedly asked for the boon that I might be born as your son. It is in fulfillment of this request that I am now taking My third birth in your womb as your son. I have given you a vision of my Divine Form so that you will recognize Me. Meditate on Me, therefore, as the Supreme Spirit and not merely as your son and you will rise to higher states of consciousness and attain My state."

Looking at His father He continued, "Arise now and go to Gokula, to the house of the cowherd chief Nanda. His wife Yashoda has just given birth to a baby girl who is none other than My Yogamaya (embodiment of the Lord's power of illusion). Leave Me there and bring her back." So saying, He turned into a newborn infant once more and the veil of *maya* descended on His parents. Devaki picked up this bundle of bliss and started nursing Him. Vasudeva was in a hurry to be off, but she would not be hurried. Who can blame her? Once having taken Him in embrace, who is it that can bear to let Him go?

Happily He went to sleep in her arms as she looked on entranced. Reluctantly, she relinquished this bundle of bliss into the anxious arms of her husband, who had been waiting for an opportunity to hold Him to his heart. He had forgotten to ask how a prisoner could walk out of a dungeon at midnight and go to Gokula! But as he rose up, he found that he was free. Wrapping the infant in his own upper garment, he held Him tenderly to his heart and went toward the massive door of the prison, which was bolted and barred with iron. To his amazement, the bolts slid back, the locks turned, the chains fell softly, and the heavy doors swung outward of their own accord. Outside, the guards and soldiers slumbered heavily and no one woke as Vasudeva, with the baby Krishna nestling within his robes, passed into the open. Here, there was a heavy storm, the winds raged, and his heart was heavy with foreboding as he listened to the sound of the gushing waters of the river Yamuna in the distance and wondered how he would ever be able to ford it and reach the other bank on such a night. But lo! as he stepped out, not a drop of rain fell on his head, for it is said that Shesha, the celestial serpent on whom the Lord Vishnu is said to rest, followed him with his hoods upraised, acting as a gigantic umbrella over the divine child. From a distance he saw the Yamuna rising in a turbulent flood, but as he came nearer the waters parted so that he walked across with only a trickle washing over his feet. The Yamuna wanted to have the honor of washing the blessed feet of him who was lucky enough to carry the Lord.

At last Vasudeva came with his precious burden to the village of Gokula and to the dwelling place of Nanda, the chief of the cowherds. Softly, the door of the farmhouse opened before him and as he entered he saw a light burning within the doorway of the first room. The lamp stood by the bed of a sleeping mother and her newborn child. Quietly, Vasudeva bent down and exchanged the children. To the herdsman's wife he gave the divine child and from her side he took her little daughter. Once more, he bent down and kissed that pearly forehead. Then, with a last lingering look at the baby's beloved face, he slowly backed out the door.

His sense of desolation after leaving the child was so great that he knew not where he went and cared less. Maya Devi (goddess of illusion), who lay in his arms, had to direct his footsteps so that he crossed the river once again, reached the dungeon in the city of Mathura, and gave the baby girl of Yashoda to his own wife Devaki. He returned to the pillar and found himself once more in chains. The doors of all the buildings remained bolted and barred as before. Hardly had he put the child on Devaki's lap than she began to squall at the top of her voice. The guards jumped up in haste and went running to Kamsa, carrying the news of Devaki's child, the child Kamsa was awaiting with dread. They had orders to wake him up at whatever hour of day or night the baby was born. Sword in hand, without his kingly ornaments, he rushed to the dungeon with his hair dishevelled and his feet stumbling on the path.

"Where is he?" he shouted. "Where is that puling, mewling babe? It is better to kill the cobra's young in its nest before it can grow up and kill me!" So saying, he snatched the child from his sister's arms.

"But it's a girl," she moaned, "and deserves to be spared. O Brother, you have killed so many of my children, all brilliant like flames. Spare me at least this one, a daughter. Am I not your sister? The prophecy mentioned a boy and this is a girl. What harm can she do to you? Return her to me, therefore, I beg of you."

In spite of her piteous appeals, Kamsa snatched the baby from her bosom and said, "It's some trick of Vishnu, the master trickster. Girl or boy, what do I care? I'll see her in hell first!"

So saying, he grasped the tiny feet and swung the baby round in order to dash Her down on the rock already bathed in the blood of six other children. But as he lifted the child aloft, She slipped from his grasp and flew into the air, and as he looked up in surprise he saw the beauteous eight-handed form of the Goddess, decked in celestial garlands and ornaments and armed with many weapons in each of Her hands, shining above him.

She declared in a laughing, musical voice, "O fool! What use is it to kill Me? The one to kill you has already been born. He lives within a radius of ten miles. I have spared you today since you caught hold of My feet. Because of that I bless you, O Kamsa, with death at the hands of Lord Vishnu—the giver of eternal life." So saying, the Yogamaya of the Lord disappeared and manifested herself under different names in other parts of the world.

Kamsa was sunk in gloom and decided to release his sister and her husband and to beg their pardon for his atrocities. At daybreak, however, he sent for his evil counselors, who advised him to kill all the babies in the outlying districts as well as all holy men, for Vishnu is said to hide in the hearts of the holy. Being thus advised by his vicious ministers, he sunk himself in that infernal crime of infanticide and harassment of the virtuous and let loose a reign of terror unparalleled in the history of the world. The persecution of the virtuous leads to man's absolute ruin. It annihilates his longevity, good fortune, reputation, and his prospects in the hereafter.

Thus ends the second chapter of The Play of God,
named "The Birth of the Unborn."

Hari Aum Tat Sat

Lord Narayana is the Supreme Reality known as Brahman. Narayana is the highest Self. Narayana is the Supreme Light. Narayana is the Infinite Self. Narayana is the greatest mediator as well as the supreme object of mediation.
—NARAYANA SUKTAM

Whatever in this world is known through perception or by report, all that is pervaded by Narayana within and without.
—NARAYANA SUKTAM

THREE

THE DIVINE INFANT

Nandakumaraya namaha

Homage to the son of Nanda

O Dearest Lord! By Thy incarnation, Gokula has surpassed all other places. It has become abundant and charming, for the goddess of wealth has made it her permanent residence. Deign to cast Thy glance on us who are Thine own people, who live only for Thy sake, and who have been vainly searching for Thee in all directions. Pray grant us Thy beatific vision.
—*SHRIMAD BHAGAVATA*

The scene now shifts to Gokula, where for the next twelve years Krishna beguiled His foster parents and the rest of the *gopis* (milkmaids) and *gopalas* (cowherd boys) in a thousand charming ways. Those fortunate ones were able to dandle the Infinite on their knees, to suckle the Nourisher of the Universe, to bind that Boundless and Formless One, and to hold Him in the circle of their loving arms. There is no chapter in the Lord's life so touching as this. It explores the heights and depths of all the various forms of love a simple, unsophisticated heart is capable of giving: *vatsalya bhava*, or the parents' love for their son, *sakhya bhava*, or the boys' love for their friend, and *madhura bhava*, or the girls' love for their sweetheart. He was everything to them — son, friend, lover, savior, and God.

The moment his father left Him beside the sleeping Yashoda, the baby opened His rosebud mouth and started yelling, as if to say, "What! Are you all sleeping when I enter your house? So also will I enter your hearts like a thief in the night, but once I'm ensconced within, I'll leave you in no doubt as to My presence!" The whole household, which had been held in a magic sleep until then, now sprang to life. Great was their joy when they

19

found that the child they remembered as a girl was really a boy, for over-sight was the only explanation that occurred to them.

"A boy! A boy!" The news spread like wildfire.

"A beautiful, bonny boy has been born to our chief!"

The happy father rushed to the room and feasted his eyes on the delightful mite of divinity that shone in his room. Loud and long were his praises to God. He made presentations of clothes, ornaments, cows, and money to all for the well-being of his son. He had never expected to become a father in this life, for his wife Yashoda was already forty-five years of age. They had almost given up hope of ever having a child and now to be blessed with a son, and a son of such a delightful aspect. His joy knew no bounds. When morning came, the entire community of *gopis* and *gopalas* came to see the child with their little offerings of but-ter and milk and curd, which were all they had to give. But these they offered in the pure crystal bowl of their hearts and so it was more acceptable to the Lord than the costliest presents. All those who saw Him loved Him as if He were their own, and this was no wonder, for God belongs to all equally. He was a source of unlimited bliss to the *gopis*, who used to finish their housework as fast as possible and crowd into Yashoda's house to pet Him and fondle Him and exclaim over His cute ways. They forgot their homes, their husbands, and even their own children and revelled in the bliss emanating from this divine child. From that day onward Vraja (the cowherd settlement of Gokula), being the residence of Hari, also became the playground of Shri (Lakshmi), the goddess of prosperity and auspiciousness.

Since Kamsa was the king of the land, all the chiefs had to pay an annual tribute. So Nanda left for Mathura to pay the taxes, with many anxious warnings to Yashoda never to leave the child alone. Hearing of Nanda's arrival, Vasudeva went to meet him, for he was very anxious to have news of his son Krishna, as well as of his son by his wife Rohini, who was also living with Nanda.

"O Brother!" he said. "I hear I have to congratulate you. It is indeed fortunate that you, who were childless until now, have a baby at this advanced age. Lucky man, to be the father of such a son. And what about my son who is now living with his mother at your house? How is he?"

Poor Vasudeva, though not an envious man by nature, was filled with envy at the thought that Nanda would be enjoying what should have been his by rights and his wife Yashoda would be having the extreme pleasure of nursing the Lord. His own wife could nurse only her tears, while her breasts dried up, unwanted and unfulfilled. Bitter indeed was this thought. At least he had been happy that the child was safe, but now, having heard of Kamsa's edict to massacre all children, he was filled with dread and warned Nanda.

Nanda said, "Alas! I have heard of all the calamities that you have had to bear, O Brother. All things are in the hands of God. Those who know this will not grieve."

Vasudeva, though he longed to hear more about his sons, did not like to keep him talking any longer, for he feared for their safety. Thus he urged Nanda, "I see ill omens and I fear for the safety of your child. Return to Gokula immediately. Do not waste time in the city and never leave the child alone or show Him to strangers." Nanda was terrified when he heard this and went directly to Gokula in his ox-drawn cart.

In the meantime, a demoness called Putana, an expert at infanticide, had begun to move about in towns, villages, and settlements at Kamsa's behest to slaughter all infants, regardless of their sex or age. She could travel anywhere in any form. One day, she came to Gokula, taking the form of an attractive young woman. She had perfected an ingenious method for killing infants. Posing as a wet nurse she smeared her breasts with poison and nursed the babies. The result was conclusive. When she reached Gokula, she heard of the birth of a baby boy in the house of Nanda and went there immediately. Putana looked like a veritable goddess when she glided into the room where the child lay sleeping. She picked Him up without realizing that it would be her last act.

Seeing her air of authority, both Rohini and Yashoda felt embarrassed to ask her who she was and to remonstrate with her for taking up the baby, even though she was a stranger. Without hesitating, Putana placed the sleeping infant on her lap and proceeded to nurse Him. It is said that the Lord deliberately feigned sleep, for He knew that if she looked into His wondrous eyes, even she, hardened sinner though she was, would repent and go away without attempting to kill Him, and then His mission would be incomplete. Even so, as she gazed at His sleeping face, an overwhelming rush of maternal love flowed from her and her breasts, which were incapable of yielding milk, gushed forth. She forgot the poison she had smeared on them, giving the child suck and crooning to Him the while. But her lullaby soon changed to a scream, for the little fellow, toothless though He was, held her breast in a vise-like grip and was sucking with gusto; He seemed to drain her of her vital energy. In mortal agony, she rushed out of the house and assumed her demonic form. At last, with a roar of pain, she fell like a mountain in the middle of the courtyard, destroying the cowshed and the hayrick. Her fall seemed to cause tremors in the earth and made the *gopis* and *gopalas* tremble in fear. This was the scene that greeted the eyes of the terrified father when he returned from Mathura.

"Where's the baby? Where's the baby?" was the frightened clamor from all sides.

Suddenly, they saw the infant fearlessly kicking its limbs in delight, lying on top of the monstrous form of the demoness. The *gopalas* hesitated in fear, but the *gopis* rushed forward, for He was more important to them than their own lives, and took Him up in their arms. They were amazed at how He could still be alive. They did not dream that He could be responsible for the monster's death.

"God must have saved Him in some miraculous way," was the general verdict.

They bathed Him and performed sacred rites for His safety, such as waving cows' tails over His body, smearing Him with dust from the hooves of the cows, and applying dried cow dung powder to the twelve vital parts of His body while uttering the sacred names of Vishnu. The child submitted to all these ministrations with secret amusement and kicked and crooned with delight.

Since they could not cremate this huge body in the compound, they had to hack it into bits and carry it far away to be burnt. They had expected a terrible stench to rise from the burning carcass, but instead the sweet smell of sandalwood filled the air. This was because Putana had suckled the divine child and thus become free from every form of sin. If a killer of infants and a vampire like Putana attained to *mukti* (liberation) because she had fed Him, then think of the glorious destiny of those who offered Him all that was nearest and dearest to them, as His parents and the *gopis* did. Those sacred feet of His, which devotees cherish in their hearts and which are the refuge of even sages, were placed on her lap while He sucked at her breast, so that even though she was a demoness she got the reward due to the mother of God. What then can be said of the good fortune of the *gopis* and even the cows, who fed Him with the greatest of love?

Never was mortal woman happier than Yashoda, wife and queen of

Nanda, foster mother of the Lord. Day after day she held him in her lap and fed Him, played with Him, and cradled Him to sleep, as if He were an ordinary baby, for not even she suspected the extent of His strength.

Putana was the forerunner of many other demons sent by Kamsa to kill the baby. They came in various forms and guises. Needless to say, none returned alive. Though at first none of the *gopalas* realized the extent of the remarkable powers possessed by this infant, slowly they began to have some inkling of the vast storehouse of power that lay between those tiny arms.

It was the third monthly birthday of the infant, when the star Rohini came around for the third time after His birth, and it marked the ceremony of His being taken out of the house for the first time. There was a large gathering and Yashoda bathed the baby amidst the chanting of *mantras* (sacred syllables). Having received the blessings of the Brahmins, she placed the drowsy infant under a cart to sleep. She kept a ring of little boys to watch over Him and went inside to attend to the guests. At this moment, the demon Shakata entered the cart, thinking that it would be easy to bring it down upon the infant and kill Him as if in an accident. But he calculated without knowing the powers of his opponent.

At the very instant the cart started to fall, He gave a kick with His tiny foot and lo! the cart and all its contents were thrown to the other side of the yard and Shakata was killed. Of his body, however, there was no sign, for it is said that since the Lord's feet had kicked him, even his physical form attained liberation. Hearing the terrible cracking sound everyone rushed forward.

"What happened? What happened?" they asked the children who had been looking after the baby.

"The cart fell down and this little baby kicked it and broke it with His feet," they said proudly.

The people gazed in astonishment at the baby, who was kicking His feet and gurgling happily as if to confirm the truth of what the children said.

"These children are capable of making up anything," the adults said in disbelief.

Yashoda snatched up her baby and caressed His rose-petal feet. "Did you get hurt, my darling?" she crooned. "Did the cart hurt you?"

"God certainly looks after your child, Yashoda!" the other *gopis* exclaimed.

Not having an inkling of the superhuman might of their child, the frightened parents arranged for many rites to be done for Him to protect Him from evil forces.

After this incident, Yashoda was frightened to leave Him alone even for a minute. One evening, she was sitting with Him in her lap, crooning to Him and repeating prayers, when she felt herself unequal to the task of bearing His weight, for He appeared to be growing heavier and heavier. What could the matter be? She felt that someone had cast an evil eye on Him, so she placed Him on a mat and went to the kitchen to get some condiments which, when waved above an infant, were supposed to ward off the effects of the evil eye. Hardly had she disappeared than the child made Himself lighter than usual, for He had known of the approach of the demon Trinavarta, who was coming in the form a whirlwind that engulfed the whole of Gokula in such a cloud of dust that the entire settlement was plunged into darkness. While the tornado was raging, Yashoda was unable to see her child anywhere, and she collapsed in fear and started to cry. Trinavarta rose up into the air with the baby, but soon he was unable to bear the infant's massive weight and found his speed dwindling, until at last he fell down with a roar onto a huge rock and dashed himself into smithereens. The *gopalas* ran to the spot where the demon had crashed and found the baby glowing like a sapphire atop the rock. Taking up the blessed child, they presented Him to His mother. They were filled with wonder at His apparently miraculous escape.

Poor Yashoda. Until a child starts to crawl, it can be expected to remain in the place where it has been put. Having a baby at such a late age, Yashoda was already an overanxious mother and to add to this, it appeared that this child was accident-prone. She could never leave Him alone even for a minute and be sure of finding Him in the same place on her return. Though He appeared to be unscathed by these experiences, she had no way of knowing that this was due to His own powers and not to some miracle. She attributed it to luck or providence. How could she imagine that within Him lay the ability to protect the entire cosmos? It may have been to set her mind at rest that one day He showed her a miracle.

As usual, she was sitting in her favorite spot on a veranda that overlooked two huge trees in the garden and worrying about all the dangers that might possibly befall Him. With infinite tenderness, she contemplated the cherubic face in her arms. At that moment the Lord opened His rosebud mouth as if to yawn and lo! the mother saw the entire universe in His little mouth. She stared mesmerized. There was no doubt. The sky, the earth, and the heavens, the stars, the planets, the sun, the moon, fire, air, oceans, rivers, and continents were all inside her baby's mouth. For a split second, she forgot herself and the baby and felt as if she were poised on the brink of endless worlds, the spectator of a mighty drama. At last she could bear it no longer and she closed her eyes. When she opened them again, the illusion, if it could be called that, had vanished, and she was just a mother holding her baby in her arms.

"Rohini! Rohini!" she called. "Come here and tell me what you see in this child's mouth. I thought I saw something strange and wondrous."

Rohini came running and with great difficulty she managed to pry open His little mouth and shove her finger inside, only to get a sharp nip for her pains.

"I know what's in this child's mouth," she told Yashoda. "He's teething. That's what you saw."

Yashoda shook her head doubtfully. The miracle she had just witnessed was already fading from her mind, but a lingering feeling of awe remained and with it a certain degree of comfort. This child was not as helpless as He looked, she thought to herself. There was no need for her to worry so much over His welfare. He was capable of looking after Himself. This thought comforted her and this was just what the Lord wanted.

At that time the great sage Gargacharya,[1] the priest of the Yadava clan, went to Vraja at the instigation of Vasudeva, who had sent him there to perform the naming ceremony of his sons. Garga Muni (sage) was noted for his skill in astrology, and Nanda welcomed him and requested him to perform the purificatory rites for his child as well as Rohini's.

Gargacharya said, "I am well known as the priest of the Yadavas and if I perform the purificatory rites for these children, Kamsa will come to hear of it, take it as an indication that his foe is here, and take steps to kill him."

So Nanda begged him to perform the ceremony in some solitary place without the knowledge of even the other *gopalas*. Since the sage knew everything and had gone there with the express purpose of naming the child, he agreed with alacrity.

---

1 *Gargacharya*—Garga the *acharya* (teacher or preceptor).

Thus, without the knowledge of anyone else, the ceremony was conducted in an empty cow barn with only Nanda, Yashoda, and Rohini as witnesses. First, Gargacharya took Rohini's child in his lap, since he was the elder, and named him Balarama, because of his great strength as well as his ability to delight everyone. Next, he lifted Yashoda's child and placed Him tenderly on his lap. The mischievous little thing gave him a sharp look as if to say, "You'd better give me a nice name, one that has never been heard before and yet one which befits me and will be remembered by all to come . . . or else. . . ."

At this moment the old man felt the baby hands give a sharp tug at his long grey beard, which dangled right down to the baby's stomach and was tickling Him. Gargacharya smiled and looked into those wondrous eyes and his heart left his keeping forever!

"Krishna!" That was the name for Him. "Krishna"—the one who steals the hearts of men, so that one who has once come into contact with Him belongs to Him forever. Krishna also means "he who is dark in color," for the baby was the color of the rain clouds during the monsoons. Gargacharya then outlined the child's horoscope and told Nanda that since He had been the son of Vasudeva in a previous birth, He would also be known as Vaasudeva. "Numerous are the names with which this child will come to be known because of His qualities and achievements. Even I cannot know them all. Mark, O Nanda! This child is equal to Lord Narayana (Vishnu) Himself in respect of fame, prowess, and excellence. Look after Him with all attention. All those who harm Him will be harming themselves, and those who love Him will be ever protected."

Krishna gurgled with delight. Here at last was one who realized His greatness. And here was license to perpetrate whatever mischief He wished to do! He decided to lead the inhabitants of Gokula in such a dance that they would never forget Him for the rest of their lives.

Thus ends the third chapter of The Play of God,
named "The Divine Infant."

Hari Aum Tat Sat

FOUR

THE BUTTER THIEF

Navaneeth-anadaya namaha

Homage to the One who plays with butter

"I meditate on the enchanting form of Nanda's darling, with eyes like the petals of a newly blown lotus, lips like the bimba berry, a face made entrancing by a beguiling smile, and whose color is that of a water-laden rain cloud."
—SHRIMAD BHAGAVATA

Very soon, Balarama and Krishna began to crawl about and they got themselves into more scrapes than any other children. There was never a dull moment for Yashoda. In all her forty-five years she had never run so much. She forgot her normal household duties while watching the boys at play. Krishna would crawl forward very fast and then turn His head and look over His shoulder when He heard the sound of tinkling bells coming from His own ankles, as if to see who was following Him. That enquiring look was irresistible. Up she would jump, run after Him, pick Him up, and kiss Him all over His cherubic face. He'd wriggle out of her arms and crawl as fast as He could, with bells tinkling and feet twinkling like twin rose petals blown in the wind. Where was He? By the time she caught up with Him, He would be with the big mother cow, pulling off her young one with one small hand and drinking milk straight from her udder as He had watched the calf do. Yashoda would scream in terror for the cow was noted for her vicious nature and she was already shaking her head in a menacing manner, bringing her huge horns closer to the child. Yashoda would stand petrified, not knowing whether to run and pick up the child or whether that would irritate the cow further. But as she stood root-ed, this fierce cow would put out its rough tongue and lick the little bottom as affectionately as she licked her own calf. Krishna would turn round and look at His mother as if to say, "See, mother. All creatures love Me, for I am the soul of all." But, poor mother, she would think it was another miracle and she would snatch Him up and tell Him never to do such a thing again.

So then He would follow her into the kitchen and put His hand into every pot until He came to the one with the butter, eating some and pasting the rest over His face, and the little kittens would come mewing and lick His face with delight. The mother was now in a dilemma, not knowing whether to attend to her household duties or to watch the child. So playful and restless was He that He had to be constantly guarded from the dangers of cows, fire, cats, knives, ponds, thorns, and birds.

Once He started to toddle, it was even worse. One day, Yashoda heard Him call her excitedly and she rushed out to see Him hanging perilously over the well. "Mother! Mother! Come and see! There's a little boy just like me in the well. Please come and take him out, Mother!"

Yashoda rushed and caught Him. "Never do that again," she admonished, and ever after that, every time she drew water from the well, she would imagine His face peeping from the water. There was no mischief He was incapable of doing. The little hands were busy with everything. One moment He would be brandishing the kitchen knife, the next He would try to pluck the hot coals from the fire. So, at every moment of the day, Yashoda kept running after Him, and for the rest of her life to come, she continued to see His face everywhere—in the coals, in the fire, in the water, near the cow, whether she was cutting vegetables or plucking flowers. Thus did He prepare her for the separation to come. This is a lesson to all housewives. It is difficult to fix our minds on a formless God while doing mundane tasks, but how easy to recall the mischievous exploits of that divine child, peeking and laughing at us in and through our most tedious chores.

Sometimes, some of the other *gopis* would beg to be allowed to take Him to their houses for the day and Yashoda would reluctantly agree, for she could not bear to be parted from Him for even a moment. Once He had been taken to a house, He would go uninvited. In fact, He would steal into their houses like a rogue, and help Himself to their butter, *ghee* (clarified butter), curd, and milk, which were their prized possessions. Such is His kindness that once we invite Him into our hearts, He'll come unbidden, steal the butter of our love, and bless us with the riches we have never asked for.

One day, the *gopis* gathered together and began to speak of Krishna's pranks to His mother. The charges against Him were numerous. "He comes and releases the calves before milking time. He steals the butter, milk, and curd and after consuming what He wants, He distributes it to His playmates, if they are there, or else to the kittens and baby monkeys who follow Him in the hope of getting something. After He has had His fill, He breaks the pots. If we scold Him, He laughs at us. What should we do to him?"

"Why don't you give Him what He wants?" asked the doting mother. "After all, He's only a child and He loves these things. Why don't you give Him a glass of milk and some butter as soon as He comes? At the end of the month you may present the bill to me and I'll meet it."

"O! But we do give Him!" they chorused. "We give Him as much as such a small boy can eat, but still He comes into the house unseen and steals more. If we hang up the curd, He makes a hole at the bottom and drinks from below as it drips down. After He has finished, His friends drink and the last drops are lapped up by the kittens!"

Another *gopi* took up the sad tale. "Once I hung the milk pot so high that He couldn't reach it even with a stick, and do you know what He did? He dragged a pounding stone from outside, I don't know how, and then He clambered up on it, broke the pot with a stick, opened His little mouth, and stood there drinking the milk that was pouring down. Half went into His mouth, some over His body, and the rest on to the floor, to the delight of the waiting kittens. Now look at Him, standing there the picture of innocence after having done so much mischief."

Krishna was hiding behind His mother and peeping out, His face quivering with pretended fright and His eyes anxiously rounded at hearing these accounts of His misdeeds. He was sucking a worried thumb and peeping anxiously at His mother's face to see how she was taking it.

Yashoda's only response was to laugh. She could not bring herself to scold her darling for any reason. "Never mind," she comforted the *gopis*. "I'll replace your mud pots with golden ones."

Thus, each of them got a golden pot in lieu of the one He had broken, and this was exactly what He had wanted, for He wanted them to enjoy all the luxuries which were there in His own house.

But still the complaints grew, so Yashoda started watching her little one very carefully to see when He went and perpetrated these misdeeds. She soon came to the conclusion that He could never have done any of the crimes that were being laid at His door, for the simple reason that He was never out of her sight for more than a few minutes at a time. "Is it possible that these *gopis* are making up these stories to get golden pots?" she wondered.

Just then another *gopi* came with a different tale. "Just listen to this, Mother," she said. "You know that I've started being very careful with my things and always keep them locked so that Krishna can't get them. Yesterday, He was really angry when He found nothing to steal, so He gave a pinch to my little daughter and made her wake up and scream just as He was leaving."

Krishna grinned when He heard this, for that child was Radha, who was going to be His beloved playmate in the future and He was asking her, "Why are you wasting time sleeping when you should be concentrating on growing up? What knowledge can you have of happiness that makes you smile now? I'll show you such delights that nothing else can be comparable." So saying, He had pinched her, and she had awakened squalling. Yashoda could not believe what the *gopi* was saying, so she said, "Well, next time He does something of the kind, just catch Him and bring Him to me and I'll punish Him."

The *gopi* agreed doubtfully, for she knew Him to be a slippery customer; however, with a little luck she managed to catch Him red-handed the next day when He was actually standing with His hands in a pot of butter. She grabbed Him by His buttery hands and dragged Him to the house. Just as they reached the turning, He said, "Look! What's that?"

She relaxed her hold and turned to look, and poof! His buttery hand slipped out of her grasp and off He went like a streak of blue light. She panted after Him, but He was all quicksilver and she was all lead! She puffed into His house and found Him sitting in His mother's lap on the swing, looking a picture of cherubic innocence.

"Aha! So this is where you have got to, is it?" she asked. "Look, Yashoda! I had caught this child red-handed stealing butter hardly ten minutes ago and I was dragging Him here to show you. Just as we reached the turn, He was off like a shot, and now look at Him, sitting here looking as if butter wouldn't melt in His mouth!"

Yashoda looked at her in astonishment. Now she was sure that the *gopis'* powers of fabrication were enormous. "What are you talking about?" she asked. "This child has been sitting on my lap listening to a story for the past hour. How can He possibly have been with you ten minutes ago?"

The *gopi* stared. She should have expected this, she thought resentfully. Naturally, a mother would side with her child. But what a bare-faced lie! How could Yashoda make up such a story? The two of them kept silent, while Krishna smiled. How God can appear to so many at one and the same time is a mystery to all. At last, seeing the *gopi's* crestfallen look, Yashoda said kindly, "Never mind. Next time you catch Him, be sure you tie Him up securely and bring Him to me, and I promise to punish Him."

Happily for the *gopi*, she was able to test the truth of this promise the very next day. Krishna allowed Himself to be caught, for after all she was Radha's mother. Determined to take no chances, she put Him inside a big empty chest in a corner, locked it up, and pocketed the key. "Just you wait there, you little rogue, and think of some new mischief while I finish my work and take you to your loving mother. Then we'll see." After finishing her work, she lugged the heavy chest up the small incline leading to Yashoda's house. "Here He is," she panted in triumph. "Here's your innocent son. I've caught Him and locked Him up as you suggested."

"When did you catch Him?" Yashoda asked curiously.

"Soon after lunch," Radha's mother replied. "He joined us for lunch and then left very properly by the front door, only to creep in through the back gate and steal butter from the larder. Mind you, this was not even for Himself, for He was too full after the heavy lunch I gave Him. I caught Him distributing the day's butter, the result of a hard morning's labor, to the cats and the monkeys."

Yashoda gasped, "Either you're mad or I am," she said. "Krishna had His lunch with us today. In fact, He sat between His father and His brother, and He's been playing here ever since. Now open the chest and let's see who is right, you or I."

Without hesitation, the *gopi* went and opened the chest, for she had no doubt who was right. Both of them peered into the chest and lo! staring at them with tear-filled eyes was the *gopi's* own daughter. Yashoda had a hearty laugh. "Well, well, I never realized your eyesight was so poor!"

The poor *gopi* was completely bewildered. How could she grasp the fact that God can appear in all places at the same time, for He is everywhere? After that, she never dared to go to Yashoda with her complaints, and her devotion and love for Krishna grew day by day. Her little daughter grew up seeing her great devotion, and from that time onward gave her heart to Him.

One day, the bigger children, including His brother Balarama, rushed out to eat the fruits of a tree growing in the compound. Krishna loved those fruits, so He toddled after them even though nobody had thought of inviting Him. They shooed Him off as being too small to climb trees. Still, He insisted on accompanying them, so they agreed to give Him the task of picking up the fruits as they fell.

"Now mind you, don't eat a single one," they warned, knowing His capacity for food. "Your job is only to collect the fruits and we'll come and divide them equally."

"All right," He said meekly.

The big boys, including Balarama, scrambled up and started dropping bunches of lovely, ripe, purple fruits to the ground. Krishna started picking them up and gobbling them as fast He could. He crammed His mouth, and His little hands were going up and down like pistons from the ground to His mouth. After some time, one of the boys chanced to look down and discovered what was going on. "Hey! Stop that nonsense at once!" he shouted. "Look at Krishna," he called to the others. "He's eating the fruit instead of collecting it!"

"Stop it! Stop!" all of them shouted from the top of the tree. All the little heads popped out from among the branches, shouting angrily at Krishna, who seemed supremely unconscious of the whole affair and continued to cram His mouth. The purply fluid was oozing down the corner of His mouth and in His hurry to eat as much as He could, He had not even cleaned the fruit. Quite a bit of mud also found its way into His mouth. The boys came sliding down and shook Him hard. "What do you think you're doing?" they shouted.

Krishna did not speak a word for the simple reason that His mouth was packed with fruit.

"All right, we'll show you," they cried and ran inside searching for His mother.

"O Mother!" they cried. "Your son is eating mud!"

Yashoda came running to find out what the commotion was all about.

"Your son is eating mud!" they cried, pointing accusingly at Krishna.

"Have you been eating mud?" she repeated sternly.

Krishna shook His curly head and started sniffing loudly as a prelude to crying. He dared not open His mouth yet, for He hadn't quite finished swallowing the fruit.

"Ask Him to open His mouth, Mother!" Balarama urged. Krishna glared at him as if He couldn't believe that His brother would stoop to such a low trick.

"Yes, ask Him to open His mouth," the rest of the boys chorused.

"Open your mouth, Krishna," Yashoda said sternly.

Krishna turned His limpid gaze on her. "Have you forgotten what happened when you looked into my mouth the last time?" was the unspoken question.

She had indeed forgotten, or probably misunderstood. If so, the time was propitious for another lesson. Or perhaps, He thought, if she wanted to see mud, she could have her fill of it!

And the Lord who had become a human child out of sport, without any loss of His divine powers, now opened His rosebud mouth. She bent forward to peer more closely and lo! she felt herself to be whirling in space, lost in time, for inside the baby mouth was seen the whole universe of moving and unmoving creation, the earth and its mountains and oceans, the moon and the stars, and all the planets and regions. She was wonderstruck to see the land of Vraja and the village of Gokula, herself standing there with the child Krishna beside her with a wide-open mouth, and within that mouth another universe, and so on and on and on....

"O God!" she thought. "Am I going mad or is this a dream or the magic wrought by this strange child of mine? Krishnaaa...," she cried, clinging to His name like a drowning person to a lifeline. "Krishnaaa...." It was a despairing cry, for she felt her head whirling. Immediately, He shut His mouth, and she got back her equilibrium. In a trice, she had almost forgotten what she had seen. "Why have you been eating...." She stopped in mid-sentence. What a fool she was! This child carried the whole universe within Himself and she was worrying about a few grains of sand! "Krishna! O Krishna!" she whispered, snatching up her boy in her arms. "Who are You? Who are You? Who are You?" she whispered, nuzzling His baby curls with her lips. Before the astonished gaze of a dozen small boys, she carried her darling inside, caressing Him and murmuring endearments to Him. The boys gazed after her in disappointment. You really couldn't tell with adults, they decided. There was no saying how they would react. They had fully expected to enjoy the spectacle of Krishna howling for mercy from an irate mother and look at her! Hugging and kissing Him!

He whom the Vedantins (followers of the Vedas) speak of as Brahman, whom the *yogis* consider the *Atman* (individual soul), and whom devotees call Bhagavan, that Supreme One was considered by Yashoda to be her own son.

Thus ends the fourth chapter of The Play of God, *named "The Butter Thief."*

Hari Aum Tat Sat

May we be able to know Narayana. For that do we meditate on Vaasudeva. May Vishnu guide us.
—NARAYANA SUKTAM

FIVE

BONDAGE OF THE BOUNDLESS

Damodaraya namaha

Homage to the One who has a rope tied round him

Whoever, at whatever time, joins the palms of his hands in supplication just once toward Thy feet, in whatever manner, dispels at once all his misfortunes and accumulates immense good. Such an act of supplication is never lost.
—*THE HYMN JEWEL OF SHRI YAMUNACHARYA*

One day, Yashoda got up early to assist the maids in churning curds. She left the sleeping Krishna and tiptoed out of the room to boil the milk and churn the curds before He woke up. Unfortunately, He woke up soon after and was quite annoyed to find her missing. Even though He was about three years old, according to the custom He had not yet been weaned, and it was His usual habit to have a good feast as soon as He got up. He shouted for His mother, but the noise made by the wooden churn, as well as the fact that she was singing songs about Him, drowned out His baby voice. By now, He was thoroughly disgruntled and decided to go down and investigate. "Ah! There she is busy churning curd when she should be feeding Me!" He thought, as He spied her from the door. Running to her, He caught hold of the churning rod and put a stop to the whole operation.

She turned to look at Him. Her eyes melted with love and her breasts started to flow of their own accord. He was such an enchanting sight. His bunch of curls was sprouting from the top of His head where she had tied it the previous evening, with a single peacock feather stuck in the middle. His eyes were smudged with collyrium due to the tears He had shed, and even now one tear was precariously balanced on His lower lids wondering whether to fall, loathe to leave those lovely eyes. His lips were

35

pink, with the full lower lip thrust out in a delicious pout. She caught Him to her in a tight embrace and, loosening her garment, she started to feed Him. Both mother and son were thoroughly enjoying this interlude, He sucking with gusto and she watching with great tenderness, when suddenly she heard the hissing noise of the milk boiling over on the fire. Placing the child down on the floor, she ran to rescue the milk. Krishna was furious. His eyes became red and His lips trembled. It was bad enough to have been deprived of His pleasure in the morning, but this was the very limit! To be dumped like a sack of potatoes when He had not finished drinking His fill! He'd show her! He took up the heavy wooden churn and brought it down with a bang on the mud pot containing the curd she had been churning. The buttermilk gushed out with a gurgle, with the blob of butter in the middle. With make-believe tears in His eyes, He looked aghast at what He had done. Deciding that discretion was the better part of valor, He hurriedly trotted off on His chubby legs. At the door He turned and looked back. The blob of butter looked too inviting. Moreover, He was still hungry. He trotted back, rescued the butter, and ran to the veranda, where there was a big rice-husking mortar. Seating Himself precariously on top of this, He proceeded to enjoy His stolen feast, throwing a few lumps to the kittens now and again. Yashoda returned after rescuing the milk and saw the mess He had made on the floor. But of the child there was no sign. She tiptoed out and saw Him sitting on the mortar, glancing here and there with the pretended fear of discovery written large in His eyes. She approached Him slowly from behind. Turning around, He caught sight of her, jumped down, and ran away as if in fear.

She gave chase to Him, who cannot be caught even in the mind of a meditating *yogi* purified by austerity. Crying and rubbing His eyes with buttery fingers, looking back anxiously at His mother who was slowly catching up with Him, He ran and hid behind the mortar. When she saw His fear, she threw away the stick she had been carrying and decided to tie Him to the mortar. Quickly, she returned with the longest and strongest piece of rope she could find. Creeping up to the stone she suddenly threw it over Him and said, "Now I'm going to tie you up!"

At these words a tuft of curls bobbed up over the stone, followed by two anxious eyes, one tiny nose, and a pair of buttery lips ending in a determined chin that lifted itself up and rested on top of the stone.

"I'm going to tie you up," she repeated, hardening her heart against the plea in His enchanting look. His eyes looked down, but was there a mocking gleam in them? He was the Unmanifest Supreme sporting as a human child, whom this *gopi* took to be her own son and was trying to fasten to the mortar. Determinedly, she wound the rope around His middle and found it short by two fingers. So she attached another rope and wound it twice around Him and again found it short by two fingers. She attached another rope with the same result. Thus, she exhausted all the rope in the house and still there was a shortage of two inches to complete the round. The other *gopis*, who had come to watch the fun, now began to laugh at Yashoda's predicament. As for her, she could not imagine what the matter was. She was still to learn the folly of trying to bind the One who is boundless. The mocking gleam was more pronounced, and the *gopis* started tittering among themselves and whispering. "She didn't believe us when we told her and see now she herself is suffering!"

The poor mother was desperate. She cast an imploring look at her little son. Seeing the pathetic state of His perspiring mother, with hair dishevelled and flowers falling from it, Krishna felt pity and allowed Himself to be bound. Not even the gods could attain as much grace from Him as He showed to this *gopi*, His mother, for the rope of love is the only cord capable of binding the Boundless.

"Just you stay there, you naughty boy," she said sternly, as she bound Him with ease and hoped to convince the others that she was fully capable of punishing the little rogue. Everyone drifted away, leaving Him alone. His mother also went inside after admonishing Him once more.

Luckily, He had thought of hiding some of the butter in the hole in the mortar. He took it out and had a small feast, but soon He became quite bored. What was He to do now, since He had given an unspoken promise to His mother to remain tied? Suddenly, He spied a pair of gigantic trees in the distance. They were growing very close to each other. In fact, between them there was such a small gap that only a very small boy like Him could manage to squeeze through. He was struck with a desire to put His theory to the test. Now was as good a time as any. He set off at a brisk trot on His chubby legs followed by a grumbling, rumbling pounding stone. In all its life it had never been treated so ignominiously. It hardly befitted a stone of its dignity to be bouncing up and down in the wake of a small boy like this! Krishna had reached the trees and passed with ease through the gap between them, thereby proving His point, but the poor stone got well and truly stuck. Krishna looked back and saw the impediment.

"One, two, three," He said and gave a slight tug. Both the trees crashed to the ground with a terrible rending noise. In their place stood two handsome celestials. They were the sons of Kubera, the god of wealth, and were known as Nalakubera and Manigriva. They had been cursed by the sage Narada in order to curb their pride, arising from the intoxication of wealth. The spell could only be lifted by the touch of the Lord, who had embarked on this particular game to fulfill the words of His devotee, Narada. With folded palms they bowed low and extolled Him.

"Bless us, O Lord, for we are the servants of Your devotee Narada. It was by his blessing that we have this opportunity to see You. In the future, may our words be always devoted to the narration of Your excellences. May our ears be always listening to the accounts of Your deeds. May our hands be ever engaged in performing work for Your sake. May our minds ever rest in constant remembrance of Your feet. May our heads always remain bowed in reverence before Your temple, which is the whole Universe."

Hearing this, the Lord was pleased. He blessed them and sent them back to their abode in the Himalayas. The celestials rained flowers on Him and addressed Him with a new appellation—Damodara, the one with a rope around His waist.

Hearing the terrific sound of the falling trees, Nanda and the gopalas rushed to the place to find Krishna sitting happily on the mortar eating the small, black berries from the tree. Nanda liberated Him who is capable of liberating all souls. Yashoda anxiously inspected Him for bruises, but could find none. Everyone commented on the miraculous way in which this child managed to escape from danger.

Another day, when Krishna was toddling through the streets on another of His nefarious errands, He saw an old lady laboriously carrying a basket of fruit that she had managed to collect from the forest.

"Give me some, give me some!" He lisped, running to her and tugging at her sari.

She looked at that cherubic face and was lost. "I generally sell may fruits in exchange for grain, but for you I'll give my whole hoard free," she said.

Krishna, the Bestower of the fruits of action to all, refused to take anything free. "My father is very rich. He has plenty of grain. Come with me and I'll give you as much as you wish," He said.

So saying, He darted off like a blue arrow and the lady labored after Him. This way, that way, she saw flashes of blue fire and soon came to His house. By this time, Krishna had darted inside, imperiously calling His mother to get the grain. But Yashoda had gone out for a visit. The house seemed deserted. What was He to do? Going inside, He grabbed as much grain as His little hands could hold and with the greatest concentration He walked with bated breath, gazing fixedly at His hands so that not even a single grain would fall. But despite His best efforts, all along His passage the grains slipped through His baby fingers. When He emptied the two fistfuls with a sigh of relief into her basket, it was doubtful whether there were more than five or six grains all together. The child beamed with joy at His own efforts and looked happily at the old lady. She smiled tenderly at Him and wiped the beads of perspiration from His forehead with her torn garment.

Then she sat down on the steps and made Him sit in her lap. She took a fistful of berries from the basket and filled His cupped palms. Two more were needed to fill them to the brim. She turned to search for two big berries to place on top and when she looked around his hands were empty. Once more she filled them, and once more the same thing happened. This kept on until the last berry was in His mouth and the basket empty. "Are you satisfied now, my precious?" she enquired anxiously.

He nodded His head vigorously so that the bunch of curls bounced up and down. He couldn't speak, for His mouth was too full. Though she had received only a few grains in return for her entire store of fruit, the old lady's heart was filled with unspeakable joy. Lifting the empty basket onto her head, she walked forward with a lilt. She had hardly gone a few steps when she felt a great weight on her head and, putting the basket down, she found that it was filled with precious gems as big as the fruits. They sparkled in the sun, glistening and gleaming—some black like Krishna's eyes, winking at her in mischief, some blue like His body as He darted before her like a flame, some pink like His palms upturned to receive her fruits. Everywhere, everywhere, her poor old eyes were dazzled by the colors and the memories they evoked. She turned back for one more glimpse of Him. Nothing could she see, but she did not mind, for inside her heart His form shone forever.

Who can explain the *lila* of this divine Being who played these pranks to the delight of the simple cowherds of Gokula? Assuming the role of a village child, He sang and danced at the command of the *gopis* as if He were a sort of puppet. He fetched and carried for them, played and pranced for them, and ran to do their bidding to show that He was One who would subordinate Himself to fulfill even the slightest wish of His devotees.

Nanda and the other elders among the *gopas* now started to feel alarmed at all the extraordinary happenings in their settlement and the number of miraculous escapes this child seemed to be having. They had a conference to decide what best could be done. An old man called Upananda declared that there was some evil spirit in that place, that God alone had protected their child and kept Him from harm. He suggested that it would be better to shift to a new place before any further calamity took place. The nearby forest of Vrindavan was noted for its beauty and had plenty of virgin pasture for the cows. This was an important point for them since they depended on their cows for their livelihood. All of them readily agreed to make the move, and they got their carts ready and started on the trek. The old men, the women, the children, and their possessions were loaded on the carts and the cavalcade set forth with the cows marching in front, the carts following, and the men and priests behind carrying bows in their hands. How picturesque was the way and how lovely the scene! The calves lowed softly as they ran to keep up with their mothers, the bells on the horns of the bulls tinkled merrily, keeping time with the bells on the wheels of the carts. The *gopalas* blew their horns and trumpets and the *gopis* sitting in the carts sang lyrics about the pranks of their beloved Krishna. Balarama and Krishna were seated in a new cart on the laps of their mothers and neither Yashoda nor Rohini felt the tediousness of the journey, listening to their prattle. They jolted along in the carts until the sun set in the west and they reached the outskirts of Vrindavan, which was bathed in the soft glow of the setting sun. The prominent landmark of the Govardhan Hill loomed in the background, the river Kalindi (or Yamuna) was like a beautiful damsel rushing with delight, as if to meet her lover, and the abundance of flowering trees and bushes drenched the air with their perfumes. They sat for some time soaking in the charm of their first night in the forest of Vrindavan. Fortunate indeed was this place, where all the trees and every blade of grass must have been great sages to have the good fortune to feel the divine feet of the Lord dancing over them, His lotus-petal body brushing them, and His perfumed breath invigorating them.

Since they were a nomadic tribe used to constant moves, the *gopas* cleared the land and set up their dwelling places in no time. Small boys up to the age of five were allowed to tend the calves. Krishna begged His mother to be allowed to go with them, Reluctantly she agreed, for she could not bear to be parted from Him. Her heart yearned after Him and her eyes followed Him until He was no more than a small blue dot in the distance, with the morning sun creating a halo around His head from the dust raised by the hooves of the calves. All the boys carried toys with them. Once they reached a grassy plain, they would allow the calves to graze while they amused themselves. Sometimes they played on the flute, sometimes with their catapults, sometimes with balls, and sometimes with masks in mock bullfights, bellowing like bulls and charging at each other. Thus, He played with those fortunate *gopalas* like an ordinary child.

But while they were leading their idyllic existence in the forest, Kamsa was in a fever of impatience back in Mathura. The three demons he had sent to Gokula had never returned, so he strongly suspected that his enemy was hiding in the cowherd settlement and he called his assistants and sent them to kill the boy Krishna, whom he suspected of being none other than his sister's son.

One day, while Krishna was standing and playing the flute, He spied a calf behaving in an extraordinary manner. It was one of Kamsa's assassins who had taken on a calf's form in the hope of remaining unnoticed. But the divine intelligence could never be baffled, and Krishna caught hold of the calf's hind legs and tail together, whirled him round and round, and hurled him to the top of a tree. As the huge carcass of the demon came hurtling down, it brought down a number of fruits and flowers. Krishna continued His interrupted flute-playing while the other boys rushed to inspect what was happening. They saw the flowers and fruits falling all around Him and asked, "What happened, Krishna? From where have all these flowers and fruits come?" Krishna told them the story and showed them the body of the dead demon.

One day, they went to the lake so that the calves could drink. While they were drinking of the crystal-clear waters of the lake, the boys were terrified to see a huge crane flapping its wings and advancing threateningly toward them with parted beak. It was a demon called Baka, and it rushed at Krishna and swallowed Him. The other boys were petrified and could do nothing. But the crane spat Him out as fast as it had swallowed Him, for it felt as if it had swallowed a live coal, so hot had the Lord's body become! Nothing daunted, it tried to pierce Him with its sharp beak, but Krishna pried it open and tore it apart as easily as one would split a blade of grass. The boys were filled with wonder and reported all the events of each day when they reached home. The elders listened to all these strange tales in growing amazement and marvelled at the prowess of this unique child in their midst.

How happy were the years that Krishna and Balarama spent in the forest of Vrindavan with their companions. The weather never grew too hot in summer, nor did the grass become dry. The trees were always laden with blossoms, and a gentle breeze blew over the foreheads of the boys. In spring they would play on the swings or they would play hide-and-seek among the trees. Sometimes they would dance like peacocks or quack like ducks, leap over the streams like frogs or make a ring and try to catch Krishna as He darted between their entwined arms. Even the animals had a special love for Him and the cows lowed happily when He went near them and caressed them. Bedecked with garlands made of wildflowers, He would imitate the stately tread of the swans and the cries of birds. Sometimes, tired after the bouts of boxing with His friends, He would rest with His head on a bed of flowers they had made for Him. In this way, hiding His identity by the power of His own *maya* and assuming the form of a common cowherd boy, He who was in reality the Supreme Divine lived a rustic's life amidst the humble rural folk. But whatever He did, He did to perfection, throwing Himself heart and soul into the role He was enacting.

Thus ends the fifth chapter of The Play of God,
named "Bondage of the Boundless."

Hari Aum Tat Sat

The first creator (Brahma) knew the Supreme Person. He in turn made Him known to Indra (the king of gods) for the benefit of all beings. Hence, even today he who knows Him and the creation thus, as pervaded and permeated and possessed by this Supreme Person, attains immortality. There is no other way for spiritual perfection.
—*Purusha Suktam*

SIX

BRAHMA BEMUSED

The celestials looked on in wonder at the sight of Him to whom all the offerings at yajnas (sacrificial ceremonies) are made, sitting in boyish delight to take His food amidst His playmates, with a flute stuck in His waist, a horn tucked into His left armpit, a staff in hand, a ball of curd-rice in His right hand, and various delicacies between His fingers, sitting in a circle made by His friends, cracking jokes and making them laugh.
—SHRIMAD BHAGAVATA

One day, Krishna got up very early, for He had decided to have a picnic in the woods. He blew loudly on His horn to wake up His companions and set out with the calves. The boys danced and frolicked as they went, carrying their slings, sticks, horns, flutes, and mud pots with their lunches. Though their mothers had adorned them with golden ornaments, they embellished themselves further with tender leaves, flowers, peacock feathers, and mineral powders. Some buzzed like bees, some cooed like pigeons, some ran under the shadows of flying birds, some pulled monkeys by their tails, some climbed trees, jumping from one branch to another, and some chased the frogs through the streams. How can one describe the good fortune of those inhabitants of Vrindavan before whose physical eyes stood He whom *yogis* fail to attain despite austerities practiced in life after life?

At this time, a demon named Agha, Putana's brother, made his appearance in the form of a huge python. He lay in wait for the boys with his mouth wide open like a cave. The boys, on seeing him, thought him to be another extraordinary feature of the scenery of Vrindavan. He had kept his huge tongue hanging out, and they mistook it for a newly made road and ran into his gaping mouth before Krishna could stop them. Instead of swallowing them immediately, the demon kept his jaw open in the hope that Krishna would enter. Though He knew who it was, Krishna entered Agha's mouth and there grew in size so that very soon Agha could not breathe. Eventually he suffocated to death. As the boys, led by Krishna, came out of the body of the monster, they saw a radiance coming out of the python and merging into Krishna.

After this, Krishna led them to the sandy bank of the Yamuna, which was an ideal place for a picnic. First, they let the calves drink their fill and let them loose near some grass. Then they placed Krishna in the middle and sat around Him in circles, looking like the petals of a lotus. They ate from plates made of leaves, bark, and petals. Think of the sight of Him, to whom the most delicious food offerings are made at costly sacrifices conducted by kings, sitting in the midst of His friends sharing their simple fare, joking and teasing them, and offering them delicacies from His own hoard. Seeing this unique sight, the creator Brahma was steeped in wonder. Desirous of seeing more of this Divine Child's play, he spirited away the calves into his own world, known as Brahmaloka.

After enjoying this delightful interlude with the Lord, the boys noticed that the calves were missing. Krishna told them not to interrupt their meal and that He would go Himself to bring back the straying calves. Still carrying the half-eaten ball of rice in His right hand and a staff in His left, He wandered off in search of the calves. In the meantime, Brahma came and spirited away the boys as well. Unsuccessful in His attempt to find the calves, Krishna returned to the riverbank to find that the boys had also vanished. It dawned on Him that this was a joke by the creator Brahma. He decided to play along with him. In the evening, when it was time to return home, they were still missing, so He took on the forms of all the missing boys and calves, the sticks and slings, and the pots and flutes. This is the experience of *yogis* in God consciousness, when they see all things, including inanimate objects, as divine.

As the calves, as the *gopalas*, as the toys and vessels, and as Himself, Krishna, the soul of all beings, entered Vraja. As this remarkable contingent returned, the *gopis* and mother cows, instead of welcoming Krishna first, as was their habit, ran to their own children and calves, for everyone and everything was *Krishnamaya* (filled with Krishna). Therefore, on that day no one saw any difference between their own children and Yashoda's child.

A *jivatma* (embodied soul), due to its past *karma* (results of past actions), is born in our wombs and we pet it, fondle it, and call it our own—flesh of our flesh. But Krishna is more than our flesh. He is the Soul of our soul. Naturally they loved Him more dearly than their own children. For one year this impersonation went on and every evening when the little cavalcade consisting of so many Krishnas returned to the village, the *gopis* bathed Him and fed Him and fondled Him and put Him to sleep in all their houses. With the cows it was the same. Thus did the Lord spend one year in the houses of the *gopis* as their own sons and in the cowsheds as the calves. In the mornings, He would set out to the forest tending Himself as calves and *gopalas*.

Balarama, who was the incarnation of the Lord's power as Shesha, noticed these startling signs of overwhelming affection by the *gopas* and *gopis* for their own children instead of for Krishna and realized that it was all a play of the Lord. He tackled His brother about this and was let into the secret.

A human year is only a minute to Brahma, so when he came back a while later he was surprised to find the scene exactly as he had left it. Krishna was sitting in the middle, the *gopalas* were seated around Him, and He was holding the half-eaten ball of curd-rice in His right hand and the staff in His left, teasing and laughing with them while the calves frisked around them merrily. Brahma was thoroughly confused. He knew for sure that he had just whisked the calves and boys away a while ago, a year ago to be exact according to human calculations, and here they were all exactly as he had seen them before! In compassion, the Lord gave him the eye of wisdom, with which he saw that all the boys and calves were replicas of Lord Vishnu—four-armed, holding the conch, discus, mace, and lotus, having the *Shrivatsa* mark and the jewel *Kaustubha* on the chest, adorned with the *vanamala*, or garland of *tulsi* leaves (from the holy basil plant), and many divine ornaments. And what was more wondrous was that even the inanimate things carried by the boys like the flutes, slings, sticks, and pots had the same form. Many celestial beings, including himself, were seen by Brahma as kneeling down and worshipping the Lord of Vraja. According to the *Bhagavad Gita*, it was the experience of the great devotees to see everything as Vaasudeva (Krishna), and this was the experience that Brahma had. His pride was thoroughly humbled and he did not know what to do.

At last, the Lord had pity on his predicament and when he looked again, Brahma saw that immeasurable consciousness, in the assumed form of a cowherd body, going about in search of His calves and companions with a ball of rice in His hand. Thereupon, Brahma got down from his divine vehicle, the swan, in haste and prostrated before the Divine Child and began to extol Him.

"O Lord of Lords! Even I who am the firstborn, having come out of Your own navel, cannot understand the mystery of Your form, which is not fashioned of material elements but of Your own will in order to bless devotees. Who can calculate Your attributes? Only the one who surrenders body, mind, and intellect to You can become eligible for liberation. I am but a spark of Your mighty flame and therefore it behooves You to pardon my stupidity. You have demonstrated to me today how the One, undifferentiated consciousness, as You were in the beginning of cosmic time, came to be differentiated and changed into numberless forms. What is this world but Your jugglery? You unfold the universe of Your own free will, assuming the role of myself, Brahma, to create, Yourself, Vishnu, to uphold and sustain the creation, and Shiva for its dissolution. O Almighty One! O Bhagavan! None can say anything definite as to where, how, when, and in what way Your play as the incarnate is going to take shape. Nor can anyone find an explanation for it. It is all part of Your divine mystery. Without You, there is no world.

You are the Truth. You are the Self-manifest. You are the Cause of all causes, the Indweller in all, the Eternally Blissful. He who is able to see You, the One Universal Spirit as manifesting in all, certainly overcomes this *samsara*, or transmigratory existence. Bondage and liberation are not actual facts but mere names arising from ignorance of the truth which is You alone. The *atman* (the divinity within each soul) has no other phase except that of truth, consciousness, and bliss, just as in the sun there is neither day nor night but only eternal effulgence. You are the indweller in all, yet people search for You outside and thus can never find You. But without Your grace, none can ever come to realize this truth. Pray confer the boon of *bhakti*, or devotion, on me so that I may be ever engaged in adoring Your lotus feet in every birth I take, whether as Brahma or man or animal. How fortunate are these women and cows of Vraja, for in the form of their sons and calves You sucked their milk for one whole year. What is the good of being a god like me? I would deem it the greatest good fortune if I could be born even as a blade of grass in this enchanting forest of Vrindavan, where I would get a chance of being bathed in the dust of Your holy feet. O Krishna! You are the sun of the Vrishni (Yadava) clan. You are the Master of the Universe and the Lord of Vraja. To You, O Krishna, my homage for eternity." So glorifying Him, Brahma prostrated before the lotus feet of the blue boy of Vrindavan, circled him three times, and departed to his own realm after receiving Krishna's blessings.

The *gopalas* and the calves who had been spirited away a year ago now appeared, but since they had been in Brahma's world, they felt that they had been away only for a few moments. There is no memory which cannot be effaced by the Lord's *maya*.

The boys said to Krishna, "You've returned so soon. You haven't even finished eating Your ball of rice. Come and sit comfortably and eat." They concluded their interrupted picnic and returned home, and the boys announced at Vraja that Krishna had killed the demon Aghasura, even though the event had occurred a year ago.

Now that He had attained the hoary age of six, Krishna was promoted to look after the cows instead of the calves, along with the older boys. He went with them to distant parts of the forest which had been hitherto forbidden to Him. One day, a *gopala* named Shridama, a dear friend of His, said to Him, "Not far from here there is a palm grove which has been forbidden to us, since the wicked demon Dhenuka lives there. He has the form of a donkey and kills all who go there. The fruits of those trees have a unique flavor. Please let us go and get a few of the fruits." Nothing loathe, Krishna said, "Come, let's go."

He was ever ready to meet the most taxing demands of His friends, so, together with Balarama, He entered the forbidden forest. They looked at each other, Balarama, the incarnation of Adishesha, and Krishna, the *avatar* of Vishnu, and an unmistakable message passed between them. With a laugh, Balarama took hold of the trees one by one and shook them hard so that the ripe, juicy fruits fell down in clusters. Hearing this sound, the donkey-demon came rushing out furiously and kicked Balarama in the chest. He was about to kick him again when Balarama caught hold of him by his hind legs and whirled him round and round with one hand and threw his dead body onto the top of a palm tree. The tree crashed down, felling a number of other trees. The boys came rushing into the forest shouting excitedly. They picked up the ripe fruits and, after eating their fill, they carried loads of fruit back home, singing merrily the while. The palm fruits, when ripe, had a slightly intoxicating effect and by the time they went home, all of them were slightly inebriated. With the death of Dhenuka, the forest was liberated. People could collect as much fruit as they liked, and the cows, too, could graze without fear.

Another day, Krishna went to the banks of the Kalindi without His brother Balarama. It was summer and the cows and the *gopalas*, who were very thirsty, drank deep from the water. All of them fell down in a swoon. At this spot the river water was extremely poisonous, for the multi-headed serpent Kaliya lived there. So strong was the poison coming from him that nothing could remain alive near the banks. The grass and trees around the place had withered, and even the birds fell down dead when they flew over this spot. The forest appeared to have retreated in dread from its edge. Even the mist and spray which arose from the waters had a noxious effect. As Krishna observed the desolation, He decided that the time had come to get rid of Kaliya and deliver the creatures of the forest from his baneful presence.

Seeing the inert and lifeless forms of the cows and His friends, the Lord cast His loving glance at them and sprinkled on them the life-giving water from His eyes. They rose up as if from a dream. Krishna comforted them and told them not to be frightened, for He would kill the serpent. The only living thing near that accursed place was a *kadamba* tree on which Garuda (an eagle, the vehicle of Lord Vishnu) had once sat. Without much ado, Krishna climbed this tree and plunged into the swirling, poisoned waters below! His friends watched breathlessly as He thrashed about in the water creating a huge whirlpool to attract the attention of the snake. Enraged at this strange disturbance of his peace, Kaliya raised his cluster of heads in order to see who had been so foolhardy as to jump in. When he saw Krishna, he flew at Him, bit Him all over, wound his coils around Him, and dragged Him down to the bottom of the infested pool. Holding Him thus in a tight embrace and darting his tongue here and there like flames all over His body, the snake gave Him bite after bite. But he found to his surprise that his teeth made no impression on Krishna's body. Instead, they broke and fell out.

Seeing their beloved playmate disappear with Kaliya to the bottom of pool, the *gopalas* were so terrified that they started to cry and some fell down in a swoon. At the same time, terrible omens were seen at Vraja. Nanda and Yashoda were very unhappy to note these ill omens and they felt worse when they discovered that Balarama had not gone to the forest that day with Krishna. They knew that it was the Lord's inevitable custom to leave His elder brother behind whenever He wanted to embark on some new escapade. They collected the other *gopas* and *gopis* and all ran to Vrindavan to search for Krishna. On reaching the banks of the Kalindi, they found the unconscious boys and the cows lowing piteously and gazing at the spot where Krishna had disappeared. Yashoda was only restrained from jumping into the river by the other *gopis*. All of them except Balarama, who alone knew the extent of Krishna's prowess, were sorely distressed. Seeing His mother and the others in agony, Krishna released Himself from the snake's hold and came up. He had been waiting for just such an audience before starting His dance. The serpent darted after Him, with hoods spread menacingly, hissing and blowing poisonous fumes through his nostrils. Fixing his red-hot eyes on Him, the snake tried to mesmerize the Lord and render Him powerless. But Krishna merely looked amused at the creature's pranks and playfully swam round and round him in full sight of the *gopalas*, so that the snake also started to revolve. Tiring of this particular frolic, the Lord lightly sprang onto one hood of the snake and began His macabre dance. When Kaliya brought up his tail in order to thrash Him, Krishna laughed and caught hold of it in His right hand. Holding the flute in His left, He played a divine melody, dancing the while on the snake's many hoods. When one head was crushed, He would jump onto another. The sky became filled with the celestials who had come to watch the show and also to provide music for His wonderful dance! The sight was so remarkable that the *gopas* and *gopis* forgot their fears and started to watch the astonishing performance in wonder. The setting sun spotlighted this strange scene of the black snake writhing in mortal agony with the jewel-like child dancing merrily to the melodious strains of the flute. His pink feet twinkled like lotus petals blown in the wind and His anklets tinkled as He jumped from head to head. The red rays of the dying sun mingled with the blood of the dying snake and made the river crimson. Kaliya's eyes, which had been gleaming like rubies at the beginning, had become dull and cloudy. Battered and bruised in body and spirit, his pride thoroughly humbled, he was a miserable wreck of his former glory. He began to think of his creator, the Lord of all beings, and mentally took refuge in Him. At this, the wives of Kaliya ranged themselves before Krishna and begged Him to spare the life of their husband. Unable to resist any plea, Krishna lightly jumped off his hoods and swam to the shore. Kaliya followed Him and, fully repenting of his deeds, came and bowed before Him.

"O Master!" he said, "You created this universe with its infinite varia-
tions. We serpents are by birth ferocious and cruel. How can we overcome our nature? You alone can help us in this. Our salvation and our
destruction are both in Your hands."

Krishna said, "Depart, O Kaliya. Go with all your kindred and subjects to the island of Ramanaka in the middle of the ocean. You are banished forever from this pool in the Kalindi, which you have poisoned and
have thus debarred other creatures from using."

Then Kaliya, bruised and bleeding, answered, "Alas! O Lord! As I
depart to the island, that bird of Yours, Garuda, who is my archenemy,
will surely see me and destroy that life which You have spared."

Then Krishna answered gently, "No, my friend. When Garuda (Vishnu's, and thus Krishna's, vehicle) sees My footprint on your head, he will
not dare to attack you, for he will know that you have been blessed by
Me. So have no fear, and depart in peace." So saying, He placed His
hands on Kaliya's heads and made him whole again. Hearing this, Kaliya
regained his spirits and, together with his retinue of snakes, he prostrated
to the Lord and departed to Ramanaka.

Thus, the dwellers of Vrindavan were freed from the terrible scourge
of the serpent Kaliya. Once more could they bathe in the reviving waters
of the Kalindi and drink their fill. Once more did the withered trees and
bushes bloom and the flowers dance, and the forest crept back to the
banks of the river.

The cowherds and cows, hungry and tired though they were, did not
return to their settlement that night but decided to spend it on the banks
of the river, for Nanda still had his doubts that the child Krishna might
have been affected by the poison. There was no way by which he could
know this. People who are poisoned by snakes are generally thought to
turn blue, but this child was naturally a blue color, so what were they to
do? Another belief they had was that one suffering from snakebite should
fast and should not be allowed to sleep, for he might never wake up. The
only way to ensure this was to stay in the forest for the night, for if they
went back, Krishna would surely beg, borrow, or steal something to eat.
So they lit a fire and lay down around it. It was a calm, still, and sultry
night. While the others slept, Nanda kept watch with Krishna. Suddenly,
a breeze sprang up out of nowhere and the cowherd chief saw to his horror that a raging forest fire, like a sheet of flame, was advancing toward
them with alarming rapidity. Quickly, he woke up the others. The *gopas*

did not know what to do, but the children had no such doubts. "O Krishna! Krishna!" they cried. "Save us from this calamity as You have saved us so often before!"

Krishna smilingly reassured them and stepped forward in the path of Agni, the god of fire, and opening His small mouth, He quietly swallowed that mighty flame in three gulps. The men looked on in wonder at Him who had saved them in this miraculous manner. Then Krishna turned to His father and asked him, "Now are you satisfied, Father?"

Fire is supposed to be the greatest purifier, capable of reducing even poison to ashes, and the Lord wanted to reassure His father that even if He had been poisoned, He would have been cleansed by the fire He had swallowed. Nanda gathered Him up in his arms and embraced Him. Who was this strange child, he wondered, now wholly divine, now completely human? What was he to believe? The only thing he knew was that he loved his little son to the exclusion of everything else and, as the sage Gargacharya had prophesied, this child had the power to save all those who loved and depended on Him.

Afterward, Krishna was taken in procession to the settlement surrounded by His friends and relatives and the cattle, singing and rejoicing at His safe return.

Now came the hot summer season, but while the Lord made His residence at Vraja, the summer resembled spring. Due to the delightful sound of the waterfalls, the chirping of the crickets, the luxuriant growth of grass, and the perfume of the lotuses and water lilies, the inhabitants of Vrindavan did not know the intense heat of the sun or the forest fires that were characteristic of summer.

One day, Krishna went to the forest as usual with His friends. They regaled themselves with various sports, like wrestling, whirling, leaping, pulling, and boxing. Sometimes they danced while Krishna played the flute, and sometimes He would dance while the others provided the music and clapped in rhythm. While they were thus playing under a huge banyan tree, a demon called Pralamba arrived in the form of a *gopala* and joined the group. Many others in various guises had come to kill the boy Krishna and had failed. So Pralamba had the brilliant idea of taking on the form of a *gopala* and thus lulling His suspicions. Krishna penetrated his disguise immediately but, willing to give him the benefit of the doubt, asked him to join their game. After all, demon though he was, he had taken on a form which was dear to the Lord. The group split into two teams with Krishna and Balarama as the team leaders. Various games were arranged, at the end of which the defeated person would have to carry his victorious counterpart on his shoulders and walk to the banyan tree. Pralamba chose to be on Krishna's side, for he thought that he could easily defeat Balarama and then deal with Krishna. At the end of the game, Krishna's party was defeated and He took Shridama on His shoulders, while Pralamba took Balarama and started walking. The Lord, who had killed ten demons with His baby hands, allowed Himself to be defeated by one who grappled with love! He is ready to carry any of His devotees who surrender to Him, as He carried Shridama.

In the meantime, Pralamba set off at a brisk trot with Balarama, jubilant at the success of his plan. Not stopping to look back or see what was happening, and unmindful of Balarama's cries to stop, he strode on past the tree, determined to take him straight to Kamsa. By this time he had taken on his own huge, demonic form, so Balarama could not jump off. Balarama turned around to look at Krishna and, from afar, the Lord made a sign to him to crush the demon's neck. Such was the power of the look that Balarama was able to strangle him to death. The *gopalas* ran forward to see the mighty form of the dead demon.

While the boys were discussing the wonders of the day, the cows had wandered afar in search of grass. Concerned about their disappearance, the boys searched far and wide and eventually traced them to a field. Having left the shade of the trees, the cows were dazed by the blinding heat of the sun and did not know which way to turn. Hearing the beloved voice of their master, they were preparing to return, when the dry grass was swept by a wave of fire that soon turned into a mighty conflagration. Terrified at the sight of the advancing flames, the *gopalas* and the cows cowered in fear and thronged around Krishna.

"Don't panic," said the quiet voice beside them. "Just close your eyes and hold Me and no harm will befall you." With absolute trust, they did as they were told. No longer did they have the slightest fear, no longer did the fire have power to harm them, for that beloved voice had spoken and they knew that He would never fail them.

"Why are you standing like statues, closing your eyes?" Now it was the little boy speaking teasingly and they opened their eyes and found themselves back under the banyan tree where they had been playing. The rubbed their eyes in surprise. Had they dreamed the terrible happenings of a minute ago? Where was their guardian angel? Was He only a little boy laughing and rolling in the grass, making faces, pulling their hair, jumping and climbing trees like all little boys, or was He a superhuman? They followed Him in glee. Why bother to puzzle their heads as to who or what He was? Let them enjoy the present while they could.

Now the rainy season was upon them. It was characterized by bright circles around the sun and the moon, angry skies fille with gathering clouds, and claps of thunder. The brilliance of the heavanly bodies was dimmed by the dark thunderheads and streaks of lighting. The land, which had shrunk in the summer heat, now became filled with luxuriant vegetation and in the night the fireflies dominated the scene, for the stars were hidden by the clouds. The frogs began their serenade and all the little streams, which had dried up, now gushed and gurgled with delight. The whole forest took on a festive appearance. Even in this season, the children would take the cows up the hill slope and into the woods, but when it rained they would take shelter under the trees or in caves, munching roots, tubers, and fruits. The splendor of the season was enhanced by the presence of the Lord.

Next came the autumn season, with its clear skies and mild breezes. Ushered in by the lotus flowers, the autumn season saw the turbid waters of the rivers and lakes becoming clear and limpid. Relieved of their rains, the clouds now shone in white brilliance. At night, the clear skies revealed the stars in all their clarity and the autumn moon rose, large and red, on the eastern horizon.

Thus, the golden days of childhood slipped by like gleaming beads threaded on the rays of sunshine.

Thus ends the sixth chapter of The Play of God, *named "Brahma Bemused."*

Hari Aum Tat Sat

SEVEN

THE ENCHANTING FLUTE

Venunadashara-
daya namaha

Homage to the
One who is an
expert flutist

Extolled by the gopalas, Krishna entered the forest of Vrinda-
van, which had become more beautiful because of His foot-
prints. He was dressed like a professional dancer, wearing a
garment of golden radiance, a garland of wild tulsi leaves with
peacock feathers in His hair, and ear ornaments of karnikara
seeds. Thus attired, He played the flute, filling its holes with the
honey of His lips.
—SHRIMAD BHAGAVATA

Though He had only reached the age of twelve, such
was Krishna's grace and beauty that none could
resist Him. He is one who can arouse the desire of
the world; how then could those poor *gopis* of Vrindavan
resist Him? They did not even try. They had fondled Him
as a baby, kissed Him as a toddler, played with Him as a
child, and now He stood before them, the epitome of all
that a man, the true *Purusha*,[1] should be. Like the Yamuna
flowing toward her goal, the ocean, so their hearts flowed
toward their Lord. Their minds were untutored, their intel-
lects poor, but their hearts were large and full of love and
they burst and flowed toward Him in a never-ending
stream, following Him wherever He went. Each morning
as He left with the *gopalas* and the cows to the forest, the
poor girls could hardly contain themselves until the
evening, when He returned. They could not concentrate on
their daily tasks, they could not think of anything else but
Him. They begrudged every minute He spent away from
them and waited only for the moment when they could see
the tip of the peacock feather adorning His hair in the far

[1] *Purusha*—Male aspect of God, formless, attributeless, the ground on which
the creation stands, as opposed to Prakriti or the manifest universe, the
creation, the female aspect of God. Also used to denote masculinity.

55

distance. Then they would forget their fatigue and loneliness and rush toward Him to welcome Him and throng around Him until it was time for Him to go home. During the day, they would picture Him standing beneath the spreading branches of a tree, perhaps leaning slightly on the trunk with one leg crossed over the other in a dancer's pose, and playing a divine melody on the flute placed close to His lips. The melody was the call of the infinite to the finite, and it awoke the chords in even the most sluggish hearts and made them yearn for union with the infinite, which is the hidden desire of every heart. This yearning is present in every human being, but sometimes we are too engrossed with the world or too poor of understanding to know what it is. All we know is that we are incomplete and inadequate as we are, but are ignorant of what it is that will make us complete. Sometimes a touch, a glance, or a word spoken by some great sage is enough to loosen our bonds and open our eyes, and then our heart leaps forward to meet its maker. Confinement to finitude is unbearable to the human being. We crave for nothing short of the Infinite and Eternal. The whole of the finite world moves and progresses toward this infinity and until it reaches there, it will remain unsatisfied. All the baubles offered by the material world fail to satisfy because they are themselves products of finitude and impermanent by nature.

As Krishna played His divine melody, the entire aspect of the forest changed. The birds flying in the air stopped to listen, the animals moved closer to Him, and even the Yamuna is said to have stopped her flow to listen to the enchanting music. All moving things became immobilized and the immovables, like the stones and rocks, started to melt and flow, such was the bewitching power of His music. Even the rocks could not withstand the eager, enticing call to the life divine, for He is Manamohana, the one who arouses the desire of all minds.

"Awake! Awake! O sleeping soul!" He seemed to be saying. "Come to Me, your Lord. Why do you slumber when I am here ready to play the dance of Eternal Life with you? Wake up, O sluggish mind! Awake, O stony heart! Come to Me, the Divine Beloved. I will make you experience the meaning of bliss!"

Without understanding this truth, it would be impossible to understand how a child of twelve could so entice grown women that they forgot every fidelity for which Indian women are renowned and ran after Him regardless of consequences. Even the hearts of the wicked, hard as granite, melted at the call of the divine flute. What wonder, then, that the *gopis*, who had already given their minds to Him as a baby, should quiver and burn with an overwhelming longing to have Him as their husband? They were not sages, they were not *yogis*, they knew nothing of philosophy or metaphysics. All they knew was that He was a man and they were women, and they longed with every fiber of their beings to have Him as their lover. Because their longing was invested in Him who was the beloved of the universe, though carnal in nature at first, it became transformed into something wonderful and indescribable. As they sat in their huts listening to the melodious strains of the flute coming from the forest, they thought to themselves, "The supreme fulfillment of having eyes is to be able to drink the beauty of His face as He stands playing the flute in the forest. How fortunate are the trees, flowers, and animals of this forest to be able to enjoy this bliss at close quarters and to see His beguiling form in front of them, while we unlucky ones are confined to this cage and unable to go!"

"What meritorious deed has this flute done to have the privilege of imbibing the pure honey of His lips without any restriction? Will that flute ever leave something for us? Will we ever be able to taste the nectar of His lips one day? How lucky are the deer who nestle close to Him and nudge Him as He plays. How lucky are the calves who stand pinned to the spot, forgetting even to swallow the milk and eat the grass in their mouths, fixing their gaze on Him as if they would drink Him in through their eyes! Surely the birds of this forest must be sages in disguise, for see how they have perched themselves on the branches above His head and are listening enthralled to the strains of His melody! See the Yamuna, how she brings lotus flowers as offerings and places them at His feet. Even the clouds stop their wanderings and send a mild spray of water over His head like a benediction. Surely the Govardhan Hill must be the luckiest of all, for it has the great privilege of coming into contact with His feet and of offering Him all the delicacies He enjoys—the fruits, canes, tubers, and nuts."

Thus constantly thinking of Him, the *gopis* spent their days and waited for His arrival in the evening. Day by day their minds were more closely bound to Him, so that soon their state was that of meditating *yogis*.

At the beginning of the winter season, the young maidens decided to take a forty-one-day vow in connection with the worship of the goddess Karthyayani[2] to procure Krishna as their lover. Every day these young

---

[2] Karthyayani is another name for Parvati, the wife of Shiva. Parvati had practiced spiritual disciplines to have the great Lord Shiva as her husband, so the *gopis* prayed to her.

girls would wake up at three in the morning and go to the river Kalindi in the bitter cold and take their baths at sunrise. There on the banks, they would install an image of the goddess made of sand and worship her with sandalwood paste, garlands, incense, lamps, fruits, and food offerings.

"O Devi Karthyayani! Thou mighty cosmic power and mistress of all! Deign to make the son of Nanda my husband." Repeating this *mantra*, those maidens of Vraja worshipped the goddess for one full month, regardless of bodily hardships, with their minds fixed on Krishna, praying that they might procure Him as their husband. On the final day of their vow, they deposited their clothes on the riverbanks as usual and sported joyously in the water singing songs about their Lord. It was still very early in the morning and the pearly mists of dawn were enshrouding the surrounding forest. While they were thus playing happily in the river, they suddenly saw the object of their desire standing on the banks, looking like the incarnation of the god of love, smiling teasingly at them. They became aware of their nakedness and covered their faces with their hands and looked shyly at Him through their fingers. Krishna smiled, for He realized that they were not yet completely pure. He decided to help them to get rid of the last traces of their egos. They had lost their sense of possessiveness regarding property, wealth, and relations, but they still had to lose their body consciousness. This was the final barrier keeping them from the fulfillment of their desires. The sense of shame comes only when we are faced with "another," and God is not "another." He is our very "self." What is the need for modesty when we are faced with ourselves? Unless this point is clearly understood, we cannot aspire to union with God. In order to make them realize this, Krishna collected the clothes lying on the banks in heaps and quickly climbed up the *kadamba* tree nearby, saying to the maidens teasingly, "Come on, girls! Come and get your clothes!"

Taken aback by these words of their hero, they shivered, neck deep in the water, and begged Him to return their clothes.

The Lord replied, "If you are indeed my handmaidens as you say, then do as I tell you. Come out of the water, one by one, and accept your clothes. Don't you know that it is a violation of a vow to bathe nude in the waters? Come forward and prostrate before Me, and thus you will be pardoned for this transgression."

Hearing this, the *gopis* threw off their egos like snakes shedding their skins and walked forward one by one with hands outstretched and eyes fixed on Him. In His eyes they saw mirrored their own selves. One by one, they got back their clothes and stood before Him with folded palms and bowed heads, waiting for His next command.

The Lord had tested them to the outer limit and they had passed with ease. Their clothes were stolen, they were told that it was against the rules to bathe nude in the water, and they were forced to abandon their sense of shame and go naked to receive their clothes. They were treated like puppets and made to salute and prostrate. In spite of all this they felt not the slightest resentment. Totally divorced of ego, immersing their minds only in Him, the divine object of their passion, they were fit to receive the final benediction of consorting with Him.

The Lord, knowing what was in their minds, had gone there with the express purpose of fulfilling their desires, and so He told them, "Having cast off the last traces of your ego, you are now ready to receive Me as your Husband, in the true meaning of the word. Passion directed toward Me will not end in sensual enjoyment. Human love is only a shadow of divine love. Who would be happy to remain in the dark when she can enjoy the glory of the sun? Who would be happy with the mere fragrance when she can have the whole flower? That is what I'm offering you now. The flower of divine love, which will lead you to eternal bliss. Your names will go down in history as the luckiest of all women. You are indeed blessed, for you have discovered the secret of divine love, which will end in liberation from this cycle of birth and death. Sensual love is the common experience of all human beings, but *bhakti*, or divine love leading to *mukti*, or liberation, is experienced by only a few rare souls who have prayed and meditated for many years and undertaken many austerities. But you girls, at the end of a mere forty-one-day vow, have been blessed, for you are being offered that which meditating *yogis* gain only after years of struggle. You are all paragons of virtue. You may now return to Vraja. The object with which you have observed this worship of the goddess will before long be fulfilled. You will sport with Me on the moonlit banks of the Yamuna in the autumn."

Hearing these words of their beloved, their cup of happiness was full, and slowly, with dragging footsteps and many backward glances, they wended their way home. The remainder of the time before the consummation of their desire the *gopis* spent in prayer and meditation, so that when the time came, they were perfect, pure, and shining. They had already attained the stage of the *avadhuta*, or the sage who wanders about naked, for clothes symbolize the attachment to false values, beginning with the body. The *gopis* had attained this state and were fit to receive the Lord as their own.

One day while wandering in the woods with the *gopalas*, the Lord said to them, "How noble are the trees. They live entirely for the sake of others. They bear the wind, rain, heat, and sleet, but protect us from them. How covetable is a birth like that, providing sustenance to all beings. They fulfill the wants of all creatures with their leaves, flowers, fruits, roots, and tubers. People take shelter beneath them, and finally they give up their very lives to provide man with fuel. Man's life in this world is meaningful only to the extent that his energies, wealth, and intelligence are utilized for the good of others." Thus to each according to his needs and his capacity, the Lord taught these boys and girls who were devoted to Him.

One day, the boys had finished eating all the food they had brought from their homes and yet they were still hungry, so they begged Krishna to procure some food for them. To meet their demands as well as to bless the wives of certain Brahmins who were performing fire sacrifices (as enjoined in the *Vedas*) in the neighborhood of the forest, Krishna asked the boys to go beg for some food from the Brahmins, for it was incumbent on them to feed the hungry. So the boys ran off and begged for food from those learned Brahmins, who were well-versed in the *Vedas*. Pretending that they had not heard, the learned ones continued to chant *mantras*, deaf to the needs of the hungry boys outside, for they were confirmed ritualists, blind to the inner meaning behind the *Vedic mantras*. The disappointed boys returned with tears in their eyes and Krishna comforted them.

"Never mind," He said. "Such behavior is to be expected from those who have only heads and no hearts. They may be full of learning but their hearts are barren and they know not the meaning of love, out of which alone kindness can flow. But don't lose heart. Go inform their wives that I and My brother are waiting here and they will give you whatever you need, for they have great love for Me."

So, once again the boys went, and this time they were welcomed with great love by those pious ladies, who had been hoping to have a glimpse of the child Krishna from the time they had heard of Him. Though they were reprimanded by their men, they rushed to meet Him, carrying with them all types of delicacies. There was one woman, however, who had been sternly debarred from going and whose husband had locked her up, though her heart was brimming with love for the Lord. So great was her longing to join Him that her spirit left its mortal cage and merged in Him even before the others reached Him. It is said that the Lord had sent the boys on this particular mission only in order to bless her.

The others ran to Him and when they saw Him, blue-complexioned, wearing a golden-colored garment, and decorated with a garland of wild-flowers, with peacock feathers in His hair, twirling a lotus in one hand and resting the other on the shoulder of a friend, they felt their hearts fill with joy. They prostrated before Him and then laid the feast in front of Him. The Lord, knowing their devotion, accepted the offerings and told them to return to their husbands. They were terrified of going back and said, "There is no chance of our husbands accepting us, since we have mortally offended them by coming here. It behooves You to deal with us, for we have offered ourselves body, mind, and spirit at Your feet. We do not desire any other way of life than Your service in the future. Pray, do not forsake us."

The Lord said, "You will not be blamed by your husbands, parents, brothers, or sons for coming to Me. Physical contact is not needed for the growth and fulfillment of spiritual love. Keep your mind fixed on Me always and you will surely attain to Me before long."

So the ladies returned with lagging steps and were surprised to find that their husbands had repented of their folly and welcomed them back cordially. They realized that it was only to bless them that the Lord of the universe had come to them to beg for some food. What irony! He, whom they were worshipping through the *yajna* (fire sacrifice ceremony), had Himself come to them in the guise of a *gopala* and they had sent Him away! But even now, though the realization came to them, yet they desisted from going to Him for fear of the king, Kamsa!

Thus ends the seventh chapter of The Play of God, *named "The Enchanting Flute."*

Hari Aum Tat Sat

EIGHT

KRISHNA LIFTS
THE MOUNTAIN

*Govindaya
namaha*

Homage to the
protector of all
living beings

*At the end of your life, your knowledge of grammar is not going
to save you, O foolish man! Therefore, adore the Supreme Lord,
Govinda (Krishna), for in that alone lies your salvation.*
—ADISHANKARACHARYA

Every year at the end of the summer season, the
cowherds of Vrindavan would offer a great sacrifice
to Indra, the king of the gods and the god of rain.
This was to propitiate him so that he would send enough
rain to make the grass grow for their cattle to feed and
not send too much, which would make the Yamuna flood
its banks and destroy their settlement. Krishna noticed
the preparations and questioned His father about it.

"Every year we make a sacrifice to Indra to show our
gratitude," said Nanda.

"What has he done for us for which we should be
grateful?" queried the Lord.

"Hush, child, don't speak like that. You have no
respect for the gods. Don't you know that it's Indra who
gives us rain? We are cowherds. Our wealth is derived
from our cattle. How will our cows thrive without grass
and how will grass grow if there is no rain? If Indra is not
propitiated, he will not give us rain or he will give too
much of it, and where will we be? Without rain, all
human efforts are of no use."

Hearing this, Krishna replied, "Living beings are
born according to their *karma*[1] and they die according to
it also. *Karma* regulates their attainment of enjoyments

---

[1] *karma*—the cosmic law of cause and effect that applies to the realm of an
individual's thoughts, words and deeds and results in his or her future circumstances.

and their suffering, fears, and welfare. To creatures who are thus subject to their *karma*, of what use is an Indra, who cannot undo the effects of those *karmas*? Therefore, it is best to do one's duty as born of one's nature and thus honor *karma*. That is worship. The three *gunas* (modes) of *Prakriti*: *sattva*, *rajas*, and *tamas*,[2] are the basis of the origin, preservation, and dissolution of the universe. By the power of *rajas* all places get rain, from which all creatures get food. What has Indra got to do with this? Being a forest tribe, we are always staying in the woods and on hills like the Govardhan. Because of the hill the rain clouds are stopped and rain falls in Vrindavan, and it's on the grassy slopes of this hill that our cattle graze and grow sleek and fat and yield plenty of milk. So let a variety of eatables be made and let food and gifts be given to all, including the outcasts. Worship the cows with grass and the hill with sacrificial offerings. This is my view, O Father! This will make everyone happy—the cows, the holy men, and Myself. If it is acceptable to you, you may follow it."

Nanda had been brought up in the tradition of paying respects to all the ancient gods, such as Indra, Varuna, and others, but he had great faith in the words of his son, who possessed extraordinary powers, as he well knew, so he carried out all Krishna's instructions. On the appointed day, under the Lord's supervision, plenty of butter, milk, and sweets, all His favorite dishes, in fact, were prepared in vast quantities.

"Do not stint on anything, Father," Krishna said teasingly. "When you make an offering to God, it should be the very best that you can afford." In and through the prank He was playing, He was also teaching them a valuable lesson—to give honor where honor is due and also to give lavishly when giving.

Carrying loads of food, the entire community trudged up the hillside. There, they lit the sacrificial fire and worshipped the holy men, the cows, and the mountain itself. To generate faith in their minds, Krishna appeared in a gigantic form as the spirit of the mountain and consumed large quantities of the food offerings! No wonder He had asked them to prepare the things He liked best. Then, in His own form as a *gopala*, He prostrated before Himself, and turning to the others He asked them, "In all the years that you have been giving offerings to Indra, has he ever come personally to accept them?" They shook their heads sadly.

---

[2] *Prakriti: sattva, rajas, and tamas*——According to Hindu cosmology, *Prakriti* (the creation) has as its basis three qualities or *gunas*. They are *tamas* (torpor, laziness inertia or ignorance), *rajas* (action, energy, desire, or passion) and *sattva* (truth, harmony, serenity or balance). All objects gross and subtle are said to be constituted by all three qualities in different proportions.

"Now see," said the Lord playfully, "how the Govardhan has accepted your offerings in person!"

After this, they circumambulated the hill and then returned to Vraja in a happy mood after having partaken of the delicious feast.

But Indra was not to be dismissed so easily. He was not going to resign his position and relinquish his accustomed offerings without a struggle. He had listened to Krishna's audacious words to His father and was determined to teach Him a lesson and punish the cowherds for their presumption in withholding the sacrifice which was his due. Thus, he assembled all his mightiest rain clouds and hurled them down with such force that it rained in Vrindavan as it had never rained before in their memory. Drops as large as buckets came pelting down, hour after hour, day after day, without a moment of intermission. The river began to overflow, the trees to be washed away. It looked as if the little settlement with all the people and the cattle would be swept away in a mighty flood if something was not done immediately. When they found that the onslaught refused to abate despite their tardy prayers to an irate Indra, the terrified cowherds ran to Krishna for help. He calmed their fears and spoke reassuringly to them. "Fear not, I will protect those who trust in Me and have no recourse but Me."

Telling them to bring their cattle and all their worldly possessions, He took them to the Govardhan Hill and then, with the greatest of ease, He uprooted the mighty mountain with His tender, boyish hand and held it aloft with one finger as easily as a child would sport with a mushroom! Snugly ensconced beneath this mighty hill, with their cattle and their belongings, the cowherds stayed safely for seven days and seven nights, while the rains lashed down in all fury. Thunder crashed and lightning flashed, the winds howled and the waters poured down in an unending deluge. It resembled the flood waters at the end of Time, for Indra was determined to make them come out of their improvised shelter and beg for mercy. Not even a giant could hold out for so long, thought He, and certainly not a small child like Krishna. Very soon, He will get tired and put down the hill or it may even come down on Him and crush the whole tribe to pulp! But nothing of the sort seemed to be happening. The *gopas* with their usual childlike capacity for living in the present were having a wonderful time in their improvised shelter. They built a fire to keep warm and brought out their usual games and entertainments, holding wrestling bouts and bullfights, while the *gopis* danced and sang and gazed adoringly at the Lord. He stood there holding the hill aloft with one hand and sometimes playing the flute with the other, sometimes tickling the necks of the calves who came nuzzling up to Him, sometimes joking and laughing with the boys, and never for a moment showing the least sign of fatigue. It was a great holiday for the whole community. They did not have to worry about their usual routine chores and could enjoy the divine presence unhampered by the pressing needs of their daily routine.

At last Indra's stock of water seemed to have been exhausted. The drops seemed to be losing their intensity and soon came to a full stop. Even the wind and thunder seemed to have lost their volume and soon the last howl and rumble died away in the distance. Seeing the sky clear of clouds, Krishna led His entourage out into the open. The land had been ravaged by the rain, but the sun was already coming out and soon the waters would dry up. The river had begun to subside and the animals came creeping out of their lairs. In the presence of all, the Lord reinstalled the mountain in its original place. The inhabitants of Vraja could not contain their excitement and joy, and all of them threw themselves at the Lord's feet and hailed Him to the skies. Indra looked down from his heaven and knew to his fury that a new star had appeared on the firmament which would eclipse him in the years to come.

With pride thoroughly humbled, he decided to go to Krishna and beg His pardon for not having recognized who He was, but he was ashamed to go by himself. He requested the celestial cow, Surabhi, to accompany him. Together they approached Krishna and prostrated before Him while He stood on the sodden sides of the Govardhan.

Indra said, "Salutations to You, O Krishna! You are the indweller in all beings and the master of all devotees. I seek shelter at Your feet, for You are the Lord, teacher, and soul of all beings. Please forgive me!"

Next, Surabhi approached Him. "You are the Lord of all that exists. May You deign to be our Indra (king) in the future so that the holy and the innocent may be protected. Allow me to perform the ceremonial bath (*abhisheka*) for installing You as our king. Verily You are born to lighten the burden of Mother Earth."

After having extolled Him thus, Surabhi performed the *abhisheka* to Him with her milk. She was followed by Indra, who, with the assistance of the sages, performed the ceremonial installation of the Lord as King of kings by pouring over Him the waters of the heavenly Ganga (River Ganges), brought in golden pots by Indra's royal white elephant Airavata.

To the ringing cries of "Hail Govinda! Hail Govinda!" they installed Him as the Overlord of all *jivas* (embodied souls). This incarnation of the Lord had the express purpose of saving all *jivas* from the wheel of existence, and thus it was fitting that He never again submit to another consecration ceremony as a king. When Krishna was thus acclaimed as Lord of cows and *jivas*, it is said that milk started to flow from the udders of all cows and the earth was bathed with their offerings. The rivers began to flow with waters of various delicious tastes, trees began to shed honey, and cereals to grow and mature without any cultivation.

After this fantastic event, the *gopas*, who had not yet understood the divinity of Krishna, were anxious to know more of the details of His birth. They could not understand how Nanda and Yashoda, who were ordinary cowherds like themselves, could produce such a prodigy. So they went to Nanda and demanded an explanation. Nanda himself did not know much except what the sage Gargacharya had told him, and this he divulged to the others.

"Hearken to me, O Gopas!" he said. "I will tell you what Gargacharya has told me about the birth and achievements of my son. Your son, he said, will help you to attain higher spiritual evolution. He will enable you to surmount all difficulties and contribute to the happiness of your people and your cattle. Those who love Him will have no cause to fear enemies, for He is equal to the Lord Narayana in respect of auspiciousness, fame prowess, and other great qualities. Therefore, O Gopas, do not be surprised by these exploits revealing His divinity and majesty."

The *gopas* who had personally witnessed these feats were delighted to hear of Gargacharya's predictions and started worshipping Krishna as Narayana.

Once Nanda, after an *ekadashi* (eleventh day of the moon) fast went to the Yamuna on *dvadashi* day (twelfth day of the moon) very early in the morning for a bath. The servants of Varuna, the god of the waters, took him to their master's abode. The *gopas* ran and told Krishna that His father had disappeared in the water, and Krishna entered the river and went to the abode of Varuna to rescue His father. Varuna was one of the protectors of the quarters, and as he was filled with joy to see the Lord, He worshipped Him with various ingredients. Then Varuna loaded Nanda with numerous gifts and sent both of them back to Vraja. Naturally, such a stupendous happening could not be kept to himself. Nanda began to bruit abroad the tale of his fantastic experience in Varuna's abode, and soon the news spread far and wide and the other *gopas* also thirsted for a similar experience. Knowing their desire, Krishna took them to a pool called Brahmahradam, or the pool of Brahma, and asked them to take a dip. There, He showed them the vision of Lord Vishnu lying on His serpent couch in the middle of the milky ocean, surrounded by celestials and sages. What was more wonderful and thrilling to the *gopas* was the fact that they recognized Vishnu to be none other than the son of their chief! They were filled with bliss and lost their sense of identity, merging in that ocean of bliss for a few exalted moments.

Thus, one by one, Krishna fulfilled the desires of all the inhabitants of Vraja—His parents, His playmates the *gopalas*, and His father's friends the *gopas*. Now all that remained before He left them was to satisfy the desires of the *gopis*.

Thus ends the eighth chapter of The Play of God,
named "Krishna Lifts the Mountain."

Hari Aum Tat Sat

NINE

THE DIVINE LOVER

Shyamasundaraya namaha

Homage to the handsome dark–hued One

Who can describe the fascinating charm of Lord Krishna, who was a unique combination of the unparalleled beauty of the goddess Lalita and the unmatched masculine grace of Shri Rama?
—FROM A TRADITIONAL VERSE

Noting the advent of the autumn season, with nights fragrant with the perfume of jasmine flowers, Krishna, assuming His *yogamaya*, decided to enact His long-promised play with the *gopis*. The full moon of the harvest season rose large and red, painting the eastern horizon with vermilion. The *Yamuna* gushed and gurgled with the rains and the forest of Vrindavan gleamed in the moonlight, filled with luxuriant vegetation and perfumed with the scents of a thousand newly opened night flowers. It was a night which poets rave about and lovers dream of. It was a night calculated to strike a spark of desire even in the heart of the sternest ascetic. What did it not do to the *gopis*, whose hearts had already been churned up by the god of love? As the moon rose like a crimson disc on the horizon, Krishna placed His lips on the magic flute and poured out His divine call of love. The music drenched the air of Vrindavan and flowed into the hearts of the *gopis*, making them forget everything else. Neither duty, nor honor, nor husband, nor child, nor house did they have. Indeed, they forgot their very bodies. Leaving everything, they flew to their tryst with their lover, but because of their total absorption in Him they did not even notice that many others were also moving in the same direction. As soon as the first plaintive call of the flute was heard, they left unfin-

69

ished whatever work they had been engaged in and ran to meet their lover. Some, who were engaged in milking cows, put down their pails; some kept the milk on the fire and left it there; some were feeding their babies or giving food to their husbands. Leaving all these chores half done, they hurried toward the forest, totally oblivious of their neglected duties. Some were bathing, or dressing, or applying makeup, but even though they had put on only one earring and applied collyrium to one eye or were only half dressed, they left everything and ran as the musk deer runs, maddened by the magic of the music of the flute. Though their men tried to stop them, they would not listen, for their minds were completely absorbed in Krishna alone. Hair flying, bells tinkling, breasts thudding, they ran through the moon-drenched streets and down the forest paths, lured by the strains of that divine melody. Some, who were locked up in their rooms by their husbands, closed their eyes and became absorbed in Him and gave up their earthly bodies then and there.

The rest reached Him panting and excited, with parted lips and heaving breasts. Their whole attitude was wanton. They saw Him only as their lover. But one more test had to be passed before they achieved their desire. The *jiva* in its quest for God has to overcome many obstacles. Only the intrepid, who never give up come what may, achieve the desired union. The *gopis* had already proved themselves devoid of ego. Now they had to prove themselves ready to follow His path even if He Himself seemed to spurn them. The Lord spoke to them, "O Fair Ones! What is it that brings you here at this time of night? Have you come to admire the beauty of the forest, bright with the silvery rays of the moon? In that case, you may return home, since you have seen it. If, however, you have come here due to your attraction for Me, then it is My duty to remind you that the highest duty of a woman consists in looking after the needs of her husband, even if he is ill-mannered, old, incurably ill, or poverty-stricken. To have illicit relationships with a lover is a bar to heaven and a stain on one's reputation on earth. By thinking of Me and meditating on Me, you will attain a high state of spiritual love, which is far better than physical love. Go back to the security of your own homes, therefore, or else be forever branded as abandoned women, crazy with love for Krishna, the cowherd boy of Vrindavan. What can I offer you which is comparable to the security of your own homes and husbands? My way is fraught with dangers. It ill befits girls like you to be seen here with a boy like Me at this time of night."

Only the soul who holds to God through all the trials and tribulations that beset the path of devotion, who holds on through the hours of darkness, when we feel that God Himself has forsaken us, is fit to attain ultimate union with Him. When they heard these harsh and cruel words of one from whom they had expected nothing but love, they fell back like stricken deer, helpless and wounded.

"O Lord of our hearts!" they begged. "Do not desert us now, after we have left everything and come to You. Our only fault is that we love You too much! Of what use, O Lord, is the love of husband and children, productive as it is of misery in the end? You have reminded us that the natural duty of a woman consists in the service of husband, children, and relatives. But are You not our closest relative and only husband, the dearest and most cherished object of desire for all *jivas*? Having stolen away our minds, which used to find delight in home life, and having put restraints on our hands and feet, which used to occupy themselves with mundane household tasks, why do You now send us away? The moment that You allowed us to have contact with Your lotus feet, from that moment it has become impossible for us to look at any other man. O Thou Universal Redeemer! Be gracious to us, who have come to You, forsaking hearth and home and husband. Hearing the enthralling melody of Your flute, who is the woman who will not be charmed and drawn away from the path of duty? Therefore, O Manamohana, charmer of minds, please place Your cool, fragrant, lotus-like palms on our fevered heads and assuage the heat within our hearts."

So saying, they sank to the ground in a state of despair. Then the Lord, who had only been testing their constancy, bent down and lifted them up one by one. With the tip of His yellow garment, He wiped away their tears and kissed their pale lips till they reddened like roses in the sun. Then, tenderly, He led them to the banks of the Yamuna, where the setting was romantic enough to enchant the heart of any woman, and played the game of love with them. They spread the soft upper parts of their attire, one on top of the other, and thus made a downy bed on which the Lord of their hearts could relax. They then sat around Him, stroking His limbs, His hair, and His face, fanning Him with leaves and nestling close to Him, while the bolder among them would even snatch a kiss. Krishna gazed at them, and ill-clad and poor though they were, in His eyes they were lovely beyond compare, for they were lit with an inner radiance which had nothing to do with earthly adornments. In all His checkered career to come, He was never to meet with love like this again.

Thus, for a short time, they were all immersed in bliss.

After some time, however, pride reared its ugly head and the thought darted unbidden into their minds that they had procured this essence of sweetness for their very own because of their cleverness and charm. The sense of duality was reestablished, and they felt themselves to be separate from Him. As soon as they felt this, they found that He had indeed separated from them! He had vanished, and with Him the light that had bathed the banks seemed also to have gone. They were alone in the middle of the night on the suddenly unfriendly banks of the river, with the forest looming behind, dark and menacing. Now that the Lord had gone, they realized the utter futility of life without Him. Life without the protective presence of God is a dark and dreary forest infested with strange and terrifying specters. There was no kind hand to help them over the stones, no strong arm to carry them over streams and remove the thorns from their path. Hither and thither they ran, falling and crying like demented persons. They addressed the trees and creepers, "O *Mallika*! O *Malathi*! O *Sandal*! O *Champaka*![1] Have you seen our beloved? O *Tulsi*! Have you seen Krishna? You are very dear to Him. He wears you close to His heart in His garland!"

Speaking thus, the *gopis* became so identified in consciousness with Him that they began to enact all the various miracles of His childhood. The creepers trailed their flowers and tendrils across their faces as if to comfort them. The trees sighed and bowed their heads to assuage their sorrow, but though they searched everywhere, they could not find Him. After awhile, they realized that the one who was most fortunate among them, who was still humble, was not in their midst. Her name was Radha, luckiest among those *gopis* who were themselves luckier than ordinary mortals. Radha was especially dear to Krishna, for it is said that she was the incarnation of His *Prakriti*, or nature. The Lord's *Prakriti* is simple, yet inexplicable. So also was Radha—sweet and beguiling at times, willful and contrary at times, yet withal, filled with adoration for her Lord alone, careless of everything but the constant memory of the Lord, the One *purusha* to whom she was the *Prakriti*.

As the *gopis* were thus searching frantically, they suddenly saw two sets of footprints in the sand, highlighted by the moon. "Ah! Here I can see two sets of footprints," one *gopi* said. "Look where they have wandered off with

---

[1] *mallika, malathi, sandal, champaka*—the names of various Indian trees and creepers with sweet-smelling flowers.

their arms entwined round each other's necks. Let us follow."

"O look!" said another. "Here He must have carried her in His arms across this little stream, for there is only one set of footprints, which have sunk deep, as if He was carrying some burden."

"And look!" pointed another, "Here they have been sitting down and He has made a jasmine garland for her, for I can see the remains of it. O fortunate Radha! How I wish I were you!"

So lamenting, they wandered on and suddenly came upon the object of their envy, Radha herself. Ever since she had heard the story of how Krishna carried Shridama on His shoulders, she had cherished a secret wish to be carried by Him in a similar manner, and at that very spot she had begged Him to carry her. He had knelt down but just at that moment, the thought occurred to her of how fortunate she was and how she would boast of her conquest to the others. As soon as her ego asserted itself in this fashion, the Lord disappeared, along with her pride, and she fell to the ground in a swoon, unable to bear this separation from Him even for a second. The other *gopis* sprinkled water over her and whispered the magic *mantra* of Krishna's name and she revived.

"Come, let us search for Him," they urged. But Radha could not move. "I cannot," she whispered. "I can only lie here and perish if He does not come."

They half carried her and went to the banks of the Yamuna, where they had sported with Him earlier, and sang a piteous song. In it is portrayed the utter misery and darkness into which the soul of a seeker is plunged when it finds itself separated from its Maker. All seekers have experienced the poignancy of this separation. For one blissful moment, they experience union with God and then, due to the limitations of the human body and the pull of the ego, they are dragged back into the mundane level of existence, and the searing pain they feel is indescribable. It's the pain of a limb which is torn from its socket. The *jiva* thirsts to break the bonds of mortality and attain immortality, but, unfortunately, physical ties forged by its past *karma* keep it in bondage until the time is ripe for its release.

"O dearest Lord!" they sang, "By Your presence here, this forest of Vrindavan has become the most beautiful place on earth. Are You not the ocean of kindness? Will You not grant us Your vision? We live only for Your sake and have been searching for You in all directions.

"O Lord of supreme delight! Your eyes excel the charm of the inner petals of these lotuses blooming in this clear autumnal lake. We are

Your unbought slaves. Why are You so harsh to us? Why do You not reveal Yourself to us?

"O Eternal Companion! You are not just the son of Yashoda, but the immanent witness in all embodied beings, born to protect the world. Many a time You have saved us from destruction by evil forces.

"Now why have you deserted us in this dark and fearsome forest? O dear and lovely One! Deign to lay Your blessed hand on our heads and confer safety on us, who are fleeing through the forest of *samsara* (transient life and worldly existence) and have taken refuge at Your feet!

"O Supreme Lord of our hearts! Deign to place Your feet which danced on the hoods of Kaliya on our parched and aching bosoms and rid us of our sorrows!

"O lotus-eyed One! We are ever ready to obey Your commands and are swooning because of our separation from You.

"O dearest One! Your loving glances and bewitching smiles are the most auspicious themes for our meditation. The nectar of Your words is extolled by the sages and confers every prosperity on those who listen to them. Our minds are deeply agitated by them.

"O Hero of our hearts! When we think of Your enchanting face smeared with dust and Your dishevelled locks when you return with the cows at sundown, we are thrilled to the core. But the thought of Your tender feet being hurt by sharp stones and thorns while grazing the cows makes our hearts break. During the day when You are away, a moment appears like an age to us who are denied Your company, and when at dusk we see You again, we curse the creator who made lashes for the eyes, thus forcing us to blink and lose a precious second of Your beatific vision.

"O Hero of our hearts! Deign to fill us with the enrapturing notes of Your music, which drop like ambrosia from the flute kissed by Your lips and which send us to a height of spiritual ecstasy, making us oblivious to every other allurement. We have rushed to You, overriding our husbands, children, kinsmen, brothers, and relatives, captured by Your divine music. Why have You then abandoned us in the darkness of the night?

"O adorable One! Your manifestation is as much for the well-being of the entire world as it is for removal of the sorrows of the people of Vraja. The only remedy for the ache which gnaws at our hearts is Your company, so please do be gracious to us, Your handmaidens.

"O lovely One! We quiver in agony at the thought of Your delicate feet treading the thorny, stony paths of the forest. Even our bosoms are too hard for You. Yet do please place them on us and we will hold them with extreme caution so as to avoid injury to them."

Thus the *gopis* sang in their agony and intense longing to meet the Lord. And suddenly, just as He had disappeared, Krishna reappeared in their midst looking verily like Manmatha, the god of love.

"How could you think that I had left you?" He asked tenderly. "Not for one moment were you out of my sight. At every step you took, I took one beside you. Every time you faltered I held you up. How else do you think you have remained safe in this jungle, infested with wild creatures, at this time of night?"

The Lord is ever with those who have placed their lives in His hands. A life once entrusted into His hands is safe forever. We may stumble on the stones of misfortune, we may be pricked by the thorns of sorrow, but, unknown to us, His hand will be there to lift us up and wipe our tears.

Having seen Him, they felt as if their life breath had returned and they clung to Him. There on the banks of the Yamuna, where the air was saturated with the fragrance of jasmine, where the Kalindi had provided sandy dunes for Him to recline, Krishna the Master of all the universe, who has His seat in the hearts of meditating *yogis*, now sat on the seat made by those simple maids of Vraja who worshipped Him with all the usual offerings of love. Fondling Him and stroking His limbs, which were reposing on their laps, they questioned Him about the different types of love.

"Some love others according to how much they are loved in return. Some love even those who have no love for them. And others have no love for anyone, neither for those who love them nor for those who are indifferent to them. Please tell us, who are the most virtuous among these?"

The Lord said, "In the case of mutual love, the motive is only self-interest. This is only a type of barter and cannot be called real love. This is the type of love which is normally found among human lovers. Among those who love others even if it is unrequited, there are two kinds—those who are by nature kind and loving and those like parents, who love their children without expecting reciprocation. As for the last type mentioned by you, those who do not love anyone even if they are loved, these are of three types—the *atmaramas*, or those who are ever absorbed in the Self, for whom everyone is included in the Self, the *aptakamas*, or those who have no wants of any kind, and thus need have no dealings with anyone, and the brute man, who has no gratitude or love for anyone, even those who love him. However, I do not belong to any of these categories. If I seem to be keeping away from you, it is only to strengthen your desire, so that you will attain Me faster. How can I not love you, who have left your home, family, and position in the world for My sake? Even if I were to serve you for countless divine years, I would not be able to repay you for this glorious act of self-surrender, prompted by love alone, untainted by selfishness, breaking asunder the powerful chain of attachment for home and worldly life."

The *gopis'* pangs of separation were assuaged by the Lord's words. He then led them to perform the mystic dance known as the *Rasalila*, "the play of Love." He took each of them separately to a special chamber in the bushes and attended to her toilette with His own hands, arranging her hair, applying her makeup, and adorning each of them with orna-ments. He then arranged them in a wide circle in which each *gopi* danced with one Krishna and He Himself stood in the middle supplying the music for the dance. Like a sapphire between two golden beads, Krishna's blue form shone between two *gopis*! Heavenly instruments joined with the flute, and flowers were rained on the heads of these fortunate damsels by the gods. The tinkling sound of their bangles, bells, and anklets mingled with the music and filled the air. The *gopis* were not aware of the fact that there were so many Krishnas! Each one felt that she was alone with her beloved and, forgetting all modesty, she clung to Him and caressed Him. He, in turn, embraced her and transported her to a state of bliss never before attained by anyone, for it was no ordinary physical union that they experienced but the ultimate union of the *jivatma* with the *Paramatma*, the realization of the great *Upanishadic mantra Tat Tvam Asi*, That Thou Art, which is attained by striving *yogis* after intense and prolonged auster-ities. This experience was granted to those poor and unlettered *gopis* of Vrindavan because they possessed one great quality which transfigured them, the alchemy of love, which transformed them and made them into creatures of light and glory. Such love transcends the boundaries of time and space and soars above both physical and mental planes. The only bond which can bind the Infinite to the finite is the bond of love, which sweeps away man-made barriers and soars into the unknown. The *gopis* had no sense of separation. Like the Ganga losing itself in the ocean, their souls were submerged in the ocean of bliss that was Krishna. Though their love was carnal in nature at first, yet through contact with Him who was the Supreme Being, it was transformed from the dross of physical passion to the effulgence of a divine union. This particular incarnation of the Lord was only to bestow salvation on all *jivas* in whatever way they approached Him—through love, fear, anger, affection, or devotion. Later on, in the *Bhagavad Gita*, He was to tell Arjuna, "In whatsoever way people approach me, in that same guise will I go to them, for people approach Me in many ways."

If He was capable of giving liberation even to a Putana and an Aghasura, who came to kill Him, why would He not grant the same status to the *gopis*, whose only fault was that they loved Him too much? They knew that they could never hope to have Him as their husband, so they longed to have Him as their lover, and He went to them in that guise. Since their love was not lodged in some limited human being but fixed on Him who is the eternal *Purusha*, it was sublimated, and they achieved that state of direct union with Him which even striving *yogis* attain with the greatest difficulty. Therefore, the *Rasalila* is also known as *Brahmaratra*, or the night of Brahman.

As the night advanced, the music faded and only the soft sound of their ankle bells could be heard. Slowly, even this died away as they became tired of dancing. Their eyes started to close like half-opened buds and their heads dropped on their beloved's shoulder. They were unaware that their garlands and ornaments had slipped away, and they were incapable of attending to their loosened tresses and garments. He wiped their perspiring faces tenderly with His own cooling hands, His arms encircled their slender waists, and they drank the nectar of His lips for which they had been longing. Some clung round the neck of their own particular Krishna, others kissed His hands, others His lips, and others stole the half-eaten betel nuts from His mouth. Their locks were falling in abandon, their clothes were loose, their blouses open, but they knew not, nor cared, for they were quite unconscious of their bodies. He was their husband, their lover, their Lord. Nearer to them than friend or relative, nearer to them than father or mother, dearer to them than life itself. He was flesh of their flesh and soul of their soul. They had no separate existence apart from Him. He alone existed. They were submerged in a state of unity in which all is One and there is no other.

Thus, on many a moonlit night like this did they sport with that Infinite One, who had taken on a finite form in order to delight the world. Though He was the All Knower who was completely detached from all things and ever poised in the bliss of the Self, yet He invested everything He did with the zest and enthusiasm of a child. He was the cosmic

Beloved, yet He made each *gopi* feel that He was her own special lover. Each full moon night as they ran to Him in disarray, leaving all their unfinished work behind at the call of His magic flute, He would take them to a special bower prepared for each one individually and repair her toilette with His own hands. He would comb their hair, put collyrium in their eyes and the sacred red dot on their foreheads, anoint them with sweet-smelling unguents and adorn their tresses with jasmine garlands. This He did, not to one, but to all the *gopis*. Then He would lead them to the banks of the Yamuna and dance the *Rasa*. After that they would sport in the river to shake off their fatigue before returning to their homes. Toward the early hours of the morning, persuaded by their Beloved, the *gopis* would return to their homes unwillingly. Owing to the Lord's mysterious power, the *gopas* did not miss their women and felt no ill-will toward Him. In fact, they worshipped Him as God.

The Lord assumes a human body and sports in ways that are suitable to fulfill His purpose for the blessing of all humanity and to draw toward Himself even those who are not spiritually inclined. Sexual passion is normally considered a hindrance to spiritual life, but since their minds were attracted to Him who was the repository of holiness and purity, the *gopis* became paragons of virtue and devotion, extolled even by the sages. In the *Shrimad Bhagavata* it is said that all those who read this particular episode in the life of the Lord will be able to subdue their own sexual craving and direct it toward Him, the Supreme Beloved.

Thus ends the ninth chapter of The Play of God,
named "The Divine Lover."

Hari Aum Tat Sat

O Krishna! Thou art the dwelling place for all good people, the ultimate goal for those in distress and the One who banishes the sorrow of Thy devotees. O Krishna! Thou art my sole refuge!
—DRAUPADI IN THE MAHABHARATA

I know that Supreme Person who is beyond ignorance and darkness and whose splendor is comparable to that of the sun. Knowing Him thus in this life, one transcends death. There is no other path to liberation.
—RIG VEDA

TEN

THE LORD OF VRAJA

Vanamaline namaha

Homage to the wearer of the garland of wild-flowers

When Krishna, adorned with an attractive tilaka,[1] begins to respond with His flute to the loud humming of the bees that are drawn to Him by the fragrance of the tulsi leaves in His vana-mala (garland of wildflowers), then do the waterbirds, like the swans and sarasa, gather, attracted by His music, and stand beside Him like self-controlled sages, silent, with eyes closed, as if in contemplation of the Divine.
—POPULAR SANSKRIT VERSE, SOURCE UNKNOWN

During the day, when Krishna went to the forest to tend the cattle with His playmates, the *gopis* spent their time imagining His activities in the forest. Their imaginations ran riot when they thought of all the things He would be doing there. They lived for that moment at dusk when He would return in a cloud of dust raised by the hooves of the cattle, His hair and garlands covered with dust, joking and playing pranks with the *gopalas* and delighting all with His loving glances.

One day Krishna told the *gopis* that the sage Durvasa had come to the opposite bank of the Yamuna and that they should all go worship him and take him some offerings. The *gopis* were ever willing to do His bidding, and they prepared many delicacies. They went to the Yamuna, only to find that the river was in spate and they could not cross. They returned forlornly and told Krishna about their predicament.

The Lord smilingly advised them to try again. "Go to the Yamuna and tell her, 'O Yamuna! If you know Krishna to be ever firm in His vow of celibacy, then please part

---

1 *tilaka*—auspicious mark on the forehead.

and make way for us to go to the other side.'"

The *gopis* were startled at this statement, for their own experience told them that this was not true. However, they did as they were bidden and lo! the waters parted and they were able to cross over with the greatest of ease. They approached Sage Durvasa, worshipped him, and placed all the baskets of delicacies before him. The sage was noted for his abstemious eating habits, yet he polished off all the vast quantities of food brought for him by the *gopis* and blessed them. On their return, they found that the Yamuna had closed her path and they could not cross over. They returned to the sage and explained their difficulty. He was naturally curious to know how they had managed to come to him. They told him of the miraculous way in which they had crossed and, with a smile, the sage said, "Go tell the Yamuna, 'O Yamuna! If you know sage Durvasa to be the most abstemious of eaters, then you should part and make way for us to cross over'."

The *gopis* were amazed. How could a sage like him make such a false statement when he had just swallowed vast quantities of food in front of their very eyes? Yet, since he was also known for his temper, they dared not remonstrate, but went meekly and did as they were bidden. Great was their amazement when the Yamuna parted and allowed them to cross. At this behavior on the part of the river, they could not contain their curiosity and ran to their mentor and asked Him the reason for these inexplicable occurrences. The Lord gave them a discourse on the law of *karma*.[2]

An action binds us only when we feel that we are the doer. The consequence of such an act is always bondage. However, when an act is done by a realized soul or by the Lord Himself, it is done with no trace of ego and no involvement of the mind. It is a completely free and natural act and thus it has no consequences. It goes beyond the law of *karma*. The Lord's actions are totally devoid of personal motivation. He is a free agent, ever immersed in the bliss of Brahman, totally detached from everything, and thus, even though He may consort with a thousand women, yet is He ever a *nitya brahmachari*, or perfect celibate. So also, the sage Durvasa had no attraction or repulsion for the food placed before him. He ate only to please the *gopis* and not because he was in any way interested in the food. Had they brought nothing for him, he would

---

2 *law of karma*—see footnote 1 on page 63.

still have been equally happy, for his happiness was derived not from the external object, but from his inner, blissful Self. Ever immersed in the Self, he knew nothing of either hunger or thirst. Thus, he had every right to be called an abstemious eater. In this delightful way did the Lord teach the *gopis* the secret of action without bondage to the wheel of *karma*.

Once during a festive season, the *gopas* went to a place of pilgrimage known as Ambikavana. After bathing in the river, they offered worship to Lord Shiva and His consort Parvati. They spent the night there on the banks of the river and while they slept, a python caught hold of Nanda's leg. The *gopas* woke up on hearing his screams and tried to drive it off with firebrands, but it would not let go. They went and called Krishna, who touched the snake with His foot. Freed from its curse by the contact of His holy foot, the serpent assumed its original form of a celestial being. He prostrated to the Lord, thanked Him for having released him from his curse, and returned to his abode.

Another day, when Krishna and Balarama were roaming in the woods with the *gopis*, a servant of Kubera, the lord of wealth, happened to pass that way and seeing the *gopis*, he abducted them. The two brothers chased him and rescued the *gopis*.

Now Kamsa sent to Gokula a demon called Arishta, who had the form of an ox. Bellowing wildly, with upraised tail and reddened eyes, he charged down the small lanes, causing havoc among the people and cattle. Seeing the confusion caused by the beast, the Lord barred his way and provoked him by clapping his hands in the manner of bullfighters. The enraged bull charged at Him with lowered horns, fixing Him with his mean and bloodshot eyes. Krishna caught hold of him by his horns and gave him a mighty shove that threw him back ten feet. The maddened bull staggered to his feet and charged once more. Again the Lord caught hold of him by his cruel and pointed horns and threw him on the ground. Pinning him down with his foot, he pulled out his horns and killed him.

After this feat, the sage Narada went once again to the court of Kamsa, for he considered it high time that the Lord moved out of Vraja to enact further scenes of His enthralling life in different arenas. He proceeded to enlighten Kamsa about the identity of Krishna and Balarama.

"Know, O Kamsa, that the eighth child of Devaki who was shown to you was actually the daughter of Yashoda, the wife of the chieftain Nanda, who resides at Gokula. She was exchanged with Devaki's son, Krishna, who now lives in Vraja as the son of Nanda. Balarama, his brother, is also Vasudeva's son, by his wife Rohini, and lives in Nanda's house. They are the ones who have killed all the demons you have sent to destroy Krishna."

Hearing this, Kamsa became furious with rage and took up his sword to kill Vasudeva. He was restrained by Narada, but he chained Vasudeva and Devaki once again in his dungeon. Then he called the demon Kesi and commissioned him to go kill the boys.

Kesi took on the form of a huge horse and arrived in Gokula snorting and furrowing the earth with his sharp hooves. Seeing Krishna approaching him fearlessly, the demon charged at Him with his mouth wide open as if to swallow Him. Evading his upraised hooves, Krishna caught hold of his legs, whirled him round and flung him a hundred yards away. But Kesi was not beaten yet. He struggled to his feet and charged once again with his teeth bared menacingly and foam flecking his mouth. Krishna thrust his bare arm into the horse's open mouth, and when the demon tried to bite off His arm, his teeth fell out! The Lord's arm now swelled in size and choked him to death.

Krishna proceeded on His interrupted journey with the *gopalas* to graze the cows. There on the hill slope they played at ranchers and cattle thieves. A demon called Vyoma came there in the form of a *gopa*. He stole many of the boys who were playing the parts of the cattle and shut them up in a remote cave. As he was coming back to steal more of them, Krishna caught hold of him and killed him. He then released the *gopalas*, and they returned to Vraja that evening and described the events of their day—how their make-believe game had turned into a thrilling adventure.

With the killing of Kesi, Kamsa became desperate. He decided that the only way to kill the boys was to bring them to Mathura, where he could personally supervise their end. He summoned the famous wrestlers, Mushtika and Chanura, and told them that he would arrange a wrestling match for them in which they would have to kill their opponents—the boys Krishna and Balarama. He also told the chief of his elephant stable to station the mighty mammoth, Kuvalayapida, at the entrance to the wrestling amphitheater to kill the boys.

"Let the Festival of the Great Bow of Lord Shiva be ceremonially inaugurated on the thirteenth lunar day, which is sacred to Shiva, and let all the inhabitants of the outlying villages be invited to participate in the festivities!" This was Kamsa's proclamation. He realized that the only way to entice the boys to Mathura was to send someone acceptable to the *gopas* to invite and escort them. So he called Vasudeva's cousin Akrura, who was a great devotee of Vishnu, and spoke to him as follows, "Dear Akrura, you must do something for me which only a close friend can do. I don't find anyone among the Bhojas to match you in sincerity and ability. Please go to the cowherd village, Gokula, where Krishna and Balarama, the sons of Vasudeva, are residing with Nanda. Invite them for the Festival of the Bow and bring them here in the chariot without any delay. You may also invite the rest of the *gopas* for the festivities so that they will not get suspicious."

Akrura was a great devotee. Hearing of Krishna's greatness, he had been longing for a glimpse of Him, but since he was in Kamsa's service, he had not dared to make the fourteen-mile journey to see Him. He was overjoyed to find that of all the people that Kamsa could have sent, he had chosen him to be the one to invite the boys and escort them to Mathura. Such are the mysterious ways of the Lord that He makes use of even His so-called enemies to serve the interests of His devotees. But at the same time, Akrura's heart trembled with fear when he realized that he was only a tempting bait to lure the children to their death at the arena, for he had heard the orders given by the king. He was in a panic of apprehension whether the Lord would realize his predicament and forgive him. Would He understand that he was an innocent instrument and had nothing to do with the plot?

Akrura spent the night in great expectation and started for Vraja the next morning in a lovely, jewelled chariot calculated to entice the rustic minds of the boys. After traveling for some time, his joy at being given the chance of seeing the Lord surpassed his despair at the purpose of his mission, and he allowed his mind to revel and wander freely over the delights he would share with the Lord when he met Him.

"The fact that I have seen so many auspicious sights at dawn indicates that today I shall see Him who is the joy-giver and enlightener of the universe, the refuge and preceptor of all holy men, the most auspicious object for the eyes. As soon as I see Him, I shall jump down and prostrate before Him. He will place His blessed hands on my head and cast His smiling look at me and I shall attain to supreme bliss. And if perchance He embraces me with His powerful arms, my bondage of *karma* will surely be broken. To none is He partial, nor is anyone the object of His enmity or indifference, but still He blesses His devotees in a manner which is appropriate to their needs, just as the heavenly wish-yielding tree, the Kalpaka, gives to each person according to his requirements."

Ruminating in this fashion, Akrura quite forgot where he was going and allowed the horses to go as they liked. At last, by the time he came to the outskirts of Vrindavan, twilight had fallen. He now began to notice the footprints of the Lord. Jumping out of the chariot in excitement, he exclaimed, "Here is the dust of my Lord's feet!" With these words he took up a handful of the dust and placed it reverently on his head. Tears coursed down his cheeks and he burst into raptures over the forest of Vrindavan.

"Ah, lucky Vrindavan! O fortunate trees! Who can extol your virtues? His divine feet have played on this ground, His clothes have caught on these thorns, His body has been stroked by these leaves. This divine breeze has ruffled His curls and carries with it the perfume of His breath."

So saying, Akrura threw himself on the sanctified ground of Vrindavan, breathed deeply of its intoxicating air, and clasped the trees and vines to his chest in a paroxysm of rapture. Then, remounting his chariot and proceeding a little further into the village, he saw from a distance the Lord of his heart standing in the courtyard looking even more beautiful than his imagination had pictured Him. Krishna was waiting outside as if to see the milking of the cows, but actually to get the first glimpse of His devotee, for His longing to see Akrura was equal to the latter's desire to see Him. He had just had His bath after returning from the forest and wore His usual yellow garment. His hair was bunched on top with peacock feathers stuck in the middle and a garland of white flowers surrounding it. The eyes in the feathers and His own eyes were wide open in eager anticipation to meet His devotee and His lips were parted in a delightful half-smile, overflowing with love. On seeing Him, Akrura jumped out of the chariot and threw himself at His feet. Immediately, Krishna lifted him up with both hands, embraced him, and led him into the house. Akrura was too overwhelmed to be able to speak. He could only close his eyes and hold Him close to him as if he could not bear to let Him go. He felt as if he were drowning in a sea of nectar. Gentle hands were stroking him and a lilting voice was enquiring tenderly about his welfare. Slowly his senses returned, but like the waker who knew the dream to be false, Akrura realized that this life was but a dream and the only reality was this bundle of bliss he held in his arms.

Nanda and Yashoda welcomed him, and all the *gopas* crowded around to hear some city news. The whole night was spent in discussing Kamsa's commands and whether the boys should accept this invitation to destruction. Krishna laughed at his father's fears and told him that the king's commands had to be obeyed; if not, Akrura would surely get into trouble if he returned empty-handed.

Reluctantly, Nanda agreed, though his heart was filled with foreboding. He ordered the *gopas* to collect milk, milk products, and other gifts to be presented to the king and to harness their carts for the journey. The announcement was broadcast all over the settlement that all those who wished to take part in the Festival of the Bow were welcome to accompany him to Mathura the next morning.

The *gopis*, to whom the Lord was their very life-breath, were overwhelmed with grief to hear that someone had come to take Him away to the city. The actual meaning of the word "*akrura*" is "not cruel," but to the *gopis* he appeared to be the personification of cruelty.

"How did such a cruel man get such an unsuitable name?" they lamented. "He has come to wrench our Beloved from our arms. O cruel fate, that separates us before we have assuaged our thirst! How are we to endure the excruciating sorrow of separation from Him even for a day? The wishes of the women of Mathura are soon to be fulfilled, for tomorrow the Lord of Gokula will be entering their city and they will be able to imbibe from the cup of His charming eyes, His intoxicating glances. Surely He will forget His rustic playmates and be charmed by the beauties of the city. What shall we do, O friends? Shall we throw ourselves in front of the chariot so that He will have to ride over us if He wants to go?"

"No, No!" said another. "That would be most inauspicious. It's bad luck to put obstacles in front of a traveler. He is sure to return soon, as soon as the festival is over."

Thus the *gopis* lamented, imagining the pangs of their prospective separation from their Beloved. The night passed in this fashion and with the break of dawn, the *gopis* began to cry out loud, "O Govinda! O Damodara! O Madhava!" (names of Krishna).

Knowing the turbulent state of their minds, Krishna sent Shridama to comfort them. They were not satisfied with his words, but they were too shy to go in front of the stranger and accost Him themselves. Little did they realize that this parting was to last for the rest of their lives.

The next morning the entire community was plunged in grief. The *gopis* thronged the lanes waiting to have a last glimpse of Him who was the custodian of their hearts. With piteous, tear-filled eyes, they gazed at

Him as He got into the chariot with Akrura and Balarama. Nanda and the other *gopas* and *gopalas* followed in ox-drawn carts laden with pots of curds and other objects for presentation to the king. As He passed them, each of the *gopis* felt a message pass from His eyes to hers, and this filled them with hope and made them forget the actual moment of parting. Even from afar, they felt His eyes brimming with love, caressing them in waves of kindness. They remained where they were, motionless like pictures drawn on canvas, watching the chariot until it disappeared from sight and only the little flag was seen merrily waving to them, as if by order of their Beloved. Soon, even that disappeared and only a cloud of dust remained. Then, even that vanished and they were left bereft, feeling as if their hearts had been torn from their bodies. At last, they returned to their empty homes to spend the rest of their lives singing about His glories with their minds absorbed in contemplation of His divine form until they merged into Him at the end of their earthly sojourn.

Thus did Krishna leave Gokula, followed by the carts of the *gopalas* and the hearts of the *gopis*. One phase of His life was over. Never would He return to Vraja as a cowherd boy to enjoy the simple pleasures of rural life. A new chapter was opening in which He would have to play the role of king-maker. There is no episode in His life as poignant as His stay with the *gopalas* of Vrindavan. As entrancing as the melodious call of His flute, this chapter in His life as "the Blue Boy of Vrindavan" is one which has thrilled the hearts of His devotees to this very age. Some of the greatest poems and paintings of the culture of Bharatavarsha have been inspired by this period of His life.

Thus ends the tenth chapter of The Play of God,
named "The Lord of Vraja."

Hari Aum Tat Sat

That Supreme Brahman, the Absolute Reality, has become an androgynous Person, dark blue and pink in color, with indrawn vitality, having lustrous eyes. Salutations to Him, who alone is the Soul of the universe.
—ADAPTED FROM THE NARAYANA SUKTAM

Whether we live in a cave or a palace, in the forest or on the mountain, in water or fire, there is no difference. He who has entrusted himself into Your keeping, O Lord, will ever be protected by You.
—SHANKARACHARYA

BOOK TWO

RAJA LILA

THE ROYAL GAME

Rugmani-Krishna

Hail to Thee,
O King of Kings and Lord of Lords,
Wielder of the mighty mace—the Kaumodaki,
               the sword—Nandaka,
Flourishing aloft the wheel—Sudarshana,
               the bow—Saranga,
Power immense and majesty supreme!
Is this a game or just a dream?
Overwhelmed am I by Thy might and glory,
Enthralled am I by Thy sermon holy.
Sole friend and lover of all humankind,
With bonds of love tie Thou my mind.
O Lord of Lords and King of Kings,
Thy sport to all enlightenment brings.
All hail to Thee,
Thou knight Divine!
Thy royal game is sport sublime.

ELEVEN

THE PROPHECY FULFILLED

Vaasudevaya
namaha

Homage to
the One who
resides in all
beings

Hail to Thee, Lord Krishna, preceptor of the universe, son of Vasudeva, the supreme bliss of Devaki, and the destroyer of Kamsa and Chanura.
—KRISHNASHTAKAM

Akrura drove the chariot fast and at noon reached the banks of the Yamuna, where he alighted to perform his afternoon worship. The boys rested in the chariot while Akrura went for his ablutions. The chariot had outdistanced the carts of the *gopas*, so they had plenty of time at their disposal. As Akrura submerged in the water and began repeating the *Gayatri mantra*[1] to the Sun God, he had a vision of Lord Vishnu reclining on His serpent couch, Adishesha[2], and he saw that Vishnu was none other than Krishna and Shesha was Balarama. All the sages and celestials were standing around and extolling Him. Akrura also saluted Him with folded palms, "Salutations to You who are pure consciousness, who are the source of consciousness everywhere, who are the infinite power of Brahman, controlling the three factors of Time, *Karma*, and Nature that determine the destiny of man. Pitifully weak-willed as I am, I find it impossible to control my mind, plagued by desires, drawn hither and thither by the strong-willed senses. Therefore do I resign myself at Your feet. It is only through Your grace that I am able to do so."

The vision vanished and Akrura came out of the water and went back to the chariot. Krishna asked him

---

[1] *Gayatri mantra*—a hymn to God, as represented by the sun, that the mind and heart be illumined, commonly chanted daily even today by many Hindus.
[2] *Adishesha*—the cosmic serpent, on whose coiled body Vishnu lies, dreaming the universe into existence.

91

mischievously, "What is it, Uncle? You seem to have come across something wonderful, either in the water or on land or in the sky. What could it be?"

Akrura answered, "Whatever the phenomenon that exists on land or in water or in the sky subsists only in You and because of You, the all-inclusive existence. What is it that cannot be achieved by one who is blessed by You, yet what is it that a devotee of Yours can desire, which he considers greater than Your blessed vision? When You are present before me, You in whom all that is wonderful subsists, what other wonder can I possible see?"

Saying thus, Akrura drove the chariot toward the city. When they reached the suburbs, they found that the party headed by Nanda had arrived in advance and was waiting in a garden for their arrival. Krishna alighted there and told Akrura to go ahead. Akrura begged Him to go with him to his house with his friends, but Krishna declined the offer and promised to visit him after His encounter with Kamsa. Akrura, though he felt sad, yet complied with the Lord's commands and proceeded to the palace to give Kamsa the news of the fulfillment of his mission.

The next day Krishna, accompanied by Balarama and the other *gopas*, proceeded in a leisurely manner into the capital of the Bhojas, City of Wonders, a novel sight for the rustics! The city gate shone like crystal, with shutters lined with gold and ornamental arches, granaries made of copper, with moats and gardens and parks. The roads were flanked by mansions with gardens, assembly halls, and rest houses inlaid with gold and set with gems. The main street was swept and watered, with markets and courtyards strewn with flowers, tender shoots, puffed grain, and unbroken rice. The entrances of the houses were decorated with plantain trees with hanging bunches of fruit, palm trees with golden-colored nuts, rows of lights, strings of flowers, and festoons of silken scarves and banners. It was as if the city of Mathura had decked herself up to meet her future Lord. Down the king's highway they sauntered, with arms carelessly flung round each other's shoulders. The women were thronging the terraces and balconies to get a view of the One about whom they had heard so much. His kingly gait and noble mien drew all eyes to Him as He strode down the road.

Suddenly, they saw Kamsa's washerman coming toward them carrying the king's clothes. Krishna recognized him of yore. This was the wretch who had spread calumnious tales about Sita during His incarnation as

Rama in another age! He had a score to settle with him. He stepped in front of him and blocked his way.

"Dear man," he said, "will you lend us some clothes? We have just come from Vraja and we find our clothes are not fashionable enough for the festival tomorrow."

The man haughtily replied, "O mannerless fools! Do you fellows who generally wander in the jungles wear clothes like these? These are the king's clothes, not meant for urchins like you. Get you hence or else the servants of the king will put you in fetters, strip you, and perhaps even kill you!"

The man's time for liberation had come. Krishna merely laughed at this abusive speech and touched him. He fell down lifeless and his assistants fled in terror, leaving all the bundles of clothes. The *gopas* who had accompanied them now helped themselves to the clothes they fancied.

Next, they went to a tailor's shop. As soon as the boys entered, he welcomed them and presented them with clothes fit for princes. The boys dressed themselves in these and Krishna blessed the tailor. They proceeded to the house of Sudama, the garland maker. He honored them and presented them with garlands made of select flowers. The boys decorated themselves with them. Sudama chose three boons, which the Lord granted him with pleasure—unflinching devotion to the All-Inclusive Being, friendship toward His devotees, and kindness to all creatures.

Then, as they walked on, they saw a peculiar sight. A sort of bundle of clothes was coming toward them, which at a closer glance resolved itself into a woman who had such a terrible hump that she was almost bent to the ground. She was rolling along, carrying perfumed *sandal* paste to the court. She was a courtesan whose duty was to prepare unguents for the court and to make herself useful in other ways as well. As she was hobbling along with eyes on the ground, she suddenly saw in front of her two feet like tender rose petals. A lovely voice enquired in the kindest tones she had ever heard, "O beautiful one! Who are you? To whom are you taking these unguents? Will you give us some?"

She was thunderstruck. To her knowledge, no one had ever called her anything but Kubja (hunchback) or Trivakra (three-humped one). She struggled to lift herself up to see the face which had spoken these words, but she could not manage it.

"O handsome one!" she said. "I'm a courtesan named Trivakra, patronized by the king for my skill in making these fragrant pastes. I shall certainly give you some of it. For who is more eligible than you to use such precious *sandal* paste?" Then she felt a strong hand beneath her chin, another was placed on her hump, and a foot was pressed on hers and lo! she was lifted up, her hump removed so that she stood tall, straight, and beautiful before that stealer of hearts!

"Let the world see the beauty of your soul in your body itself, O Sairandhri (maidservant)," He said.

She gazed and gazed at this divine being who had wrought such a miracle. Her heart overflowed with love. What could she give Him, poor and stupid as she was? Sensing her confusion, He asked gently, "For whom are you taking this *sandal* paste?"

"Who else but for You, my Lord?" she stammered. Taking the *sandal* paste meant for the king, she anointed Him with it. As He was about to move on, she was filled with panic. What if she never saw Him again? The thought was unbearable. Shamelessly, she caught hold of the cloth round His neck and, hanging on to it, she whispered, "Come with me to my house. It is impossible for me to be without you!"

When the girl solicited Him thus in the presence of His elder brother, the Lord looked at the faces of the other *gopas* and said laughingly, "After I have finished the task for which I have come, I shall think of going to your house."

Balarama looked on with disapproval at the sight of his younger brother encouraging the advances of this shameless woman, who had the temerity to hang around His neck in broad daylight before the interested gaze of so many spectators. He walked ahead without a word, and Krishna smiled and followed him while Kubja gazed after Him longingly, her love mirrored in her eyes.

Next, they proceeded to the hall where the great Bow of Shiva was kept and worshipped. Many guards had been posted at the entrance. Naturally, they did not expect anyone to force their way in and though they shouted, "No one is allowed to touch the bow," He took it up, strung it, and with one twang broke it in the middle as easily as an elephant breaks a sugar cane. The terrific sound of the breaking bow filled the sky and all the quarters. Everyone trembled with fear and Kamsa felt a shaft of pure terror shoot through his heart. He realized that this was but a prelude—the first chords of the stupendous opera which was to culminate in his demise. After that he could never remain quiet for a moment. He could neither stand nor sit. Everywhere he saw his enemy

Vishnu—on the chair, on the bed, under it, and in every nook and cranny. Sleeping and waking, Kamsa had been continuously thinking of Vishnu for the past twenty years. How could such devotion go unrewarded? Such concentration is rare even among *yogis*. Until his death the next day, Kamsa could not even eat a ball of rice without breaking it to see whether Vishnu was hiding inside.

The guards took up arms and surrounded Krishna and the *gopas*, who took up the broken pieces of the bow and drove them off with it. Then they left and went about seeing more of the marvels of the city. In the evening, they returned to the park where their carts were stationed. They slept soundly while Kamsa, after hearing the news of their doings from the guards, did not have a wink of sleep. Early next morning, he gave orders for the commencement of the wrestling match. The arena was swept and watered. The galleries were adorned with wreaths, flags, and bunting. Trumpets and drums sounded. People from the city and the countryside occupied the galleries in order of precedence, while the royalty had special seats. With a trembling heart and a bold front, Kamsa sat on his royal throne, surrounded by his ministers and chieftains. Amidst the sound of trumpets and the characteristic clapping of arms of the wrestlers, the contestants entered the arena. Nanda and his followers, who had been invited by Kamsa, made presentations to him and occupied one section of the gallery.

The wrestlers had secret orders to show no mercy and to dispatch the boys at the earliest opportunity to the abode of Yama, the god of death. When they reached the entrance to the arena, Krishna saw the elephant Kuvalayapida, who was being prompted by his cruel trainer to charge at Krishna. Tightening His garments and tying up His locks in true wrestling style, Krishna ordered the elephant keeper to keep his beast under control and make way for Him. The irate keeper directed the elephant to charge at Him and catch Him in his trunk, but Krishna slipped out of its hold, gave it a mighty blow on its forehead, and ensconced Himself between its legs. Provoked by the blow and the fact that it could not see Him, the animal smelt Him out and again caught Him in his trunk, but the Lord slipped out once more and, catching hold of his tail, pulled it back as He used to do the calves at Gokula. Then He ran in front of it and, as the elephant chased Him, He pretended to fall, quickly rolling away so that the elephant pierced the ground with its tusks and got stuck there. Krishna now plucked out its tusks and beat it to death, together with its keeper. Armed with the elephant's tusks and surrounded by the *gopalas*, Balarama and Krishna now entered the arena. According to the state of his own mind, each person saw Krishna in a different light. A hero to the common folk, Cupid embodied to women, their beloved friend to the *gopas*, a terror to evil ones, an infant to His parents, just a boy to the ignorant ones, the Supreme embodied Truth to the *yogis*, their chosen Savior to the Yadavas, and the lord of death himself to Kamsa! Like two actors entering the stage, the two boys strode into the arena. Everyone was thrilled to see them, for they had heard many rumors about their prowess.

The mighty wrestler Chanura, veteran of many matches, approached them and said, "O Son of Nanda! O Rama! You are both famous as heroic young men and experts in wrestling. Hearing this the king has invited you today, in order to watch your skill in wrestling."

Krishna replied, "We are nomadic forest dwellers who have only engaged ourselves in wrestling contests of a playful nature with boys of our own age and strength. Though we are anxious to please the king, how can we challenge professionals like you?"

Chanura replied, "Neither You, who killed the mighty pachyderm Kuvalayapida, nor Balarama can be called mere boys! You are undoubtedly qualified to wrestle with us. You may show your prowess against me and Balarama can compete with Mushtika."

So saying, he led them to the middle of the arena. The Lord was nothing loathe to have a good bout of wrestling! He plunged Himself with great enthusiasm into this, as He did everything He was called upon to do, as if He were totally involved in what He was doing. Actually, He was totally detached, ever immersed in the bliss of His own Self, from which He never wavered, however much He gave the impression of being involved. Entwining, hand to hand and leg to leg, they closed with each other. Fist against fist, elbow against elbow, head against head, and chest against chest, they clashed again and again! Whirling and throwing, embracing and strangling, pushing and pulling, each tried to overpower the other. Much distressed to see this unequal contest between the slender young boys and the devilish-looking professionals, many of the spectators started to walk out in protest. "Shame! Shame!" they cried. "Let us not watch this slaughter. A fight should be between equals. What is the fun of watching this? Sin will accrue to us also!"

But just as the murmurs were getting louder, they saw the slender boy lifting the mountainous Chanura, whirling him round and round, and dashing him to the ground. This was child's play to Him who had held aloft the Govardhan mountain for seven days! As for Mushtika, Balarama slew him carelessly with a blow of his left hand. Another pair of gladiators now came forward and offered battle, for it was obvious that it was indeed a battle, and again a third pair, only to be slain by the two boys! As the third round ended, the rest of the wrestlers fled, and the cowherds could no longer be restrained. They rose as one man from their place in the gallery, jumped into the arena, and embraced their heroes amidst laughter and shouts of triumph. Then all together, to the accompaniment of the tinkling of their ornaments, they began to perform one of their folk dances to the great delight of the assembly. Krishna, as usual, threw Himself with zest into this, as He had taken part in the macabre dance of death a few moments ago.

By now, Kamsa was in a panic. The carefully planned assassination had turned into a farce. Foiled at every turn, he was like a madman, shouting and giving a hundred contradictory orders. "Stop the music!" he shouted to the drummers, who were pounding away to a crescendo, as he had told them to do when the boys were killed. The poor drummers weren't told that they were not to play if the wrestlers were killed.

"Catch the boys! Arrest the chieftain Nanda and his followers! Kill that crooked Vasudeva and that treacherous father of mine, Ugrasena, who has joined my enemy's side!" Thus he shouted in a frenzy. The soldiers tried in vain to catch Him who cannot be caught by might alone. Krishna slipped like quicksilver through their grasp and, making His body light, jumped onto the high dais with ease. The music stopped. There fell a sudden hush over the whole crowd, as for the first time uncle and nephew came face to face. At last, Kamsa saw in front of him the form that had haunted his nights and days for nearly twenty years. His imagination had painted many lurid pictures of Vishnu as He would appear to him, but never one which resembled this! For a second he looked into those glorious eyes, those twin pools of kindness and, instead of fear, he felt a great relief, as if at last, after many buffetings and storms at sea, he had come in sight of a safe harbor. It was but a momentary respite. Then, with true *kshatriya* (warrior class) valor, he ran forward with upraised sword to kill the defenseless boy. Krishna caught hold of the tuft of hair on his head, from which the crown had slipped off, and threw him onto the ground from the top of the dais. There he lay in the dirt and dust of the arena—the mighty king of the Bhojas, terror of the Yadavas. Krishna jumped down lightly onto his chest and at the touch of the Lord's feet, his soul, which had been thirsting for liberation, rose up like a pale glow and melted into the aura surrounding Krishna. Then Krishna dragged the body of the dead tyrant around the arena as a lion might drag a dead elephant, so that all his subjects might see that their king was dead.

Meanwhile, the eight younger brothers of Kamsa rose in defense and came forward to avenge their brother's death. They were beaten to death by Balarama, armed with the elephant tusk. Then came the two royal women, each to lament at the side of her dead husband. After consoling the ladies, Krishna and Balarama went to release their parents, Devaki and Vasudeva, from their fetters and touched their feet with their heads. Recognizing them to be one with the Lord of the universe, Devaki and Vasudeva stood before them with folded hands, until there fell upon their minds once more the veil of *maya*. Then they forgot the greatness of their children and embraced them with the love and tenderness which had been suppressed for twelve long years.

Krishna now spoke to them with great kindness, "O Father! O Mother! It behooves you to pardon us for not serving you at a time when you needed us most—when you were imprisoned and oppressed by the wicked Kamsa. A man is not able to redeem, even in a hundred years of life, the debt he owes to the parents who gave birth to and nourished the body, which is the basis for the achievement of all objects in life, including liberation. Vain were the days of our past life as we failed to be of service to you when you were living in great fear of Kamsa."

Having comforted his parents thus, the Lord released Ugrasena, His grandfather, and proclaimed him King of the Yadavas.

Thus ends the eleventh chapter of The Play of God, *named "The Prophecy Fulfilled."*

Hari Aum Tat Sat

TWELVE

UDDHAVA AT GOKULA

*Mathuranathaya
namaha*

Homage to the
Lord of Mathura

*O Lord of Mathura! Your lips are sweet, Your speech is sweet,
Your face is sweet, Your smile is sweet, Your heart is sweet, Your
gait is sweet. In fact, O Lord, everything about You is filled with
sweetness.*
—*MATHURASHATAKAM OF MADHVACHARYA*

The Yadavas had a curse that they should have no
king, but all the same, since His grandfather
Ugrasena was the senior-most member and the
one worthy to rule, Krishna made him the ruler of the
Yadavas and appointed Uddhava, a cousin of His and a
pupil of the sage Brihaspati, as the Prime Minister.
Then He gathered together all His clansmen, who had
fled to various hiding places due to fear of Kamsa, welcomed them back to their rightful capital, and resettled
them in their homes. The city of Mathura entered a new
phase of life. Once more, the citizens could walk about
fearlessly, secure in the might of Krishna and Balarama
and delighting in seeing glimpses of their faces now and
again.

It was only now that Nanda realized the bitter truth
that the child he had adored and brought up for twelve
years as his own son was not his, but Vasudeva's. How
blithely had he set out for the capital a few days ago!
How happily had he assured his wife that he would
return with their beloved son. Now he found his son to
be a king and he himself left to return home, alone and
empty-hearted. With what words could he comfort his
wife? In that whole town that had gone mad with joy, he
alone grieved. But Krishna, sensing his deep unhappiness, went and comforted him.

99

"Dear Father!" He said. "We were nourished, fondled, and cared for by you with extreme affection. She is the real mother and he the real father who take up and care for as their own such infants as are deserted by their kith and kin. You, O Father, have done this for us when our parents were unable to look after us. Even Devaki, who gave birth to Me, has never had the joy of nursing Me, as mother Yashoda had. Even Vasudeva has never had the pleasure of watching my childhood pranks, as you have. O Father, I do not belong to this person or that. I belong to those who love Me. To him who looks on Me as a son, I will go as a son, not only now but in the ages to come." His voice rang out as He said this, as if He was making a promise to posterity. Nanda felt immeasurably comforted and able to return to Gokula in a happier state of mind.

Vasudeva now arranged for all the various rites which had to be done for *kshatriya* children and which had not been done by Nanda. Though Balarama and Krishna were all-knowing and were the source of all knowledge, they had hidden that inherent knowledge under the cloak of humanity. Vasudeva realized that they had to have formal education befitting their status. They had been trained only in the art of looking after cows! For some time, the fond parents enjoyed the delight of having their sons back with them, but then they were forced to send them to Guru Sandipani, who lived in Avanti, and there they had to stay for the duration of their studies. In order to demonstrate to the world the glory of the *gurukula* system of staying in the preceptor's house, they devoted themselves to the service of the teacher, attending on him as servitors and bestowing on him the honor due a divinity. The learned Sandipani imparted to them all the *Vedas*, including the *Upanishads*. He taught them the science of warfare, as well as the *mantras* connected with all the divine weapons, and also the ethical codes, the law codes, the science of logic, and the administrative codes. Pupils generally took their own time about learning and left the *gurukula* only after they had imbibed as much as they were capable of learning. But these unique princes grasped all aspects of knowledge at the very first instruction. They had such powers of concentration that they mastered the sixty-four subjects in sixty-four days.

It was during this time that Krishna formed a friendship with the poor Brahmin boy Sudama. Once when they had gone to the forest to collect firewood, they were overtaken by a terrific storm. There was no place to take shelter, so the boys huddled together and told each other stories to keep up their spirits. All they had to eat was a small bundle of beaten flakes of rice that the *guru's* wife had given them. When morning came, they were discovered by the *guru* and his wife, who had been searching for them. They were deeply touched by the boys' action in having risked their lives collecting firewood for their sake, and they blessed them. In later years when they met again, Krishna reminded Sudama of this incident and attributed all His greatness to that blessing given by the *guru.* Here, the Lord reminds us that the blessing of a great soul, especially a preceptor, is something to be striven for and that it is the one thing that will set a person on the right path of life.

At the end of the course of study, each student had to give the *guru* a *dakshina*, or fee, for having taught him and looked after him for such a length of time. In those days, unlike modern times, it was the teacher's duty to look after both the material and the spiritual welfare of the student and no payment was expected or demanded until the course of study was completed. Even then, there was no fixed fee. Each student gave according to his means. When Krishna asked Sandipani what he wanted, the old man refused to take anything, for he had no desires. So Krishna approached his wife, who said diffidently, "Lord, though You have behaved like an ordinary child here, I have heard that You are the incarnation of Lord Vishnu. I had but one child—a boy, who was drowned in the ocean at Prabhasa. I would like to have him back."

"So be it," said Krishna.

Accompanied by Balarama, He went to the great port of Prabhasa. Approaching the ocean, He ordered Varuna, the Lord of the Waters, to bring back His tutor's son. Varuna replied that he had been taken away by a demon called Panchajana, who had the form of a conch. Hearing this, the Lord entered the ocean and killed the demon, but He could not find the boy. He then took the conch, Panchajana, which formed part of the demon's body, and went with Balarama to the abode of Yama, the god of death. He demanded that Yama return the son of His preceptor. Yama was but a vassal of the Supreme Lord and he bowed to Him and returned the boy. Krishna took the child and gave him to His *guru* as a *dakshina* from all three of them, since Sudama, his friend, could not afford to give anything on his own. Having received the blessings of the *guru* and his wife, Krishna and Balarama returned to Mathura after taking a fond farewell of Sudama and urging him to keep in touch. The people of Mathura were filled with joy to see their saviors.

As soon as He returned to Mathura, Krishna heard of the misery of His foster parents and the *gopis* after His departure. He decided to send His close friend, Uddhava, with a letter from Him. In choosing Uddhava, He had two purposes. One was to comfort His people and the other was to make Uddhava understand the meaning of selfless love. Uddhava was one of the most learned and brilliant men of the age, but the *avatar* of the Lord Krishna was not merely to preach the path of *jnana*, or knowledge, but also the path of *bhakti*, or devotion. It is very difficult for the man of knowledge to forget his learning and approach the Lord with a simple and innocent mind. However full of learning we might be, yet all earthly knowledge is but a drop in the ocean of the all-comprehensive wisdom of the Lord. We are all but nursery children in His eyes, and it is with the innocence of a child that we should approach Him. Perhaps Uddhava was a little ashamed to be the messenger of a love letter to milkmaids, but since his love and obedience to Krishna was exemplary, he set out immediately. By the time he reached Vrindavan, it was evening, the most beautiful part of the day at Gokula, the time for which the *gopis* would wait anxiously, for it brought the return of their beloved Lord. The cloud of dust raised by the hooves of the returning cows was highlighted by the last rays of the setting sun. The air was filled with the bellows of the bulls, the lowing of the cows, and the buzzing sound made by the milking of so many cows. These sounds mingled with the haunting melody of the flutes of the *gopalas* and the songs of the *gopis* singing about the exploits of their hero, Krishna.

Little lights were being lit in every house as Uddhava reached Gokula. Seeing the chariot and his form from afar, the *gopis* thought that Krishna had come back. This was no wonder, for Uddhava resembled Krishna in height, age, and style of dressing since he always wore the cast-off clothes and garlands that Krishna had worn the previous day, such was his love for Him. No wonder that the *gopis*, who had no other image in their hearts but Krishna, who saw Him constantly, waking and dreaming, mistook Uddhava for their beloved. They rushed out with joyful cries, "He has come! He has come! The Lord of our hearts has come!"

Seeing Uddhava, they fell back a pace. Then, realizing that he was a messenger from their beloved, they went close to him, forgetful of their womanly modesty, unmindful of the fact that he was a stranger whom they had never before met. They caught hold of his hand, tugged at his upper garment, and pelted him with questions. Uddhava laughingly ward-ed them off, though inwardly he was quite shocked. Never in all his well-regulated life had he come across such shameless behavior in women! How could he comfort them, he wondered? He was rescued from his predicament by Nanda and Yashoda, who took him to their home and honored him as if he were Krishna Himself. After he had rested and eaten, Nanda asked him, "O Uddhava, does Krishna still remember the people of Gokula? Does He remember his poor parents, His friends, the cows, and the hills and dales of Vrindavan? Will He ever come back even once to look up His old comrades? We have been saved from many a danger by His grace. Every spot here is filled with memories relating to Him. We can hardly attend to our normal duties these days, for our minds are totally absorbed in thinking of Him and His exploits while He lived with us." As he was reminiscing like this, both he and Yashoda were overcome with emotion and could hardly speak. Their tears flowed and they remained silent and absorbed in Him.

Uddhava marveled at this state of devotion and spoke to them thus, "O Great Ones, you are the most praiseworthy among all mankind, for your minds are firmly fixed on Krishna, who is none other than the Supreme Lord Narayana. He is the soul of all and the cause of all, who has assumed a human form for the fulfillment of certain divine purposes. What other end is there for you to achieve? O Noble Ones, do not grieve. He is ever beside you, for He is enshrined in your hearts. He has no father or mother, no wife and son. There is none related to Him and none who is a stranger, He has no birth and no body. He has manifested in this world of His own free will and not due to any bonds of *karma*, in order to bestow liberation on all. Though free from the *gunas* of *Prakriti*,[1] yet He assumes these *gunas* for the sake of sport. Krishna, who is none other than the Supreme Being, is not your son alone. He is the child of all. He is the father of all. He is the mother of all. He is the soul of all. There is no entity that can be said to have an existence apart from Him."

Thus, while they were talking of Him who was dearest to all their hearts, the night passed. The next morning, Uddhava set out to meet the *gopis*. They took him off to where Radha was sitting beneath a tree, immersed in contemplation of her lover. She scarcely noticed him nor

---

[1] *gunas of Prakriti*—see footnoe 2 on page 64.

did she pay much attention to the eager questions of the others. Ever absorbed in the memory of the days and nights of rapture she had spent with her beloved, she lived in a world of her own, peopled entirely by Krishna.

The others, in the meantime, were pelting Uddhava with a hundred questions. They did not give him a chance to speak, for their hearts were full of the things they wanted to tell Krishna, and what better person could they tell it to than His friend? They cared not for his prestige or erudition. The only worth he had in their eyes was that he had come from their Lord.

"Were you sent by that hard-hearted one to comfort His parents?" was their first question. "He could never have sent you to comfort us, for surely He must have forgotten us after seeing the sophisticated beauties of the city. Where is He now? Tell us. Tell us the truth. Is He not in the arms of some beauteous damsel in the city of Mathura?"

Uddhava tried to stammer out a few words, but his studies had never taught him how to deal with the lovelorn. Then they started weeping and crying.

"How can we forget that body that has lain so close to us? How can we forget those arms that have held us so close? How can we forget those eyes that have gazed deep into ours, those rose-petal hands that have stroked away our tears, and those tender lips, from which we have sucked the nectar of divine life? Will we ever be able to see Him again? Will we ever be able to hold Him close to our breasts again and touch His feet and feed Him with the things He likes best? The only reason we do not die is because He is still alive. So long as there's a hope of ever seeing Him again, we can never give up our lives!"

Uddhava listened to this intimate monologue, astounded and bewildered. As yet. he was unable to decide what manner of women they were. He could not believe that they were loose and immoral, for such devotion is not to be found among that class of women, and he could not yet recognize the depth and extent of their devotion, for he had never seen the like before. To the *gopis*, they themselves did not exist as separate individuals. They existed in Him and for Him. They had started living only after meeting Him and in future they would continue to live only in the hope of hearing about Him, talking about Him, and maybe of meeting Him. It was a total submerging of their separate personalities in Him who was the *Uttama Purusha*, or the perfect person. Though their bodies appeared to be different, yet in truth they had no existence apart from Him. In all the aspects of their lives, whether mundane or exalted, they had but one thought, Krishna, Krishna, Krishna, and then again Krishna! Whatever they saw was a part of Him. The breeze was His breath, the rose His lips, the sunset His clothes, and the clouds His color. They carried on their duties like automatons. Sometimes they would sing, sometimes laugh, sometimes cry, as different thoughts about Krishna came to their minds.

Uddhava tried to speak to Radha, for he had heard Krishna mention her many times, but she seemed oblivious to anything but His name. Then suddenly, she saw a honeybee and started speaking to it as if it were a messenger from her beloved, "Ah honey sucker! You are like my Lord—going from flower to flower and owing allegiance to none, leaving the flower the moment you have exhausted its nectar. Where have you come from? You have been sucking honey from His garland, I see. And look, you have some red powder on your feelers. That must be from the forehead of some beauty from Mathura, which got into His garland while she embraced Him, and now you have smeared it on yourself while sucking from His garland. Go away. I cannot bear the sight of you! Having made us drink of the inebriating nectar of His lips once, He has abandoned us, who have given up everything for His sake—our sons, our husbands, our homes, and our prospects here and in the hereafter." Turning to Uddhava, she continued, "We are the widows of Vrindavan. Bereft and forsaken are we, for our husband has left us and now we will never be whole again." So saying, she buried her face in her hands and burst out crying. Uddhava marveled at the imagination which was so immersed in thoughts about Krishna that it could weave a story about Him even at the sight of a bumblebee! Radha's sorrow is the sorrow of the *bhakta* (devotee) who realizes that God does not belong to her alone, but to everyone who loves Him. It was a harder lesson for her than for others because for a short time it had seemed to her that He was hers alone.

Uddhava tried to comfort them. "Listen, O Gopis! You have attained the highest fulfillment of life and the whole world must adore you, for you have succeeded in surrendering your minds completely to the Lord of all. Normally, people attain devotion through the practice of many disciplines, vows, and austerities, but even without any of these, I find in you an extraordinary manifestation of love for the divine, which is rare even among sages. Now listen to the message He has sent for you."

"O Beloved Ones, I have never left you and will never leave you. You have never been separate from Me, for I am manifest in the whole universe. If I have not come to see you, it is only because I have still to accomplish what I have come for. But do not grieve, for your grief is My grief and your joy My joy. For love such as yours there can be no end. I, who am boundless, have been bound by your love. Blessed are you among women, for your names will ever be remembered by the world to come. When I am far away physically, meditate on Me, and thus you will be able to commune with Me. Devoid of other thought, allow your minds to enter into Me, and then you will attain Me without delay."

Hearing this, the *gopis'* grief was slightly assuaged. They told Uddhava, "O Noble One, this river Kalindi, this mountain Govardhan, these forests, these cows, the sound of the flutes, all these are indelibly connected in our minds with Him. His footprints, placed over these vales, will never allow us to forget Him. Our minds have been completely possessed by Him, so how can we possibly forget? O Lord," they cried, "O Lord of Lakshmi! O Lord of Vraja, dispeller of sorrows! Master of Gokula! Be kind enough to lift up this settlement of ours, which is fast sinking into the sea of sorrow!"

At this heartrending cry, Uddhava reminded them of Krishna's message and of their identity with Him in spirit. To comfort them and His parents, he stayed on in Vraja for some months, during which he thrilled the whole community with songs and poems about Krishna's deeds. What was more important was the lesson he learned from them, namely, that love such as this was superior even to knowledge. Before he left Vraja, Uddhava, the foremost of the Yadavas, brightest student of Brihaspati, prostrated himself in the dirt at the feet of the cowherd girls of Vrindavan and extolled them thus, "You are indeed the only ones who have attained the real purpose of human birth, for you have attained that *mahabhava*, or extreme yearning for Govinda, the soul of all, which is aspired to by all, but attained by very few. Of what use is birth in a high social milieu? Of what use is money or status or beauty if it does not bring this intense love for the Infinite Being? Yet by His grace, you humble nomads of the forest have been blessed with this state. Love for God produces the same results, irrespective of one's learning or social status. Not even Lakshmi, the consort of Vishnu, has received the grace that has been showered on the *gopis* of Vrindavan! May I be born as a bower or a creeper or even a blade of grass in this blessed spot which is covered with the dust of the feet of these *gopis* who have abandoned the unbreakable bond of love for

their own relations and even the path of virtue approved by society to follow the way of the divine, which is only an aspiration even for the sages.
Again and again do I salute at the feet of these women of Vraja, whose
mental attitude purifies the three worlds."

At last, bidding farewell to the *gopis* and Nanda and Yashoda, Uddhava got into his chariot to return to Mathura. The meeting of the *gopis* with
Uddhava was like the mingling of the two rivers of *bhakti* and *jnana*, or
devotion and knowledge. Uddhava's knowledge flowed into the *gopis* and
strengthened their minds while their *bhakti* seeped into Uddhava's heart
and melted his pride. The result of the confluence was the *jnana-bhakta*, a
rare combination. It was only now that Uddhava realized that Krishna
had sent him not merely to comfort the *gopis*, but to show him an example of a truly exalted and unselfish love. Poor Uddhava. Little did he realize, as he waved good-bye to the weeping *gopis*, that one day he, too,
would have to part from his beloved master. Only then would he be able
to understand fully the anguish felt by the *gopis*.

Krishna never again returned from Mathura to Vrindavan. It is as if
He wants to teach the lesson that life is an ever-rolling wheel of Time. The
wise person is the one who, like the child, lives entirely in the present,
unburdened by the memories of the past, however sweet, unworried by
the prospects of the future, however dark. Krishna's life became that of a
prince and the adviser of princes, though He never occupied the throne
Himself. Henceforth, He lived in the palaces and courts and council
chambers of monarchs with as much ease and grace as He had lived in
the hills and dales and forests of Vrindavan.

It is said that on one occasion, unable to bear their separation from
Krishna, the *gopis* and *gopas* made a great pilgrimage to the city. It was
the time of the harvest festival, when the earth lies fallow for a while, so
that people may rest. When He heard that they had come, He had them
brought with all state and dignity into the audience chamber meant for
kings! Krishna received them with the greatest of love, dressed in the
robes and jewels of a prince. But the rustics would not look at Him. With
eyes cast to the ground and heads averted, they stood there, the *gopas*
and *gopis* of Vrindavan, uttering not one word, casting not one glance in
the direction of the Prince who stood before them, overwhelming them
with His magnificence. Then Krishna understood what was the matter
and, going out of their presence for a moment, He put off the robes and
jewels of state and came back to them clad in the simple attire of the

cowherds. On His head was the tiny circlet with the peacock's feather. In His right hand He carried the flute, round His neck was the garland of wildflowers (*vanamala*), and His feet were bare. When they saw Him like this in the form of Gopalakrishna, the cowherd Krishna, they were over-joyed. They begged Him to play the flute for them and they romped and frolicked and sang all day with Him in the royal gardens, even as they used to do in the meadows and woods of Vrindavan. Recalling the happy days of the past, they reminded Him of His boyhood pranks and the Lord played and danced with them with as much abandon and as much skill as He played the game of kingmaker.

Thus ends the twelfth chapter of The Play of God,
named "Uddhava at Gokula."

Hari Aum Tat Sat

May He protect us. May He nourish us. May we both work together with great energy. May our study be vigorous and effective. May we never hate each other. May peace, physical, mental, and spiritual be on us forever.
—UPANISHADIC PEACE PRAYER

As all the waters which fall from the sky reach the one ocean, so also prostrations to any god will reach Keshava (the Supreme, as embodied in Krishna) alone.
—POPULAR VERSE

THIRTEEN

LORD OF DWARAKA

Dwarakanathaya namaha

Homage to the Lord of Dwaraka

This body, which is now attractive, is bound to age one day and will disintegrate gradually by its very nature. O foolish man! Why try to perpetuate it through medicines? Utter the sweet name of Shri Krishna instead, which is the sure remedy for all ills.

—MUKUNDAMALA

Krishna, recalling the promise He had made to Trivakra, went to her house with Uddhava in order to fulfill this promise, for it was the purpose of His *avatar* to go to each devotee in the form in which his or her inmost heart cried out. Trivakra, being a courtesan, knew of no other ways to please the Lord than with her body, and since she had nothing else to offer, He accepted it with as much joy as He did the *vanamala* of the garland maker and the blows of Kamsa.

Soon after, the Lord, accompanied by Uddhava and Balarama, went to Akrura's house in order to fulfill the promise made to him. Akrura worshipped Him with all honor and addressed Him thus, "O Lord, today my house has been rendered more holy than the hermitages of ascetics, for it has had the great good fortune to have as its guest the Supreme Parent and Teacher of the world, who is the embodiment of all the divinities. Who is the man who will seek shelter in anyone other than You, the lover of His devotees, the universal well-wisher? Not only do You grant the desires of Your devotees, however trifling, but You are the One who grants Your very Self, attaining which there is no further fall (into the meshes of worldly delusion). You have embodied Yourself in age after age whenever the ancient path of right living and enlightenment, the *Sanatana Dharma*, which has been revealed by You, is in danger of being lost.[1] O Janardana, it is the height of good fortune that You have condescended to come of Your own accord to my humble abode. Grant me the ability to cut asunder the cord of attachment, Your *maya's* creation, for son, wife, wealth, house, and body."

Kamsa had two wives, Asti and Prapti, the daughters of the mighty King of Magadha called Jarasandha. This king was supposed to be an invincible warrior with the strength of a hundred elephants. After the death of Kamsa, his wives returned to their father and begged him to avenge the death of his son-in-law, their husband. He swore to raze the town of Mathura to the ground and exterminate the race of the Yadavas completely. This would be an easy matter, he thought, for they were ruled by the doddering old monarch Ugrasena, assisted by that puny upstart cowherd boy! What could they do against the might of the Magadha empire?

News of the impending invasion by Jarasandha was brought to Krishna and He mobilized the Yadava forces to repel the attack. He mustered up as much of a fighting force as He could in so short a period and made Kritavarma the general. The Yadavas had scattered in diverse directions during the rule of Kamsa and had just returned and taken up the threads of their lives. Krishna had hardly had time to put the state in order. But when He heard reports of the impending attack, He was forced to make fast preparations. The city was ill-prepared to withstand a siege. Krishna knew well the defects of the city and decided that He had to provide a better asylum for His people. For the moment He could do nothing but to make the best use of everything at hand, since Jarasandha was advancing toward Mathura with an army of twenty *akshauhinis*, or battalions.

The Yadava army managed to repulse the attacks of the Magadha hosts many times. In fact, it is said that Jarasandha attacked fifteen times and was repulsed every time. But Krishna knew that they could not hope to hold out much longer. The people were already distressed, normal life had come to a standstill, and yet the forces of the Magadha king, which were being continuously replenished, kept attacking. Time after time the huge army of Jarasandha was completely destroyed by Krishna and Balarama. In fact, the latter managed to catch the king alive and was about to kill him when Krishna stopped him, for the time of his death was not yet nigh. Just when Jarasandha was about to start on his eighteenth

---

[1] *Sanatana Dharma*—Literally "The Eternal Religion," the name Hindus give to their religion; correct name for Hinduism.

expedition, he was joined by Kalayavana, a fierce warrior of foreign origin, who was itching for a fight with some worthy opponent and thought he could find it in Krishna. So he marched to the city of Mathura and laid siege to it.

The Lord was very much concerned about the predicament of the Vrishnis, now threatened simultaneously with attack on two fronts, and decided on a stratagem. He slipped out of the city, taking care to allow the Yavanas to see Him as He pretended to escape. Kalayavana had been given a description of the Lord as wearing a lotus garland and having peacock feathers in His crown. He was exultant when he saw Him slip out stealthily, or so he thought. He followed Him with great excitement, determined to kill Him single-handedly, for if Krishna fell, Mathura would fall. But the Lord was not as easy to catch as he had expected. Slim and slight was His boyish figure, adorned with a simple lotus garland, but He darted hither and thither and led Kalayavana on a merry chase into the hills surrounding the city and disappeared into a cave. Krishna had a special purpose for taking him there.

An ancient king of Bharatavarsha called Muchukunda had procured a boon from Indra, the king of the gods, for having helped him defeat the demons. The boon asked by the king was that he should be allowed to sleep in peace for many years until the advent of the Lord as Krishna, for he was anxious to behold this form of the Lord. Indra granted him this blessing and also promised him that, if anyone woke him up before the appointed time, that person would be turned into ashes. This king, Muchukunda, was sleeping in the cave into which Krishna entered. Naturally, Kalayavana was ignorant of all this. He followed the Lord into the cave and saw the form of the sleeping king. In the dim light of the cave, he mistook it for Krishna. Not waiting to ascertain further details, he directed a well-aimed kick at the sleeping form and said in a loud voice, "Get up, O Yadava! You cannot hope to escape my wrath by resorting to these childish tricks!"

Being thus rudely awakened from his sleep of eons, King Muchukunda turned a baleful eye on the miscreant. Kalayavana was immediately changed into a heap of ashes. Krishna thereupon emerged from behind the rock, from which vantage point He had been watching the proceedings with interest. Muchukunda's second boon had been that he would able to see Vishnu in His *avatar* as Krishna and when he saw the divine form which he had been dreaming about for years, he immediately rose up and then prostrated. "Who is it that I am seeing before me? In this mountain cave filled with gloom, the brilliance emanating from You is dispelling the darkness with a glowing light. O Great One, please tell me all particulars about Yourself, for I consider You to be an incarnation of Lord Vishnu."

To him the Lord replied smilingly, "O Honored One, My births, deeds, and names are so numerous that even I cannot recount them all. It may be possible to count the particles of dust on this planet but not the number of My births. But know that in this birth I am incarnated in the line of the Yadus as the son of Vasudeva and am known as Vaasudeva. Because you have worshipped Me in the past and have desired to have a vision of Me in this form, I have presented Myself in this cave. O Royal Sage, choose whatever boons you want and I shall grant them accordingly."

The king said, "O Lord, my life until now has been wasted in vain pursuits centering on the feeling that the body is the Self. Your mighty power called Time reduces to mere dust even a kingly body encased in silks. So now, having come to my senses, I do not seek any other blessing than the service of Your feet. Who is it that, having once known You, would ask for any other boon, which is only the means for further bondage? O Spirit Supreme! O Refuge of the helpless! I have been reduced to wretchedness by the enemies called passions within me, and I have sought refuge in You. Protect me, O Lord, from the dangers within me."

The Lord replied, "Know, O King, that I did not tempt you with boons in order to test your mastery over your desires, but only to show how a devotee with unswerving love for Me can never be attracted by worldly distractions. I bless you with unshakable and unwavering devotion to Me always and under all conditions. Do you go and practice austerities to remove the effects of your past *karma*. In your next birth you will be born as a saint with universal love; after that you will attain Me."

Muchukunda, being thus blessed by Krishna, made full prostrations to Him and left in a northerly direction for the ancient shrine of Badrinath, where he meditated on the form of the Lord as Narayana and attained liberation.

As soon as He returned after killing Kalayavana and blessing Muchukunda, Krishna found that Mathura was being besieged by Jarasandha for the eighteenth and last time. Krishna and Balarama now employed another ruse to lure Jarasandha. They took to their heels as if in fright, right in front of Jarasandha's eyes, and climbed up a hill. Jarasandha followed them but could find no traces of them. So he heaped firewood around the hill and set fire to it. When the flames started leaping up, Balarama and Krishna, making use of their *yogic* powers, jumped clear of the flames and made their way back. Jarasandha returned home feeling satisfied that he had seen the last of his two troublesome enemies, and told anyone who cared to listen that he had just returned after making a bonfire of the two Yadava brothers.

It was at this time that Raivata, the king of the land of Anarta, offered his daughter Revati in marriage to Balarama. Part of the kingdom was also given as a dowry. For some time now, Krishna had been thinking that Mathura was in too vulnerable a position to be defended and that they should change their capital to a safer place. The island of Dwaraka, which lay just beyond the peninsula which Balarama had received as a bride price, was a natural fortress, surrounded as it was by the ocean on all sides. By His *yogic* powers Krishna made a wonderful city of this island, with properly planned highways, flower gardens, beautiful mansions and palaces, parks, temples, and lakes. He employed the celestial architect Vishvakarma to get the town built. The Yadavas were transported to the island fortress of Dwaraka while Krishna and Balarama lured Jarasandha away.

Under the guidance of the Lord, the Vrishnis became one of the most powerful people in Bharatavarsha, as India was known in those days. Those were stirring days in the country, and the position of Krishna in the powerful Vrishni state placed Him in the front of affairs. Kings sought His approval and the alliance of His people. It was never His way, however, to interfere in affairs in person. Instead, He chose certain agents who advanced the course of history for the fulfillment of the cosmic purpose. For Himself, He regarded the whole of life as if it were a sort of play, at which He was the audience. Thus, He allowed events to work themselves out even though this led in the end to the self-destruction of all things. But the body was not His concern; He had come to ensure the spiritual evolution of all mankind and to reestablish on a firmer footing the ancient law of righteousness, the *Sanatana Dharma*.

In this objective, His main agents were the Pandavas, who belonged to the Kuru dynasty, which ruled over a vast portion of the north. The great epic, the *Mahabharata,* deals in great detail with the fortunes of this dynasty and contains the first authentic account of the life of Krishna.

The life of Krishna would not be complete without an account of the Pandavas. Veda Vyasa, the grandson of the great sage Vasishtha, was the author of the *Mahabharata*. He was the son of the sage Parasura and the fisherwoman Satyavati, who later married the Kuru king, Santanu. King Santanu's first wife was the goddess Ganga, by whom he had a son called Bhishma. After the birth of their son, Ganga left him and the king was bereft for many years. At last, he met Satyavati, whom he wanted to marry, but her father refused to allow him to marry her unless he promised that her children would be his heirs. Santanu was loathe to agree to this since his eldest son Bhishma had already been proclaimed as heir apparent and he was a most noble lad, beloved by all. But Bhishma came to know of his father's predicament, and he took an oath that he would remain a lifelong celibate and would never demand the kingdom.

Thus Santanu married Satyavati and had two sons called Vichitravirya and Chitrangada. Chitrangada died at an early age. When it was time for Vichitravirya to marry, Bhishma represented him at the *svayamvara*[2] of the daughters of the King of Kasi and brought away the three princesses called Amba, Ambika, and Ambalika. On the way, Amba revealed that she had already given her heart to the King Salva, and so Bhishma sent her back to him. The latter, however, refused to accept her, since she had been forcibly abducted by Bhishma in the presence of all the other suitors. So Amba returned and asked Bhishma to marry her, but he refused. She swore vengeance against Bhishma. She went to the forest and practiced severe austerities, gave up her life, and was reborn as Shikhandini, the daughter of King Drupada of Panchala. As she grew up, she remembered her past, went to the forest again to practice severe austerities, and became transformed into a male known as Shikhandin, the destined slayer of Bhishma.

Vichitravirya, after some years of marriage with his two wives Ambika and Ambalika, died, leaving no issue, and Satyavati's father's ambition came to naught. Determined to preserve the line of the Kurus, Satyavati tried to persuade Bhishma to marry his sisters-in-law, but he was unshakable in his resolve to keep the oath of celibacy he had taken up only for her sake. Satyavati was forced to summon her eldest son, the sage Vyasa, and beg him to cohabit with her daughters-in-law, thus allowing the lineage to continue. According to rule, a childless widow could beget chil-

2 *svayamvara*—"self-choice," referring to a ceremony in which a woman, usually a princess, chooses her husband from among the assembled suitors. For most women, marriage was arranged.

dren through a holy man who had transcended body consciousness in order to continue the line of her departed husband, and the children would be known as her husband's children.

Ambika and Ambalika had to be coaxed to accept Vyasa, who had the unkempt appearance of a *yogi*. The former closed her eyes in horror as he approached, and her son, called Dhritarashtra, was born blind. Ambalika turned pale with fright at the sage's visage and she had a son called Pandu, who was extremely pale. The Queen Mother persuaded Ambika to accept Vyasa once more, but she sent her maid instead. The maid received the sage with all due honors and was blessed by a highly virtuous and wise son called Vidura, who was supposed to be the incarnation of Yama, the god of death and righteousness.

Until the children came of age, Bhishma directed the affairs of the Kuru kingdom. As Dhritarashtra was blind, the younger son, Pandu, was crowned king and made commander-in-chief of the army, and Vidura, who was a repository of wisdom and knowledge, was made the Prime Minister. Once again, Bhishma looked around for suitable brides for his nephews. Gandhari, daughter of the King of Gandhara (modern Afghanistan), agreed to wed the blind Dhritarashtra. Determined that she would not enjoy the sight of a world which her husband could not see, she blindfolded herself with a scarf for the rest of her life. To protect her interests, her elder brother Shakuni was sent to live in the Kuru capital of Hastinapura.

Vasudeva, the father of Krishna, was the son of Sura, who had a daughter called Pritha, who later came to be known as Kunti, for she was adopted by the King Kuntibhoja. As a young girl, she had received a boon from the sage Durvasa that she could invoke any god she chose with a *mantra* and he would bless her with a child. The innocent Kunti, in order to test the efficacy of the *mantra*, invoked the sun god, Surya, who gave her a divine child born with shining armor and earrings, later known as Karna. Since she was still unwed when she begat the child, she placed the baby in a casket and floated it down the Ganga, where it was rescued by a charioteer from Hastinapura called Adhiratha. He and his wife Radha brought up the child as their own. Since his foster mother was Radha, the boy was called Radheya.

Soon after this incident, Kunti was given in marriage to Prince Pandu of Hastinapura, who later also wed Madri, the Princess of Madra. Once, when Pandu was hunting in the forest, he shot and killed a mating deer, who cursed him that he would die if he ever had relations with his wives. The grief-stricken Pandu then decided to renounce the world and live in the forest, but his two queens were determined to keep him company. After some years in the forest, Pandu became anxious to have progeny, but since he had the curse he knew he could not procreate sons with his wives. It was at this time that Kunti told him of the *mantra* given to her by the farseeing sage Durvasa. Pandu was overjoyed and suggested that she invoke Yama-dharma, the god of righteousness. From him Kunti gave birth to a son called Yudhishthira, who was famous for his righteousness. A year later, Kunti invoked Vayu, the lord of winds, and by him she begat a strong son called Bhima. In the meantime at Hastinapura, Gandhari gave birth to a hundred sons and one daughter; the eldest son was known as Duryodhana. As soon he was born, all sorts of ill omens were seen. Vidura prophesied that this child would bring about the destruction of their dynasty and that he should be destroyed at once, but Dhritarashtra refused.

Meanwhile in the forest, Kunti invoked Indra, the king of the gods, and was blessed with a famous son called Arjuna. Madri now wanted a son too, so Kunti taught her the *mantra* and she invoked the twin gods, the Asvini Kumaras, who gave her twins called Nakula and Sahadeva. These five sons of Pandu came to be known collectively as the Pandavas, and they were the ones chosen by Lord Krishna to direct the course of events in the history of Bharatavarsha.

Just prior to Arjuna's birth, an event of the greatest importance had taken place in a little prison cell at Mathura. The Lord Vishnu had incarnated Himself as Krishna, son of Vasudeva and Devaki. There was a strong bond between Krishna and Arjuna, and it was to him that the Lord gave the wonderful message known as the *Shrimad Bhagavad Gita*.

The Pandavas were brought up in the forest for sixteen years, until Pandu died. His second wife Madri immolated herself in his funeral fire, and Kunti was left alone to look after the five boys. The sages of the forest persuaded her to take her sons to Hastinapura and stake Yudhishthira's claim to the throne of the Kurus, for he was the eldest son. Bhishma welcomed them with open arms and arranged for their education, together with the hundred sons of Dhritarashtra, who were collectively known as the Kauravas. Duryodhana was the same age as Bhima, the second of the Pandavas. He was a haughty and wicked child, doted on by his blind father Dhritarashtra and encouraged in his wickedness by his uncle, Shakuni. When they came to Hastinapura, the Pandavas enjoyed for the first time the luxuries of palace life. They were taught the princely arts by their tutor Kripa. Later, the great teacher and archer Dronacharya was brought there by Bhishma to teach the princes.

Much to the chagrin of their cousins, the Pandavas excelled in everything—studies, games, and the art of warfare. They were also wise, obedient, and polite. Bhima, especially, was a thorn in the side of his cousin Duryodhana, whose boyish envy was fanned to flames by his uncle and evil counselor, Shakuni. Aided by him, Duryodhana tried many methods to kill Bhima, including poisoning and drowning. But, by the grace of the divine, Bhima escaped from all these dangers and became stronger than ever.

At the end of their period of studies, Drona arranged for a tournament, in which the princes could show off their prowess. Arjuna was Drona's star pupil and his favorite, so he was kept until the last. After he had exhibited his skill in archery, another young man, wearing golden armor and earrings, came into the arena and proved himself equal to, if not superior to, Arjuna. This was no other than Karna, the eldest son of Kunti and the half brother to the Pandavas. Of course, no one could guess his identity and all thought him to be the son of the charioteer Adhiratha. Duryodhana, however, was quick to see his possibilities, so he promptly struck up a friendship with Karna and bestowed on him the title of Prince of Anga. This gave Karna the status necessary to challenge the Pandavas, if need be, for only those of equal status could challenge each other. Karna was deeply grateful to Duryodhana for this and swore allegiance to him for the rest of his life.

The military training of the princes now drew to a close. Drona then demanded his *guru dakshina*, or fee. Drupada, the King of Panchala, was his old enemy. Drupada and Drona grew together as children and were close friends, though Drupada was heir to the throne and Drona a commoner. During their playful exploits, Drupada promised Drona that when he obtained the throne, he would share it with Drona. Years later, when Drona was an impoverished teacher of martial arts and in difficult straits and Drupada king, he returned to Drupada's land and reminded Drupada of his promise. Drupada laughed in his face and told him that the offer was meaningless childhood prattle. Drona demanded for his *guru dakshina* that Drupada be captured alive and brought to him. Arjuna was the one who managed to do this. Drona's love for Arjuna grew with this accomplishment and he released Drupada unharmed, for all he wanted was to humble his pride. Drupada, however, became obsessed with thoughts of revenge upon Drona. He was also filled with admiration for Arjuna's prowess. He swore that his son, Drishtadyumna, would kill Drona and that his daughter, Draupadi, would marry Arjuna.

When Yudhishthira came of age, he was crowned *Yuvaraja*, or crown prince. The blind king would have preferred to crown his own son, but he had to bow to the wishes of the people as well as to those of the elders like Bhishma, Drona, and Vidura. Within a year of installation as heir apparent, Yudhishthira proved himself fully worthy of the choice, though he was only eighteen years of age. In the meantime, Bhima and Duryodhana had become Balarama's pupils in order to learn the art of mace fighting. In fact, Duryodhana became his favorite pupil! Arjuna's forte was archery, and Drona taught him all he knew, some of which was kept a secret even from his own son, Ashvatthama, whom he knew to be unworthy of this gift. Drona also advised Arjuna to be devoted to his cousin Krishna, who was the embodiment of divinity.

Public support was entirely for the Pandavas, and Duryodhana's jealousy increased day by day when he saw how everyone doted on them and how Arjuna had even conquered several kingdoms.

Far away in Dwaraka, Lord Krishna knew of the plots being brewed in Hastinapura and feared for the safety of His cousins. In order to try to avert the threatening storm if possible, He sent Akrura to Hastinapura. Akrura went and stayed for some months in the capital of the Kurus to gauge the pulse of the city, and he realized that, although on the surface everything seemed smooth, the palace was a bed of intrigue in which plots and counterplots were being hatched by Duryodhana in order to evict the Pandavas from the kingdom and grab the throne for himself. Kunti spoke to him in private and told him that she lived in the palace like a doe surrounded by a pack of wolves. Except for Vidura, there was none she could trust or talk to, and she lived in mortal fear for the lives of her sons. "Krishna! O Krishna!" she cried, "Pray protect me and my children, who are in extreme distress. I do not find any other support than Your lotus feet!"

Akrura comforted her as best as he could and told her not to worry, for the Lord was well aware of her plight and had sent him especially to console her. Akrura then approached Dhritarashtra and warned him against the folly of treating his brother's children badly. The blind king agreed with all that was being said to him, but he proved himself too weak to go against the wishes of his son Duryodhana.

The growing popularity of the Pandavas only served to fan the flames of jealousy which were gnawing at Duryodhana's vitals. At last, unable to bear it any longer, he approached his father and threatened to commit suicide if something was not done to "remove" the Pandavas. The father demurred at first, but eventually gave in. He summoned Yudhishthira and invited him and his brothers to spend a holiday with their mother at the holy city of Varanavata, considered sacred to Lord Shiva. In the meantime, Duryodhana, aided by his henchman Shakuni, his brother Dusshasana, and his friend Karna, had constructed a guest house at Varanavata made of lac, a highly inflammable material, for the Pandavas. The plan was to burn them alive after a year, when all suspicions had died down. But thanks to their wise and virtuous uncle, Vidura, who was constantly alert to Duryodhana's machinations, Yudhishthira was warned of the possible danger. Vidura had also seen to it that a secret passage was made from the palace to the forest through which they could make an escape when the need arose.

The people of Varanavata were delighted to have their crown prince in their midst, but the Pandavas were well aware of the time bomb on which they were sitting, and Kunti directed Bhima to keep watch and alert them when the time for action arose. He made a study of the surrounding forest and planned their escape. Exactly a year later, on the fateful day of *amavasya*, or the new moon, when the night was at its darkest, the attack was supposed to take place. However, Bhima invited Purochana, who had been commissioned by Duryodhana to do the fateful act, for dinner at the palace and having plied him with liquor, Bhima himself set fire to the building and escaped with his brothers and his mother into the forest. News of the disaster spread like wildfire through the country. The Kauravas secretly rejoiced, while others mourned. Only Vidura, Bhishma, and Krishna knew that the Pandavas had escaped. From then on, the Lord kept a close watch over their movements. He guided them through their stay in the forest and ever afterward during their stormy career, for they were His chosen instruments in the propagation of the eternal *dharma* in Bharatavarsha.

Thus ends the thirteenth chapter of The Play of God, *named "Lord of Dwaraka."*

Hari Aum Tat Sat

FOURTEEN

THE ABDUCTION OF RUKMINI

Madhavaya
namaha

Homage to
the Lord of all
knowledge

Victory to the Supreme Divinity
  born as the delightful child of Devaki.
Victory to Shri Krishna
  who is the enlightener of the race of the Vrishnis.
Victory to Mukunda (Krishna), who removes the burden
  of the earth caused by the wicked.
—*MUKUNDAMALA*

Soon after the defeat of Jarasandha, the marriage of his brother, and their consequent shift to Dwaraka, Lord Krishna made His first marital alliance—with Rukmini, the daughter of King Bhishmaka of the country of Vidarbha. The king had five sons and one daughter, noted for her beauty. The eldest child, a son, was Rukmi and the youngest was the daughter, Rukmini. She had a character to match the loveliness of her face and many were the princes who aspired for her hand. But she did not give a thought to any of them. Her grandfather was a great devotee of Lord Krishna, and from childhood she had grown up hearing stories about Him. She vowed to herself that she would marry none other than the Prince of the Yadavas. The sage Narada used to visit the palace often and regale her with stories of the greatness of Krishna, who was none other than the Lord Vishnu incarnate. He also informed her that she herself was the incarnation of Lakshmi Devi, the consort of Vishnu, and that He alone was the fitting groom for her. Thus, from the age of five onward, her heart was completely fixed on the Lord. Though her father and grandfather were very happy with her choice, her eldest brother Rukmi was determined to give her in

121

marriage to his friend Shishupala, the Prince of Chedi, who was Krishna's cousin. Jarasandha, who was still rankling from his defeat at the hands of the upstarts Krishna and Balarama, was also nursing his grievance and biding his time to put down the might of the Yadavas. He had formed an alliance with King Bhishmaka of Vidarbha and King Damaghosha of Chedi. He gave his own granddaughter to Rukmi and urged him to get his sister to marry Shishupala, the son of Damaghosha. So Rukmi, without consulting either his father or his sister, arranged for a *svayamvara*, or wedding ceremony, for his sister at Kundinapura, the capital of Vidarbha. Normally, many kings were invited to a *svayamvara* and the bride could make her choice from among them, but this *svayamvara* was only a farce, for he had determined to get her to marry the groom of his choice. He knew of her predilection for Krishna and feared that she might refuse if she were given an ultimatum to marry Shishupala. All arrangements were made and invitations were sent to all places, except Dwaraka, before Rukmini was told. She was horrified and pleaded with her father to intercede, but he was too old and frail and was a ruler in name alone. All decisions were in the hands of his son, and Rukmi would brook no arguments. In vain she begged her other brothers but they were deaf to her pleas. At last, on the morn of the day previous to her wedding, alone and bereft, she lay in her bedroom sobbing her heart out when suddenly, there was a timid knock at the door, She did not hear, so the door opened a crack and in stepped a Brahmin of noble mien.

"My Lady! Why do you weep so?" he asked. "It is your wedding eve and you should be rejoicing rather than weeping!"

"I would rather it were the eve of my funeral," Rukmini said in a low voice, averting her face so that he could not see its disheveled state.

"I'm but a humble *Brahmin*, but I have known you from the time you were a child and I would gladly do anything I can to help you. You have but to order me."

Startled at this last minute offer of help from such an unexpected quarter, she looked up and was struck with a daring idea. Her cheeks flushed and her heart beat fast at the audacity of what she had in mind but, without pausing to conjecture and weigh the pros and cons, she made an immediate decision, since that appeared to be her only hope. It is said that the Lord Himself. in order to test her determination, had waited till the last moment and then had instigated this plan of sending the Brahmin to her aid.

"O revered one! Will you take a letter to my Lord Krishna, scion of the Yadava race, residing at Dwaraka and bring back a reply before the wedding on the day after tomorrow?" Rukmini asked timidly.

"Certainly," said the Brahmin. "I will willingly do anything for you." Not by a word or a flicker of an eyelid did he betray the fact that he thought it unusual for a gently nurtured girl, a princess of her standing, to be writing letters to someone she did not know, especially on the eve of her wedding! Neither did Rukmini cast a thought to the correctness of her behavior. All she knew was that if she could not have Lord Krishna as her husband, she would rather die, and since death held no charms for her at the moment, she had to make an all-out effort to save herself. Rukmini's behavior both before and after this episode is so full of womanly modesty and charm that it is difficult to imagine how she ever bolstered up the courage for such a bold move. However, the explanation is simple. Like the *gopis*, her love was so great that her ego was completely obliterated and her natural tendencies could not act as an obstacle to her union with the Lord. She felt that she was about to submerge in the waters of *samsara*, and the only one who could save her was the Lord of her heart, who was also God incarnate. Naturally, she clutched at whatever means were offered to her.

"Make haste, O noble one!" she said. "Take the fastest horse and speed away to Dwaraka and back, for if He fails to arrive at the appointed time, I shall surely put an end to my life!"

The Brahmin disappeared in a trice. What powers he utilized to make the long journey from Vidarbha to Dwaraka in such a short time is anybody's guess. Rukmini spent the rest of the time in an agony of suspense, at times elated, at times cast into despair. Sometimes she would think, "He's the Lord of all. Surely He will not forsake me." Then she would say, "I'm so unworthy, how can He ever want to marry me?" Thus, she spent the day and night alternately crying and praying and longing with all her heart that He would answer her prayers.

When the Brahmin reached Dwaraka, it looked as if he was expected, for the guards of the gate allowed him to enter immediately and he was taken without any loss of time to the Lord's presence, where Krishna Himself welcomed him and took care of all his wants. After he was rested, the Lord enquired about the purpose of his visit as if He knew nothing about it.

"What part of the country are you coming from? Why have you taken the trouble to cross the sea and come to Me? Are you in some trouble? Is there anything I can do for you?"

Without preamble, the Brahmin, who knew well the urgency of the situation, bowed and said, "O Lord! I have not come for my own sake but for the sake of your devotee, the Princess of Vidarbha, who has sent a letter through me for your kind perusal."

"Read it! Read it!" Krishna commanded, and the Brahmin read out the tender message.

"O Bhuvanasundara (handsomest one in the entire world)," the letter began, "having heard of Your wonderful qualities, my heart has left its keeping forever. O Granter of liberation, who is the girl of noble birth who has attained marriageable age who will not choose You for a husband if she could have You? Therefore have I chosen You and offer myself to You, if You will deign to accept me as Your wife. Do not allow the Prince of Chedi to appropriate me, for I belong to You alone! Whatever merit I might have acquired by way of sacrifices, austerities, and charities, I now offer in exchange for the honor of being accepted as Your wife. If You will deign to accept this offering of my very self, then do You present Yourself at the *svayamvara* which has been arranged for me. Defeating the armies of Chedi and Magadha, do You capture and marry me according to the *rakshasa rites*,[1] the bridal money paid on the occasion being nothing else but Your might! If You are wondering how I might be carried away, I will give You a hint. On the morn of the wedding day, there will be a grand procession going to worship at the shrine of the goddess Parvati, situated just outside the palace. The bride will accompany this procession. This will be the most convenient time for You to stake Your claim. O Lotus-eyed One! If You fail to be gracious to me, I shall not despair. I shall fast unto death. This I shall do life after life until I get You as husband."

Was there a flicker of a smile in the depths of those all-knowing eyes when He heard this gently worded threat? It is difficult to say, but when He had read this moving epistle, the Brahmin looked expectantly at His face and said, "I have brought this private message to You, O Lord of the Yadavas. Now whatever is to be done in this matter should be done immediately, for the *svayamvara* takes place tomorrow."

Krishna caught hold of the Brahmin's hands and said, "Away, O noble

---

[1] *rakshasa rites*—a marriage ceremony where the groom kidnaps the bride and carries her off.

one! Let us go immediately to Kundinapura and rescue the princess! I cannot get any sleep thinking of her!" He who dwells in the hearts of all had already known what was in her heart and had been waiting anxiously for her message.

He ordered His charioteer, Daruka, to bring His chariot immediately. He hustled the Brahmin into the chariot and left immediately for the country of Vidarbha without waiting for the return of His brother Balarama, who had gone on an expedition. When the latter returned, he was quite annoyed to find that Krishna had acted in His usual impetuous fashion and had left without taking a fighting force. Having heard of His destination, he was sure that He would not be able to abduct the princess without some sort of skirmish, for he knew well of Rukmi's antagonism toward them and of his alliance with Jarasandha. So he followed Krishna as fast as he could with a battalion. The Lord's four fleet-footed horses were known as Saibya, Sugriya, Meghapushpa, and Valahaka, and they made short work of the distance between the Anarta country, in which lay Dwaraka, and Kundinapura, the capital of Vidarbha, and arrived there on the morn of the *svayamvara*.

Kundinapura was well decorated for the *svayamvara* of its princess. The streets were swept and sprinkled with rose water. Multicolored flags and ornamental arches decked with garlands adorned the roads and the perfume of burning incense emanated from all the houses. All the citizens were attired in their best, adorned with jewelry, *sandal* paste, and flower garlands. Learned Brahmins chanted *mantras* from the Rig, Sama, and Yajur *Vedas* to offer protection for the bride from all adverse psychic forces, while others, who were well versed in the Atharva Veda offered oblations in the fire to the accompaniment of chants for the pacification of the planets. Just as Bhishmaka, the King of Vidarbha, was doing for his daughter, Damaghosha, the King of Chedi, was doing for the well-being of his son Shishupala, the proposed bridegroom. The bridegroom party started for Kundinapura surrounded by an army with a full cavalry of elephants and horses, foot soldiers, and chariots decorated with golden chains. They were given a royal welcome by the princes of Vidarbha and taken to a special apartment reserved for them. A large number of kings, such as Jarasandha, Salva, Dantavakra and Paundraka, who were all allies of Shishupala, were also assembled.

The whole night Rukmini had kept vigil from the top of the palace, looking out for the Brahmin's arrival. Morning dawned with no sign of

him. Desperately, she prayed to the Lord to save her from her predicament. While she was thus praying, her left arm, eye, and thigh started
throbbing, which was a sure sign of good fortune. Very soon, the Brahmin
arrived and gave her the joyful news of Krishna's arrival in the city and
His vow to carry her off by force, if necessary. Her joy at hearing this was
so great that she could think of no adequate recompense for the bringer
of such news. Her eyes filled with tears of joy and gratitude and she prostrated herself before him. The Brahmin blessed her and departed.

Next, the court ladies came to attend to her toilette. She was dressed
with infinite care, for she was going to meet her beloved for the first time.
She peered anxiously into the mirror. Would He like her? Would He think
her beautiful? She was plagued with a thousand doubts, yet brimming
with joy. The ladies wondered what had made the pensive maid of the
previous day blossom into an excited and ravishing bride!

Hearing that the Yadava princes had come to attend the *svayamvara*, Bhishmaka was delighted. In his heart of hearts, he wanted his
daughter to marry Krishna, but he knew that his son had deliberately
not sent Him an invitation and rejoiced that He had come uninvited.
He went personally to receive Krishna, showered Him with every mark
of love and respect, and escorted Him to the best residence, which by
rights should have been given to the bridegroom. Hearing of Krishna's
arrival, the citizens flocked to have a glimpse of His unique personality.
They murmured among themselves that He alone was the fitting groom
for their beloved Princess Rukmini.

The time was approaching for the bridal procession to start for the
temple of the goddess Parvati. Accompanied by a glittering array of married ladies, Rukmini set out on foot to worship the Divine Mother, but
her mind was absorbed on the lotus feet of her Lord. Observing a vow of
silence, she walked down the avenue lined with soldiers bristling with
swords, for Rukmi had heard rumors of Krishna's arrival and His vow to
abduct the bride. Trumpets, conchs, and kettledrums blared. Rose petals
were strewn down the road and Brahmin ladies adorned with jewels, flowers, and *sandal* paste preceded the bride. Singers, bards, and minstrels
extolled her beauty as Rukmini walked down the route to the temple, but
she heeded them not. Her attention was entirely focused on trying to
have a glimpse of that beloved form. She peeped in vain through the folds
of her transparent veil, but she could not see Him. On reaching the temple, she washed her hands and feet, performed the purificatory rites with

water, and entered the shrine, outwardly composed but inwardly agitated. She prayed to the Divine Mother, as the *gopis* of Vrindavan had done long ago, to help her to procure the Lord Krishna as her husband.

"O Mother Parvati, again and again do I prostrate myself before you and before your children Ganesha and Kartikeya. May you be pleased to grant my prayers to wed the Lord Krishna. May you be pleased to grant my prayers to have the Lord Krishna as my husband."

Worship was offered to the goddess as well as to the Brahmin ladies who had accompanied her, and they in turn blessed her and gave her the consecrated remains of the offerings. Now she could break her vow of silence and she came out of the temple holding the hand of her lady-in-waiting. As she came out, she lifted her veil for a second, as if to make an offering of her beauty to the Supreme Being as embodied in Lord Krishna. Crowds had gathered outside to catch a glimpse of her entrancing beauty, and she cast them a bewitching smile, which so enraptured the watching princes and kings that they lost control over their hands. Their weapons fell from their nerveless grasp and they closed their eyes as if to enfold her beauty and treasure it in their hearts forever.

Delicately stepping forward on her rose-petal feet, she scanned the lines of royalty for one beloved face. Suddenly, she sighted Achyuta, the Unchanging Being, He who never falls and who never allows His devotees to fall. Sitting in His eagle-crested chariot and smiling tenderly at her was He to whom her heart had been given from the age of five, dearer to her than her own self. Boldly, she stepped forward to the chariot that had been conveniently placed in the middle of the path. Now that she was sure He had come, she lowered her eyes as befitting a modest bride, but as she reached the chariot her delicate hand, laden with jewels, was raised, as if to make it easier for Him to grasp it. Seeing this, Krishna smiled, and bending down, He lifted her up to the seat beside Him, slowly and deliberately, in full view of her brother and the other princes, like a lion lifting its prey from the midst of a pack of jackals.

He then whipped up the horses and flew through the crowded streets. The citizens made way for Him and cheered wildly, for they were filled with joy at the thought that their prayers had been answered. As if mesmerized, the rest of the kings watched this drama of the princess being abducted right under their noses. Then, pandemonium broke loose. Precious minutes were lost trying to clear the roads of the citizens and soldiers, who blocked it as soon as the lovers had gone.

Violently angry at the slight on their names, the other kings pursued the pair. They were stalled by Balarama and the Yadava army, who had arrived on the scene in the nick of time. Sensing His bride's fear, the Lord reassured her with a smile. Seeing the determined resistance of the Yadava forces, Jarasandha and the other kings gave up and returned, for such incidents were commonplace in most *svayamvaras*!

Rukmi, however, was determined not to give in, for he had given his word to his friend Shishupala and did not know how he could face him if the bride was not brought back. He caught up with the eloping couple and challenged Krishna to a duel. Krishna defeated him, but refrained from killing him at Rukmini's entreaties. He satisfied Himself with cutting off Rukmi's topknot, which was considered to be an insult worse than death. Balarama reprimanded Krishna for having done such a thing to His brother-in-law, but Krishna merely smiled, for He knew that a time would come when this brother would have reason to do a much graver injury to him.

In the meantime Jarasandha took upon himself the thankless task of comforting the bridegroom, who was still sitting in blissful ignorance of the stirring events which had just taken place. He had been lost in a beatific vision in which he was sporting with his beautiful bride in the enchanted gardens of the palace that he had specially built for her and which he had even named after her, so sure had he been of his prize. He was rudely jolted out of his reverie by the booming voice of Jarasandha.

"Wake up! Wake up! O heroic prince! Let us be off!"

"Where? What?" stammered Shishupala. "Has the auspicious time come for the groom to enter the marriage hall? Has the bride returned after praying at the temple?"

"She has not only come but she has also gone!" said the unfeeling Jarasandha. He then enlightened the poor groom as to the true state of affairs.

Shishupala was quite heartbroken and Jarasandha consoled him. "Do not lose heart over such a trifle as the loss of a bride. I'll find you a much better one. Look at me. I remain equal in victory and defeat. I was defeated by Krishna seventeen times, yet I'm not bothered. Today they are victorious because time is in their favor. When the tide of time turns in our favor, we will defeat them and recapture your bride."

"But I don't want someone better," protested Shishupala. "I want Rukmini. I've even named my new palace after her!"

"Well, you'll just have to rename it," said Jarasandha coldly, "for Rukmini has been abducted by that rascally cowherd Krishna while you have been sitting here and dreaming!"

"Can't we go after Him?" Shishupala enquired anxiously.

"We did, and we were defeated, but Rukmi has not given up. He chased after them."

"Was he able to bring her back?" Shishupala asked agitatedly.

"No," said Jarasandha shortly. "Krishna insulted him by removing his topknot and he has sworn not to return to Kundinapura until he has killed Krishna!" Without wasting time in further useless conjecture, he proceeded to hustle the dejected Shishupala out of the groom's palace and back to his own country.

Defeated and deprived of his army and name, Rukmi resolved to stay alone at a place called Bhojakata, where he nursed his grievance against Krishna and swore not to enter his capital until he had killed Him and rescued his sister and thus erased the blot on his fair name.

In the meantime, Dwaraka, the capital of the Yadus, was preparing itself to welcome the royal couple. The citizens were thrilled to hear of the romantic abduction of the Princess of Vidarbha by Krishna and the couple was met with joyous hails of welcome. The wedding was conducted on as grand a scale as if it had been the marriage of Lord Vishnu with Lakshmi Devi, as indeed it was, for was not Krishna the incarnation of Vishnu and Rukmini of Lakshmi?

Thus ends the fourteenth chapter of The Play of God,
named "The Abduction of Rukmini."

Hari Aum Tat Sat

FIFTEEN

THE CURSED GEM

Jagannathaya namaha

Homage to the Lord of the Universe

O *Janardana (Krishna),*
I have no recourse to anything else,
I have surrendered completely to Thee.
By Thy grace alone,
may I be saved.
—POPULAR VERSE

A nother young girl who was pining for love of
Krishna was Satyabhama, the only child of the
Yadava chief, Satrajit. Since he had no sons, he
had brought her up to learn all the manly pursuits. Consequently, she was both haughty and high-spirited and
considered herself superior to all the men she met. It was
only when she saw Krishna that her pride was humbled
and she felt herself to be, quite simply, a woman. Her
father had already promised her in marriage to a young
Yadava stalwart called Shatadhanva, but when Krishna
came to know of her love for Him, He decided to fulfill
her desire to become His wife. To accomplish this, He
had to undergo many difficulties, even to the extent of
giving Himself a bad name; thus He proved that He was
willing to undergo any trial to serve His devotees.

Satrajit had been in straitened circumstances at one
time and had done severe *tapasya* (spiritual discipline)
to the Sun god Surya, who had given him a beautiful
jewel called the Syamantaka. This gem had the ability to
produce eight times its weight in gold daily, if it was
worshipped with the proper rites. It was, moreover, a
talisman against disease, misfortune, and theft. Needless to say, Satrajit prospered, but too much wealth had
its ill effects. He started to lapse from the high code of

131

dharma that he had followed and started living a life of vain and useless luxury. Realizing this, and in order to save him from his own folly, Krishna requested that he hand over the jewel to Ugrasena, the king, but Satrajit refused. Proud of his precious possession, he did not want to part with it and worshipped it daily. That love and devotion which should be given only to God was given to the jewel. The habit of worshipping mammon more than God has always landed human beings in trouble. He suspected that everyone was after his jewel; he suspected Krishna particularly of having designs on it. What he did not suspect was that Krishna had designs on his precious daughter and that, too, with her full consent and connivance!

As Satrajit suspected everyone, he had very few friends. The only two he felt he could trust were his brother Prasena and the man he had chosen to be his prospective son-in-law: Shatadhanva. The latter would come and sit for hours, nodding wisely at everything Satrajit said and boring Satyabhama. She was quite determined that she would not marry him, but was too fond of her father to suggest Krishna's name as an alternative. So she bided her time and prayed to the Lord to disentangle her from this web. The time came soon enough. One day, her uncle, Prasena, came to Satrajit and begged to be allowed to wear the jewel when he went out hunting. In vain, Satrajit tried to dissuade him from this foolish act, but Prasena had set his heart on it and would not give in. At last, Satrajit acceded to his young brother's wish and Prasena set out for the forest with the Syamantaka hanging like a gleaming ball of fire around his neck, a cynosure of all eyes. During the course of the day, he became separated from his companions and found himself alone in the middle of the forest. Suddenly, he was faced with a hungry lion who was attracted to him by the glittering jewel around his neck, which it mistook for a lump of flesh. The lion killed Prasena and made off with the jewel. In turn, it was attacked and killed by Jambavan, the king of bears, who took possession of the jewel and presented it to his daughter Jambavati.

When the hunting party returned without his brother, Satrajit was sunk in gloom. No amount of searching disclosed any trace of either the man or the missing jewel. Satrajit came to the conclusion that his brother had been killed by Krishna in order to get the Syamantaka, which He had been coveting for some time. Satyabhama's heart sank when she heard this, for though she knew it to be absolutely untrue, it seemed to put the lid on all her hopes. The rumor was bruited abroad and soon reached

Krishna's ears. He laughed and shrugged it off, but both Balarama and Uddhava were insistent that He do something to clear His name. So, accompanied by them and some of the other Yadavas, He set out for the forest in which Prasena had gone hunting.

Penetrating deep into the woods, they soon came across the body of Prasena decomposing where he had been killed by the lion. A short search revealed the fact that the gem was missing. Following the lion's tracks, they climbed to the mountaintop, where they found the carcass of the lion, slaughtered by the king of bears. Not finding the jewel on the lion, they followed the tracks of the bear, which took them to the mouth of a fearsome-looking cave. The general opinion was that it would be foolish to venture in, for the cave was reputed to be the dwelling place of an old and mighty bear who killed everyone on sight. But Krishna decided to press on. He knew how anxiously Satyabhama was awaiting His reappearance, for her only chance of happiness lay in His safe return with the jewel. "We have set out to find the Syamantaka," He said, "and find it I will before I return."

Krishna forbade anyone else to accompany Him, for it was something He had to do Himself. In fact, this was the fulfillment of a promise made during His divine incarnation as the *avatar* Lord Rama. He told Uddhava and Balarama to return to Dwaraka if He did not appear within twelve days. The cave belonged to Jambavan, the ancient bear who had helped Lord Rama at the time of the war with the demon Ravana. At the end of the war, when the Lord asked him to choose a boon, Jambavan had asked Him to marry his daughter Jambavati. But in that incarnation the Lord had sworn to take only one wife and that was Sita. He therefore promised to fulfill Jambavan's wishes in His incarnation as Krishna and also told him that his daughter would retain her youth until then. It was for this girl that Jambavan had killed the lion and snatched the jewel.

As Krishna entered the cave, He found it lit up with the brilliance of the Syamantaka, with which the girl was playing. When she saw the handsome stranger, she ran to call her aged father. Leading a cloistered life in the cave, she had not been acquainted with many men before. As for Jambavan, he was so old that he could barely see at all. Since he lived alone in the forest with a young and beautiful girl, his usual method of greeting strangers was to hit first and ask questions later. He had no means of knowing that this stranger was none other than his Lord and Master, Shri Rama, who had now taken the form of Krishna and come to fulfill His promise. He greeted Krishna with powerful blows of his adamantine fists. The Lord was happy to accept any offering from His devotees. Some offered flowers and others blows. Nothing loathe, He gave back blow for blow and punch for punch! For twenty days and nights they grappled thus with each other. At last, with his joints dislocated, enfeebled and exhausted, Jambavan began to get worried, for he felt that there was none who was capable of resisting his blows but his Divine Master. Filled with doubt, he pried open the overhanging lids of his eyes with his gnarled hands and looked at the bright vision before him. Lord Krishna stood there in the form of Shri Rama. With a cry of remorse, Jambavan prostrated before Him and extolled Him.

"I know You to be the all-pervading being and the controller of everything. You are the soul of Time. You are the creator and sustainer. You are the Supreme Being, the Lord of all divinities. I know You now to be that Rama who built a bridge over the ocean and destroyed Lanka. Pray forgive me for my ignorance in having fought with You!"

The lotus-eyed Lord stroked the battered body of His devotee with loving hands and spoke to him, "The blows of My devotees are as precious to Me as their flowers. I have come to this cave to retrieve the Syamantaka, which I have been accused of stealing. Now tell me what is your desire, for I have come to grant it."

Jambavan clasped the Lord in his hairy arms and rejoiced in the fact that his old eyes could still see the form which he had carried around in his heart for so many centuries. "Today my life has been fulfilled by Your vision and I want nothing for myself. But I'm too old to protect my daughter and I would like you to accept her, together with the jewel."

Krishna smilingly agreed for He remembered the promise made in another age and another role.[1]

When He returned to Dwaraka with Jambavati and the jewel, He found the city in a turmoil, for the rest of the party had returned some time ago and spread the news. Everyone was cursing Satrajit and praying to the Divine Mother to restore their darling Prince, Krishna. Satyabhama, too, was in dire distress, and her joy when she saw Him return knew no bounds. Krishna summoned Satrajit to the Yadava assembly and there, in full view of everyone, He gave him the jewel Syamantaka and also explained to him how it had been traced. With his

---

[1] The story of Jambavan is told in the *Ramayana*.

head bent in shame for having doubted Him, Satrajit received the jewel and returned home. He racked his brains as to how he could win the Lord's favor as well as erase the sense of guilt from his own mind. While he was cogitating thus, Satyabhama decided to take matters into her own hands and whispered to her father that the best way to earn Krishna's forgiveness was to emulate Jambavan's example. In order to redress his grievous wrongs in having hit the Lord, he had given his daughter in marriage to Him! The hint was obvious. It was in Satrajit's hands to make equal amends for his own outrageous behavior. He brightened visibly at the suggestion, for even though he had already chosen someone else for his daughter, this seemed the best way out of his problem. Happy at having found a solution, he went straightaway to Krishna and offered Him his daughter, together with the jewel. The Lord accepted the former and refused the latter, and the wedding was conducted with no loss of time, much to the chagrin of Shatadhanva, the erstwhile suitor who had been rejected.

Rukmini and Satyabhama are supposed to be the incarnations of the two consorts of Lord Vishnu, Lakshmi Devi and Bhuma Devi—the goddess of wealth and the earth goddess. It is said that Lord Krishna had sixteen thousand one hundred and eight wives. One hundred are said to be the personifications of the principal *Upanishads*. As for the remaining, it is said that the human mind is capable of having this many *vrittis*, or mental vibrations, in every breath. Lord Krishna, being the master *yogi*, had perfect control over His mental modifications, as symbolized by the control He had over His numerous wives.

Unlike His other wives, Satyabhama had a mind of her own. She demanded her rights, not merely as a wife but as a helpmate in all fields, including warfare, for which her father had given her ample training. So, while the rest of His wives sat at home and engaged themselves in womanly pursuits, she often accompanied Krishna wherever He went, sometimes even to war!

It was soon after His marriage with Satyabhama and Jambavati that the fire incident took place at Varanavata, in which the Pandavas and their mother Kunti were supposed to have perished. The Lord knew that they had escaped, but he also knew that the time was not yet ripe for them to return to Hastinapura, so He went with Balarama to the land of the Kurus in order to fulfill the duties of a relative. Meeting Bhishma, Drona, Vidura, and others, He joined them in their mourning.

During the Lord's absence from Dwaraka a plot was hatched by Akrura and Kritavarma in order to tease Shatadhanva. One day, they met Shatadhanva, the jilted suitor of Satyabhama, and asked him in mock sympathy, "Why are you looking so glum these days?"

This was just the opening Shatadhanva had been longing for, and he poured out his tale of woe, of how he had been the apple of Satrajit's eye, if not of his daughter's, and how he was completely ignored by him now. In fact, he would look the other way if they chanced to meet on the road. Akrura and Kritavarma were duly sympathetic over this.

"The only way to redress this wrong," they told him, "is to go and confront Satrajit and ask him for an explanation. He promised you both his daughter and his jewel, so if you were deprived of one, at least you deserve to have the other. He shouldn't be allowed to get away with such a blatant breach of promise."

Thus goaded, Shatadhanva fortified his flagging spirits with some potent wine and went to Satrajit's house in the middle of the night, armed with a dagger. His senses befuddled by the alcohol he had imbibed and his self-pity aroused by the words of the other two, he forgot all rules of *kshatriya dharma* and murdered the sleeping Satrajit in cold blood, escaping with the jewel. The women of the household woke up and started to wail. Shatadhanva was terrified at what he had done and ran off to Kritavarma's house with the jewel. The latter refused to have anything to do with him and threw him out before someone arrived and implicated him in the plot. Shatadhanva then turned to Akrura for advice and told him that it was entirely due to his sympathetic attitude that he had resorted to such violent measures. Akrura also hastily backed out and swore that he had not meant him to do any such thing and that he would have nothing to do with a plot that would antagonize Lord Krishna, whom he knew to be God incarnate. He advised Shatadhanva to leave town as fast as he could. Being a trusted member of the Council of Elders, he wanted to have nothing to do with such a suicidal plot. Shatadhanva felt himself to have been sadly let down by his two supporters and as he ran off he threw the ill-fated jewel into Akrura's house, for he knew that the possessor of the jewel would certainly be suspected of the murder.

Next morning, there was a hue and cry that Satrajit had been brutally slain for the sake of the Syamantaka and a warrant was immediately issued for the arrest of anyone who was in any way connected with the crime. Seeing the dead body of her father, Satyabhama swooned and was totally bereft of her usual courage. She had the body preserved in oil and left immediately for Hastinapura to apprise Krishna of the mysterious circumstances resulting in her father's death. Though He was well aware of everything, the Lord did His best to comfort her. He had always known that a man who set so much store by his wealth would surely come to grief because of it. However, to placate His wife He returned to Dwaraka in order to discover the murderer. Hearing of Krishna's arrival, Shatadhanva procured the fastest horse he could get and fled from Dwaraka. Balarama and Krishna, who already had some suspicions about him, heard about his flight and gave chase. They caught up with him at the city of Mithila, where Shatadhanva's horse dropped dead. He started running on foot. Krishna also got down from His chariot and chased him. They had a short scuffle in which Shatadhanva was killed, but a search for the jewel proved futile. Balarama was sure that he must have entrusted the jewel to someone at Dwaraka and that they should go search for it. However, since the King of Mithila was a good friend of his, Balarama decided to stay with him for a while. During this time, Duryodhana came once again to take lessons in mace warfare from him and somehow managed to endear himself to Balarama. Duryodhana was capable of beguiling many with the charm of his personality when he chose to do so.

Krishna returned to Dwaraka and informed Satyabhama that her father's death had been avenged but that the jewel was still missing. Hearing all this, Akrura and Kritavarma were terrified, for Shatadhanva was the third person to die because of the ill-fated gem. Krishna knew the jewel to be in Akrura's possession. He also knew that Akrura, being a good man, would use the wealth for noble purposes and not for self-aggrandizement. He advised the pair of them to go on a pilgrimage to the holy city of Kasi and stay there for thirteen years, after which they could return safely. Akrura took the Lord's advice and left for Kasi, where he lived the life of a sage and used the gold produced by the gem to benefit the city and help the pilgrims. Of course, this was not known to anyone, but Balarama was not satisfied with the way the whole matter had been settled and suspected that Krishna was hiding the truth from him. In order to clear his doubts, Krishna recalled Akrura at the end of thirteen years and told him to display the jewel publicly before the assembly. This was done and the jewel was given back to Akrura with this admonition, "This jewel is too dangerous for ordinary people to wear. Only a person possessing great austerity and spiritual worth, like you, is competent to wear it. So take it back and may it bring all auspiciousness to you."

Thus, the Lord showed the world that even this cursed gem, when kept in the hands of a devotee, did no harm to him and could even be put to good use, for a devotee always uses his wealth to serve others and not for his personal and selfish ends.

Thus ends the fifteenth chapter of The Play of God,
named "The Cursed Gem."

Hari Aum Tat Sat

SIXTEEN

THE PANDAVAS

Achyuthaya namaha

Homage to the One who never falls from His real nature

I know what righteousness is, yet I am unable to do it,
I know what unrighteousness is, yet I am forced to do it!
O Hrishikesha (Krishna), Thou art the dweller in my heart.
As Thou guidest me, so shall I act.
—*POPULAR VERSE*

After having sent Akrura to Kasi with the Syamantaka, the Lord turned His attention to the plight of the Pandavas. He sent Uddhava to discover their whereabouts, for He knew well that they had escaped. Uddhava hated to be parted from Krishna even for a minute, but His slightest wish was Uddhava's command, so he proceeded to the forest, where, with the help of a *rakshasa* boy, he managed to trace the missing Pandavas. The *rakshasas* were a group of cannibalistic tribes living in the dense forests of Bharatavarsha. They were strong and uncultured. Bhima, however, was the equal of any *rakshasa* in strength. He had killed the *rakshasa* Hidimba, who had tried to molest them, and married his sister Hidimbi, who had fallen for his muscular charms. She had taken them to the *rakshasa* encampment in the dense forest, and there the *rakshasas* had accepted Bhima as their king; he came to be called Vrikodara, or the wolf-bellied one. Subsequently, he had a son called Gatotkacha by her. When Uddhava found them, they were living in a treehouse and, though Bhima was enjoying himself, the rest were having a hard time of it. They could not reconcile themselves to the barbarous practices and cannibalistic eating habits of their dear brothers-in-law. They greeted Uddhava with great joy and begged him to ask Krishna to rescue them from their plight, for they did not know which was worse—to be eaten alive by the *rakshasas* or to court murder at the hands of the Kauravas! Uddhava assured them that their welfare was nearest to Krishna's heart and that all things would come to pass as He willed.

Krishna, in the meantime, had gone to the court of Drupada, the King of Panchala, at his invitation. The kingdoms of the Kurus and the Panchalas were two of the most important ones in Bharatavarsha and if they could unite, they could easily put down the might of the wicked king, Jarasandha. Unfortunately, Drupada had a grudge against Bhishma for having employed his enemy, Drona.

Drona and he had studied together as boys and in a fit of boyish enthusiasm Drupada had promised his impoverished friend to share his kingdom with him when he became king. Though it was but a casual promise made in childhood, Drona never forgot it. When he was in desperate straits, with no means even to give milk to his only son, Ashvatthama, he went to Panchala to claim his share of the kingdom. Drupada was quite put out at having been taken so literally and offered him as much wealth as he would need, but Drona proudly refused and swore vengeance. Later, he became tutor to the Kuru princes and at the end of their course of study, as has been said, he demanded that they should capture and bring back Drupada to him as *guru dakshina*. The high-spirited boys set out and Arjuna, aided by Bhima, captured the king in a surprise attack and brought him before their preceptor. He was freed only after he gave up his entire kingdom to Drona, which the latter returned to him in a magnanimous gesture, as he no longer wanted it. From that time onward, Drupada nursed his revenge and fed his children, Draupadi and Drishtadyumna, on tales of revenge. He was determined that Draupadi should marry Arjuna, whom he considered the bravest warrior in Bharatavarsha, and humble the pride of Drona, who loved Arjuna more than his own son. When he heard of the death of the Pandavas in the house of lac, he was terribly disappointed, but his priests told him not to despair, for their predictions could not go wrong and his daughter would certainly have Arjuna as her husband. It was at this time that Krishna approached him and advised him to hold a *svayamvara* for Draupadi in which he should arrange a challenging test, the winner of which would win the bride.

The test, arranged by Guru Sandipani, was a very difficult one. A whirling emblem of a fish was suspended with five strings to a pole fixed in the middle of a pool. Just beneath the fish was a disk with a hole in the middle. The contestants were to be given a bow and five arrows, which they had to shoot through the hole and bring the fish down by looking at its whirling reflection in the pool. There were only five people in the whole of Bharatavarsha who were capable of doing it. Of these, three belonged to the Yadava clan: Krishna himself, Satyaki, and Uddhava. All three had refused to participate, since Krishna did not want it. The other two were Karna and, of course, Arjuna, who was believed to be dead.

Having received Uddhava's report on the situation of the Pandavas, Krishna sent Vyasa to the *rakshasa* encampment to advise them to proceed to the city of Ekachakra disguised as Brahmins and await the call of destiny.

All the greatest princes and kings of the land were invited to the Draupadi *svayamvara*. The hundred Kauravas as well as Shakuni, Karna, Drona, and his son, Ashvatthama, were there. Jarasandha of Magadha had come, though he was old enough to be Draupadi's grandfather. Shishupala, Prince of Chedi, Salya, the King of Madra and uncle of Nakula and Sahadeva, as well as Bhishma and Vidura were there. The Yadavas, headed by Krishna and Balarama and accompanied by Uddhava, Satyaki, and others, had come as spectators, for they refused to take part in the contest. The Pandavas, who had been staying at the nearby town of Ekachakra, had also come to the tournament, disguised as Brahmins.

Draupadi was a flaming beauty, tall and dark, with lustrous eyes and long black tresses. As was the custom, at the start of the *svayamvara* she was escorted into the hall by her chaperones and introduced in turn to the various princes who had assembled to try their luck at winning her hand.

As she came to Krishna, she gazed long at Him, for she had heard much about His miraculous deeds, but had never met Him. Who was the woman who could look into His bewitching eyes and be able to resist their charm? Krishna shook his head slightly, as if to say, "I have other plans for you." From that moment of wordless communion, she became an ardent devotee of the Lord and turned to Him at every crisis in her life.

At last, the tournament began. One by one, the defeated princes and kings slunk back to their seats. Even Karna, the acclaimed bowman, was unable to fulfill the taxing demands of the contest. At last, when everyone else had failed and it looked as if Draupadi would remain a maiden, a slight and slim youth got up from the ranks of the Brahmins and stepped forward, asking permission to try his hand even though be was not a *kshatriya*. Drishtadyumna, Draupadi's brother, who was master of ceremonies, gladly gave his consent. Krishna alone recognized Arjuna and gave him a brilliant smile of encouragement. The youth stepped forward, lifted the bow with ease, strung it, shot the five arrows in quick succession through the revolving disc, and brought the target down, to the amazement of the assembly. There was pandemonium in the crowd. The Brahmins were jubilant and the *kshatriyas* voiced their disapproval, as they had been humiliated. Amidst the confusion, Draupadi walked over with her lilting gait and garlanded the youth. Duryodhana, as usual, was the first to resort to violence, for he had been badly smitten by Draupadi's charms. He tried to attack Arjuna, but Bhima plucked a tree and defended him. Next, Duryodhana incited Karna to challenge him, but Arjuna defeated him. This was the prelude to a general skirmish that was brought to an end by Lord Krishna, who declared that Draupadi had been won in a fair contest and, if the others did not like it, they could air their grievances in private and not in public.

The next day, the Lord went to meet the Pandavas and his aunt, Kunti. He promised her that he would never forsake her sons. From that day on, Kunti became an ardent devotee. Arjuna and Krishna were supposed to be the incarnations of the ancient *rishis* (sages) Nara and Narayana, who were themselves incarnations of Lord Vishnu. They are ever engaged in doing *tapasya* (spiritual disciplines) at *Badrikashrama*[1] for the welfare of mankind. Thus, there was a strong bond between Krishna and Arjuna.

The Lord now returned and disclosed to Drishtadyumna the identity of the Brahmin youth who had won his sister. Both he and his father, Drupada, were delighted when they heard this, since this was just what Drupada had been hoping for. So he invited the Pandavas to the palace and arrangements were made for a grand wedding at which all five brothers wed Draupadi. Their mother, Kunti, had made the Pandavas promise that they would share everything they possessed, little realizing to what extent they would honor her words. Krishna and the other Yadavas were also present.

When this news reached Hastinapura, Duryodhana felt terribly humiliated. Not only had his dastardly plot failed, but the Pandavas had also snatched the girl of his choice from beneath his nose. Now they were

---

[1] *Badrikashrama*—the area of Badrínath in the Himalayas, one of the four main shrines in India.

in a stronger position than ever before, for Drupada was no mean opponent and Krishna had made it clear that He was entirely on their side.
Encouraged by his uncle, Shakuni, and his friend Karna, Duryodhana,
with the Kauravas, marched on Kampilya, the capital of Panchala, where
the Pandavas were residing in honor. Duryodhana wanted to try to nip
their power in the bud. But the Kauravas met with a resounding defeat,
which only served to increase Duryodhana's wrath. Finally, after much
persuasion from Bhishma, Drona, and Vidura, the blind King Dhritarashtra forced Duryodhana to invite the Pandavas back to Hastinapura. Yudhishthira, who was ever anxious to comply with the wishes of his elders,
agreed and the Pandavas, accompanied by their mother and their new
wife, returned in triumph to Hastinapura, where they were welcomed
with a great show of cordiality. For some time they lived in apparent ami-
cability with their cousins, and it appeared as though the enmity between
them had ceased. But Shakuni, as usual, fanned the ever-smoldering coals
of Duryodhana's hatred and Karna promised to defeat the Pandavas single-handedly. Encouraged by this, Duryodhana forced his father to divide
the kingdom and send the Pandavas away from Hastinapura. Dhritarashtra was too weak to refuse his son anything, so he summoned Yudhishthira and informed him of the decision to divide the kingdom. The portion
given to them was known as Khandavaprastha and had been the ancient
capital of the Kurus during the time of their ancestors, Yayati and Pururavas. Now it was but a forest, overrun by wild animals and *rakshasas*. The
brothers were horrified at this trick of the old king, but Yudhishthira, as
usual, could not refuse any request made by Dhritarashtra, who was like a
father to him. Moreover, Krishna told him to accept, provided the king
gave him enough craftsmen, cattle, and gold to establish a city. So Yudhishthira agreed and Krishna and Arjuna went to Khandavaprastha in
order to clear the forest. When they arrived, they were met by an old man
who declared himself to be Agni, the god of fire. Due to the amount of
ghee he had consumed at a *yajna* (fire sacrifice), he was suffering from
indigestion and he begged the two of them to help him get rid of his disease. The only cure for him was to consume the forest of Khandva, which
was filled with medicinal herbs. But since the forest belonged to Indra,
the god of rain, Agni was unable to consume it, for as soon as he tried to
do so, Indra would bring a shower of rain and put him out! Arjuna immediately promised to help him and Agni presented him with Varuna's bow,
called Gandiva, two quivers with an inexhaustible supply of arrows, and

an armor which could not be pierced. He also gave him a chariot and fleet horses. Agni then presented the *Sudarshana Chakra* to Krishna, which was the weapon of Lord Vishnu. Krishna acted as Arjuna's charioteer and the two of them drove round and round the forest at lightning speed, enabling Arjuna to shoot a continuous stream of arrows, which acted as a shield over the forest, while Agni licked up the entire forest with his tongues of flame. Because of this dome of arrows, Indra was unable to penetrate into the forest with his showers. Mayan, the architect of the demons, was in the forest when it was being burned and since Arjuna allowed him to escape, he was very grateful and agreed to build them a wondrous city. To appease Indra, Krishna promised to name the new city Indraprastha. Thus, in one master stroke the Lord engineered everything so that the forest was cleared, Arjuna got his divine weapons, and the help of Mayan was obtained to plan the assembly hall of the new city.

The Lord also got the help of Vishvakarma, the architect of the gods, to build the city of Indraprastha on the banks of the Yamuna, on the spot where modern Delhi stands today. It was a wonderous city with all conveniences, rivaling Dwaraka in beauty and splendor. Mayan built them the Great Hall of Illusions, which came to be known as the Maya Sabha and was a wonder to all who saw it. On an auspicious day, Yudhishthira was crowned King of Indraprastha. He was the ideal monarch. The welfare of his subjects was his main concern and he created another *Ram Rajya* (rule of Lord Rama, a Golden Age). He was *dharma* incarnate and with Krishna to help and advise him, he ruled wisely and well. For the first time in their storm-tossed lives, the Pandavas felt happy and secure.

Soon after they took up their residence in Indraprastha, Arjuna, accompanied by Krishna, set out on a hunting expedition. At the end of the day, tired and thirsty, they went to the banks of the Yamuna to refresh themselves. They were struck by the sight of a beauteous damsel strolling along the banks. When questioned by Arjuna, she informed him that her name was Kalindi. She was the daughter of the sun and lived in a house beneath the river, where she had sworn to stay and practice austerities until she met Him, who was the incarnation of Lord Vishnu, for she had sworn to wed none but Him. Arjuna told her that the object of her devotion was standing but a yard away. She was delighted to hear this and prostrated at the Lord's feet and begged Him to accept her. So they returned to Indraprastha with Kalindi and got the blessings of Yudhishthira. The Lord than returned to Dwaraka and sol-emnized His marriage to her.

Krishna had a half sister, Subhadra, who was younger than He. She had grown up to be a lovely girl and Balarama was anxious to have her married to a suitable bridegroom. Arjuna had met her on one of his visits to Dwaraka and they had been attracted to each other, but only Krishna knew of this attachment. Before he could broach the matter to his broth-er, Arjuna was forced to go on a pilgrimage for one year. In the meantime, Duryodhana had expressed a wish to marry Subhadra, of whose beauty he had heard. Balarama promptly agreed to this proposal, since he had a weak spot for Duryodhana and quite fancied the idea of an alliance with the Kurus. Krishna was none too happy to hear this news, for He knew Duryodhana's nature only too well and did not want his only sister to suf-fer at the hands of this unprincipled and haughty man. However, He kept silent, for He knew that His brother had given his word and could not back down, so some stratagem would have to be devised if His cousin Arjuna was to wed His sister.

Arjuna's year of pilgrimage was coming to a close. He decided to end it at Dwaraka and to see Krishna as well as Subhadra and perhaps broach the subject of his marriage to Balarama. During this year, his beard had grown and he was clad in the soiled and crumpled clothes of the wayfarer, quite unlike his usual debonair self. Thus it happened that no one recog-nized him when he entered the city, where he was well-known. Thinking it to be a good joke, he sat under the shade of a banyan tree with half-closed eyes as if in meditation. Soon people gathered around to watch the holy man and from them Arjuna gathered the latest bit of gossip—that Subhadra was betrothed to Duryodhana. It was now that poor Arjuna really felt like renouncing the world! What a bitter blow fate had dealt him! To have the cup brought to his lips and then to have it dashed to the ground was too much to bear. What had Krishna been doing to consent to such a thing? Thus he ruminated and sat under the holy tree, sunk in deep and gloomy reverie, which quite convinced the ordinary folk that he was a great saint. He hardly ever smiled, he was always meditating, and he expressed no desire even for food.

That night it rained in torrents. Krishna, who was spending the night in Satyabhama's palace, suddenly started chuckling. When she asked Him what the matter was, He replied, "The thought of Arjuna pretending to be a *sannyasi* (renunciate) and sitting under the banyan tree in the pouring rain when his mind is full of Subhadra is making me laugh." Very soon, Balarama heard of the arrival of this great sage in their midst. He could never resist a holy man and went posthaste to meet him. "Hail, O Holy One!" he said, "Blessed is our city to have the sight of noble sages like you."

Arjuna was slightly embarrassed at first and tried to hide his face, but seeing Balarama to be quite sincere and totally unsuspicious of his identity, he gathered his wandering wits together and proceeded to act the part of a true *sannyasi*. Balarama went off, well pleased with his latest find, and returned later dragging a reluctant Krishna with him. The latter gave him a piercing look. Arjuna felt himself to be quite exposed and hurriedly closed his eyes so as not to see any more of those looks. Balarama humbly requested the holy one to spend the rainy season at their residence. The only time a *sannyasi* was allowed to live in a householder's home was during the time of the monsoons, when the rains made it impossible for him to sleep in the open. Arjuna gave a quick glance at Krishna and acceded to the request. "O Brother! Beware of bringing strange young men into our house, even though they may profess to be *sannyasis*. Our sister is a young girl of marriageable age. You know how I feel about such young *sannyasis*; they are not to be trusted. They are not old enough to have renounced the pleasures of life. Think well before inviting him to our house." Though Krishna spoke in a low-pitched voice, it was at just the correct note to penetrate the *sannyasi's* ears. Arjuna hurriedly closed his eyes and recommenced the chanting he had interrupted in order to hear what Krishna was whispering. Balarama glared at his younger brother and told him to mind His manners. After getting Arjuna's consent, he went off leaving the field clear for Krishna. The *sannyasi* opened one eye slightly and, finding a blue color in front of him, closed it again and started chanting "*Aum Nama Shivaya*," the *mantra* of the great Lord Shiva, in a loud voice.

He felt a tap on his shoulder which could not be ignored. He opened his eyes again cautiously to find himself alone with Krishna. The crowd had dispersed and Krishna gave him a charming, reassuring smile.

"Well, my dear friend," he said, "I hadn't realized that you had taken to the holy life. Why did you suddenly decide on such a course, my dear boy? Did something happen to give you a distaste for life? I heard that you had gone on a pilgrimage for a year but I never dreamed it was for life."

"O, You recognized me!" Arjuna said with relief, for he was finding the strain of impersonation too much to bear, coupled with the mental agony of thinking of Subhadra's approaching nuptials. "It was just a joke," he said feebly, as he caught Krishna's mocking glance.

"Whatever it is, I would seriously advise you to buy some saffron dye from the market and take up *sannyasa* (the life of renunciation) in earnest. That appears to be the only way to cure your malady." With this cryptic remark, Krishna left Arjuna.

Arjuna cogitated for some time. He had fully decided to leave the city and not accept Balarama's hospitality, for he feared that he would be exposed, but after listening to Krishna's advice he decided otherwise. What had He meant by asking him to take up *sannyasa* seriously? Did He mean that his case was hopeless and he had better renounce the world? Surely that could not have been His meaning, for *sannyasa* was not a thing to be bought with a packet of dye from the market. So Krishna must have some devious plan which necessitated his carrying on with the deception. Whatever it was, Arjuna had absolute faith in the Lord, so he set out to deck himself as a true *sannyasi*, complete with freshly dyed saffron robes and a rosary made of *rudraksha* beads[2] around his neck, with another tucked away in a little bag in which his right hand was always hidden, while he was supposedly muttering his prayers on the beads. This little bag was essential to the success of his plan, for it was obvious to the most casual look that his hands were not those of a true *sannyasi*, who would be expected to have a callused middle finger caused by the constant repetition of countless beads being rolled over it. Arjuna, on the other hand, had a callused forefinger, as befitting an archer. Thus armed, he was taken in state to the palace, where Subhadra herself was given the pleasant task of catering to the holy one's needs. It was considered very lucky for a young girl to get the blessings of a holy man, especially in order to procure a good husband and many sons, both of which Arjuna was perfectly capable of and willing to bless her with! Needless to say, Arjuna revelled in this bit of unexpected luck. With open eyes, he watched her beauteous form as she undulated in and out of the room, carrying out her self-appointed tasks of cleaning his room, bringing his food, and so on. When she left him, with closed eyes he meditated on the same form. Subhadra, too, had her own suspicions about the *sannyasi*

---

2 *rudraksha beads*—seeds of the *rudraksha* tree, sacred to Shiva.

from the very first day. The way he patted her head when she prostrated before him was far from being paternal. She watched him closely and, though he took care to hide his right hand, she discovered that his exposed left hand also had a callused forefinger. She knew well that it was only Arjuna who could have it, for he was famous for his ambidexterity and could shoot equally as well with his left as with his right hand. After this discovery, she became a little more bashful, but even more eager to serve the handsome young *sannyasi*. Thus, the courtship progressed smoothly during the four months of the monsoon. With the end of the rains, the wedding season would commence, so Krishna had to devise a plan to remove Balarama from the vicinity for a while. It so happened that Balarama went to enquire about the discovery of an ancient temple on top of a hill and Krishna announced to Arjuna that a chariot with his own four horses would be stationed at the palace gates to take Subhadra for a religious function. He also hinted that an opportunity once lost may never return. Arjuna, who was never slow on the uptake, lost no time in grabbing the hand of the willing Subhadra, who happened to come into the room just at that time. He hurried her quite unresistingly into the chariot and whipped up the horses.

The news of the *sannyasi's* abduction of his sister was carried to Balarama, who returned at once from the renovation site. Without waiting to consult Krishna, he sent off some soldiers after the erring couple. Since the *sannyasi* was not expected to carry any weapons, he thought the capture would be an easy matter. But he had reckoned without his sister's foresight. Not for nothing was she the sister of such valiant brothers! Taking over the job of driving the chariot, she gave Arjuna the bow and arrows which she had concealed, with which he managed to stall the approaching soldiers.

In the meantime, Balarama stalked into the palace and angrily demanded an explanation from Krishna. He was chagrined to find his brother innocently engaged in a game of dice. He could not believe that such a thing could have happened without his knowledge, if not His connivance.

"Did I not warn you, my dear brother, of the dangers of allowing strange young men into the house when our sister was here? But you refused to listen to me. Now why do you blame me?" asked the Lord, with an innocent expression.

Balarama ranted and raved, for his temper was not improved by hearing this truth. He swore to kill the *sannyasi* with his own bare hands. At last, Krishna took pity on him and disclosed the *sannyasi's* identity.

"Why didn't you tell me this at first? Why do you go about everything in this devious fashion?" Balarama asked.

"Well, brother," Krishna replied reasonably, "had I told you of Arjuna's liking for Subhadra you would immediately have asked me to mind my own business, for you had already arranged for her marriage with Duryodhana. You would not have been able to go back on your word. I knew that Subhadra also was keen on marrying Arjuna. In this way, you are completely clear of all blame, since you knew nothing about it. Duryodhana can find no fault with you for having broken your word."

Balarama's anger was appeased when he heard this, and he decided to make the best of a bad job. The couple was brought back and the wedding celebrated at Dwaraka itself. Krishna accompanied them back to Indraprastha with a huge dowry of gold, horses, and servants. His parting words to His sister were, "I suppose I can take away my chariot, since you have no more use for it!" Subhadra blushed and thanked her enigmatic brother, to whom the whole of life was one big game.

In the course of time, Subhadra bore a son to Arjuna, the great Abhimanyu, who was equal to his father in valor and expertise in archery.

Thus ends the sixteenth chapter of The Play of God, *named "The Pandavas."*

Hari Aum Tat Sat

SEVENTEEN

THE DIVINE HUSBAND

Srinivasaya namaha

Homage
to the One
who is the
abode of
auspiciousness

Thou alone art my father as well as my mother,
Thou alone, my relation and only friend.
Thou art my knowledge as well as my sole wealth,
Thou art my everything, O Thou Lord of Lords.
—TRADITIONAL HINDU PRAYER

The remaining marriages of Krishna took place soon after this incident. Mitrabinda, the Princess of Avanti, was His cousin. Her brothers, Vinda and Anuvinda, had studied with Him at Sandipani's ashram, but now they had come under Jarasandha's influence and were forcing their sister to marry his grandson. She begged Krishna to rescue her and once again, in the face of all the other kings, Krishna abducted her as He had done Rukmini.

Bhadra was also a cousin. She was offered in marriage to Him by her brothers. This was the only marriage which took place without any untoward incident! Satya was the daughter of Nagnajit, King of Kosala. He had declared that only the person who was capable of subduing his seven vicious bulls at the same time would be allowed to marry her. Hearing of her love for Him, Krishna went to Ayodhya, the capital of the Kosalas, to try for her hand. Nagnajit was a very pious man and felt honored that the Lord had come to win his daughter's hand. He would willingly have given her in marriage to Him, but since he had already issued such an edict, he could not go back on his word. Hearing this, the Lord girded up His loins and entered the arena into which the wild bulls had been let loose. Multiplying Himself into seven forms, He subdued the bulls simultaneously with the

151

greatest of ease. The king happily bestowed his daughter on the Lord and the marriage was celebrated at the bride's residence. Many of the kings who had failed to gain Satya as their bride now came to attack the bridal party on its way to Dwaraka. Arjuna, who was accompanying the Lord, routed all of them with ease.

Lakshmana was the beautiful daughter of the King of Madra. He held a *svayamvara* for her with a contest similar to the one held at the Draupadi *svayamvara*. Krishna attended accompanied by Arjuna, since Lakshmana had begged Him to come to her rescue. He shot down the whirling fish with ease and took her away in the face of stiff opposition from the other kings.

At that time, a mighty king called Bhauma, or Narakasura, had been terrorizing the neighboring states. He had captured the daughters of sixteen thousand kings, all of marriageable age, and clapped them in jail as a kindly precaution, he said, against would-be abductors like Krishna! What he did not realize was that the damsels were longing to be so abducted and had sent Krishna a piteous plea for help. At the same time, Indra, the king of the gods, approached Krishna to solicit His aid in killing Narakasura. Not content with stealing damsels, Narakasura had gone to heaven and helped himself to Indra's mother Aditi's earrings, which had miraculous powers. This complaint had barely been noted when Varuna, the god of waters, added to the list of Narakasura's iniquities. Having paid a visit to Varuna, he couldn't resist filching Varuna's umbrella, which had remarkable properties. He had also occupied Indra's seat on top of the mountain, Meru. The complaints against him seemed to be adding up, so Krishna decided to take prompt action. In the meantime, the sage Narada had brought a flower from the celestial tree, the Parijata, from Indra's garden for Rukmini. Immediately upon seeing it, Satya-bhama wanted nothing less than the whole tree for her garden, so she went off to find her Lord and found Him in conference with Indra. She considered this a good omen, so she whispered to the Lord her desire to have a sapling from the celestial tree. Krishna agreed, provided Indra had no objection, and Indra cordially invited them both to come to heaven after Krishna had defeated Narakasura and regained his mother's earrings.

The Lord set out for Pragjyotisha, Narakasura's capital, mounted on His eagle vehicle and accompanied by His wife Satyabhama. The city was fortified by several layers of barriers, consisting of ranges of mountains, water, fire, and wind. Within that were the cords of the demon Murasura, which no one could break. Krishna shattered the external fortifications of mountains with His mace, the water and fire with His discus, and the weapons with His arrows. He also shattered the courage of Narakasura's warriors with the powerful sound of His conch, the *Panchajanya*. Murasura rushed out at Krishna with his three-pronged trident upraised. He hurled it at Garuda and Krishna broke the trident with three arrows. Murasura hurled his mace at Him, which was also shattered by the Lord. At last, bereft of weapons, he rushed at Him as if to throttle Him with his bare hands and had his head cut off by the Lord's discus, the *Sudarshana*. Seeing all his barricades broken and his leader slain, Narakasura came out with his elephant brigade. Thereupon, there ensued a terrific battle between the two, which ended in Narakasura's head being cut off by the *Sudarshana*. His mother, the earth deity, then presented to the Lord the earrings, umbrella, and other precious articles that her son had stolen. She knew of Krishna's greatness and she extolled Him and begged Him to spare the life of her grandson Bhagadatta. Krishna acceded to this request, made a triumphal entry into the prosperous city of Pragjyotisha, and released the sixteen thousand young women whom Narakasura had taken away by force. As soon as they saw Him, they mentally resolved to wed none but Him, so Krishna accepted all of them and sent them to Dwaraka to await His arrival.

Next, He proceeded to Indra's celestial abode and restored Aditi's earrings and Varuna's umbrella. As soon as Satyabhama saw the celestial tree with its golden bark and intoxicating perfume, she clung to Krishna's arm and begged Him not to forget His promise to get the tree for her. The Lord looked at her pityingly, as if to say, "O Bhama, how foolish you are. Having procured Me, the essence of sweetness, do you crave for this petty tree which can grant you only worldly pleasures?" But she was adamant, so He gave in to her request. So also, when we ask the Lord for childish trifles which are pleasant to the senses but have no lasting benefit, the Lord may yield, for the power of prayer is great and every individual is given the freedom to carve out his own future. Eventually, we will find that the gift is a worthless one and will bring us nothing but sorrow. Thus, each one of us has the voice of God within our hearts, but if we disregard it, He may appear to give in, not because He is too weak to stop us, but because we are given the freedom to choose, and according to our choice, have to accept the consequences.

So Krishna reminded Indra of his promise, but that foolish monarch conveniently forgot his obligations once he had what he wanted, like most of us, and sent his forces to fight with Krishna! The Lord defeated them and returned to Dwaraka with the delighted Satyabhama carrying her trophy. At Dwaraka, He married the sixteen thousand princesses in as many palaces, taking on as many forms at the same time. They were housed in their own special mansions so that there would be no complaints.

As soon as Satyabhama reached her own home, she decided to plant her treasure. The spot chosen was directly beside the wall separating her residence from that of Rukmini so that her rival would have clear proof of her Lord's preference for her! Just then, the sage Narada arrived on the scene and offered to plant it for her since he was well-versed in the method of planting celestial trees, being a resident of those regions. Narada had a decided partiality for the modest and unassuming Rukmini. The outcome of his horticultural activities was that when the tree grew and started flowering, Bhama found to her dismay that all the branches hung over the wall into Rukmini's garden. The flowers fell in profusion and carpeted Rukmini's compound, perfuming the entire atmosphere. If Satyabhama wanted even a single flower, she had to beg for one. So, while she had all the troublesome tasks of watering and manuring and pruning, Rukmini could sit back and enjoy the perfume of the flowers, which literally fell into her lap. Thus, Rukmini, who thought that there was no perfume comparable to the one emanating from the feet of her Lord, was drenched in celestial fragrance, whereas Bhama, who craved for other excitement, was left bereft.

Once, the sage Narada, who was a celibate himself, had a doubt as to how the Lord treated His sixteen thousand one hundred and eight wives and how they looked upon Him. The thought of keeping even one wife seemed a burden to him, so how did Krishna manage to please all His wives and yet find time for all his other activities? One day, he decided to find out for himself. Armed with his *vina*, or musical instrument, he visited his favorite, Rukmini. There he found Krishna relaxing on the swing bed, with Rukmini fanning Him. He jumped up as soon as He saw the sage and welcomed him and pressed him to partake of some fruits and nuts. Narada sat for a while and then departed, for he still had sixteen thousand one hundred and seven more houses to visit. He stepped into Satyabhama's house next. Here he found Krishna engrossed in a game of dice with her. He was steadily losing and as soon as He saw the sage, He jumped up, upsetting the board, and welcomed him with open arms. "Ah, Narada! How long is it since we met! How are you and where are you coming from?"

Narada's jaw dropped, for had they not met but a moment ago? He hastily extricated himself from the Lord's embrace and withdrew to Jambavati's house. Here he found that even the season had changed. While it was still spring at the other two palaces, it was summer here, and the two of them were sporting in the lake in order to get cool. The same tableau was enacted here—Krishna pretending surprise at seeing him and Narada feeling nervous and abashed. Poor Narada stuck to his self-imposed task and climbed in and out of any number of palaces. In each of them he was met by a smiling Krishna and a devoted, happy, and contented wife, both of them seemingly enthralled with each other's company! Though each of His wives had a hundred maids as her personal attendants, every one of them attended herself to all Krishna's wants, welcoming Him when He arrived, offering Him *arghya*[1] and water to wash His feet, preparing His food, massaging His feet, fanning Him, applying *sandal* paste and unguents over his body, decorating Him with flower garlands made with their own hands, combing and arranging His hair, and even feeding Him. All of them told Narada that they considered themselves more in the capacity of His servant than His wife. They delighted in doing the most menial service for Him. By the end of the day, Narada had lost count of the number of palaces he had climbed into and out of. Exhausted, he decided to give up his futile pastime of trying to plumb the depths of the Lord's glory. In a mood of repentance, he flung himself down beneath a tree to rest, when he suddenly found a man bearing down on him.

"Hail, O Sage!" said the man, who was swaddled in a cloak. "Have you given up so easily? Why don't you finish the task you have set yourself? You have exactly four hundred and sixty-five houses more to visit!"

So saying, the man disappeared and Narada thought he heard a delighted chuckle near him. He stood up with both hands clasped and mentally prostrated sixteen thousand one hundred and eight times to the Lord for having doubted Him and daring to test Him.

"Forgive me," he whispered. "You are the sum total of all. Everything exists in You. How then would You find it difficult to be in as many places as You like at the same time?"

It may be impossible for a human being to keep so many women happy, but for God nothing is impossible. Just because he was a sage and a realized soul, Narada saw that he had no greater claim on Him than His

---

1 *arghya*—traditional respectful offering of leaf, flower, grass, and *sandal* paste.

wives, who worshipped Him with their bodies, minds, and souls.

Of all His wives, there was none so sweet and docile as Rukmini. She was Lakshmi Devi incarnate, the consort of Lord Vishnu. She was the ideal *Aryan* wife, asking for nothing, demanding nothing, finding her greatest happiness in the service of her husband, who was also her Lord and God. At no time in her life had she ever opposed His wishes or in any way expressed her opinions at variance with His, as the headstrong Satyabhama was wont to do. One day, the Lord decided to test the placidity of the calm lake of her mind by dropping a pebble of discontent into it. Was it as calm at the bottom as it appeared on top or were the storms of passion lurking below the surface?

One afternoon, He was resting on the swing bed with Rukmini gently fanning Him and deriving immense pleasure from this small service. She presented a picture of rare beauty as she stood beside the Lord. Her jeweled anklets made a sweet, tinkling sound as she moved about and her bangles kept time with the movement of the gently waving fan. Seeing her looking so lovely and serene, the Lord said, with a mischievous smile, "O Princess, many a ruler who was equal in wealth to the divinities, who was as noble, as charming, and as endowed with looks, generosity, strength, and valor came to your *svayamvara*, including Shishupala, the Prince of Chedi. Without caring for any of them, why did you choose Me, who am inferior to them in all things, who out of fear has taken up shelter in the middle of the sea, who has abandoned all claim to the royal throne, and whose way of life is steeped in mystery and transcends the ways of the world? I am One without any possessions and am fond of those with nothing. Therefore, O beautiful one, wealthy people do not seek My favor. Marriage and friendship should only be between people who are compatible with respect to birth, wealth, and position. Therefore, O Princess of Vidarbha, if it was without knowledge of these failings that you chose to marry Me, then it is still not too late for you to seek some noble *kshatriya* prince like Shishupala, who will be a real match for you and enable you to fulfill your aspirations in this world and the next. I took you by force only to destroy the pride of those evil kings. We who are established in the indifference of wisdom[2] have no need for women, offspring, or wealth. We are ever satisfied with the bliss of the *Atman*, the true Self, and we act the role of the uninvolved witness in the affairs of the world."

At the beginning of this remarkable discourse, Rukmini had looked up

---

2 "indifference of wisdom"—it is the Hindu belief that a person established in true wisdom is freed from all personal worldly desires.

startled, wondering what she had done to provoke this tirade. But as the harangue continued unabated, her lips started quivering, her eyes filled with tears, and a terrible sorrow clutched at her heart and threatened to tear it apart. Any minute now, she expected to hear the fateful words banishing her from His divine presence, forbidding her ever to return again. The final straw was the mention of the hateful word Shishupala. If there was anyone whom the gentle princess detested, it was he. Her tender heart could bear no more. Her bangles slipped off her limp arms and without a sound she crumpled to the ground. Seeing this drastic reaction to His teasing, the Lord jumped up from the cot, lifted her up tenderly, tied up her disheveled locks, massaged her face with His lotus palms, did everything to bring her back to consciousness, and then proceeded to soothe and pacify her. At last, her lovely eyes fluttered open.

"O beautiful one," He said. "do not be angry with Me. I was only teasing you for the pleasure of hearing your reply. Differences of opinion happen in all marriages. In fact, that is the only gain to be had from marriage. What you should have done was to defend yourself against My unjust accusations and then we could have spent a happy hour arguing and quarreling with each other, as all husbands and wives do. I never expected you to take My teasing so seriously and swoon." Thus He comforted her and tenderly kissed away her tears. At last, with heaving breasts and smothered sobs, Rukmini spoke.

"I find no pleasure in anything but Your service, O Lord," she said with quivering lips. "Your smiles, Your glances, Your commands—these constitute my life breath and if I cannot have these, I would rather die." Then, taking up each of the points which He had declared to be detrimental to Him, she pointed out that these very points were a matter of pride to her.

"O lotus-eyed Lord! What you said about my not being a fitting match for You is indeed true. For where are You, the all-pervading being, the master of all powers and excellences, and where am I, a creature constituted of the three *gunas* (made of the stuff of the material world)? It is true that You have taken Your residence in the deep sea, for You are the pure consciousness which is ever resident in the ocean of our hearts. Your ways are mysterious and no doubt none can conceive of them. You are indeed a pauper, for there is nothing outside You that You can possess. You are the embodiment of all values. Men abandon everything the world prizes to follow You. These are the noble ones with whom You have affinity. This is a true marriage and not the relationship of the body. It was by hearing of Your greatness from

the ascetics who have no possession but You that I came to love You, reject-
ing all lesser mortals. Having driven away the assembled kings by a mere
twang of Your bow, You took me away, for I am Your rightful property. Who
is the woman with even a modicum of sense who would go after a man, who
is nothing but a walking corpse, in preference to You, who are the abode of
all excellences? Who is the woman who will care to leave You after having
once experienced the perfume of Your lotus feet, the abode of Lakshmi, the
goddess of fortune? I have sought shelter in You, the Lord of all the worlds,
the Supreme Soul, and the fulfiller of the aspirations of everyone, here and
in the hereafter, for You are the only match for me. (The *Paramatma* is the
only match for the *jivatma*).[3] Revolving as I am in this cycle of birth and
death, may Your feet be my shelter, Your feet that destroy the false identification of the body with the spirit and that remain ever with the devotee as
his sole support in the ocean of *samsara*. Only those women who are
steeped in ignorance and who have never known the fragrance of Your lotus
feet would go after human husbands, who are nothing but corpses clad in
skin and bones and flesh." Rukmini's sentiments are those which have been
felt by many women, like Mirabai,[4] who have given their hearts over to the
Lord. After having married the Lord within their hearts, the thought of
touching a man becomes abhorrent to them. Shunned by their husbands,
scorned by their relatives, and condemned by society, they are helpless and
can only remain true to the ideal cherished within their hearts. One who
has known pure gold can never be satisfied with dross.

The Lord said, "O noble one! It was only to hear these words of yours
that I teased you. It would be difficult to find even one household with a
wife like you. Your single-minded devotion and dedication to Me shall go
uncompensated, for they are too noble and pure to be compensated by
anything I can do for you." Thus He blessed and comforted her. This
small episode in the life of the Lord shows how He played the role of the
typical householder to perfection, as He played every other role.

Thus ends the seventeenth chapter of The Play of God,
named "The Divine Husband."

Hari Aum Tat Sat

---

[3] *Paramatma / jivatma*—The highest Self is the only true companion of the individual self.
[4] Mirabai—A famous 16th Century Hindu saint who considered herself married to Krishna and thus
had no interest in other men.

EIGHTEEN

THE SONS OF KRISHNA

*Satthwatham-
pathaye namaha*

Homage to the
Lord of the
Satthvathas

*I constantly contemplate Krishna, the attractor of all, whose
face, with the gentle smile playing over it, is as charming as a
lotus flower in bloom and who transcends the relationships of
cause and effect. Yet He lived as the son of Nanda and was
worshipped by ascetics like Narada.*
—MUKUNDAMALA

The wives of Krishna considered themselves His
servitors and bowed to Him in all things, but the
devotion of the *gopis* of Vrindavan was even higher
in quality, for they gave their devotion with no hope of
reward. Radha, in particular, was the outstanding example. Many are the stories told of her association with the
Lord while at Vrindavan. She was supposed to be very
high-spirited, like Satyabhama, and she had many tiffs
with the Lord when she found Him dallying with the
other *gopis*. Like all women, she wanted Him wholly for
herself and He wanted to teach her the lesson that He
belonged to all. Anyone who called to Him with love was
showered with His grace. Thus, during the short term of
His stay at Vrindavan, He cleansed her of the dross of
selfishness, so that at last her love was burnished like
pure gold. It had to stand the test of a physical parting
from Him and this she could do only because she was
spiritually one with Him. Neither space nor time could
alter the perfection of their relationship. His wives could
hardly come up to this standard and they had always
been curious about Radha, for they had heard much
about her. Even Uddhava never tired of singing her praises. At last, at their earnest request, the Lord decided to
invite her to Dwaraka for a day. He warned His wives

159

that she should be treated on a par with Him, for she was a part of Him and any slight to her would be tantamont to a slight to Him. They agreed to everything and eagerly looked forward to meeting her.

One day she arrived, escorted by her companions, looking like a wild rose transplanted from its natural habitat to the artificial glitter of court life. Though the others felt shy and strange, she herself seemed oblivious to the strangeness of her surroundings until her eyes fell on Krishna. She gave a glad cry, rushed forward without any inhibitions, and flung herself into His welcoming arms! The others watched in astonishment. Even Satyabhama, the boldest of them, never presumed to do anything like this in public. Krishna was not embarrassed a whit. He returned her embrace, gently led her around the palace, and introduced her to His wives, who had all lined up. Then He left her in Rukmini's charge, for He realized that His wives were longing to have her to themselves in order to question her, and they dared not do it in front of Him.

They found her to be naive and childlike. She was quite unimpressed by the wonders of the city or the palace. Her lovely face became animated only when Krishna's name was mentioned or any of His exploits repeated. At last, they gave up trying to interest her in the various aspects of palace life, and sat down and talked about Him who was uppermost in all their minds. Then Radha was blissfully happy. Like a *yogi*, her mind was totally unattracted by the external world and reveled only in the Lord. They spent the whole day happily listening to His exploits in Gokula and Vrindavan. At night, Rukmini led her to her room and put her to bed as tenderly as she would a child. Then she brought a cup of hot milk and placed it beside her bed, warning her to be careful when she drank it, since it was very hot. But Radha, of course, lived in her own world and gulped the milk down without even realizing how hot it was. Rukmini next went to the Lord's room to see to His needs before He slept and found Him massaging His throat.

"What is it, Lord? What has happened to your throat?" she enquired. The Lord smiled and said, "The hot milk you gave to Radha has burned My throat, though it would not have harmed her. She has drowned her separate individuality in Me and so she is ever protected, but I feel her pain, for I am enshrined in her heart."

Rukmini stood aghast. Now she began to have a glimmer of the greatness of Radha and the greatness of Krishna, who could feel the pain of His devotees. No tear could be shed by them without His feeling the prick in His own eyes. The devotee, on the other hand, who is ever immersed in Him, feels no pain at all.

Radha is the picture of the soul who is ever immersed in divine love. Like a lamp burning in a sheltered place, the fire of her love burned steadily for her Lord alone. Having once experienced the bliss of *atmic* realization in the episode of the *Rasalila*, she could no longer find joy in the pleasures of the mundane world, just as the *yogi* finds no amusement in the joys of the senses. To the one who has drowned in the ocean of bliss, the pleasures of the world appear like the toys of childhood. Radha returned to Vrindavan, there to meditate on the Lord until the end of her earthly life, as did the rest of the *gopis*.

For the first five years after His marriage to Rukmini, Krishna did not have any children. Understanding her disappointment, He placated Lord Shiva and was blessed with His eldest son, Pradyumna. Lord Vishnu had only one son, Manmatha, the god of love. He had been reduced to ashes in the flame of Lord Shiva's wrath for having dared to interrupt His *tapasya*. This He did to help Parvati win Shiva as her husband. Rathi, the wife of Manmatha, had begged Lord Shiva to grant the life of her husband, but she had been told to take birth on earth and await the arrival of Manmatha. This is why Krishna had to placate Lord Shiva, who relented, and Manmatha was born as Pradyumna, the eldest son of Rukmini. But Rukmini was unable to enjoy her baby, for he was stolen in infancy by Sambasura, the sworn enemy of Manmatha. Sambasura threw the baby into the sea and thought he had seen the last of him. But a huge fish swallowed the babe and was caught by a fisherman, who brought the fish to the kitchen of Sambasura himself, where Manmatha's wife Rathi had already incarnated herself as Maya Devi, his cook. She had been told by the sage Narada to expect her husband in this miraculous way. So she cut open the fish very carefully, rescued the beautiful baby from inside, and brought up the child tenderly. When Pradyumna came of age, he found his supposed mother to be behaving toward him more in the nature of a wife than a mother, and he asked her the reason for this change. She told him the whole story and handed over to him the divine weapons she had in her keeping. Armed with these, he defeated Sambasura and the couple returned to Dwaraka. Rukmini's heart leaped with joy when she beheld the handsome young man who had entered the court with a lady. Though she had never set eyes on him since birth, she felt strongly attracted to him and she

begged Krishna to find out who he was. The whole story was then narrated by the sage Narada and the couple was welcomed with great joy.

Each of the wives of Krishna is said to have given birth to ten sons.
Each of them thought herself to be His favorite, for He always seemed to
be with her in her palace. Only a few of them realized that He was ever
immersed in His own inherent bliss and His mind was never drawn by
any of them. Like an actor playing a role in a drama, He played the role
of husband to all these countless ladies. Despite all their amorous
devices, they failed to capture His mind.

Pradyumna also married his uncle Rukmi's daughter, Rukmavati, and
had a son called Aniruddha by her. Rukmi, who was Rukmini's brother,
had sworn never to enter his own city until he had defeated Krishna, who
had abducted his sister. He had built another city at Bhojakata and was
staying there, biding his chance to get even with Krishna. At the *svayamvara* that he had arranged for his daughter Rukmavati, Pradyumna enacted the same scene which his father had done years ago and abducted the
bride. When Pradyumna's son Aniruddha grew up, he married Rukmi's
granddaughter, Rochana. On the auspicious occasion of this wedding,
Krishna, Balarama, Rukmini, Samba, Pradyumna, and many others went
to Bhojakata, since a sort of truce had been declared.

After the wedding, Rukmi challenged Balarama to a game of dice. In
the course of the game, Rukmi started insulting the Yadavas as being
mere cowherds. He was even caught cheating. Inflamed by this, Balarama
hurled his mace at him and killed him. In the general pandemonium that
followed, Krishna alone remained silent, for he had promised Rukmini
that he would not harm her relatives. Thus, the wedding ended in confusion and the Yadavas returned with Aniruddha and his bride Rochana.

The romantic story of how Aniruddha married Usha, the daughter of
Banasura, is well worth narrating. The latter was the son of Mahabali,
who had once offered the earth as a gift to Lord Vishnu in His *avatar* as
Vamana, the dwarf man. Banasura was a great devotee of Lord Shiva and
lived in the beautiful city of Sonita. He had a thousand arms, with which
he used to play a thousand instruments while Lord Shiva danced the
thandava (Shiva's dance of the infinite). Shiva gave him many boons and
one that Banasura chose was that Shiva Himself should come and guard
his city. He was very proud of his own strength, as well as the fact that he
was being guarded by Shiva. Banasura found his thousand arms were
proving a burden to him, as they were itching to fight with someone, but

in all the three worlds he could find no worthy opponent. Shiva was amused to hear this and told him that an opponent worthy of his mettle would be found soon after he found his flagstaff broken.

Banasura had a beautiful daughter called Usha. Her favorite companion was the minister's daughter, Chitralekha, who was an expert artist as well as an exponent of *yoga*. One day, Usha had a graphic dream in which she met a handsome prince and fell in love with him. The experience of the dream was so vivid that she lost interest in everything else and started pining for her dream lover. Chitralekha, seeing her in this sorry state, demanded to know the reason. When she heard the story, she told Usha not to feel disheartened and that she would paint portraits of all the eligible princes of the realm with her remarkable gift. Thus, she started painting portraits of the princes of each of the great royal families. At last, when she came to the Yadavas, Usha started to show signs of animation. When she saw Krishna's and Pradyumna's portraits she became quite excited, for the likeness to her dream prince was unmistakable. At last, when Aniruddha's handsome countenance appeared under Chitralekha's skillful fingers, her joy knew no bounds. But when she heard who he was, she fell into gloom once more, for she feared her father would never agree to the match. But Chitralekha was a resourceful girl. She told Usha to go to bed with a happy heart, and exerting her *yogic* powers, she went to Dwaraka and wafted the sleeping Aniruddha in the middle of the night into Usha's arms. When he woke up he proved to be most cooperative in acceding to their wishes that he should wed Usha in private, for he, too, had been dreaming of her for the past few days. Thus, they got married and he lived in her quarters in secret. This idyllic state of affairs, however, could not last long. Usha started showing signs of pregnancy. Her father soon came to hear of this. He invaded his daughter's private apartments, discovered the handsome stranger, and had him forcibly put into jail, despite Aniruddha's resistance and Usha's pleas.

In Dwaraka, Aniruddha's relatives wondered about his disappearance. As usual, the sage Narada came to the rescue and informed them of his whereabouts. The Yadavas, headed by Krishna, went on a rescue operation to Sonitapura. They laid waste the gardens surrounding the city, which infuriated Banasura and intrigued him also, since he found his flagstaff broken. Accompanied by Lord Shiva seated on His bull vehicle, Banasura went to meet the Yadavas and there ensued a tremendous battle between Hara and Hari—Shiva and Krishna—that was thrilling to behold. The Lord cut off Banasura's numerous arms one by one like the branches of a tree. At last, when he had only four left, Shiva intervened and begged Krishna to spare the life of His devotee. Krishna stopped the fight, spared Bana, and told him that a devotee of Shiva would have nothing to fear from Him. Banasura released Aniruddha and gave his daughter Usha happily to him, and the Yadavas returned back in triumph.

The Lord's victory over Shiva is the culmination of His victories over the ancient gods. His first was with Brahma (god of creation) in the incident of the cows and the *gopalas*, next over Indra (king of the gods) during the uplifting of the Govardhan mountain, as well as in procuring the celestial tree, over Varuna (god of the oceans) in the rescuing of His father from the waters, over Manmatha (Cupid, god of love) during the *Rasalila*, over Agni (god of fire) during the drinking of the forest fire, over Kubera (god of wealth) at the defeating of Shankachuda, over the Vidyadaras at the release of the snake *Sudarshana*, and now over Shiva in the war with Banasura. Thus, the superiority of Krishna over the ancient *Vedic* gods was established during the *Krishnavatar*.

At different periods of history we find different gods taking precedence and this has led to many misconceptions and factions within the fold of the Hindu religion itself. The Lord Himself says that He manifests Himself from age to age and every incarnation is adapted to suit the needs of the particular age. In the *Kali Yuga*, or Iron Age, in which we are living now, the path of *bhakti*, or devotion, is advocated and the main propagator of this path is Lord Krishna Himself. That is why in this age He is exalted above the other gods.

Krishna's eldest son by Jambavati was called Samba. He was the incarnation of Skanda, the general of the gods. He had heard of the famous capture of Rukmini by his father and he decided to emulate His example. The bride chosen by him was Lakshmana, the daughter of Duryodhana by his wife Bhanumati. Neither father nor daughter had so far shown any inclination toward such a union, but Samba did not let such a slight thing deter him in his ambition. He went uninvited to the *svayamvara* and made off with the bride. This was a common occurrence in those days, as has been seen. But Samba had gone alone and had reckoned without Duryodhana, who had no desire to have his daughter abducted, least of all by a member of the Yadava clan. He promptly caught Samba and clapped him in jail to cool his ardor. Hearing of the ignominious ending of His son's romance, Krishna decided to go Himself. He was stopped by Balarama, who said that Krishna was incapable of dealing politely with Duryodhana, who, being Balarama's disciple, would listen to whatever he said. Krishna laughed at this reading of Duryodhana's character but allowed His brother to have his own way.

Balarama went to Hastinapura and demanded an audience with Duryodhana in the garden outside the palace. When he came out of respect for his tutor, Balarama ordered him to free his nephew, Samba. Duryodhana grew furious at this command. "What!" he roared. "Has the jackal started commanding the lion? Since when have you cowherds become daring enough to command me, the King of the Kurus? Who are these Yadavas? Upstarts, all of them, led by the cowherd Krishna. Everyone knows He fled in terror of Jarasandha and is now hiding at Dwaraka, where He knows Jarasandha cannot penetrate!" Saying this, he strode off angrily. Hardly had he reached the palace when he found the entire city of Hastinapura shaking and quivering as if in the throes of some mortal agony. Balarama had not said a word in reply but he was boiling with rage. Without a word he had gone to the city walls and had placed his favorite weapon, the ploughshare, beneath the ramparts and was slowly uprooting the entire city and tipping it into the Ganga. Duryodhana was brought to a sudden realization of the folly of his rash words and he rushed back to placate Balarama. When the angry giant had been appeased, Duryodhana took him back in state to the city, released Samba, and got him married to his daughter Lakshmana. He sent them back with many horses, carriages, and ornaments, as befitting a princess of the Kurus.

One day, Krishna's sons, Pradyumna, Banu, Samba, and Charu, had gone to the outer gardens of the city in search of some new source of amusement. Feeling thirsty, they approached a well in the hope of finding some water, but the well was quite dry. However, right at the bottom they noticed a huge lizard. Out of pity, they tried to lift it out but were unable to do so. They reported the matter to their father, who came and lifted it out with His left hand as if in play. On being touched by the lotus hand of the Lord, the lizard threw off its body and assumed the form of a celestial. Though the Lord is the knower of all things, He enquired of the personage who he was.

The celestial replied, "I'm called Nriga and I was the son of Ikshvaku. I was famous in my time for my great generosity. I have gifted as many cattle to deserving souls as there are stars in the sky. They were all young milk cows with calves, gentle in nature and fair in appearance, with horns and hooves capped in gold and silver, and covered with silks. Not only have I given gifts of cows but also of gold, elephants, houses, and brides to worthy recipients. Once, I happened to present a cow who had already been gifted to someone else and which had strayed back without my knowledge. Seeing his cow taken away by another, the first man intercepted the second and they started arguing. Eventually, they came to me to settle their argument and to decide to whom the cow belonged. I offered each of them a *lakh* (one hundred thousand) of cows if one of them would release his claim, but both refused and walked away. At the time of my death, I was asked by the emissaries of Yama, the god of death, whether I would prefer to suffer for the consequences of my one mistake or enjoy the felicities accruing from my countless good deeds. I chose the former first and found myself falling down into this well as a lizard. O Lord, devoted as I was to holy men and charitable deeds, I have retained the memory of my past life and now because of the touch of Your divine hands, I have been given this form. Grant me the boon that whatever the condition in which life places me, I shall ever have devotion to Your lotus feet." So saying, he circumambulated Krishna and got into the heavenly vehicle that had come to transport him to the celestial regions.

The Lord took this opportunity to give some advice to His sons, who took Him for granted and who needed to be taught a lesson on the folly of wasting time in useless pursuits. He pointed out to them that the greatest wealth is spiritual wealth and the holy man is the custodian of this wealth and deserves the highest respect. Higher than a king is the holy man, richer than a king is he. One should never slight or take revenge on a holy man even if he curses you, for his curses will eventually prove beneficial. Thus did the Lord advise His sons, for He knew that a time would come when they would be guilty of this transgression and thus bring ruin upon themselves as well as on their race.

It will be noticed that the Lord seldom wasted His time in giving unwanted advice. Advice that is given unasked will never be appreciated by the recipient. God waits patiently for us to approach Him and ask for His help and only then does He step forward and extend a helping hand. Actually, the hand is always outstretched, grace is always flowing, but if we do not grasp the hand, it will be of no use to us. He waits patiently until the soul is evolved enough to realize that it needs divine aid. Then the soul realizes that the Lord has ever been there, all the time near to it, closer than the closest, dearer than the dearest.

Thus we find in the life of Krishna that there are only two other instances when He gave advice. One was to His friend Arjuna on the battlefield of Kurukshetra and the other was to Uddhava at the end of His sojourn on earth. Both were times when they were desperate for advice and had approached Him in a mood of self-surrender.

Thus ends the eighteenth chapter of The Play of God, *named "The Sons of Krishna."*

Hari Aum Tat Sat

NINETEEN

THE DIVINE RULER

Mukundaya namaha

Homage to the One who is the giver of liberation

Salutations to Thee, O Krishna.
Salutations to Thee, the Supreme Being.
Salutations to Thee, O Govinda,
who removest the sorrows of those who seek relief from their
difficulties by prostrating to Thee.
—SHRIMAD BHAGAVATA

How the Lord conducted Himself as the perfect householder has already been seen, but He was equally perfect in the discharge of His duties as a ruler, for Ugrasena was king only in name. It was Krishna who wielded complete power over the Yadavas and had transformed them from a set of loosely knit tribes into a mighty power to be reckoned with, even by Jarasandha, the mightiest of the kings of Bharatavarsha.

Each day at the approach of dawn, the cocks would begin to crow and the buzzing sound of the bees, stimulated by the fragrant breeze wafting from the newly opened flowers, was the signal for the birds to waken and begin their chirping, as if they were the bards detailed to arouse the Lord from His slumbers. But this auspicious moment preceding dawn was felt to be repugnant to His wives, who were lying in His embrace, for it proclaimed an imminent parting. Rising at the time known as *Brahmamuhurta*,[1] the Lord would perform the ceremonial wash with water and meditate on the blissful Brahman, the one without a second, undecaying, self-effulgent, bliss consciousness, ever established in Himself, and transcending the trammels of ignorance. Then He would

---

[1] *Brahmamuhurta*—the hours of Brahman, between 3:00 and 6:00 a.m., considered a very auspicious time of day, especially for meditation.

169

take His bath, don new garments, perform *sandhya vandana*,[2] finish His
Agnihotra[3] sacrifice before the sun rose, and then sit silently repeating the
Gayatri mantra.[4] Then He would make offerings to the orb of the rising
sun, Surya Narayana, the symbol of the Supreme, as well as to the other
gods, then to the forefathers, and also to the sages, who are aspects of
the Supreme. He would then convey His respects to the elders and holy
Brahmins. He would also make gifts of cows to worthy recipients and
touch with His hands various objects which were considered sacred and
auspicious. Then He would dress and decorate His body, which itself was
an ornament for the whole world. After this, He would bestow on suppli-
cants and servants whatever they desired. By that time, His charioteer
Daruka would come and bow before Him. He would welcome him by
holding his folded palms in His own. A mirror, a cow, a bull, a holy man,
some ghee, and certain divine images would then be shown to Him
before He got into the chariot, accompanied by His friends Uddhava and
Satyaki. As He drove off, He would turn around and give a last charming
smile to His wives.

Starting in this way from the palaces of all His consorts, Krishna
appeared outside as a single person and, surrounded by all the Yadava
chiefs, He would enter the assembly hall known as Sudharma, wherein
those present did not experience hunger, thirst, or pain. Seated there on
the imposing lion throne, He would discharge the duties of the day.
Before starting the serious business, it was the custom to regale the Lord
with the frolic of master comedians and dancing troupes. Then the bards,
minstrels, and heralds would proclaim His valorous doings, learned Brahmins would chant the *Vedas*, and orators would describe the mighty feats
of the great kings of the Yadava line. Only then would the assembly take
up the main business of the day.

One day, while the Lord was thus holding His morning audience, a
messenger came from the King of Karushna, called Paundraka. Many
people had led this Paundraka to believe that he was the incarnation of
Lord Vishnu and the poor man had styled himself as the real Vaasudeva.
He proclaimed that he was the Supreme God, forbade the worship of all

2 *sandhya vandana*—traditional daily worship of the sun (as an embodiment of the Supreme) done
   in the morning at sunrise, at midday, and in the evening at sunset.
3 *Agnihotra*—worship of fire as emblematic of God, done at sunrise and sunset.
4 *Gayatri mantra*—see footnote 1 on page 91.

other gods in his country, and put all the *rishis* and Brahmins who insisted on reading the *Vedas* and performing the *Vedic* rituals into the dungeon. Every week, a man was sent to ask these people if they had come to their right senses and were ready to accept Paundraka as the only God. If the answer was in the affirmative, they were let out; otherwise they were left to rot until they agreed. One of those who had been cast into the dungeon in this manner was Punardatta, the son of Guru Sandipani, whom Krishna had once brought back from the land of the dead. Paundraka had grown more and more evil due to his power and when he heard of the existence of Krishna, who also styled Himself as Vaasudeva, he could not bear it. So he sent a messenger to the Yadava court with a proclamation.

"I'm the true incarnation of Vishnu, I'm Narayana, or Vaasudeva, the Primeval Being who has incarnated Himself to uplift the world from its misery. I hear that you have dared to usurp my title and my insignia, like the *Shrivatsa* on the chest, the jewel *Kaustubha*, and the appearance of four arms when necessary, carrying the discus *Sudarshana*, the conch *Panchajanya*, the mace *Kaumodaki*, and the lotus. Leave off using these emblems and surrender to me immediately, or else come and fight and let us prove to the world who is the real incarnation!"

This piece of folly was read aloud in the open assembly and was heard with great amusement. Krishna also smiled and assured the messenger that his master's wishes would be complied with and that He would visit him within a few days and clear his doubts once and for all.

Paundraka, meanwhile, was preparing himself to meet his maker. He managed to procure a ruby of extraordinary size, which could pass as the *Kaustubha*, had his body painted a deep blue color, and got two extra arms, made of wood, holding the conch and discus, respectively. This contraption was fixed onto his shoulders. The greatest difficulty came in making the sign of the *Shrivatsa* on his chest. The sign, as found on Lord Vishnu and on His incarnations, is in the shape of the foot of the sage Bhrigu and is a peculiar formation of the hair rather than an actual print. After considerable cogitation, the poor misguided fool got an iron foot made and branded himself with it. The agony of this procedure may well be imagined. But when the fester had gone down it could well pass as the *Shrivatsa*. All these preparations were made with the help of his friend, the King of Kashi, at whose residence he was staying. Following His message, Lord Krishna, accompanied by an army and His friends Uddhava and Satyaki, who did not want to miss the fun, proceeded to Kashi, where

Paundraka was awaiting His arrival. The Lord had brought all His accouterments with Him, His discus, the *Sudarshana*, His bow, the *Saranga*, His mace, the *Kaumodaki*, and His sword Nandaka. Seated in His chariot drawn by His famous four white horses, wearing shining yellow garments and a crown topped with peacock feathers, for which He was famous, He shone with a radiance that put to shame the glory of the sun at noon. As He came to the outskirts of the holy city of Kashi, the citizens thought to themselves, "If there is a God on earth, this must surely be He! How lucky we are to have even a glimpse of Him. Yet how unlucky, for instead of paying homage to Him, we are forced to worship this fool Paundraka!"

Hearing of Krishna's arrival, Paundraka arrayed himself in a lovely yellow robe and, sporting all his absurd accessories, he came out of the city with two *akshauhinis* (divisions) of the army. His friend the King of Kashi followed with another army. The Yadavas laughed when they saw Paundraka impersonating the Lord in every detail.

From the distance of a few yards, Paundraka said in a loud voice, "Halt! Do you now admit that I'm the true Vaasudeva, the only incarnation of Vishnu?" He feared that a closer inspection would reveal the flaws in his getup.

Krishna obediently halted and said, "Yes, indeed, I readily admit the truth of your claims. I call myself Vaasudeva only because I happen to be the son of Vasudeva. I'm quite ready to be friends with you, provided you set free the people you have incarcerated in your dungeons."

Paundraka proudly said, "I have no need of friends like you! Be prepared to fight, for there is no place on this earth for both of us!"

So saying, he and his army attacked the Yadava host with various weapons such as tridents, wooden maces, iron-tipped maces, javelins, spears, and arrows. At last, tiring of this play, the Lord laughingly told him, "O Paundraka, whatever weapons you have asked me to give up, I'm now giving to you. Here, catch them!"

So saying, He threw the discus at Paundraka, who was unable to do anything but gape as it hurtled toward him and neatly severed his head from his body. His friend the King of Kashi soon followed him. Paundraka, who had been mentally identifying himself with the Lord all the time, got released from his mortal coils and attained identity of form with the Lord. Mysterious are the ways of *karma*: each one gets liberation in his own way.

The Lord is above all laws and has no need to follow the rituals and

regulations which are meant for ordinary mortals in order to attain liberation, yet we find that He was always the first to set an example of right
and well-regulated conduct according to the ancient rules set down in the
Vedas. He taught that human beings could attain liberation only by following *svadharma*, or the set of rules for which each was best suited, both
mentally and physically. Each one is born in a certain type of environment
and has certain psychological aptitudes which, if followed, will benefit
both oneself and the society, whereas if one tries to ape the customs and
manners of another mode of life that is at variance with one's own nature,
both the individual and the society will suffer. The person will suffer
because he or she will not like the work they are doing, and the society
will suffer because the individual will be giving less than their best. The
truth of this can be seen in modern society. Krishna always tried to inte-
grate the individual with the society, for man (or woman), being a gregari-
ous animal, is happiest when they have the respect and approval of their
fellows.

At this time there occurred a full and prolonged eclipse of the sun. A
holy immersion in the sacred waters of the lake known as Syamantapanchaka was considered most auspicious on the day of the eclipse. This lake
was situated in the holy spot of Kurukshetra, where Parasurama, another
incarnation of Lord Vishnu, had created five lakes with the blood of the
kshatriyas he had slaughtered. In order to expiate this he had performed
great penances at this place and an immersion in this lake was considered
most holy. Large numbers of people, including the Yadavas, the Kurus,
the *gopalas*, and the *gopis* assembled in this holy spot in order to submerge themselves in the sacred waters at the time of the eclipse. The joy
of the *gopalas* and *gopis* when they saw Krishna after so many years knew
no bounds. The Pandavas, with their mother Kunti and wife Draupadi, as
well as their other wives, were all there. Dhritarashtra, Gandhari, Vidura,
and the Kauravas, headed by Duryodhana, were also there. There was a
grand reunion of friends and relatives, perhaps the last before the great
holocaust of the Mahabharata war. The next time the Pandavas and Kauravas met would be for the battle at Kurukshetra.

All of them spent three delightful months there and the Lord satisfied
all according to their needs. Krishna embraced Nanda and Yashoda and
consoled them in all ways. Devaki also embraced Yashoda and shed tears
thinking of the great service she had rendered to her.

The *gopis*, finding their beloved Lord after so many years, gazed at

Him longingly, cursing the fact that they were forced to blink now and again and thus waste precious instants. He embraced them all and comforted them thus: "Clouds in the sky are scattered here and there by the wind. So also the Creator brings together and separates human beings. We have been parted physically from each other, but you are ever in my mind. Do not think your devotion to Me will go unrewarded, for it will enable you to cut the coils of mortal life and attain union with Me, who am the Infinite source of Bliss." In the days that followed He gave them instruction on *Atmavidya*, or the science of the Self, by reflecting on which they attained liberation.

At the end of their stay, their prayer to Him was this: "O You who carry the lotus of the world in Your navel, Your feet are the object of contemplation by great *yogis* with deep understanding and meditative capacity. But, O Lord, they are the sole support of ignorant folk like us and the only means for lifting us out of this dilapidated well of human existence. May those holy feet ever shine in our hearts."

After having blessed the *gopis*, the Lord made enquiries of Yudhishthira and other friends and relatives about their welfare. They, for their part, felt themselves to be purified by His presence and told Him, "No harm can befall those who have come into contact with Your divine presence even once; then what about us, who have been blessed by Your vision constantly and have been protected by You at all times?"

One day, Draupadi approached Krishna's consorts and asked each of them to narrate the story of her marriage to Him. All of them delighted in describing the romantic way in which He had wed them. Draupadi then wanted to know whether they regarded Him as man or God. All of them agreed that as a husband He was perfect, as He was in everything He did, even if it was only playing a game of ball with His youngest child. But their attitude to Him was as if He was the Supreme Lord. They considered themselves honored to be able to serve Him in the most menial capacity, for in that lay their salvation.

To that holy spot had come all the sages, who wished to have a glimpse of that personage whom they had been cherishing in their hearts during meditation.

The Lord welcomed them and said, "In this world, people try to acquire spiritual merit in various ways, undergoing severe austerities, worshipping images, going on pilgrimages, and so on. These methods take a long time to purify the mind, but the very sight of holy ones like

Him around the great assembly hall known as the Maya Sabha, or Hall of Illusions, built for them by Mayan, the architect of the *asuras*, whom Arjuna and Krishna had rescued when they helped Agni to consume the forest of Khandva.

This hall was a wonder of wonders and Krishna Himself had told Mayan to fill it with deceptive contraptions, for He knew that the end of the era of *Dvapara* was approaching, ushering in the advent of *Kali*.[6] The destiny for which He Himself had taken this incarnation had to be fulfilled. The hall attracted many people from far and near. In some places there appeared to be a lake when there was nothing at all, a door when there was only a wall, a wall which was really a door, a mirror when there was none, and so on. In fact, the hall was filled with optical illusions and had a particular capacity to fool the evil and the pompous especially. Mayan had also presented the mighty mace, the Shaturagadini, to Bhima and the beautiful conch Devadatta to Arjuna. Into this fantastic Sabha the Pandavas welcomed Krishna and the other Yadavas who had accompanied Him, and He stayed with them for some months, seeing to all the formalities which had to be done before the commencement of the *Rajasuya*.

Thus ends the nineteenth chapter of The Play of God, *named "The Divine Ruler."*

Hari Aum Tat Sat

That Supreme Brahman, the Absolute Reality, has become an androgynous Person in the form of Lord Krishna, dark blue and pink in color, with vital forces ever drawn upward and having lustrous eyes. Salutation to Him who alone is the Soul of the Universe.
—NARAYANA SUKTAM

---

6 *Dvapara, Kali*—According to Hindu cosmology, the Earth goes through cycles of four epochs or *yugas* starting with a Golden Age where there is a high level of spiritual realization in the general populace. The last two are the Dvapara Yuga, which is said to have ended with the death of Krishna, and the Kali Yuga, or age of iron, that had its advent at the time of the same event. The Kali Yuga, which is the present age, is said to be a time of general ignorance and low values.

TWENTY

THE RAJASUYA SACRIFICE

Bhaktavatsalaya namaha

Homage to
the One who
shows kindness
to devotees

I bow to that All-Blissful Madhava (Krishna), by whose grace the dumb become orators and the lame are able to cross mountains.
—BHAGAVAD GITA MEDITATION VERSE

As the sage Narada had told Krishna, it was he who had first put the idea of holding a *Rajasuya* sacrifice into Yudhishthira's head. The sage informed Yudhishthira of the plight of his father Pandu in heaven, who was unable to sit on the same throne with Indra, since his sons had not performed the *Rajasuya* sacrifice. From the time he heard this, Yudhishthira started to feel rather guilty and his life changed from one of peace and tranquility to one of restlessness and uncertainty. Personally, he was not in favor of holding the *Rajasuya*, since it meant conquering all other kingdoms and forcing them to accept his suzerainty and pay him tribute. On the other hand, the thought of his father's desire to sit beside Indra on the throne, as well as the enthusiasm of his brothers, who were all for holding the *Rajasuya*, caused him great concern. Hence, he had told Narada to invite Krishna so that he could get His opinion. After having spent some happy days in the Lord's company, Yudhishthira, with his usual humility, asked Krishna whether He really considered him worthy of conducting such a stupendous sacrifice as the *Rajasuya*. Krishna assured him that he would certainly be able to conduct it, provided he subdued Jarasandha, since he was the only one capable of challenging the might of the Pandavas. Krishna proceeded to tell him the story of Jarasandha's birth.

179

"King Brihadratha of Magadha was childless, so he worshipped the great sage Chandakausika, who gave him a mango and told him to give it to his wife to eat. Since the king had two wives, he shared the mango equally between them, and in due course each delivered half a baby. The unhappy king threw the two parts on the waste heap outside the city gates, where they were picked up by a *rakshasi* (demoness) called Jere. The halves accidently came together in exact opposition and formed themselves into a perfect baby boy. Jere handed over the baby to the king, who named him Jarasandha after the woman who had given him life. This man has now become an evil and haughty king and has captured many kings in order to offer them as a sacrifice to Lord Shiva. He has attacked the city of Mathura many times and I had to shift my people to Dwaraka in order to protect them. Jarasandha is considered invincible, but he has a weak point, and that is the place where he was joined as a baby. To attack him with an army would be futile, but he can be defeated in a duel with one who knows this weak point and Bhima is the one who can do it."

Krishna then outlined their plan of action. *Digvijaya* was the first item of the *Rajasuya*. In it, the king sent his emissaries to all other kings and demanded the vassal fee by which they showed themselves willing to accord him the position of emperor. Krishna suggested that Arjuna, Bhima, Nakula, and Sahadeva be sent in all four directions in order to conquer all the kings. This was done and most of the kings willingly sent the vassal fee to Yudhishthira, for he was well loved by all. Hence, he got the name Ajatashatru (one without enemies).

Now only Jarasandha remained. His case demonstrates the great truth that devotion to God has no merit unless coupled with virtue and righteousness. He was a great devotee of Shiva and had captured many kings in order to make human sacrifices to Shiva. Krishna pointed out to the Pandavas how devotion should go hand in hand with kindness to one's fellow beings. *Dharma* should be accompanied with *bhakti* to be fruitful. Krishna suggested that He Himself would accompany Arjuna and Bhima and they would go disguised as Brahmins into the capital city of Jarasandha and there challenge him to a duel. At first, Yudhishthira was against the whole idea, but, as usual, he gave in and the trio departed.

Clad in robes of bark and with matted hair, they entered Mahishmathi, the capital of Jarasandha. Had they gone in their own garb, they would have been made to wait for days outside the fortress before gain-ing an audience with the king. As they were *sadhus* (holy mendicants), Jarasandha granted them an audience immediately and received them with great respect. Refreshments were offered to them, which they refused to take. Somewhat offended, he demanded to know who they were and what they wanted.

Krishna said, "We are your foes and we desire instant combat with you. Since you are steeped in *adharma* (unrighteous behavior), it is our duty to bring you to your right senses. So, you can choose one of us to fight a duel with you."

Jarasandha was amazed when he heard this and looked at them closely and said, "who are you and why do you pretend to be Brahmins when you are obviously *kshatriyas?* You have refused to partake of any of the refreshments offered to guests and you have come with this strange request. So who are you?"

"You are right," said Krishna, "in guessing that we are not Brahmins, but *kshatriyas*. We are your enemies and hence we have refused your hospitality. Know Me to be Krishna, the son of Vasudeva of the Vrishni clan. This is Arjuna, the middle one among the Pandavas, and this is Bhima, his elder brother, destroyer of Hidimba and Bakasura and invincible in battle. You may now choose with whom you would like to fight."

Jarasandha threw back his head and roared with laughter. "Oh, you are Krishna are you?" he asked sneeringly. "I have defeated you eighteen times in battle and made you run away and take refuge in the city of Dwaraka, where you live in dread of my wrath! How can I fight with you? As for Arjuna, he appears to be a mere boy. It is not meet that a hero of my stature should come to grips with such a stripling. The only one with whom I can even consider fighting is Bhima, for, puny though he is when compared to me, yet he is better than both of you!"

Krishna laughed and said, "O King! I think you have forgotten what happened at the Gomantaka hill when you set fire to it and went away after having boasted of your victory. And perhaps you have also forgotten the Draupadi *svayamvara*, when this 'stripling,' as you call him, defeated all the assembled kings and snatched the prize from beneath your noses. However, we shall not waste time in talking of the past, but get ready to meet our future!"

Bhima, who was itching for a fight, immediately prepared himself. The weapon chosen by both was the mace, for they were both experts in it. Selecting a level ground as the arena, the two warriors closed in combat and began to exchange blows with their diamond-hard maces. They were well matched and Jarasandha proved a more formidable adversary than either Hidimba or Bakasura. As for Jarasandha, he had never met such an opponent. He had fully expected to defeat Bhima in a few hours and now the fight was dragging on for days. At twilight when they stopped for the day, Bhima would retire, worn and weary, with his bones broken and his body crushed, but Krishna would gently massage him and make him whole again, so that on the morrow he would fight with renewed vigor. On the sixteenth night, Bhima told Krishna, "O Madhava (Krishna), I find it very difficult to overcome this man."

Krishna comforted him and infused new spirit into him by imparting his own spiritual powers to him and He reminded Bhima of Jarasandha's weak point, about which He had told him at Indraprastha. "Once you manage to bring him down, tear him apart and throw the pieces in different directions, being sure to reverse the position of the pieces. If the halves are not reversed, they have the power to come together again. This is the boon given to him by his foster mother."

The next day the fight began with great vigor on Bhima's side after the Lord's ministrations, but the mighty King of Magadha was flagging. Bhima watched carefully for his chance and overthrew him and tore him apart, but, unfortunately, he forgot the instructions for reversing the pieces. He had hardly turned jubilantly toward Krishna when he saw the look of horror on His face. He turned around to see his victim's two halves reuniting, and Jarasandha sprang up with a terrible oath, for he realized that his secret was out. With strength born of despair, he sprang at Bhima with the ferocity of a tiger. All rules of fair play were thrown overboard, as these two mighty giants grappled with each other for their lives. At last, with superhuman effort, Bhima managed to pin down his foe. He knelt on him with his knees pressing his chest and his arms forcing him down and cast a despairing glance at Krishna. The Lord smiled that bewitching smile, which made Bhima forget his woes and invested new life into him. With a deliberate gesture, Krishna took up a piece of straw, tore it apart, and, reversing the sides, threw the pieces in opposite directions. Seeing this, Bhima suddenly remembered his instructions and, with a quick movement, he jumped up. Catching hold of the king's legs, he tore them apart once more and flung the pieces wide in the prescribed manner. That was the end of the mighty King of Magadha and all the citizens rejoiced, for he had ruled with a hand of iron, brooking no disobedience of any sort and punishing offenders with the utmost severity.

Jarasandha's son Sahadeva was a devotee of the Lord and he was placed on the throne. He promised to follow the ancient code of *Sanatana Dharma* and also to help Yudhishthira in the *Rajasuya*. The imprisoned kings were now released and without exception they promised to support Yudhishthira. Being redeemed from the horrors of Jarasandha's dungeon and blessed with the vision of the Lord's beauteous form, the kings fell at His feet and extolled Him as the Spirit Supreme. "Allow us to have unremitting remembrance of Your feet even if we have to embroil ourselves in other births." This was their plea to Him.

Krishna sent them back to their respective countries with all due honors and returned to Indraprastha with the two brothers. He had killed two birds with one stone, accomplishing the destruction of Jarasandha as well as procuring the allegiance of so many kings. Yudhishthira's joy at seeing them return was great. He prostrated at the feet of the Lord and said, "The divinities themselves carry out Your orders like slaves, yet, O Lotus-Eyed One, it is part of Your divine *lila* that You should carry out the instructions of people like me, who can only pretend to be lords."

The preparations for the *Rajasuya* now began in earnest. The Lord Himself supervised the selection of each and every thing and He would have nothing but the best for His devotee, Yudhishthira. The best priests in the country were invited to perform the sacrificial ceremonies. Royalty from all over Bharatavarsha, together with their subjects, was invited, and they thronged to Indraprastha.

The priests plowed the sacrificial field with a golden plowshare and there initiated King Yudhishthira in the vows and disciplines of the sacrifice, following the *Vedic* instructions. Even the utensils were made of gold. Each of Yudhishthira's relations was put in charge of a different function. Bhima was in charge of catering, for he was an expert cook as well as a gourmet. Sahadeva was in charge of reception and Nakula in the collection of stores. Arjuna was engaged in serving the Elders, while Draupadi attended to the serving of food. The Kauravas were all there and Duryodhana, who was supposed to have something in him of Kubera, the god of wealth, was placed in charge of the treasury. Karna, who was noted for his love of charity, supervised the doling out of gifts. All the others were also allotted different duties. Yudhishthira refused to give any work to Krishna except that of overall supervision, but the latter insisted that He should be given something specific. At last, Yudhishthira, referring to an important ceremony of the *Rajasuya*, said, "You are the One who should be honored by us by washing Your feet! How can I give You any work?"

The Lord deliberately misinterpreted his words and proceeded to wash the feet of all the guests who arrived as well as clearing the leaf plates on which people ate! Such was Yudhishthira's humility and devotion that the Lord Himself undertook these menial tasks. If His grace is such that it can make the mute eloquent and the lame cross mountains, what could it not achieve for Yudhishthira, who had surrendered his all at His feet? The *Rajasuya* was a magnificent success. There was no place where Krishna's eyes did not reach. At one time He would be found in the music hall entertaining the guests with His flute, at others in the kitchen tasting a new dish to find out how it was, at other times in the dining hall serving the guests and even removing the leaves on which they ate, at others escorting guests to the chambers specially prepared for them.

Indraprastha was filled with all sorts of amusements—parks, dancing halls, and all types of entertainments were laid out for the guests, who did not like to remain in the sacrificial hall all the time watching the religious ceremonies. All the foremost kings, sages, and Brahmins of Bharatavarsha had come. The very gods themselves were supposed to have come and personally accepted the offerings made to them. Everyone went away utterly satisfied and full of praise for Yudhishthira. Money, jewels, horses, elephants, and cattle poured into the land from all the kings who had agreed to be his vassals. Rukmini, the incarnation of Lakshmi Devi, the goddess of wealth, had come with Krishna and He had told her to be on guard that there should be no dearth of anything in the *Rajasuya*, so naturally money flowed like water into Yudhishthira's coffers.

The only person who had come reluctantly was Shishupala, Prince of Chedi, who had been nursing a grudge against Krishna all these years since the abduction of Rukmini. His parents, who were devotees of the Lord, had also come. In fact, his mother was Krishna's aunt, but Shishupala refused to come unless he was given a self-contained apartment where he would have no necessity to meet Krishna. So, while the rest of the company enjoyed themselves with merrymaking from morn till midnight, regaling themselves with all the wonderful entertainments that had been provided, Shishupala alone incarcerated himself in his own private hidey-hole, not even daring to take a stroll in the beautiful gardens in case he met his hated rival. He listened with envy to the sweet strains of music, laughter, and shouts, which drifted down as if from another world. His hatred of Krishna had become an obsession, so that, like Kamsa, he could only think of Krishna night and day. At last, he could bear it no longer. "I'll venture forth," said he to himself. "Why should I fear anyone? I haven't done anything wrong. Let Him face me if He dares! I'm sure He's trying to avoid me."

Bolstering up his courage with such illogical arguments, he strode forth, affecting a nonchalance he did not feel. As luck would have it, the first person he saw as soon as he stepped out was the object of his hatred, striding toward him with a purposeful air. Shishupala pretended not to notice Him and walked on with a disdainful smile, hoping that Krishna would have the decency to make way for him. But Krishna did nothing of the sort and a collision seemed unavoidable, so Shishupala was forced to stop. Immediately, Krishna said, "Ah, Cousin! You're just the man I wanted to see. Why is it that we haven't seen you around? I was just coming to enquire if you were all right."

Shishupala gave Him a haughty look and, not deigning to reply, he moved on. Krishna looked at him with a smile. Foolish though he was, He had a soft spot for him.

Another person who was completely disgruntled at the way the *Rajasuya* was proceeding was Duryodhana. Seeing the Pandavas' affluence and the prestige and honor being gained by his cousin Yudhishthira, he felt quite sick with envy. Between the two of them, he and Karna concocted a plan to ruin Yudhishthira and make the *Rajasuya* come to an ignominious end for lack of funds. Since he had been kept in charge of the treasury and Karna in charge of gifts, they decided to give so lavishly that the treasury would soon be empty. Gleefully, the pair set to work giving fifty where only one was needed, but they failed to take into consideration that Yudhishthira had entrusted everything to the hands of the Lord, whose eyes were everywhere. From the beginning, He was wise to the tricks of the pair and had warned Rukmini. She blessed Yudhishthira so that every time the crooked pair emptied the coffers, wealth came pouring in from the vassal kingdoms. So, the consequence of Duryodhana's evil designs was just the opposite of what he had hoped for. The impecunious Brahmins who had come expecting only a reasonable sum to be given as gifts, found themselves being pressed into accepting vast amounts of money and other goods. Bewildered, yet delighted, at this unexpected good luck, they praised and blessed Yudhishthira in front of the angry Duryodhana.

On the day when the libations with *soma* juice[1] were made, Yudhishthira personally proceeded to honor the sacrificial priests. Vyasa made the announcement that thereafter Draupadi would be the emperor's wife alone and that they would have no physical relationships in future. The other four brothers would have to revere them as parents. They bowed in assent. The coronation of the emperor and empress was now performed on a grand scale. At the end of the ceremony came the *arghyapuja*, or worship of the noblest man present.

Yudhishthira had already decided in his own mind that Krishna alone was fit for that signal honor, but since there might be a difference of opinion among the rest, he asked his youngest brother Sahadeva, who was noted for his wisdom, to speak up. Without hesitation, Sahadeva said, "The worshipful Lord Krishna, the protector of all devotees, alone is worthy of this honor. This entire cosmos is His manifestation. This whole universe is His form. By His grace alone all these rituals have become fruitful and mankind can attain to the fourfold goals of *dharma, artha, kama,* and *moksha.*[2] What is the doubt, therefore, that He alone be worshipped as the foremost among the honored guests? By so doing, we shall be worshipping all beings, including ourselves. A tree may be very large, O King, with many branches spreading in many directions, some filled with flowers, some with fruits, and some with leaves. In fact, the branches and leaves may be so numerous that our attention may be caught by them alone, but when the time comes to water the tree, does anyone doubt where the water should be poured? Therefore, if you wish the fruits of your sacrifice to be without end, offer the *arghyapuja* to Krishna, the Soul of all, the Perfect, the Supremely Peaceful One, in whose eyes nothing is different from Himself."

Yudhishthira was very pleased by this speech of his wise, young brother. The Lord is the root from which this variegated tree of the

---

1 *soma juice*—juice of a plant growing in the Himalayas, which is offered as a libation in rituals (*yajnas*).
2 *dharma, artha, kama,* and *moksha*—righteousness, possessions, enjoyment, and liberation.

world has sprouted and spread. What doubt then, that it is His feet which should be washed in the final *puja* (worship ceremony)?

Bhishma, the grandsire of the Kurus, now added, "In this great and glorious assembly, Krishna shines as the sun in the midst of His own rays. Without Him, the hall will lose its lustre. He alone deserves the signal honor."

The sage Vyasa promptly endorsed this and declared Krishna to be God incarnate. So everything was prepared for the *arghyapuja*. The Lord was seated on a jeweled throne and Yudhishthira, accompanied by his brothers and Draupadi, came forward with jewel-studded, golden pots containing perfumed water. Placing the lotus feet of the Lord tenderly on a golden plate, Yudhishthira washed them lovingly with tears of joy and love overflowing from his eyes. His brothers and Draupadi followed suit. The water which was thus consecrated was sprinkled reverently on their own heads and then over the entire assembly. Making rich offerings of silks and ornaments to all, Yudhishthira stood with tears welling up in his eyes, overcome with emotion and unable to speak, so great was the bliss which threatened to overwhelm him. Everybody saluted the Lord, sitting resplendent on the throne and looking so charming that they felt themselves bathed in the radiance emanating from Him. Shouts of "Jai Krishna (victory to Krishna)! Jai Vaasudeva! Jai Govinda! Jai Madhava!" rent the air as they showered flowers on Him.

At this auspicious time, Shishupala, prompted by death himself, jumped up and said scornfully, "A bastard (Yudhishthira) has asked the son of a river (Bhishma) for advice. And the person chosen for *arghyapuja* is a poor cowherd who has eaten earth, stolen butter and *gopis'* clothes, dallied with them, killed His own uncle, Kamsa, and schemed to have the powerful Jarasandha killed. In this noble gathering of illustrious kings and holy *rishis*, could you not find anyone superior to this basest of the Yadavas? He is not the equal in birth or position of any one of us here and should never have been invited in the first place. To choose Him in preference to all others is an insult to this august assembly. O Yudhishthira! Don't think that we have submitted to you through fear or dread of your powers, it is because we honor your nobility and wisdom. Now that you have shown yourself to be devoid of both, it is better we do not stay to be further insulted. Come, O Kings! Let us kill this upstart Yadava immediately and defeat the Pandavas, who have subjected us to these intolerable insults!"

So spoke Shishupala after having bottled up his hatred for so many years. Immediately, the assembly broke up into factions, some siding with Yudhishthira and others Shishupala. The *Rajasuya* seemed in danger of degenerating into a vulgar brawl. Krishna alone took no notice of Shishupala's speech, as a lion does not notice a jackal's howls. Bhima, Arjuna, and Sahadeva, however, could not tolerate these insults and would have flung themselves on Shishupala and made an end of him then and there, but Yudhishthira held them back and tried his best to pacify Shishupala. Many in the assembly, unable to bear these insults to the Lord, closed their ears and walked out, for one incurs sin by even listening to the vilification of a holy personage.

Long ago, the Lord had made a promise to his aunt, Shishupala's mother, that He would calmly bear a hundred insults from her son, so He listened with a smile while Shishupala kept ranting. At last, Shishupala, having exhausted all the slurs he could hurl at both Krishna and Bhima and enraged at having met with no retaliation, sprang at Krishna like an angry cobra with hood upraised to strike, and challenged Him to a duel. Arjuna and the others immediately surrounded the Lord in order to protect Him. Krishna got up in a leisurely manner from the jeweled throne and moved His friends gently aside. He strode forward to meet the angry Shishupala, who had more than exhausted the quota of the hundred insults allotted to him. As Shishupala charged toward Him brandishing his sword, the Lord hurled His discus, the *Sudarshana*, at him with a look of infinite compassion on His face. In that split second before death overtook him, Shishupala remembered his previous lives and folded his hands and paid homage to his Master. The discus severed Shishupala's head from his body and a glow of light emerged from him and melted into the aura surrounding the Lord. Shishupala, like Kamsa, had lived for so long thinking only of Him that he had achieved identity with Him.

This miracle following Shishupala's end made Yudhishthira wonder who he had been, so he asked Narada to explain how a man who from childhood had spent his time disparaging Krishna could achieve union with Him.

The divine sage then explained how once the guards of Lord Vishnu's abode at Vaikuntha, known as Jaya and Vijaya, had barred the entry of the boy sages known as the Sanatkumaras into the presence of the Lord and the sages had cursed them that they would have to take birth on earth. They had appealed to Lord Vishnu, who had given them a choice. They could either take seven births on earth as His devotees or three extraordinary births as His enemies! Either way, they would have constant memory of Him and attain Him at the end of the stipulated period of time. They opted for the path of enmity, for it would enable them to return to Vaikuntha faster, but they pleaded that at each of these three births as His enemies, they should meet their end at the hands of their beloved Master alone. To this He had agreed. In their first births they had been born as the dreadful demons, Hiranyaksha and Hiranyakashipu, who were killed by the Lord in His incarnations as Varaha (the boar) and Narasimha (the man-lion), respectively. In their second births, as Ravana and Kumbakarna, they were killed by the Lord in His incarnation as Shri Rama. These were their final births, in which they were born as Shishupala and Dantavakra. The sage Narada now concluded his tale. "Shishupala has now been given salvation and Dantavakra will soon follow suit."

At the end of the *Rajasuya*, the emperor, together with his consort, was seated in a chariot decorated with golden chains drawn by excellent horses and taken around the city. After this, the priests made him take the ceremonial bath, together with Draupadi, in the holy river. This was known as the *avabrithasnana*. Drums blared and with joy the people showered flowers. Everyone who had attended the *Rajasuya* took a ceremonial bath in the river, since it was considered to be most auspicious. This was the concluding ceremony and the guests departed after having been honored by the emperor. The Pandavas persuaded Lord Krishna and the Kauravas to stay a while longer and enjoy their hospitality, as well as the sights of the city of wonders. Though the invitation was made in all good faith, yet it was to lay the foundation for the war between the cousins, as will be seen.

Seeing the splendor of the Pandavas' palace and the glory that the *Rajasuya* had brought them, Duryodhana felt sick with envy. He longed to possess all this for himself but did not know how he could accomplish it. One day, Yudhishthira was sitting on a golden throne in the Maya Sabha, or Hall of Illusions, looking like Indra, the king of gods, surrounded by his brothers, with Krishna sitting beside him. Just then, Duryodhana, wearing a diadem and many necklaces, approached the hall, surrounded by his brothers. Holding a sword in his hand he came in, showering abuses at the guards to show off his importance. As has been said before, the Maya Sabha was filled with optical illusions. Duryodhana thought it demeaning to ask questions and air his ignorance, which had already brought him to grief once before, when he had bumped his head hard against the wall as he had tried to pass through what he had thought to be a door. But that had not been so bad, for there had been no one with him and as he gave a quick glance around he had not seen anyone, though he did hear a suspicion of girlish laughter, which sounded vaguely familiar.

But on that particular day, surrounded by his brothers and in full view of the assembly, he came to what he thought was a lotus lake in the middle of the ball and carefully skirted it only to be met with the mocking laughter of Draupadi and Bhima and the titters of the others. Infuriated by this, he strode forward until he came to another pool, which he imagined to be another illusion. With a careless smile and a knowing look, meant to convince the onlookers of his superior knowledge of such things, he plunged in, only to find himself sprawling in an undignified heap in the water, his diadem awry, his clothes drenched, and his necklaces knotted up. Draupadi, unable to control her mirth this time, was in stitches. Bhima's guffaws filled the hall and almost all the other spectators were convulsed at the sight of the pompous Duryodhana in such a predicament. Yudhishthira alone, who could never bear the sight of another's distress, ran to comfort him and offered him rich and costly garments to replace the ones that had been ruined, but Duryodhana was not appeased by this and swore vengeance on Draupadi as well as the Pandavas. "In just such an open court as this," he swore to himself, "will I make her the laughingstock of the multitude!"

The Lord, in whose presence all this took place, remained silent. In fact, it is even suspected that it was His mischievous and encouraging look that emboldened Draupadi and Bhima to give way to their mirth! His ways are inscrutable, and who knows but this might have been engineered by Him in order to bring about a cause for the war.

The Kauravas left in a hurry and held an emergency council meeting as soon as they reached Hastinapura.

Shakuni taunted Duryodhana. "Did you see the prosperity of the Pandavas? I'm sure we were invited only so they could flaunt their wealth before us and humiliate us. Unless we do something soon, we will be destroyed."

Duryodhana was still brooding over his ridiculous fall. "Did you see how Bhima and Draupadi laughed aloud at my discomfiture? When I think of it, my blood boils. I will never rest in peace until the whole world laughs at Draupadi!"

Thus the Kauravas sat and plotted and thought of a hundred different schemes to get even with the Pandavas.

Lord Krishna and Balarama also left Indraprastha soon after, for they heard that Dwaraka was being besieged by King Salva of the Saubha. He had been Shishupala's friend and during the time of the Rukmini *svayamvara* had been witness to his embarrassment, and he had taken a vow before all the other kings that he would rid the world of the entire race of Yadavas. In order to accomplish this, he had done severe *tapasya* to Lord Shiva, who had given him an aerial vehicle called the Saubha, which was as big as a palace and which could be made invisible. Salva had bided his time and when he heard of Shishupala's death, he felt that it was the opportune time for him to attack Dwaraka, especially since he knew that both Krishna and Balarama were away and only Pradyumna had been left to hold the fort.

He attacked Dwaraka from the Saubha and destroyed the outer woodlands and gardens. Then he directed the attack against the various bastions of the city so that his army, which was marching overland, could easily penetrate it. Flashes of lightning, hailstones, cyclonic storms, and clouds of dust were released from the Saubha, which was equipped with all the latest types of weapons. Pradyumna and the other sons of Krishna ably defended the city for twenty-seven days. At last, Pradyumna was injured by a blow on the chest by Dyumna, Salva's minister, and he swooned. His charioteer took him away from the battlefield immediately. Pradyumna was very angry with his driver when he came to his senses, and he insisted on returning to the fray immediately.

Luckily, at this opportune moment the Lord arrived on the scene and charged forward into combat with Salva. When the latter found himself outmatched, he resorted to magical tricks and made Vasudeva's form appear before the Lord and then cut off his head. For a moment it seemed as if Krishna Himself trembled to see the fate of His dear father, but immediately He realized that it was but an illusion, and He rushed forward and killed Salva and destroyed the Saubha. Dantavakra, close friend of Salva and Shishupala, now came forward and Krishna made an end of him with His mace, the *Kaumodaki,* and, just as in the case of Shishupala, a strange light was seen to pass from him and melt into the Lord's aura, for he had also been one of the twin guards of Lord Vishnu, as explained by Narada.

The killing of Dantavakra marks the end of the second phase of the Lord's life—His *Raja Lila* or *Dwaraka Lila.* The next phase is almost entirely connected with the fortunes or misfortunes of the Pandava brothers.

Thus ends the twentieth chapter of The Play of God,
named "The Rajasuya Sacrifice."

Hari Aum Tat Sat

Whether we live in a cave or in a palace, in the forest or on a mountaintop, in water or in fire, there is no difference. He who has entrusted himself into Your keeping, O Lord, will ever be protected by you.
—ANONYMOUS

As the akola seed returns to the tree at night, as the iron filings rush to the magnet, as the faithful wife never deserts her husband in good and bad times, as the creeper clings to the tree and the river rushes to the ocean, so let my mind run to Thee, O Lord, and stay there forever.
—ANONYMOUS

O Krishna, Thou art the dwelling place for all good people, the ultimate goal for those in trouble, and the One who banishes the sorrow of Thy devotees. O Krishna, Thou art my only refuge!
—DRAUPADI, IN THE MAHABHARATA

BOOK THREE

UTTAMA–LILA

THE GAME SUPREME

Is this Thy *lila*, O Lord,
Thy game supreme,
To lift up the lowly
and make all holy?

Krishna—Arjuna

This frail reed Thou hast fashioned such,
Uplifting, ennobling by Thy very touch.
That which was despised by all,
Was enlivened, exalted by Thy call.
Considered hollow, worthless, scorned,
By Thy grace has become adorned.
Drinking the nectar of Thy rosebud lips,
It has poured out this unending song of bliss,
The description of Thy divine glories,
Couched in the form of enthralling stories,
As narrated by Thee to me, O Vanamali!

This *lila* is offered by Thy servant, Devi.

TWENTY-ONE

THE GAMBLING MATCH

Hrisheekeshaya namaha

Homage to the Lord of the senses

O Krishna, Thou dweller of the city of Dwaraka,
where art Thou, O darling of the Yadavas?
Why hast Thou forsaken me, alone and orphaned in this
terrible plight?
—ATTRIBUTED TO DRAUPADI, SOURCE UNKNOWN

While the Lord was thus engaged with Salva, momentous happenings were taking place at Hastinapura. At the emergency council meeting held by Duryodhana after his ignominious departure from the Maya Sabha, his friend Karna, to comfort him, proposed with his usual impetuosity that they should immediately march to Indraprastha and wipe out the Pandavas!

Shakuni said scornfully, "We will never be able to beat the Pandavas in an open battle, especially now, when they have the entire Bharatavarsha on their side. Though Karna is always boasting of his prowess, he has already been defeated once by Arjuna. So let's not talk of battle. I have a plan which will deprive the Pandavas of all their possessions without shedding a drop of blood. Yudhishthira has a weakness for gambling and I'm an adept at dice. If we can persuade him to accept a match on some pretext or other, I can assure you that I'll deprive him of everything."

Duryodhana was delighted by this simple solution to his problem and pestered his aged parent to send an invitation to the Pandavas. Since a pretext had to be found to invite them, a magnificent assembly hall similar to the Maya Sabha but inferior to it, was constructed. It was called the Jayanta Sabha, the Victory Hall. The invitation

197

had to be sent through a person revered by the Pandavas or else they might not accept it, so Duryodhana persuaded his doting father to write the invitation and instruct Vidura to take the message. The latter protested in the most vehement terms when he was given the order.

"Why are you stooping to such an atrocity?" he asked his nephew. "This will surely lead to your downfall. If you really covet the wealth of the Pandavas you have only to ask them openly. I assure you that Yudhishthira will be happy to hand over everything to you and retire to the forest, and his brothers will never disobey him."

Duryodhana was furious when he heard this and called his uncle an ungrateful wretch. "You eat our food and enjoy our shelter, but your heart is always with the Pandavas. Do what you are told!" he shouted.

Dhritarashtra also insisted that Vidura should go. It is strange that Bhishma, who was the soul of *dharma*, did not intervene. At last, Vidura agreed, for he thought that he had a chance of persuading Yudhishthira not to accept the invitation. He was welcomed with the greatest of affection by the Pandavas and Draupadi. He handed over the message and urged Yudhishthira not to accept it, since he was sure it was a trick concocted by Duryodhana and Shakuni. Yudhishthira then asked his brothers for their opinion. All of them except Bhima advised him to decline, but somehow he decided to accept.

"How can I refuse an invitation sent by my uncle who stands in the place of my father?" he asked.

Once again Vidura urged him to decline, but Yudhishthira remained firm in his decision.

"After all, it's only a friendly match," he said, "and I'm as good a player as my cousin. Moreover, if I do not accept, it will be an insult to you, for you have been sent to fetch me. It will also be an affront to my uncle, who has issued the invitation. Even if it leads to my downfall, let it not be said that Yudhishthira swerved from the dictates of honorable behavior." This was an occasion when Yudhishthira's adherence to *dharma* led to his ruin.

Vidura could do nothing more than to counsel him to be on his guard at all times. The Kauravas could hardly believe the good news. For once, Duryodhana was delighted with Vidura and he lifted him up onto the throne and said, "Uncle, I'm eternally grateful to you. Now I shall have a chance to make the world laugh at Draupadi and I shall also teach Bhima a lesson."

The Pandavas, accompanied by Draupadi, set forth to Hastinapura in five magnificent chariots. Reaching the city, they went to pay their respects to all the Elders. Later, they were escorted to their assigned quarters and Draupadi went to Gandhari's apartment. The next day, they were taken to admire the Jayanta Sabha. They were quite sincere in their admiration, especially Yudhishthira, who was determined to maintain cordial relationships at all costs. After this, Shakuni took over.

He said, "You have proved your superiority in all things, O Yudhishthira! Now let us test your skill in dice playing. We can thus pass the hours pleasantly."

Though he had a weakness for the game, Yudhishthira did not yield easily. He replied firmly, "It is well known that gambling is a terrible sin. Tell me frankly what you want from me and I shall gladly give it." Then, going to Bhishma, he whispered, "Are you and the Elders approving of this gambling match?"

Bhishma whispered back, "What is to happen will happen." Vidura alone made a final, desperate attempt to halt the impending catastrophe, but Duryodhana insolently ordered him to shut his mouth.

At this, Karna jeered. "Why are you so frightened of trying your fortune at a throw of dice? If this be so, how terrified you must be of trying your fortunes on the battlefield!"

This infuriated Arjuna and he strung his bow. This small incident appeared to help Yudhishthira to make up his mind, and he told Shakuni that he would play. Then Shakuni announced that he was going to throw the dice on Duryodhana's behalf and Yudhishthira protested. Shakuni silenced him by sneeringly asking whether he was looking for another excuse to back out. At this, Yudhishthira gave in with a sigh to what was inexorably the hand of fate beckoning him to his doom. The two of them sat down facing each other. Yudhishthira chose the white dice and Shakuni the blue.

Duryodhana said, "I shall wager on behalf of my uncle anything of equal value, if not more, to what Yudhishthira wagers."

Yudhishthira was in the habit of invoking the blessings of the Lord before starting any undertaking, but on this momentous occasion it seemed to have slipped his mind.

As soon as they had arrived, Duryodhana had greedily eyed the jewelled and magnificent chariot in which Yudhishthira had come, so that was the first thing to be wagered and lost. Following this, one by one he lost almost all his worldly possessions, for Shakuni was both a master player and a master cheat. His jewelry, elephants, horses, chariots, army, palaces, and finally his entire kingdom were lost. Shakuni's repeated shouts of victory and Duryodhana's triumphant exclamations started to become monotonous. No one in the assembly dared to intervene, perhaps for fear of Duryodhana's uncontrollable wrath. Strangely enough, it never occurred to Yudhishthira to mentally ask Lord Krishna for help. For once, the noble Yudhishthira seemed to have taken leave of his senses. He was now left with nothing, but Shakuni had not finished with him.

"I have nothing more to stake," Yudhishthira murmured.

But Shakuni taunted, "You have your brothers and one of them may prove to have the luck which you seem to lack!"

"I stake my brother Nakula," he said and flung the dice. "I have won," said Shakuni, as usual.

One by one he wagered all his beloved brothers and lost them all. After this, he no longer cared what happened to himself and hardly needed any encouragement from Shakuni to stake himself. With head bowed in shame, Yudhishthira sat as if carved of stone while uncle and nephew exchanged a meaningful look. Shakuni was in full command of the situation. "You still have your empress—Draupadi," he tempted. "If you wager her, perhaps she will be able to turn the tide. I am giving this advice out of sympathy for you."

At this, both Vidura and Bhishma raised their voices in protest and Arjuna took up his bow and Bhima his mace. Fearing that Yudhishthira might decline, Duryodhana quickly said, "If Draupadi is staked and Yudhishthira wins, I'm prepared to return all he has lost so far!"

His mind dulled by pain, his senses clouded with sorrow, Yudhishthira grasped at this last straw, hoping for a miracle to retrieve his failing fortunes. He staked his beloved queen as if she were some common baggage to be bought and sold in the marketplace. With bated breath, all watched the last, fatal throw of the dice. The result was preordained; Duryodhana's triumph was complete. The whole assembly was in an uproar. Duryodhana's voice roared above the rest. "The Pandavas are now our slaves. Let this be publicly announced here and in Indraprastha. Everything there now belongs to me. Let the Pandavas be taken to the kitchen to get acquainted with their new duties. Vidura! Go and fetch Draupadi from the women's quarters!"

Vidura said in fury, "Don't you see that you are heading for destruction? It is not too late to stop this farce even now. If you do not listen to me, you and your brothers will be destroyed."

Duryodhana retorted, "Yudhishthira gambled everything away of his own free will. If we have resorted to *adharma*, as you say, how is it that fortune has favored us and not the Pandavas?"

Bhishma protested mildly and Dhritarashtra said nothing. Since Vidura refused to go and fetch Draupadi, Duryodhana sent an agent. Unlike other women in her predicament who would have lamented, Draupadi refused to go at Duryodhana's behest.

"Go back and find out whether my husband lost himself first and then gambled me, or vice versa," she ordered. If he had lost her after having lost himself, it would not be considered valid, since he was already a slave and a slave had no right to stake anything. Duryodhana was furious when the messenger returned with this news. He ordered his brother Dusshasana to bring her forcibly, if necessary, to the open court and ask her questions in public.

Draupadi was having her monthly period and she was seated in a separate apartment, clad in a single piece of cloth, as was the custom. Heedless of her pitiful state, the wicked Dusshasana charged at her with a cruel laugh. Like a doe chased by a tiger, Draupadi fled to his mother Gandhari, and taking refuge behind her, she pleaded to be protected against her son. To Gandhari's eternal shame, she failed to give her the refuge that any woman deserved, let alone her own stepdaughter. She virtually pushed Draupadi into Dusshasana's arms with these words, "Throw off this pretense of modesty! After all, they are your brothers-in-law who are summoning you. So go!"

Now that he was openly supported by his mother, Dusshasana lost no time in grabbing Draupadi by her long tresses. When she resisted, he dragged her forcibly through the streets of Hastinapura to the assembly hall of the Kurus. All the citizens exclaimed in sympathy but none dared lift a finger to help. Draupadi, however, was a woman of great courage and determination. She did not weep and plead as any other woman might have done in her position. With head held high, she turned to her husbands Bhima and Arjuna. She did not expect them to fail her at this critical juncture. But they hung their heads down and would not look at her. To her dismay, she realized that they were equally helpless. Daunted not at all, she turned to the elders and enquired confidently, "Did the emperor lose himself first and then stake me? If so, the whole thing is null and void since he was no longer a free man and had no right to gamble with anyone. If, on the other hand, he staked me first, still it would be against the rules, for he has no absolute right over me, as I belong to all five of them!"

With a voice throbbing with fury Draupadi continued. "In this ancient house of the Kurus, reputed from time immemorial for the dispensing of *dharma*, *adharma* has reared its head. Here is this man drunk with power asking his brother to drag a woman into the court. Here is my husband, the image of *dharma*, sitting quietly. In the presence of all of you, I asked a simple question to which I was not given a reply. Did my husband wager me before or after he lost himself? Am I their slave? Answer me." She was seething with anger and looked daggers at her husbands. Yudhishthira would have been happy if the earth had swallowed him up then and there. The loss of his kingdom did not pain him so much as the burning glance of his beloved queen.

Draupadi turned to Bhishma. "Grandfather, can you not give me an answer?"

Bhishma, for the first time in his life, gave an equivocal answer. "I am indeed at a loss to give a proper answer to your question. A man cannot gamble something after he has lost himself, it is true, but a man has a right over his wife whether he is free or not. Accordingly, I cannot say whether you are free." Draupadi looked around like a stricken deer. Duryodhana and Karna were exultant and insulted her further by calling her a common woman owned by five men.

At last Vikarna, the youngest of the Kaurava brothers, rose and boldly spoke up for Draupadi. Karna told him to shut up and insultingly told Draupadi that she was now free to choose another husband from among the Kauravas. Duryodhana gloatingly ordered Dusshasana to remove the royal garments from the Pandavas, for they were now slaves and not qualified to wear such clothes. Vidura could bear it no longer and he cursed Duryodhana from the depths of his heart. "All of you will die one day at the hands of your righteous cousins," he said.

Duryodhana scoffed at his uncle's curse and ordered Dusshasana to proceed. Determined to adhere to *dharma* at all costs, the Pandavas threw down their upper garments.

Then Duryodhana commanded, "Undress their woman now! Take off her clothes and show her to the court for the shameless creature that she is. Let her see how helpless her husbands are to aid her."

Dusshasana, nothing loathe, jumped forward and started tugging at her one piece of cloth, stained with blood, which she was clutching to herself in desperation. Poor Draupadi! She knew that she was beyond all human aid. Neither the strength of her husbands nor her own wits had been able to save her. She had five husbands, all of them great warriors and kings among men. She herself was an empress in her own right, yet now, when she was in dire distress, there was none to lift a little finger to save her.

She had been holding her arms across her breasts in order to preserve the tattered remnants of her pride, but realizing her utter helplessness, she lifted up both her hands in supplication while Dusshasana laid his hands on her garment and tugged it. In utter despair, she cried aloud, "O Krishna, darling of the Yadavas, dweller at Dwaraka! Where are You? Why have You forsaken me who am helpless and alone and faced with disaster in this terrible predicament?" With this piteous cry she stood with hands uplifted in supplication and surrendered her body, mind, and spirit mentally to the Lord. The Lord was fighting with Salva at the time. For some moments, he lost interest in the battle and came to her aid, and that was the time when Salva was able to strike Him.

To the wonder of all who were assembled there, though Dusshasana pulled and pulled, yard after yard of material came out, but Draupadi still remained clothed. No amount of unwinding and tugging could denude her completely. Minutes passed while Dusshasana kept pulling and pulling and Draupadi kept chanting and chanting the names of the Lord. The entire floor was covered with heaps of cloth, yet Draupadi was still clad as before.

Thus Draupadi's agony changed to ecstasy. Even after the exhausted Dusshasana had collapsed on the floor utterly worn out by his labors, Draupadi kept chanting and singing the Lord's praises in ecstatic adoration. This is one of the most sacred incidents in the *Mahabharata* and is an example to all women that they are never as helpless as they think, so long as they have devotion to the Lord.

In fact, the entire life of the Pandavas is a great example to all devotees. They were most dear to Krishna, yet we find their lives to be filled with hardships. At one moment they were taken to the pinnacle of glory at the *Rajasuya*, when the whole of Bharatavarsha rose up to acclaim them as emperors, and the next moment they were branded as slaves. Humiliated and insulted by the very man they despised, they were buffeted hither and thither by the waves of misfortune and forced to endure the agony of seeing their beloved wife insulted and the frustration of being powerless to help her! What is the lesson to be learned? God's ways are mysterious. He is not interested in our material prospects or our physical problems. The sole aim of the divine is to fulfill the cosmic purpose of our achieving unity with Him, and for that no means are neglected. The selfish, individual ego has to be transmuted in the alternating fires of fortune and misfortune, honor and dishonor. All these dualities, which have such meaning and purpose in the life of the ordinary individual, have to be surmounted in the life of the Godman, to which state Krishna was leading His devotees the Pandavas, and that is why they had to pass through these trials. But in all their travails, the Lord Himself was at their side, ever helping and encouraging them. Even though sometimes He was not there physically, as was the case during Draupadi's predicament, yet it was apparent that He had never abandoned them even for a single moment.

As a means to overcome this setback caused by the miracle, Duryodhana crudely bared his thigh, exposed it to Draupadi, and invited her to sit on his lap. This was the final insult. She could bear it no longer. A dreadful curse broke from her lips. "One day, O Duryodhana, you will surely die on the battlefield with your thighs broken and vultures and wolves howling around you!"

Bhima, too, could contain himself no longer. Glaring balefully at Duryodhana, he swore, "May I never reach heaven if I do not kill all the Kauravas single-handedly. Duryodhana I shall kill by breaking his thighs! I swear this by Krishna, Durga,[1] and Shiva. I also swear to drink the blood of the wicked Dusshasana after killing him and to tie Draupadi's hair with my blood-stained hands. Until I achieve this, I shall not drink water with my hands, but only from the splash made by hitting my mace on water!"

Arjuna now took an oath to kill Karna, Sahadeva to kill Shakuni, and Nakula to kill Uluka, Shakuni's son. Finally, Draupadi also took an oath. "My hair will remain untied until Bhima anoints it with the blood of Dusshasana and at that time the hair of the Kaurava widows will droop down in bereavement."

The Kauravas roared with laughter at hearing these seemingly improbable events. Yet the law of *karma* is always just, and terrible is the effect of the curses of noble people who have been unfairly wounded. Time was to give truth to the words of the Pandavas.

Hearing all these terrible oaths, the blind king was alarmed and shaken out of his usual stupor. "Stop! Stop!" he cried. "Release the empress Draupadi!" Heedless of his father's commands, Duryodhana commanded

---

[1] *Durga*—The wrathful aspect of Kali, the Divine Mother (female aspect of God).

Draupadi to go inside and attend to his wife.

With great dignity, Draupadi answered, "I will go only after having bowed to the Elders. Due to the forcible way in which I was dragged here, I was unable to do so when I entered, but let it not be said that the Empress of Indraprastha was lacking in respect."

Slowly she went forward and bent before Bhishma, Drona, Vidura, and Dhritarashtra. Terrified by the oaths of the Pandavas, the latter said, "Ask for two boons, my daughter, and I shall grant them to you, for it is because of your nobility that God Himself has saved you today." Immediately, she asked for the release of her husbands together with their kingdom.

"So be it," said the king.

Before Duryodhana could remonstrate, Vidura hustled the Pandavas into their chariots. Duryodhana flew at his father and swore to kill himself unless the Pandavas were brought back and he was restored what he had so handily won.

Dhritarashtra demurred, but as usual gave in, and the Pandavas had hardly reached Indraprastha before they were recalled and invited to a single throw of the dice by the king, who had forced his son to come to some sort of compromise. The losers were to go into exile and live in the forest for twelve years and then to spend the thirteenth year incognito in some city. If they were discovered during this final period of one year, they were to repeat the entire process. Duryodhana agreed, for he did not expect the Pandavas to return alive or to remain undiscovered during the final period of one year. A fast messenger was sent after the Pandavas with the command that Dhritarashtra had asked them to return. Despite the pleas of his brothers and Draupadi, Yudhishthira foolishly ordered the horses to be turned back, for he insisted that he would not go against the dictates of *dharma* and disobey his Elders.

Once again, he was challenged by Duryodhana and Shakuni and the terms of the wager were explained. Dhritarashtra hastened to add that half the kingdom would be given back the moment they returned. Yudhishthira said not a word. He gave one last look of appeal at the grandsire's face, as if to confirm what had been said. There was a look of mute appeal on Bhishma's countenance, as if begging his forgiveness and asking him to understand. Yudhishthira thought he understood. For the past so many years Bhishma had but one thought and that was to preserve the unity of the Kuru dynasty against all odds. Despite many upheavals and in the face of insurmountable obstacles he had done so, even at the cost of his own happiness. Now he realized that unless the Pandavas were removed, Duryodhana would surely find a method of killing them. He had tried many times in the past and had failed, but who knew when he would succeed? Exile was the only way to avert this tragedy. Thus, the game was played and lost and Yudhishthira agreed to go, without so much as a murmur. "I shall always abide by what the Elders advise," he said. At that time, to the astonishment of everyone, Draupadi insisted that he should gamble just once more for their freedom, for she said that she wanted her husbands to go into exile as free men and not as slaves. Duryodhana and Shakuni insultingly asked what Yudhishthira had left to stake.

The latter answered, "I shall stake all the *punya* (spiritual merit) which I have accumulated so far."

Duryodhana was elated and, being sure of the outcome, pledged all Yudhishthira had lost in addition to their freedom. Just before the dice were thrown, Draupadi reminded Yudhishthira to chant the twelve names of Lord Krishna and thus invoke His blessings before throwing. For the first and last time, to the wonder of all, Yudhishthira won! With his usual high code of honor, he refused to take back the kingdom and accepted only their freedom. His kingdom, he said, he would claim only after the successful completion of their thirteenth year of exile. Thus, thanks to Draupadi's devotion, the Pandavas could depart with dignity. They left with Draupadi and their chief priest Dhaumya, discarding their kingly apparel and clad in deerskin and bark. They, who until now had been clothed in all the finery of the kingdom, were now clad in the attire of ascetics. Inscrutable are the ways in which divine justice works.

As they left, many omens were seen, boding ill for the Kauravas. Mother Kunti went to live with Vidura, for she refused to stay in Duryodhana's palace. Draupadi's five children by the five brothers were sent to their grandparents at Panchala and Subhadra went to Dwaraka. Followed by a host of weeping citizens and Brahmins, the Pandavas reached the outskirts of the city. Yudhishthira persuaded the citizens to return, but the Brahmins refused to go, since they said it would be wrong on their part to live in a kingdom ruled by an unrighteous king, and they insisted on accompanying him to the forest.

Thus ends the twenty-first chapter of The Play of God, *named "The Gambling Match."*

Hari Aum Tat Sat

THE EXILE

*Thou alone art my father, Thou alone art my mother, Thou
alone my beloved son and my dearest friend; Thou alone my one
confidant and my preceptor. Thou refuge of all the worlds, I am
Thine, Thy servant, Thy attendant. Thou art my goal, I take
refuge in Thee. This being so, I am verily a burden on Thee.*
—POPULAR VERSE

The Pandavas traveled fast. They wanted to get
away as far as possible from Hastinapura. Yudhishthira's first consideration after leaving the
city was how to feed the hoards of Brahmins who had
followed him. On Dhaumya's advice, he prayed to the
sun god, Surya, and procured the *akshaya patra*, or
bowl of plenty, from which any amount of food of any
type could be had. The only condition was that Draupadi should eat only after everyone else ate, like the ideal
Indian housewife, for after she ate, nothing more could
be procured from the bowl for that time. With this they
set out to the forest called Kamyaka. Vidura, who had
been harshly treated by both Duryodhana and Dhritarashtra and asked to get out, met them there and
spent some time with them. However, Dhritarashtra
could not live for long without his stepbrother and sent
Sanjaya to bring him back, much to Duryodhana's chagrin. Sage Vyasa and Sage Maitreya were the next to
visit them. They went back to Hastinapura and tried to
advise Dhritarashtra.

Vyasa said, "Your sons are doomed. The banished
princes will nurse their grievance and return with a
vengeance to destroy you, as well as the kingdom. Coax
your son to make peace with them, and let there be an
amicable settlement." Dhritarashtra hemmed and hawed
and did nothing, as usual.

Next, Maitreya tried to reason with Duryodhana, but the latter insulted him by smiting his thigh and the sage cursed him "Bhima's oath will come true and you will lose your life when your thighs are broken by him!"

All these events had taken place while Krishna was fighting with Salva. As soon as He heard the news, He went Himself to the Kamyaka forest accompanied by all the heroes of the Vrishni clan, as well as by Draupadi's brother Drishtadyumna. They were pained to see the condition in which the emperor was living. Krishna tested Yudhishthira by offering to help him get his kingdom back immediately, but the latter refused, for he didn't want to break his word.

When she saw Krishna and her brother, Draupadi's grief was intensified. Their righteous anger was such a contrast to her meek husbands. "O Janardana! I am the favored queen of the five Pandavas, who are the greatest heroes of the world. I am the daughter of the King of Panchala and the sister of the heroic Drishtadyumna, yet see what they did to me. I was dragged by the hair and insulted in front of the Elders! What do I care if Yudhishthira is called the sole monarch of the earth when my hair, which was purified by the sacred waters of the *Rajasuya*, was grabbed by Dusshasana? Had it not been for Your grace, I would have been completely disrobed in full gaze of my heroic husbands." She had been bottling up her emotions all these days, but when she saw the look of compassion on the Lord's face, she broke into uncontrollable sobs. Krishna cupped her face in His lotus palms and wiped away her tears with the hem of His upper robe.

"O Panchali," He said. "Be patient for a while. At the end of thirteen years the women of the Kuru clan will weep as you are weeping now. When Arjuna's arrows quench their thirst in Karna's blood, they will weep. When Bhima's hands are red with Dusshasana's blood, they will weep. When Duryodhana lies on the battlefield with his thighs broken, they will weep. Nothing can stop this inexorable law of cause and effect—the law of *karma*. The heavens may fall, the snowy peaks of Himavan may tumble down, and the seas may dry up. The earth may split into a million splinters, but My words will never fail. Therefore, dry your tears, my dear sister, and try to forgive your husbands, who were powerless to help you." After this, He comforted Yudhishthira and the others and returned to Dwaraka, promising to come whenever they needed Him.

Dhaumya now advised them to go to Dvaitavana, which was a picturesque forest more like an overgrown garden, filled with flowers, fruit, and beautiful peacocks and birds. It was also the abode of many *rishis*. Yudhishthira lived in these sylvan surroundings as happily as he had in Indraprastha. He was a great soul who had risen above the dualities of life and basked as happily in his adversity as he had in his prosperity. He enjoyed the company of the sages and realized that suffering was a necessary condition of the spiritual life and that true greatness was to rise above it.

The great sage Markandeya came to them at that time and told them the story of Shri Rama, the son of Dasharatha, who had to spend fourteen years in exile in the forest with His brother and His beloved queen, who was abducted by Ravana, the demonic King of Lanka.

Hearing of the carefree life the Pandavas were enjoying in the forest, Duryodhana was once again troubled by his former ailment, jealousy. He racked his brains to find some method of destroying them if possible. At that time, the sage Durvasa came to the palace accompanied by his ten thousand disciples and demanded hospitality for as long as he chose to stay. He worried Duryodhana constantly with his unreasonable demands at odd times of the day, for the sage took great pleasure in testing people. Duryodhana bent backwards in his efforts to please the sage, for the latter's bad temper was proverbial and he didn't want to risk a curse! At last, Durvasa pronounced himself satisfied and told him to ask for a boon. The crafty Duryodhana immediately thought of a plan to get the sage to curse the Pandavas and thus bring about their downfall.

Very meekly, Duryodhana said, "O Holy One! My cousins, the Pandavas, live a simple life in the forest. Do please go there at about three in the afternoon with Your disciples, for they will consider themselves blessed if holy ones like you visit them."

"So be it," said Durvasa and promptly went to the Kamyaka forest at a time when the Pandavas and their retinue had already finished their meal for the day. Draupadi had eaten and cleaned the vessel after eating. Her heart sank when she saw the sage and his hungry-looking disciples. She had not only eaten but had washed and put the bowl away. Durvasa informed Yudhishthira that he would go to the river with his disciples, take a bath, and thus return with a healthy appetite for lunch. Draupadi was in a real dilemma and as usual when desperate, she appealed to Krishna.

"O Krishna, You are the tree which shelters all good people and the savior of those in trouble. You alone can remove the sorrows of Your devotees. You, O Lord, are my sole refuge."

So saying, she sank to the ground in an attitude of utter supplication. As she opened her eyes she saw the beauteous form of the Lord approaching her with his usual tender smile. She ran forward to explain her predicament, but He brushed her aside and said, "O Panchali, I'm so hungry. Give Me something to eat first and then we'll talk."

"O Lord," she pleaded, "this is not the time for joking. I've already eaten and washed the *akshaya patra* and the sage Durvasa and his ten thousand disciples have come. There is not a grain of food in our humble hermitage. What should I do?"

"Never mind," Krishna said encouragingly. "Being a princess and most unused to hard work, I'm sure you would not have washed the bowl very well. There must be something left in it for Me. Go and get it."

Sadly, Draupadi went to get the bowl, which she had scoured and put away a few moments ago. Krishna searched the bottom very carefully and brought out a microscopic bit of spinach leaf and a grain of rice, which were sticking to the bottom, much to Draupadi's shame. Placing His precious find in His palm, He asked Draupadi to pour a little Ganga water into it and drank the concoction with evident relish.

"Ah! Now I'm replete," He said. "Let Bhima go and invite the sage and his disciples for their meal."

"But, Lord, what shall we feed them?" Draupadi pleaded.

"Never mind all that. Let Bhima go," said Krishna.

Bhima went to the riverbank to find that the sage and his disciples had finished their bath and were burping as if they had just had a full meal. When Bhima invited them, they protested that they could not eat anything, since they suddenly felt very full. In fact, they had been on the verge of creeping off without returning to the hermitage, for they feared that a hearty meal had been prepared for them to which they would not be able to do justice. Durvasa, of course, realized by his *yogic* powers that the reason for all these untoward happenings was Duryodhana's jealousy. He was so angry at having been made a stooge that he cursed Duryodhana with a speedy end and blessed the Pandavas with all success in their mission.

When asked for an explanation for this miracle, the Lord explained that He had eaten the morsel with the *bhavana*, or conception, that He was the Lord of the universe and immediately the entire universe with all its beings was simultaneously satisfied and felt replete. He blessed Draupadi and the Pandavas and left for Dwaraka.

The Pandavas spent six years in the forest very happily and had many adventures. Vyasa advised Arjuna to do *tapasya* to Lord Shiva[1] and procure the formidable *Pashupata* weapon from Him. The brothers had perforce to be separated, and Arjuna went and did severe *tapasya* to Shiva. Hearing of Arjuna's *tapasya*, Duryodhana compelled a *rakshasa* friend of his called Muka to take on the form of a wild boar and kill him. Muka agreed and went to the forest. At the same time, Lord Shiva and His consort Parvati came in the guise of a wild hunting couple in order to bless Arjuna. They stalked the boar that had come to kill Arjuna. As the boar charged, Arjuna woke from his *tapasya* and discharged an arrow at it. Simultaneously, an arrow from the divine hunter also pierced the boar. It fell down dead and Arjuna claimed the kill as his own, while the hunter insisted that it was killed by His arrow. The argument soon led to a duel. Arjuna's arrows seemed powerless to penetrate the hunter's skin. Soon he found his quiver exhausted and his bowstring cut by the hunter. In a fury, he flew at Him and smote Him with a blow from his bow. It is said that everyone felt the pain of the blow, for Shiva was none but the Supreme.[2] Without a change in His demeanor, He chided Arjuna, "How unfair of you to strike me with your bow. I can do likewise but I shall refrain. Come let us now wrestle with each other."

So they grappled with each other and Arjuna felt himself imbued with new energy at the mere touch of the Lord's hands. But, though Arjuna fought gallantly, his blows made no mark on the hunter, who carried on with ease. Sore and perplexed, Arjuna hastily made an image, a *linga*, of Lord Shiva and worshipped it with a garland. He then turned around and saw the hunter standing before him adorned with the garland he had just placed reverently round the *linga*. Arjuna then recognized the hunter to be none other than His beloved God, Shiva, accompanied by His consort Parvati and their son Kartikeya! He threw himself at His feet and begged for forgiveness. Shiva was well pleased with His devotee's courage and expertise in warfare and told him to ask for any boon. Arjuna was a true devotee and humbly said, "I have been blessed with a vision of Your divine form. I have wrestled with You and Your feet have touched me. I am thus thrice blessed. What more can I want?"

---

[1] *tapasya* to Shiva—It is a Hindu belief that by doing austerities of various kinds (*tapasya*) directed to God or great spiritual beings, material or spiritual benefits may be gained.

[2] "Shiva was none but the Supreme"—In India there are many who are devoted to Lord Shiva as the Supreme, just as many others are devoted to Lord Krishna. Though there is some times a rivalry between the devotees of each about who is greater, those with a more universal view see Krishna and Shiva both as embodiments of the Divine.

212 · *The Play of God – Visions of the Life of Krishna*

But at the Lord's insistence, he asked for the Pashupata weapon. Shiva gave it to him and warned him of its destructive potency. He told him to use it only in desperate situations.

"You will be able to defeat your enemies and, helped by Krishna, you will cleanse the world of its atrocities," He said.

After this, Arjuna's father, Indra, requested him to accompany him to his heavenly abode in order to help him defeat certain demons with the Pashupata. He did so, and the grateful Indra loaded him with many divine weapons and blessings. However, he had managed to invoke a curse from the celestial beauty Urvashi for having resisted her overtures. She cursed him that, having behaved like a eunuch, he would have to spend one year of his life as one! This, however, proved to be a blessing in disguise, for he made good use of it in their thirteenth year of exile, which had to be spent incognito.

After Arjuna's departure, the Pandavas spent their time with great difficulty, for he was a general favorite and always managed to keep them in good spirits with his ready wit. On top of this, Yudhishthira had to put up with Bhima's and Draupadi's constant nagging that it was his weakness that had brought them to this pass and that it was ill-befitting a *kshatriya* to take things so meekly. At this time, Sage Brihadvasa came to them and cheered Yudhishthira by teaching him the royal art of dice playing, called *akshahridaya*, so that no one would ever be able to defeat him again. Then came Sage Vyasa who advised them to go on a long pilgrimage. First they went to the sacred forest called Naimisha and then gradually wended their way along the western coast of the peninsula until they came to Prabhasa, the port adjoining Dwaraka, where they were met by Krishna and Balarama. The latter was furious with Duryodhana and urged Yudhishthira to fight the Kauravas then and there. Krishna said, "Brother, Yudhishthira is advising patience not because he is not powerful but because he wants to keep his word. Truth is greater to him than wealth. Let us respect his wishes. The time is not too distant when he will regain what he has lost."

After spending many happy days with their beloved friends, the Pandavas wended their way northward until they reached Binusaras, which was the source of the Ganga. Then they proceeded to the *ashrama* called Badri, where the ancient sages Nara and Narayana were said to be meditating. Here they were overtaken by a terrific storm, in which Draupadi nearly died. Yudhishthira took her head on his lap, while Nakula and

Sahadeva gently stroked her torn and blistered feet.

Yudhishthira, in a burst of self-condemnation, said, "O Panchali! Your father gave you to us with the promise that the Pandavas would give you great happiness. But, my poor wife, after marrying us, you have known nothing but pain. Please try to forgive this erring husband of yours."

Draupadi did her best to comfort the king. Soon the beauty of the *ashrama* crept into their hearts and they almost forgot their woes. One day, a beautiful flower with an intoxicating perfume wafted toward Draupadi and fell at her feet. Draupadi begged Bhima to get her more of these flowers. Bhima was only too happy to oblige and set out like a hound following the perfume of the flower. Very soon, he found his path blocked by a gigantic monkey. He requested the ape to let him pass, but the monkey said, "I'm too old and feeble to move, but if you like you may remove my tail from your path and carry on."

With a tolerant smile, Bhima tried to lift the monkey's tail with his left hand, but found that it wouldn't budge an inch. Next, he used both hands, with the same result. Surprised at this, he used his mace to dislodge the tail and found his mace cracking! He went and prostrated to the huge simian and begged him to tell him who he was. The monkey smiled and said, "I'm your brother Hanuman, the son of Vayu."[3]

At this, Bhima fell at his feet and begged his pardon. Hanuman clasped him in his hairy arms and assured him that he would do all that he could to ensure their success in the coming war. He offered to sit on Arjuna's flagstaff and frighten the enemy, thus helping them to win the war. The brothers embraced each other and Bhima went on his way. Hanuman had told him that the name of the flower was Saugandhika and it grew in the garden of Kubera, god of wealth. Kubera allowed Bhima to pluck the flowers and Bhima returned to Draupadi and covered her with the flowers she had coveted.

It was now five years since they had parted from Arjuna and they were most anxious to meet him again. It was at Badrikashrama that the glad reunion took place. After hearing about all of Arjuna's wonderful adventures, the Pandavas set out on their return journey to the plains. Eleven years of their exile had passed. Only two more years were left.

Thus, the Pandavas passed through the fires of austerity and hardship,

---

3 Hanuman— one of the central characters in the Indian epic *The Ramayana*, a monkey, who is revered by Hindus as the perfect devotee of Ram (God) and who as a result of this devotion is said to be all powerful and invincible. He helped rescue Lord Ramachandra's wife, Sita, from the demon Ravanna.

keeping their minds ever on the Lord, growing in wisdom, humility, and strength. On one occasion, they decided to invite Krishna for lunch. Arjuna thought he could summon Him at any moment, but found that all his prayers and pleas were of no avail. Then Bhima flung up his mighty mace into the air and standing directly below the falling weapon he said, "Krishna, if you do not come immediately, I shall die beneath the weight of this mace!" The Lord appeared immediately and Arjuna, who had always prided himself on being the Lord's favorite, realized the worth of Bhima's devotion.

On another occasion, the Lord visited them, accompanied by His wife Satyabhama. When the latter saw how her five husbands doted on Draupadi, she was impelled to ask her for a hint as to how she managed to please all five, when she herself found it difficult to manage just one. Draupadi smiled and said "My greatest happiness lies in attending to the slightest wants of my husbands. I treat all five alike. Their happiness is my happiness, their sorrow my sorrow."

This episode was no doubt engineered by the Lord, for Satyabhama was a self-willed woman with no fear of voicing her opinions. Krishna loved her dearly and did not think it necessary to curb her high spirits; yet He did want her to hear the qualifications of a perfect wife from a woman like Draupadi, who also had a mind of her own. Draupadi was far from being a meek and mild creature, yet she managed to get her own way by pleasing her husbands, not by dominating them. Thus, she kept her own personality intact, yet remained a perfect wife.

Duryodhana's days of peace were coming to a close. In order to cheer him up, Karna came up with a brilliant suggestion. "My friend," he said, "you are now Lord of the world. Why do you have to worry about the fact that the Pandavas' exile is coming to a close? They are wandering about in the forests like beasts. Come, let us make a trip to the forest of Dvaitavana on the pretext of inspecting our cattle. Seeing the splendor of your retinue, the Pandavas will become green with envy, and when that woman Draupadi sees our wives dressed in all their finery, she will be livid. Come, let's go and watch the fun."

This scheme was joyfully accepted by Duryodhana, and all the Kaurava brothers set out with their wives on a pleasure trip. When they heard that the Pandavas were camped near a lake, they decided to go there for a swim. But a *gandharva* (celestial singer) was already sporting in the lake with his wives and he ordered Duryodhana's men to tell their master that he would not tolerate any disturbance. Duryodhana was highly scornful of this order and marched toward the lake, but both Duryodhana and Karna were routed, not to mention the others. The *gandharva* finally grabbed the king by his hair and dragged him off. Their women were also taken away. In despair, Duryodhana's men ran to Yudhishthira, told him their shameful story, and begged him to rescue their king. Bhima refused to go at first, but Yudhishthira insisted and the brothers set out on their rescue operation. After a preliminary skirmish, the *gandharva* revealed himself to Arjuna as Chitrasena, his friend who had taught him music and dancing during his sojourn in Indra's heaven. The Kuru monarch and his brothers and women were handed over to the Pandavas, much to Duryodhana's chagrin. Yudhishthira released him and advised him not to do such spiteful deeds again. Duryodhana was filled with anger and sorrow. Not only was he unable to humiliate the Pandavas, as he had wanted, but they had forced him to eat humble pie. In fact, he owed his very life to Yudhishthira's generosity. He felt it would be better to die than to return to Hastinapura and was all set to take his own life. Karna and Dusshasana made him desist from this unworthy act and took him back to the city.

Once, when the Pandavas had gone out hunting, Duryodhana's brother-in-law, Jayadratha, passed that way. Seeing Draupadi at the door, he was smitten by her beauty and forcibly abducted her in his chariot. The Pandavas returned and gave chase and, though Jayadratha's forces were formidable, they were no match for the fury of the Pandavas. Bhima was all set to stomp him to death like a viper, but Arjuna dissuaded him and reminded him that he was the husband of Dussala, Duryodhana's little sister, and should be spared.

Jayadratha was too ashamed to return to his city. He remained in the forest, did intense *tapasya* to Lord Shiva, and asked Him for the boon of being able to vanquish the Pandavas.

Lord Shiva replied, "You will never be able to vanquish the Pandavas, who are protected by Lord Vishnu in His *avatar* as Krishna. But I will grant you this boon, that you will be able to do them some grave injury."

Jayadratha had to be satisfied with this, and he returned to his city determined to do some harm to the Pandavas, forgetting the fact that he was the one who had wronged them and not the other way around.

In their twelfth year of exile, the Pandavas were tested severely by Yamadharma, Yudhishthira's father, the god of righteousness. He created a poisoned lake to which the brothers went for water and all four of the younger ones died by drinking the water. At last, Yudhishthira went to find out what had happened and saw them all lying dead on the shore of the lake. A voice from the lake informed him of how they had died and offered to bring them back, provided he answered the questions which were put to him. Yudhishthira agreed and the *yaksha* (a spirit), as the voice called itself, began questioning him on every aspect of ethics and righteousness, all of which Yudhishthira answered perfectly. Some of the questions are worth noting.

"What makes a Brahmin?"

"Virtue and good behavior, not birth or education."

"What is the most surprising thing in the world?"

"The fact that day after day everyone sees death occurring, yet we all feel it will not happen to us."

"Who is the one who can be called wealthy?"

"The one who treats alike happiness and sorrow, pain and pleasure, loss and gain, past and future."

Thus, Yudhishthira answered many such questions put by the *yaksha* with wisdom and humility, for he knew that the lives of his brothers depended on his answers. At last, the voice said, "I'm pleased with your answers and I shall grant you the life of one of your brothers. Whom shall it be?" Unhesitatingly, Yudhishthira asked for Nakula's life.

The voice enquired, "Why do you not ask for the life of Bhima or Arjuna, who are your own brothers?"

Yudhishthira replied calmly, "I cannot swerve from *dharma* even for the sake of affection. Among my mother's sons, at least I am alive. To balance this, let one of the sons of my stepmother Madri also be brought to life."

The voice now materialized itself as Yamadharma, the god of death and righteousness. In order to test the integrity of his son, he had devised the poisoned lake and he was extremely pleased by the answers given by Yudhishthira. He restored all his brothers to him and said, "I assure you that no one will recognize you in your thirteenth year of exile. But remember that both victory and righteousness will ever prevail wherever Lord Krishna is, so you must follow Him in all things."

Thus, their twelfth year of exile came to a dramatic conclusion. Yudhishthira sent off his retinue of servants and followers to Dwaraka and his preceptor Dhaumya to Drupada, for he did not want any of them to know of their whereabouts. The brothers discussed the matter among them-

selves and decided to spend their thirteenth year incognito in Upaplavya
at the court of Virata, King of Matsya. Each one chose a disguise and an
occupation fitting to his temperament. Yudhishthira, the true Brahmin,
called himself Kanka, a Brahmin who was skilled in the art of dice playing
and decided to become a courtier. Bhima chose to call himself Valala, a
person skilled in the culinary arts, and decided to apply for the post of
cook at the palace. In his spare time, he could amuse people by wrestling.
Arjuna utilized Urvashi's curse, which turned out to be a blessing, for he
could go as a eunuch called Brahannala to teach music and dancing to the
king's daughter, Uttara. Nakula, who was skilled in the equestrian arts,
took the name of Damagranthi. He could tame the king's horses and proposed to become master of the stable. Sahadeva, who was an expert on
cattle, called himself Tantripala and applied for a post in the king's dairy.
Draupadi had perforce to take on the occupation of the queen's companion and dresser and called herself Sairandhri. Having decided on their
plans, they concealed their weapons inside the hide of a dead cow and hid
the bundle on top of a tree in the middle of a burial ground, so that
inquisitive eyes would not dare probe too closely.

They then took a fond farewell of each other and proceeded to the
city of Upaplavya separately. They were easily accepted by the king in
their new identities. Sudeshna, the queen, was at first reluctant to accept
Draupadi, for she was frightened that her husband might fall victim to
her charms. But the latter said that she was an expert in all matters pertaining to a lady's toilette and gave the name of Satyabhama, Lord Krishna's wife, as reference. She also hinted that she was married to five
gandharvas who would have no compunction in throttling the life out of
anyone who dared to molest her. Thus, having set the queen's mind at
rest, Draupadi was also employed.

Though Virata was the King of Matsya, all power was vested in the
hands of his commander in chief, Kichaka, who was also his brother-in-
law, the younger brother of the queen. Since he was an expert in warfare,
all kingdoms including that of the Kurus treated him with respect and
fear. During the first ten months of the Pandavas' stay, Kichaka had been
away on one of his numerous military expeditions. As soon as he
returned, he went to his sister's apartments loaded with gifts for her and
there, unfortunately, he set eyes on Draupadi and was smitten by her
charms. But all his persuasions failed to entice the maid, whom he
expected to be an easy prey. Poor Draupadi had to suffer innumerable

insults from him. He refused to take "no" for an answer, as he could not believe that a mere maidservant could be totally impervious to his wealth and personal charm. At last, unable to bear it any longer, she appealed to Bhima to save her.

They concocted a plan. Draupadi invited Kichaka to visit her in the night in a certain room. Kichaka was thrilled to find that at last the citadel had fallen, as he had fully expected. He went attired in all his finery, but Bhima had taken Draupadi's place and instead of two soft arms, he found two bands of steel gripping him in a stranglehold from which he could not escape alive. The next morning, everyone was horrified to find Kichaka dead and questioned Draupadi, who hinted that the deed might have been done by her *gandharva* husbands, since the queen had refused to help her.

The year was coming to an end and Duryodhana began to get desperate, for his spies had been unable to discover the Pandavas' whereabouts. It was at this time that he got the news that Kichaka, the invincible general of the land of Matsya, had been strangled to death by an unknown assailant on account of a woman. Duryodhana was jubilant when he heard this, for he was sure that the assailant could be none other than Bhima. He made a pact with his allies, the Trigartas, and they decided to make a combined raid on the kingdom of Matsya to steal Virata's prize cattle. Now that Kichaka, the commander-in-chief of the army, was dead, the country was defenseless. The Trigartas were to charge from the south and lure Virata's army away, while the Kauravas approached from the north and stole the cattle. Duryodhana was sure that he would be able to unmask the Pandavas, who would undoubtedly come to aid their benefactor, King Virata.

The attack from the south threw the king into a panic, but Yudhishthira offered to go with the cook, the master of the stable, and the master of the cattle in order to repulse the Trigartas. Virata was persuaded to lend them some armor and the entire army went with them, defeating the enemy easily. In the meantime, as planned, the Kauravas were coming down from the north, and this news was brought to a city peopled by women and children alone. This time, Draupadi came to the rescue and advised the queen to entrust her young son, Uttara Kumara, into the capable hands of the dancing teacher, Brihannala, who she claimed, was an excellent charioteer. "With him wielding the reins, your son will surely defeat the invaders," said Draupadi.

After a show of reluctance, Arjuna consented to drive the chariot for the young prince and the two set off in hot haste to the north. The faint-hearted prince had to be forced to accompany him. But as soon as they left the city gates, Arjuna exchanged places with him and told him to have no fear, for he would do the fighting, provided the prince charioted him properly. This the prince agreed to do, so Arjuna took him to the tree where their weapons had been hidden and took out his bow, Gandiva, and his quiver of inexhaustible arrows. It is said that the day on which Arjuna retrieved his bow was *Vijaya dasami* day, the victorious tenth day of the yearly worship of the goddess Durga. The day also marked the end of their thirteenth year of exile.

Thus armed, they proceeded toward the north, where the cattle rustlers were rounding up the prize cattle. Uttara Kumara quaked with fear when he saw the advancing host, but Arjuna bolstered up his courage and told him to drive on. Like an avenging angel, Arjuna fell upon the Kuru hoards, who recognized him despite his strange garb. Seated in the chariot driven by the trembling prince, Arjuna wrought havoc in the ranks of the marauding army and rescued the king. He fought with the full fury of a man wronged and the Kauravas were forced to retreat. Duryodhana turned tail and fled, but Arjuna pursued him, taunted him with cowardice, and forced him to fight. He was severely wounded. Arjuna desisted from killing him, for he was reserving him for Bhima, but in order to humble his pride he knocked off Duryodhana's crown.

Duryodhana shouted at him, "All of you will have to go back into the forest for another thirteen years, for I have discovered you!"

Arjuna flung back, "Consult your Elders. They will confirm that the stipulated period of thirteen years ended an hour ago. But don't be afraid; I shall spare your life since I don't kill cowards in flight. Moreover, my brother Bhima has sworn to kill you!"

Now Karna came forward and challenged him, but Arjuna forced him to admit defeat and Karna had to retreat.

Thus, having routed the Kuru army, the victorious pair drove back to the tree, where Arjuna replaced the weapons. They then drove back to the palace. The king was quite bewildered by the extraordinary happenings of the day. He congratulated his young son on his brilliant victory, but the prince confessed that it was the dancing master who had saved the day! This puzzled the king even further, so Yudhishthira explained the whole story to him. The king was very happy that he had unwittingly provided a haven to the Pandavas. He offered to give his daughter Uttara in marriage to Arjuna, but the latter refused the offer since she was his pupil and was thus in the position of a daughter to him. However, in order to cement the alliance with the Matsya kingdom, he accepted her as a daughter-in-law and bride for his son Abhimanyu, the nephew of Lord Krishna. This was joyfully received and the message was sent to Dwaraka. Abhimanyu was a handsome youth and a brilliant archer and he came accompanied by Krishna and the other Yadavas.

The Pandavas went with Virata to the outskirts of the city to welcome Krishna and Balarama. They fell at His feet and said, "By Your grace, O Lord, we have finished the thirteen years. You are our sole refuge. We will do whatever You want us to do. You mean everything to us." Krishna was overcome with pity when He looked at His dear cousins. He lifted up the weeping Draupadi, dried her tears, and told her, "O Panchali, do not weep. The time for tears is over. The day is near when the smiles should come back to your face. I will set about fulfilling the promise I made in the Kamyaka forest thirteen years ago."

The Pandavas had thus patiently and brilliantly gone through their period of exile. They had undergone terrible hardships, but their suffering had only helped to cleanse and purify them. They had met many great sages and received their blessings. Arjuna had procured numerous divine weapons. They had visited all the holy and sacred spots of Bharatavarsha and had emerged nobler than before. They were now ready to face whatever the fates held in store for them. They were confident that with the help of the Lord they would be able to support the cause of righteousness and emerge victorious.

Thus ends the twenty-second chapter of The Play of God, *named "The Exile."*

Hari Aum Tat Sat

He who worships Me constantly and exclusively through the performance of his duties, knowing My presence in all beings, soon attains to steadfast devotion.
—LORD KRISHNA IN THE ADVICE TO UDDHAVA, SHRIMAD BHAGAVATA

TWENTY-THREE

THE LORD AS AMBASSADOR

Jagadeeshvaraya namaha

Homage to
the God of
the Universe

I shall ever look to the maintenance of the material and spiritual welfare of those who think of Me constantly and worship Me with single-pointed devotion.
—SHRIMAD BHAGAVAD GITA

King Virata allotted a village to the Pandavas from which they could consult their friends and allies and decide on their future plan of action. Yudhishthira invited Lord Krishna and his other well-wishers and requested them to give their opinion as to how they could best proceed. Dhritarashtra had promised to give them back their share of the kingdom as soon as they came back from their thirteenth year of exile, but it was also clear that Duryodhana was in no mood to abide by this promise.

Lord Krishna was the first to speak. "The Pandavas and Kauravas are equally related to us, and the course of action that we adopt must be fair and acceptable to both sides. The Pandavas have successfully fulfilled the terms of their exile. Hence, I aver that the Kauravas, in turn, must keep to their part of the bargain—restore half the kingdom to them, and live in peace and harmony."

Balarama now spoke, "In my opinion, the completion of the thirteen years of exile entitles the Pandavas to nothing more than their freedom and not to the kingdom. Duryodhana should be persuaded gently to give half the kingdom, but he cannot be compelled to do so, since Yudhishthira knowingly gambled away the Pandavas' share. Now that he has enjoyed the whole kingdom for so long, I think it unlikely that Duryodhana will agree to part with it."

The furious Satyaki now jumped up and said, "I don't agree at all. Our virtuous cousin Yudhishthira was compelled to gamble. Even though he knew that Shakuni was an adept at dice, he chivalrously accepted the challenge since he did not wish to displease his uncle, and Dhritarashtra has promised to give back half the kingdom after the successful completion of the exile."

The others unanimously agreed with this and all promised their wholehearted support. Lord Krishna wound up the discussion. "Peace is always preferable to war," He said, "because in a war neither party really wins. Only suffering results. Thousands of women become widows. What the Pandavas lost by gambling, let them try to redeem through an ambassador of peace and goodwill. The messenger should be soft-spoken, patient, and full of wisdom. The sage Uluka in Virata's court has all these qualities, so let him be sent as an ambassador of peace. In the meantime, let us also be prepared mentally to fight, in case Duryodhana refuses our overtures of friendship."

Uluka was thus sent to Hastinapura and was received by all the Elders and the Kauravas. He spoke, "I come as Yudhishthira's ambassador of peace and goodwill. He always adheres to *dharma* and wants nothing that is not rightfully his. King Dhritarashtra promised to return his share of the kingdom on the Pandavas' return from exile. He asks you to keep your promise, therefore, and let your sons and nephews live in peace. But do not make the mistake of thinking that Yudhishthira's love of peace stems from cowardice. The Pandavas are invincible in war."

Bhishma now spoke. "Uluka has indeed spoken words filled with wisdom. The Pandavas in their goodness will forget the wrongs that have been done to them, as well as their terrible oaths. Their term of exile was fully over before Arjuna revealed himself during the cattle raid. They now have strong allies. It is best, therefore, that we should keep to our side of the bargain."

Drona, Kripa, and Vidura all supported Bhishma and urged the king and his sons to accept the terms.

Karna now jumped up and said, "The Pandavas have no rights at all. They are just trying to frighten us. We are more than a match for them on the battlefield!"

Bhishma reprimanded him, "Enough of your bragging. Many times have you boasted of defeating Arjuna, but he has defeated you twice, at Draupadi's *svayamvara* as well as at the recent cattle raid. Moreover, remember that they are supported by the divine Lord Krishna."

Dhritarashtra, torn between fear of the Pandavas and greed and love for his sons, never seemed to have a mind of his own. Weakly, he told Duryodhana to try to live amicably with his cousins.

Duryodhana, knowing his father's lack of strength, said defiantly, "I shall not yield to any threat! The Pandavas have no right to the kingdom, which they gambled away voluntarily. I certainly made no promise to give it back to them. Let them achieve on the battlefield what they could not regain by gambling and can certainly not regain through negotiation."

Vidura and Drona tried to instill some sense into Duryodhana, but he did not heed them and insolently walked out of the assembly. Finally, Dhritarashtra, trying to play for time, told Uluka to tell Yudhishthira that he would send his Prime Minister, Sanjaya, with his final decision. Uluka returned with this message. Both sides realized that war was inevitable and peace only a remote possibility, even though Yudhishthira was still hoping for the best. Both camps started canvassing for support from all friendly kings. Duryodhana, who had already made up his mind to fight, was the first to approach them and thus managed to collect eleven *akshauhinis*, or divisions. The Pandavas, who were hoping till the last moment for peace, could only muster up seven. An *akshauhini* consisted of two thousand elephants, four thousand chariots, eight thousand cavalrymen, and twenty thousand foot soldiers.

It may be wondered why the Lord did not will Duryodhana into agreeing for peace. As has been said before, human beings are free to experience the effects of their past *karma* and the Divine will not deliberately thwart the exercising of their free will. Of course, the Lord did His best to make Duryodhana listen to reason, as will be seen, but when he refused to do so, it became apparent that the course of *dharma* was at cross-purposes with that of peace. Therefore, war became a necessity.

Shakuni was fully aware of Krishna's prowess and urged Duryodhana to go to Dwaraka to solicit His support. Yudhishthira dispatched Arjuna to Dwaraka at the same time for the same purpose, since it was necessary to make a formal request for the Yadava forces. It so happened that the cousins arrived at the same time at Dwaraka.

The all-knowing Lord was prepared to meet them. He retired to His couch and informed His attendants that He was not to be disturbed. A seat was placed at His feet. Duryodhana arrived a few seconds before Arjuna and, thinking Krishna to be asleep, he removed the seat to a position at the head of the couch, as befitting a great king, and seated himself. Arjuna came in soon after and stood patiently at the feet of the Lord, meditating on Him. Naturally, when Krishna opened His eyes, He saw Arjuna first. "Ah, Arjuna! What brings you here?" He asked.

At this, Duryodhana loudly announced his presence, so Krishna turned to him and said, "Are you also here? To what do I owe the honor of these visits?"

Duryodhana declared, "I have come to ask for your help in the impending war. Both Arjuna and I are equally related to you, but since I was the first to arrive, you should pledge your support to me."

The Lord smilingly replied, "I don't doubt your word, O King, that you were the first to arrive, but it so happened that I saw the son of Kunti first. But have no fear. I shall undoubtedly lend My support to both of you, since I am equally related to both, as you have just claimed. Satyaki is determined to support the Pandavas, and I do not know what My elder brother intends to do. For My own part, I can promise to give the Yadava army led by Kritavarma to one side, while I Myself will go to the other."

Duryodhana interrupted before Arjuna could open his mouth. "That's not fair. Everyone knows of Your superhuman feats. The side You fight for will surely win, so You should promise not to take up arms during the battle."

Krishna looked highly amused at this unfair suggestion, and He laughingly turned to Arjuna and gave him first choice. "Choose, O Mighty-Armed One! Do you want Me alone and unarmed or do you want the crack regiment of the Yadava forces led by our general, Kritavarma? The first choice is yours, for I have seen you first. Moreover, you are the younger of the two."

Arjuna unhesitatingly chose the Lord and Duryodhana equally happily accepted the army. He had a few anxious moments while Krishna was speaking and before Arjuna made his choice, but the Pandavas were always quixotic and never knew how to grab an opportunity! He took a hasty farewell of both of them and went to solicit the support of his *guru*, Balarama, before Arjuna could approach him. Actually, he was quite certain that Balarama would side with him, but he was doomed to disappointment, for Balarama refused to fight on either side. "I cannot fight against Krishna, who will be on the side of the Pandavas, and I cannot fight against you, so in the case of war being declared, I shall go on a pilgrimage. I hope you will fight according to the *kshatriya* code of conduct that I have taught you."

After Duryodhana had left, Krishna asked Arjuna, "Why did you choose Me when you knew I was not going to fight?"

Arjuna replied, "My Lord, I only want You beside me driving my chariot. Then I can face the entire world and even the celestials themselves!"

Krishna smiled and blessed him, and thus it came to pass that though the Lord did not take up arms during the war, He took the reins of Arjuna's chariot into His capable hands and led the Pandavas to victory in the great Mahabharata war that was to come.

Now Dhritarashtra sent Sanjaya to the Pandavas with his final decision, as he had promised, and made a last desperate attempt to seize the kingdom for his sons without shedding their blood. Sanjaya went to the Pandava assembly and read out the message: "War is a terrible thing and both parties will suffer. My sons are obstinate, but why do you, O Pandavas, who follow the path of righteousness, not strive for peace? Spiritual pursuits are more profitable than material prosperity and it ill becomes persons of your worth to fight for the sake of a kingdom. Far better for you to go and stay at Dwaraka as Lord Krishna's guests than give cause for a family feud."

This remarkable speech on the quality of renunciation was heard with amazement by all those present. Even Yudhishthira felt that this was another stratagem by the wily king to grab the whole kingdom for his sons without jeopardizing their lives, for he feared the wrath of the Pandavas in battle. Instead of getting his sons to see reason, he was playing on Yudhishthira's love for *dharma*, which bordered almost on weakness.

Turning to Krishna, Yudhishthira spoke, "Weighing my own opinion, as well as that of my brothers, I can come to no final decision. I know not my *dharma* in this situation. Therefore, abandoning all *dharmas*, I take refuge at Your lotus feet. I shall abide by Your decision."

Very soon after, the Lord was to give the same advice to Arjuna on the battlefield of Kurukshetra, but Yudhishthira forestalled him. Torn between his love for peace and his desire to follow the *kshatriya dharma*, which urged him to fight this righteous war, he placed the entire responsibility of the decision at the feet of the Lord and made a complete surrender of his ego. Krishna was filled with admiration for this great soul who was prepared to live in humiliation for the sake of peace. But the Lord never forsook those who took refuge in Him, and even if they did not want to avenge their wrongs, He saw to it that their wrongs were avenged.

Turning to Sanjaya, Krishna spoke on Yudhishthira's behalf. "A thief who steals wealth unseen and one who seizes it in open daylight are both to be condemned, O Sanjaya! What is the difference between such a one and the sons of Dhritarashtra? The Pandavas' share is indisputable. Why should they submit meekly and watch while that share is seized by the avaricious Kauravas? Why should they be forced to accept My hospitality when they have a kingdom of their own? A paternal kingdom is surely preferable to sovereignty received from friends. When the daughter of Drupada, of fair fame and unsullied reputation, was seized by Dusshasana, all the Kurus, the young and old, were present. You yourself were present, O Sanjaya! Yet what stopped you from propounding your views on righteousness and morality then? When Karna insultingly asked Draupadi to choose one of the Kauravas as her husband, why did you not protest? When the sons of his brother departed to the forest clad in bark, why did the old king feel no sorrow? But now, when the time has come to redeem his pledge and return their kingdom, he talks of mercy and uprightness! Is he still bent on watering this mighty tree of evil passions of which his son Duryodhana is the trunk, Shakuni its branches, the Kauravas its blossoms, Karna its fruit, and he himself its roots? Yudhishthira, on the other hand, is a big tree of righteousness. Arjuna is its trunk, Bhima its branches, the sons of Madri its flowers and fruit, and I Myself, with all *dharma* at My command, its mighty roots. Tell the king that the sons of Pandu are as ready now as they ever were to wait on him if he chooses to follow the code of *dharma*. Let him choose! Let him give back their patrimony and thus bring about peace, or let him banish them and thus opt for war. In the meantime, I shall make a last bid for peace, since I know that Yudhishthira wants it. I Myself will come to Hastinapura and try to make the king see reason!"

Hearing this, Sanjaya departed and faithfully reported what had transpired and advised the king to act firmly and wisely. He also warned him about the might of the Pandavas, aided as they were by Lord Krishna, hoping that fear would act as a deterrent where wise counsel seemed to have failed. Vidura, his stepbrother, whose sayings were famous for their wisdom, as well as Bhishma and Drona, all advised him, but still the king wavered. When he heard that Krishna was coming as envoy for the Pandavas, he immediately started to make preparations to welcome Him in a grand manner, thus hoping to win Him over to their side. Vidura advised him not to make a fool of himself, for Krishna was capable of sifting the chaff of ostentation from the wheat of real devotion, but the king was determined to try. He told Vidura, "You must personally supervise the reception to be given to Krishna. I want to present Him with many costly gifts."

Vidura smiled scornfully. He could read his brother like a book. "I'm really amused to hear your childish prattle. Do you think you can bribe Krishna with your petty gifts? He is the greatest soul that has ever been born on this earth or will ever be born. What can you give Him who is the Lord of all? Don't insult Him, brother. If you really want to please Him, honor Him by granting His wish. He is coming here in the hope of making you and your son realize the horrors of war and recognize the injustice done to the Pandavas. He is an envoy of peace. If you want to welcome Him, stop your preparations for war and agree to His suggestions."

Bhishma said, "Whether He is honored or not is immaterial to Krishna. Even if anyone were to insult Him, He would overlook it. He is fighting for Truth—for righting the wrongs done to the Pandavas. If you want to please Him, do as He suggests."

Duryodhana said, "All of you are always on the side of the Pandavas. I have a master plan by which the Pandavas will become my slaves. I will imprison this man and then where will they be?" Everybody was horrified by this suggestion, but Duryodhana was already scheming with his uncle how best to achieve this.

Before leaving on His mission of peace, Krishna discussed with the Pandavas their line of action. Yudhishthira, as usual, championed the cause of harmony and said, "I would like to live amicably with my cousins, as I value peace above all things."

Krishna replied, "Though what you say is true, you have to consider the opinions of Draupadi and your brothers."

Bhima said, "We should demand our full share, failing which we should fight for it. The Kauravas are well aware of my physical strength, Arjuna's prowess in archery, and the power of Draupadi's tears, as well as the fact that you, O Lord, have pledged to help us. Surely they will realize that they cannot win the battle."

Arjuna now spoke up. "Lord Krishna, You know well what is going to happen, for all things are clear before Your vision. All I can say is that if we do not make good our oaths now, when will we ever be able to do it?"

Nakula continued, "We seem to have lost all sense of pride. I am for war even though Duryodhana may be persuaded to treat us fairly, as promised by his father." Sahadeva spoke last. "What the king has said, O Lord, may be virtuous, but speaking for myself, after having seen the plight of the Princess of Panchala in the open assembly, my wrath can never be appeased until I see Duryodhana slaughtered. He has committed every dastardly crime that a man can commit against us. He has tried to kill us by arson, drowning, murder, and deceit and still my brother is disposed to be forgiving. But I can never forget. Only honor can accrue to a *kshatriya* if he dies in a righteous battle. I'd rather court death on the battlefield than lead a life of idle luxury in any one of the villages which they may bestow on us! But what is the good of talking? You, O Lord, know everything. If You want to stop the war You can do it, so do You act as you think fit.

Krishna laughingly replied, "Tell me how you think I can stop the war."

Sahadeva replied, "The solution is simple. Kill Arjuna, install Karna on the throne, bind up Bhima, shave off Draupadi's tresses, and allow me to tie You up!"

Krishna was highly amused at this and said, "How do you propose to tie Me up, O Sahadeva? Even my mother Yashoda was not able to do this when I was only a baby! So how can you do it?"

Sahadeva insisted that he could do it, so the Lord took him to a solitary spot, took on the form of ten thousand identical Krishnas and told him to proceed if he could. Sahadava remained calm and unruffled by this spectacle, closed his eyes, meditated on the Lord and prayed to Him, "Let me be able to bind You, O Lord, with the rope of my eternal love and devotion to You."

Hardly had he prayed thus when the Lord found himself bound! He said, "Sahadeva, you have indeed discovered my weak point—that the only thing that can bind Me is the power of love. Now do you release Me!"

"Not till you promise to protect us always," said Sahadeva with a laugh and released Krishna from his shackles.

Returning to the others, Krishna said in jest that Sahadeva had opted for peace, which encouraged Yudhishthira to say, "O Lord, then You must go to the Kaurava court as our ambassador and ask politely for the restoration of our share of the kingdom. If Duryodhana refuses, ask for a small portion of our territory. If this, too, is denied, ask for five villages for the five of us. Ask not for just any five villages. I want Varanavata as a reminder of the attempt to burn us alive there; Vrikaprastha, where they tried to poison Bhima; Jayantha, where they cheated at dice and got our kingdom from us; Indraprastha, which was ours by right; and the last I leave to Duryodhana to choose. If even this is denied, ask for five houses. And if he refuses even this, then it shall be war."

Draupadi had been standing beside Krishna listening to the arguments of her husbands and was plunged in grief. With eyes bathed in tears and unbound hair flowing in luxurious abundance, she addressed Him. "O Janardana (Krishna)! Is there any woman on earth as unfortunate as I am? I am the daughter of King Drupada, sister of the mighty Drishtadyumna, and Your own devotee. I'm the daughter-in-law of the illustrious Pandu and the queen of his sons, who resemble five Indras in splendor. By these five heroes I have begotten five sons, all equally mighty. Yet, O Krishna, I was seized by the hair, dragged into the open court, and insulted in the very sight of my illustrious husbands. When the Pandavas sat silently beholding my agony, what would I have done if You had not come to my rescue? I would have been stripped in public! Fie on Partha's (Arjuna's) bowmanship, fie on Bhima's strength, since Duryodhana and Dusshasana are still alive! If I deserve any favor at Your hands, if You have any compassion for me, O Krishna, let Your wrath be directed toward the sons of Dhritarashtra."

With blazing eyes, she took up her curly tresses in her hand and approaching Him she continued, "O Pundarikaksha (Lotus-Eyed One), when You go to make peace with the Kauravas, remember these tresses of mine which were so roughly pulled by the wicked Dusshasana. At that time, my mighty husband Bhima swore that he would tie it up with his hands stained with the blood of that sinful wretch and now he sits quietly and agrees to peace! If my noble husbands refuse to fight, my aged father and his warlike sons will avenge me in battle. My sons, with Abhimanyu at their head, will fight for my honor. What peace can this bitter heart of mine know unless I see Dusshasana's arm severed from his trunk? That arm which pulled my hair so cruelly! That arm which tugged my garment and tried its best to denude me. Thirteen long years have I spent, suffering untold hardships in the expectation of better times, hiding my wrath like a smoldering fire beneath the ashes. But now, pierced by my husbands' words, that heart of mine is about to break."

So saying, she began to weep. Krishna tenderly removed her locks from her face and wiped away her tears with His *pitambara* (yellow garment) and comforted her thus: "Soon will you see, O Panchali, the women of the Kuru race weep as you do now. Simultaneously with your hair being bound up, the tresses of the Kaurava women will droop down. They against whom your wrath is directed have already been slain by the power of the Lord as Time. Have you forgotten the promise I made to you in the Kamyaka forest and again at Upaplavya? At Yudhishthira's commands, Bhima, Arjuna, and the twins will accomplish that which has been decreed by the Lord. Their hour has come and if they do not listen to My words, the sons of Dhritarashtra will surely lie on the earth and become food for dogs and jackals. The mountains of the Himalayas may shift their site, the earth may split into a thousand fragments, and the firmament itself with its myriad stars may fall down, but My words will never be futile. Cease your tears, therefore, O Panchali! I swear to you that you will soon see your husbands crowned with every prosperity and your enemies slain on the battlefield."

Turning to the others, Krishna wound up the discussion. "The world must know of the greatness of Yudhishthira and no blame should accrue to the fair name of the Pandavas, and so I shall make one last, final effort to make peace. As long as Duryodhana does not try to embody his evil thoughts into action, there is hope for him. But on the other hand, it is not correct for us to sit idly and tolerate *adharma*. If he does not agree to Yudhishthira's most reasonable request, we shall have to declare war. I shall now undertake to be your ambassador at the Kaurava court and make a last attempt to settle the dispute peacefully."

Conchs blew and trumpets blared as the Lord set out for Hastinapura in His chariot studded with gems, driven by His trusted charioteer Daruka and drawn by His favorite horses, Sugriya, Meghapushpa, Saibya, and Valahaka. The two wheels of the chariot resembled the sun and the moon. Uddhava and Satyaki accompanied Him and Arjuna went as far as the city gates. As they entered Hastinapura, the crowds surged around to behold the living legend that He had become. It is said that not a single soul was left in the houses. The old and the blind, the lame and the sick were all brought out to see the Lord. Feasting their eyes on His enchanting form, they forgot their woes and returned home restored to their former health. His enrapturing smile bathed them in a sea of bliss and they could not bear even to blink in case they missed even a second of that delightful vision. At Dhritarashtra's orders, the entire city had been decorated to welcome Him and many bejeweled arches had been put up. Duryodhana had given orders that the grandest palace should be put at His disposal; he had wanted to go personally to the city gates to receive

Him, but Shakuni had stopped him, as he said it was demeaning for a mighty monarch like him to go to receive a mere cowherd.

With great humility, Krishna saluted the Elders, who had come to welcome Him, and politely refused the offer of the palace. He went with His devotee Vidura to his humble dwelling. It is said that Bhishma's hospitality was declined because of his ego of knowledge, Drona's because of his ego of being a Brahmin, and Duryodhana's because of his ego of being a mighty monarch. Vidura alone had surrendered his ego at the Lord's feet.

Vidura could hardly believe that his humble abode had been chosen in preference to the grand mansions and danced with joy when the Lord entered his insignificant dwelling place. "What penance must this humble hut of mine have done to be graced by Your holy feet, which even the great sages and gods long to have a sight of?" he said.

He shouted to his wife to come out, for the Lord had come to their abode. She had been taking a bath, but on hearing this she rushed out without completing her toilette and prostrated before Him. She was actually Krishna's stepaunt, the daughter of His grandfather, Devakan, by a *sudra* (servant) wife. The couple lived very frugally, since they did not like to stay in Duryodhana's palace and receive his ungracious patronage. But they were both totally devoted to the Lord and lived a contented life.

There was nothing in the house except some bananas to offer the Lord, and these she lovingly put on a beautiful leaf and placed before Him. In her excitement, she forgot what she was doing and reverently fed Him with the skins and threw the fruits aside! It is said that the Lord patiently ate all the skins without a word of complaint, for anything that His devotees offered to Him with love was accepted by Him with relish. Vidura was in the same bemused state and was watching the Lord's face with joy. It was only after the whole bunch was finished that the devoted couple realized what had been happening. Afterward, for dinner, it is said that He ate His favorite dish made from the leaf called *bethua* (a kind of spinach) that grew in abundance around their modest house, preferring it to the sumptuous banquet prepared for Him and served on golden platters in the palace of Duryodhana.

After dinner, they discussed the purpose of His visit. Vidura advised Him not to proceed, since Duryodhana had already decided on war and was likely to do Him bodily injury if thwarted.

Krishna replied, "The learned consider him a wretch who does not strive until the end to save a friend from an improper act. It is to serve both parties that I have come here. If, after listening to My words, the foolish Duryodhana does not accept them, he will be inviting his own fate. If, without sacrificing the interests of the Pandavas, I can bring about peace among the Kurus, I will have served the purpose of *dharma*, and the Kauravas themselves will be liberated from the meshes of death. But if, on the other hand, they seek to injure Me, rest assured, O noble one, that all the kings of this earth united together are no more a match for Me than is a herd of deer before an enraged lion."

The next morning He sent Vidura with Satyaki and Uddhava ahead of Him to the assembly hall. In the meantime Duryodhana, furious at having his hospitality spurned, had given strict orders to the assembled people that no one should stand up to greet the Lord when he came and that he would set fire to the homes of any who dared to disobey him.

When the Lord walked in with His usual disarming smile, one by one everyone rose up and prostrated as if moved by an irresistible impulse. It is said that Duryodhana's throne tilted forward and propelled him toward the Lord's feet!

Krishna smiled and said, "I'm really moved by your devotion to me, O Suyodhana (Duryodhana)."

After saluting the Elders and greeting everyone else, He was escorted to a jeweled seat. Unable to contain his chagrin, Duryodhana began, "It was unkind of you, O Govinda, not to accept my hospitality. I had prepared the best palace for you and a magnificent banquet."

Turning His radiant eyes on him, the Lord replied, "One takes food from the house of another only when the offer is made with love, or if one is starving and has no other recourse. At present, O King, you have not inspired love in me by any act of yours, nor has your invitation been given with love, neither am I on the verge of starvation. Without any reason, you have hated your dear and gentle cousins, imbued with every virtue, from the very moment that you set eyes on them. Know this, O Duryodhana, they who hate My devotees hate Me as well, for all virtuous people are My very self. Moreover, food which is defiled by wicked thoughts is never acceptable to Me. On the other hand, the humblest fare, if offered with love, I shall joyfully partake, even if it be only a leaf, flower, fruit, or even a drop of water."

He then relented and added, "You are well aware of the code of conduct by which one cannot become the adversary of one whose hospitality he has enjoyed. If my mission is successful, I shall be happy to accept your offer and be your guest."

Dhritarashtra now courteously greeted Krishna and requested Him to declare the purpose of His visit. A deep silence fell over the audience as the Lord started to speak in a sonorous voice, which filled the entire hall and thrilled the audience to immobility.

"I have come hither so that peace may be established between the Kurus and the Pandavas. The Pandavas have successfully completed their thirteen years of exile. They have suffered greatly, but they are still prepared to forget and forgive. The terrible danger that threatens to overwhelm the entire clan of the Kurus, O King, has its origin in the conduct of your sons. Therefore, the establishment of peace depends entirely on you. Deprived of their father in infancy, the Pandavas look upon you as their father. Treat them, therefore, as your sons and behave toward them as a father. Remember they are your brother's children and it is your duty to protect their interests. For the sake of virtue, profit, and happiness (*dharma, artha,* and *kama*), O King, make peace with the Pandavas and restrain your sons from their headstrong conduct!"

Then, turning to Duryodhana, He continued. "I work for the sake of universal good, O Duryodhana! I desire your good just as much as theirs. You hail from an illustrious race that has always adhered to *dharma*. You will attain great fame and prosperity if you restore to the Pandavas that which was promised to them thirteen years ago."

The bards now related the story of the ancient sages Nara and Narayana, the twin *avatars* of Lord Vishnu who had now taken on the incarnations of Arjuna and Krishna to establish *dharma* upon the earth. Hearing all this, the old king trembled with fear for the fate of his sons and told Krishna, "My son never listens to me or to those of his Elders who try to advise him. Do You advise him and try to make him change his mind."

So once again with great patience, Krishna turned to Duryodhana and tried to make him see reason. "O Duryodhana," He said, "your father as well as the others desire peace. Why do you not obey them? Why do you rush headlong into that which will surely destroy your entire race? He who rejects the words of well-meaning friends and Elders, regarding them as opposed to his interests, and instead accepts the opinions of the wicked, will only be plunged into distress. The Pandavas are willing to accept you as *yuvaraja* (heir apparent) and your father as sovereign of the empire if you give back to them half the kingdom which is rightfully theirs. Please listen to the counsel of your friends and bring peace to the land and prosperity to yourself, or else be forever condemned as the exterminator of your race."

At this, Bhishma and Drona also urged Duryodhana to follow the Lord's advice, but the haughty Duryodhana could hardly contain his anger and burst out, "The Pandavas gambled away their kingdom voluntarily. Completion of their exile entitles them only to live as my subjects, not to any share of the kingdom. Their father Pandu was made king only because my father was blind. I am the son of the elder brother and since I'm not blind, the kingdom is rightfully mine. Let them live as your guests in Dwaraka if they like."

Shakuni encouraged him by adding, "This is the first time that I have heard of the loser in gambling asking for the return of his lost stakes."

Krishna sternly replied, "The gambling match was forced on Yudhishthira, and you played on behalf of Duryodhana, which again was quite unprecedented. Besides, in front of the entire court, the king gave a solemn promise that half the kingdom would be returned to them. Why should the Pandavas live on My hospitality when they are entitled to a kingdom in their own right? I now ask everyone here to consider carefully the consequences that will result if the Pandavas are not given back their rightful share. Do not mistake their love of peace for weakness. If you deny them their due, they will surely declare war. This in turn will lead to loss of lives, poverty, famine, and suffering. Parents will lose sons, children will lose fathers and women will become widows. There will be an extermination of the very flower of the Kuru race. Think well, therefore, before you decide."

Karna interrupted, "What do you have to say about Yudhishthira's disgraceful act in gambling away his wife? Such a person does not deserve a kingdom!"

Krishna replied, "Yudhishthira was incited and taunted into it by Shakuni, who capitalized on his weakness as well as his evil times. He was promised the return of his kingdom at the end of thirteen years."

Turning to Duryodhana, He continued. "Duryodhana, you do not realize the horrors of war and thus you do not appreciate the value of peace. If war takes place, the cries of the bereaved will rend the air. Everyone will curse the one who caused it and you alone will have to bear the brunt of their curses. The Pandavas are powerful and invincible. They have heroes like Arjuna, Bhima, Abhimanyu, Gatotkacha, and Iravan on their side. Do not think that you can defeat them easily with your superior numbers. Think of your previous defeat at their hands at

Kampilya and Matsya. The younger brothers are itching for a fight, but they will implicitly obey their elder brother, who is bent on peace. Their request is most reasonable. They have sent Me to negotiate for peace out of their love for it and not out of their fear of war."

Bhishma, Drona, Vidura, and even Ashvatthama now advised Duryodhana to opt for peace. Bhishma declared that he did not want to see the end of the Kuru race during the last years of his life. Drona predicted that a Kaurava victory in battle would be impossible with Krishna and Arjuna in the opposite camp. Vidura, too, spoke firmly and wisely. Karna, Dusshasana, and Shakuni, however, encouraged Duryodhana to defy Krishna, and finally Duryodhana said, "O Krishna! Why do you utter such harsh words to me alone? All of you, including the old king, hate me. Yet, I do not behold any fault in myself. I will not bow down to anyone, be it Indra himself, let alone the sons of Pandu. We are *kshatriyas*. If we die in battle, heaven awaits us. That share of the kingdom which was formerly given to them by my father shall never again, O Keshava (Krishna), be given to them while I live. Formerly, it was given to them while I was still too young to make a decision for myself, but they will never get it again. If they want it, let them fight for it!"

Krishna then said, "In the interests of peace, Yudhishthira is willing to accept even a small portion of land."

When this was refused by Duryodhana, Krishna asked for five villages, and when this too was turned down, he finally asked, "Will you not at least give five houses for the five brothers?"

Duryodhana thundered, "Not even five pinpoints of land will I give them! I'm against the principle of giving, however little it may be!"

Ashvatthama now appealed to Duryodhana that he who was so generous in giving Karna a kingdom could well afford to give five houses to his own cousins. He reprimanded Karna for misleading Duryodhana, but the latter was deaf to all pleas.

Krishna spoke sternly to him once more. "You say you have not committed any offense against the Pandavas. Conniving with your uncle, you wrested their possessions from them in an unfair game of dice. Not content with that, you dragged their wife into the open assembly and humiliated her. You tried to burn them to death at Varanavata and to kill them with poison, snakes, and cords. Now you are trying to cheat them of their rightful heritage, even when they are only asking for a minute portion of their patrimony. But beware, O Suyodhana! You will have to give it all to them after you are laid low on the battlefield!"

Furious at these words, Duryodhana marched out of the assembly, followed by his satellites. Krishna spoke to the assembled Kurus, "Not only Duryodhana but all of you will be guilty of destroying this race if you do not stop Duryodhana from pursuing his folly. The time has come to forcibly seize and bind this wicked prince, as Kamsa, the wicked son of Ugrasena, was killed by Me to save the race of the Yadavas. For the sake of a family, an individual may be sacrificed. For the sake of a village, a family may be sacrificed. For the sake of a country, a village may be sacrificed and for the sake of his soul, a man may sacrifice the whole world. Therefore, bind fast this Duryodhana and make peace with the Pandavas."

Hearing these prophetic words, Dhritarashtra immediately called his wife Gandhari and summoned back Duryodhana in the hope that he might listen to his mother. But even this proved futile.

At last, Krishna spoke once again. "Since, like a miser, you deny the Pandavas even five houses, give me your hand and swear by striking this pillar that you are ready for war!"

The insolent Duryodhana flung back, "It is below my dignity to give my hand to you, a mere cowherd, pleading the cause of men whom I humiliated and disgraced and who have been living like wild animals in the forest. I really wonder how food went down their throats after they behaved in such a cowardly fashion thirteen years ago, meekly bearing my taunts as well as the humiliation to their wife!"

With this parting shot, he arrogantly walked out of the assembly before it broke up. Krishna realized that nothing and nobody could deter Duryodhana from his ill-advised and disastrous action. So He turned to the Elders and said, "All of you have tried your best to drive some sense into Duryodhana's head. I have also done my best. None need blame the Pandavas for bringing about this calamity." So saying, He calmly saluted the Elders and left the court, accompanied by Uddhava and Satyaki.

Thus ends the twenty-third chapter of The Play of God,
named "The Lord as Ambassador."

Hari Aum Tat Sat

TWENTY-FOUR

DECLARATION OF WAR

Haraye namaha
Homage to Him
who destroys the
sorrows of life

*O Eternal Companion! Certainly Thou art not just the son of
Yashoda, but the immanent witness in all embodied beings. In
response to the prayer of the creator Brahma, Thou hast risen
among the Yadavas to protect the world.*
—SHRIMAD BHAGAVATA

No sooner had Krishna left than Duryodhana returned to the assembly and directed the full blast of his fury on Vidura. He had been nursing a grudge since childhood for Vidura's having given him advice that was always against his personal inclination and contrary to the advice given by his maternal uncle, Shakuni. One was the epitome of virtue and the other of vice. All the venom that had been collecting for years was now discharged in a vituperative flow. "You ungrateful man. You eat my food and live as a vassal in my kingdom, but you have the ingratitude to play host to this cowherd and also to feed him with my food after he had rejected my hospitality. But what else can be expected from the son of a maid, who always bestows her favors on the highest bidder."

Vidura was stung to the quick, not merely by the personal insults, which he had always received from Duryodhana, but because of the fact that they had been uttered on a spot which had been sanctified by the holy footprints of the Lord. As a result of this, he strung his famous and invincible bow and, aiming an arrow straight at Duryodhana's throat, he spoke, "You vile wretch! Can't you realize that my hospitality is tantamount to yours? For insulting my mother, I should sever your head, but I will not do it, since you are in the position of a son to me,

237

being my brother's son. I wanted to serve you in the eventuality of a war, but now I have decided against it. My bow will no longer be at your service during the war!"

So saying, to the amazement of everyone, Vidura broke his bow in two—the bow which was as famous as Arjuna's Gandiva—and walked out of the court. Despite his age, Vidura, armed with his bow, would have been invincible and the Kaurava side felt quite dejected at this turn of events.

Bhishma remarked, "Whatever doubts I had as to the outcome of the war are now dispelled. Without Vidura's bow, the Kauravas are doomed."

Duryodhana said in a flattering tone, "I do not depend on this aged man to win the war. I have you, Drona, Karna, and Ashvatthama to annihilate the Pandavas." Karna boasted, "Don't depend on these old and feeble men, O Duryodhana! I shall kill Arjuna and the Pandavas for you."

Bhishma laughed scornfully and asked, "Have you forgotten your defeat at Arjuna's hands a few days ago at Matsya?"

Duryodhana now began to conjecture how best he could destroy Krishna, for he feared that victory could never be theirs so long as He helped the Pandavas. Karna suggested burning Vidura's house while the Lord was sleeping within. All the others suggested various impractical schemes. The only Kaurava brother with some sense was Vikarna, the youngest, who as usual warned them gravely of the unrighteousness of putting a messenger to death. As usual, he was brushed aside.

Duryodhana said, "This Krishna is advising them to bind me up. Let's do the same thing to Him before He does it to me. We will tie up this lion. Once He's removed, the Pandavas will be like snakes without fangs."

When Dhritarashtra heard this he was in a panic. "What madness is this?" he asked Duryodhana. "You are trying to do something that even the gods cannot do. It's easier to catch the wandering breeze or the sun with your bare hands!" But Duryodhana was deaf to all advice.

Back in Vidura's hut, the Lord heard of Vidura's resolve not to fight and was delighted, for He was well aware of his prowess with the bow and did not want him as an adversary. Very soon, Duryodhana sent a messenger inviting Krishna to the assembly the next day. Though the Lord was well aware of the plan afoot to capture Him, He was not a whit put out and strode into the hall escorted by Vidura and Satyaki. As He entered, the Kauravas and Karna rushed at Him in order to capture Him. Satyaki would have challenged them with upraised sword, but the Lord restrained him.

Turning to Duryodhana, He said in a voice like thunder, "O Duryo-dhana! Thinking Me to be a mere mortal, you are trying to capture Me, but know Me now for what I am. Behold My Cosmic Form. Know that in Me are the Pandavas and Vrishnis and Andhakas. Know that in Me are all the gods—the Adityas, the Rudras, the Vasus, the *siddhas*, and *rishis*."

Saying this, He started to laugh, and as He laughed, from His body that now resembled a blazing fire, there issued myriad gods, each like lightning. On His forehead there appeared Brahma, the creator, and on His breast Rudra (Shiva), the destroyer; from His mouth Agni, the Adityas, and the other gods with Indra. From His two arms came Shankarshanana (Balarama) with the ploughshare and Arjuna with the Gandiva, and behind were Bhima, the sons of Madri, Pradyumna, and all the Yadavas. The form had many arms, some bearing the conch, the discus, the bow Saranga, and the sword Nandaka, the accouterments of Vishnu. The other arms upheld many weapons, and from every pore there issued rays as blinding as the sun. The entire assembly except Duryodhana stood up in terror. All except Bhishma, Drona, Vidura, and the *rishis* closed their eyes. The latter extolled Him with various hymns and the Elders prayed silently, "O Pundarikaksha! Forgive us for having associated with these wicked people and for helping them, for we have eaten their salt and cannot help but obey!"

It is said that out of His compassion, the Lord gave even Dhritarash-tra, misguided fool that he was, temporary vision so that he could behold this mighty form, and Gandhari also removed her bandage in order to behold this unique sight.

Dhritarashtra prayed, "Having once seen Your *Vishvarupa* (Cosmic Form), I am blessed and do not desire to see anything anymore."

Once more, the voice thundered, "O Duryodhana, steeped in *adhar-ma* you planned to kill Me, an ambassador! I can kill you and all the Kauravas with a mere look, but I shall not do so, for the Pandavas have sworn to kill you. Kurukshetra is waiting for its bloodbath and Yama (the god of death) is ready to enfold you in his arms!"

The voice died away into silence and, as the stunned assembly opened their eyes, they saw the Lord walk out of the hall arm in arm with Satyaki and Uddhava. As He left, Dhritarashtra cried out, "O Keshava! Tell the sons of Pandu that I am innocent of this crime, that my son will not listen to me!"

As He left, Krishna summoned Ashvatthama to His side. Duryodhana followed to see what was happening. Krishna dropped His ring and Ashvatthama stooped to pick it up. He then pointed to the dark clouds that were forming in the sky and Asvatthama gazed upward. Having seen Asvatthama perform these actions, the suspicious Duryodhana inferred that the latter could not be trusted, as he had just sworn upon earth and heaven that he would help the Pandavas. Krishna bade Ashvatthama farewell and beckoned to Karna and led him to a secluded spot, where the Lord then disclosed to him the secret of his birth—that he was actually the son of Kunti by the Sun god, Surya. Since he was begotten while she was still a maiden, she had floated him down the river, where his foster parents, Adhiratha, the charioteer and Radha, his wife, had found him and brought him up. Krishna concluded by urging Karna to accept his patrimony, recognize the Pandavas as his brothers, and take his place beside them in the war that was to ensue.

Karna heard all this in silent astonishment and finally spoke. "No doubt I have a moral right to be called the son of Pandu, but I was brought up by a *suta* (charioteer) and all my family rites, including my marriage, were conducted accordingly. For the past so many years I have enjoyed the status of King of Anga due to the kindness of Duryodhana. He is depending on me to kill Arjuna in the coming battle. I can never abandon him now, not even for the sake of my own life. I know that ours is a lost cause, but my life, though unsuccessful, has its own rainbow. By the rays of the setting sun the rainbow of my life will be let through my tears. Let me at least see a hero's death, though I might not have lived a hero's life. I am consumed with repentance for my past behavior. I realize now that the sons of Dhritarashtra will perish, but one thing do I pray for, O Keshava. Let all the *kshatriyas* who are slain on that most holy field of Kurukshetra attain heaven. One more thing do I beg of You, O Krishna. Keep this discourse a secret, for I do not want Yudhishthira to know of it."

Krishna looked at him with great pity and replied, "So be it, O Karna. The battle will commence on the new moon day one month hence and it shall be as you wish. All the heroes who fall in battle will attain heaven."

Karna bowed to the Lord and said, "If we come out of this great battle alive, may we meet here again? If not, O Janardana, we shall surely meet in heaven!" Then, looking into the Lord's compassionate eyes, he added sadly, "Perhaps it is only there that we shall meet."

Krishna clasped him to His bosom, for He was well aware of the worth of this mighty hero, who had had the cards stacked against him from the time of birth. Sadly, Karna returned to the city and Krishna went to the house of Kunti, which adjoined Vidura's. She was delighted to see Him. With tears streaming from her eyes, she embraced Him and said, "Seeing You has made me as happy as seeing my own sons. But, O Lord, I'm fearful of the future. Is there to be no peaceful solution? Has your coming been in vain?"

Krishna replied, "Every attempt at peace has been thwarted by Duryodhana. So now we have to plan to ensure a Pandava victory. A lot depends on you. Do you have any news of the whereabouts of your firstborn, whom you conceived before marriage and abandoned in fear and shame?"

Kunti was aghast at having her closely guarded secret brought into the open like this and said, "How did you come to know of this? Ever since that day I have known no peace. I have no idea where he might be. He might have been drowned in the river for all I know."

Krishna replied, "There is nothing I do not know. That long-lost son of yours is none other than Karna, the mighty hero on the Kaurava side and Duryodhana's bosom companion. Now think carefully. Would you prefer to have Karna alive or the other five? If Karna kills Arjuna, as he has sworn to do, the others will kill themselves, for they are like a five-headed serpent that will perish if one of its hoods is cut off."

Kunti was extremely agitated and said, "I shall reveal myself to Karna and persuade him to join his brothers. Surely he will not refuse."

"That's a very good idea," said the Lord, "but if Karna rejects your plea, as I think he will, you should ask for two boons from him. One is that he not kill any of your sons except Arjuna in battle and the second is not to use his *Nagastra* (cobra missile) more than once."

Kunti's heart melted for the sake of her newfound son and she asked fearfully, "Won't Karna's life be jeopardized if he gives these boons?"

"Of course it will," said Krishna, "but it is too much to ask for the lives of all your six sons, as well as to want to erase *adharma* from the world! Karna's inborn nobility has been defaced by association with the wicked. If he takes this opportunity to join his noble brothers, well and good; otherwise, you will have to accept the inevitable."

"You are God Incarnate. How can I debate with you?" she asked sadly. "You have incarnated in order to destroy *adharma* and destruction is only a sport for You, just as creation is a game. I have never been a mother to Karna and now I have to be the instrument for his destruction!"

Krishna left her and summoned Indra, the king of the gods, who was also Arjuna's father, and told him, "Your son's life is in great danger. Karna has sworn to kill him in the forthcoming battle. Proceed immediately to Karna, therefore, disguised as a mendicant and beg for his *kavacha* and *kundala* (armor and earrings), with which he was born and which make him invincible. Karna will never refuse to give anything to anybody, for he is the most generous man alive."

One marvels at how the Lord made every effort to bring out the best points in His devotees so that the world would ever extol them, even at the cost of bringing disrepute to Himself. In the ensuing war, He was to do this many times, stooping to seemingly unrighteous acts to bring to light the virtues of devotees like Bhishma, Drona, and Yudhishthira.

Indra lost no time in proceeding to Karna's palace. It was the latter's practice to give anything to anyone before midday. After this, he would worship Surya, the sun god, for whom he had a decided partiality, even though he was ignorant of his parentage. Indra, disguised as a mendicant, arrived a little late but was still received most cordially, for Karna could never resist a beggar. Karna asked him what he wanted and the old man promptly asked for his *kavacha* and *kundala*. Karna was taken aback at this strange request from an old mendicant, yet he unhesitatingly went inside and proceeded to tear off the armor and earrings with which he had been born. The sun god's voice now proclaimed to him that the old Brahmin was none other than Indra, the father of Arjuna, and that he should give him anything other than his *kavacha* and *kundala*. To his eternal glory, Karna, the most charitable man alive, shrugged off this advice from his father, tore off his armor and earrings, and returned to the supplicant. He was smeared all over with blood, yet spoke gently, "I'm indeed fortunate to be able to give something to one who is known for his generosity (one of Indra's names is Parjanya, the giver of rain and thus of life). I am proud that in receiving from me, your hands are at a lower level than mine."

Thus did the Lord establish Karna as superior even to Indra in the giving of gifts! Indra, realizing that his identity had been revealed, said in shame, "The world will no longer say, 'like Parjanya in giving,' but 'like Karna in giving.' But I must give you something in return. What would you like?"

Karna replied, "My Lord, giving loses its grace and merit if I ask for something in return, but on the other hand, I do not want your name to fall into disrepute. The world may blame you for having wrested my most precious possessions from me without having given anything in return, so, to safeguard your name, I will ask for something. I would like to have your *Shakti* weapon, if it pleases you."

Indra was amazed at the magnanimity of this great soul and gladly gave him the weapon and praised him. "Know, O Karna, that your name will live forever as that of the most munificent man alive. Take my Shakti weapon. It will enable you to kill one of the most formidable heroes on the Pandava side." So saying, he vanished from sight.

The next day, Kunti came to see her firstborn. She went to the river where Karna was worshipping the midday sun. Surprised at seeing her, he escorted her most respectfully to his palace. Kunti gazed lovingly at him, noting for the first time his resemblance to her other sons, and spoke tenderly to him, "Your mother must indeed be proud of you."

Karna said bitterly, "Do not mention that word to me. My mother is a heartless woman who abandoned me as a baby."

"Do not judge her harshly. There were many reasons why she had to act as she did. Didn't Krishna tell you?" she asked softly.

"Yes," said Karna. "He told me that I am actually a Pandava, but I want to verify that you are indeed my mother. Many women have come and claimed this title. The sun god has given me a golden mantle, which will burn up anyone who is not my mother. Will you allow me to put it on you?"

Kunti gladly agreed. He placed the mantle on her and she remained unscathed. Karna's eyes filled with tears and he fell at her feet. "So it's true that I'm really your son and the brother of the righteous Pandavas. I am truly blessed. For the moment, let me forget everything and remember only that I have found my mother!" So saying, he laid his head on her lap. Kunti caressed him and for a few blissful moments both of them forgot the catastrophe that was threatening them. At last, Kunti broke the silence. "Now that you know who you are, it is only right that you should join your brothers and take your rightful place as their leader. They will gladly accept you, and Yudhishthira will give you the position of *Yuvaraja* most happily, for he is the soul of righteousness."

Karna's face clouded and he said sadly, "That can never be, O Mother! I can never abandon Duryodhana, who has been my friend, benefactor, and only well-wisher for so many years!"

Just then he heard a voice coming from the solar orb advising him to follow his mother's advice, but even then Karna's heart did not waver. With bitterness, he said, "You abandoned me as a baby. No enemy could have done more. And now you have come, not for my sake, but for the sake of your other sons, who might be slain by me! But I would be a poor friend indeed if I deserted Duryodhana now, at this critical juncture. At a time when I was forlorn and helpless, he gave me not only friendship but even a kingdom and a high status and aided me in my wish to marry the princess of my choice. Tell me truly, Mother, am I to abandon such a man just because I have found a set of brothers who hate and despise him? To the world he may be wicked, but to me he is a great man!"

"Duryodhana is indeed fortunate to have you for a friend, my child," Kunti said. "No doubt I deserve all that you think of me, and your loyalty to him makes me proud of you. Maybe this was why Krishna sent me to you, so that I would discover your greatness. The law of *karma* is inexorable. Each one must reap what he sows. Fight, then, for Duryodhana if you must, but promise me two things."

"I'm truly blessed to be able to give boons to a mother I have hardly met," said Karna, "but please don't hesitate to ask for whatever you may want from me and I will surely not hesitate to give it to you."

Somewhat apprehensively, Kunti said, "Promise me then that you will not kill your brothers in battle."

Karna spoke sadly, "You have asked for the one thing that I cannot give, for you must know that I have promised to kill Arjuna in battle or be killed by him. But one thing I can promise you. I will not slay any of the others. I cannot let Duryodhana down, so fight I must with Arjuna until one of us is slain. But even then, O Mother, be satisfied that the number of your sons will remain the same. Now what is the other boon you wish to ask?"

"Promise me that you will not use the *Nagastra* weapon more than once against Arjuna," she said with trepidation. She knew that she was being grossly unfair to him, as she had been from his birth, yet she was also helpless to avert the decrees of fate, and she was bound to make a last desperate effort to save her five sons even at the cost of the sixth!

Karna laughed bitterly, "O Mother, my suspicions were correct. It is only your love for your other sons which has prompted you to approach me today and reveal your identity! But why are you worried? The Lord Himself is Arjuna's charioteer and it is ordained that victory will follow where Krishna is. My efforts will come to naught even if I refuse your request. It is obvious, therefore, that He Himself must have prompted you to request this boon in order to test my adherence to *dharma*! Therefore, I grant you the boon, O Mother. In any case, a heroic archer will not use an arrow more than once. But now that I have given you two boons, don't you think it proper that I should request something from you?"

Kunti gladly consented, for her heart was heavy with sorrow at the thought of her eldest son's fate.

Karna said, "Promise me that you will not reveal my identity to your other sons for the time being. If Yudhishthira knows who I am, he will offer me the kingdom and I, in turn, will give it to Duryodhana. It is best to keep silent on this matter. The second request is that if I'm killed by Arjuna, you shall come to the battlefield, take my body on your lap, and mourn over me, thus announcing my identity to all the world."

Kunti burst into tears as she granted him the two boons. Lovingly, she embraced him and blessed him. Fondly, she gazed at him, unable to tear her gaze away from his noble mien, for she felt that she would never see him alive again.

After she had left him, Karna sat and mused for long over the strange sequence of events that had made him what he was. Imbued as he was with all noble qualities, evil association alone had brought out the worst in him. Generous to a fault, there were many incidents in his life that proved his munificence. For Duryodhana he was prepared to give the greatest gift of all, the gift of his life. Had he been given the environmental opportunities and upbringing of the other Pandavas, there is no doubt that he might have excelled Yudhishthira in his virtues. The encounters with Indra and Kunti, instigated by the Lord, were calculated to bring out his best points. Another incident prompted by the Lord that brought out his munificence and generosity is worth mentioning here.

Soon after the *Rajasuya*, the Lord thought that Yudhishthira was getting a little too proud of his own generosity. He took him and Karna to the Himalayas, converted two hills into pure gold, gave one to each of them, and told them to use it in order to help people. Both of them were extremely pleased, since they were both generous souls. Yudhishthira engaged some workmen to dig the hill and distributed the gold daily to those who came to him for help. This went on for some months, until the whole hill was exhausted. Karna, in the meantime, issued a proclamation in the city that any desiring to have some gold could go and dig for themselves from the hill. Needless to say, the whole hill was cleared within ten days. This was a salutary lesson for Yudhishthira. He realized that if the word "munificent" could be applied to anyone, it could only be to Karna and that his own liberality was not a patch on the others! Thus, in many ways the Lord took pains to see that the world realized Karna's greatness.

Krishna then returned to Upaplavya, where the Pandavas were staying, and gave Yudhishthira a precise account of the happenings at the Kuru assembly. He ended by saying, "They will not, O Son of Pandu, give you even a pinpoint of land, much less the kingdom, without a battle. With death awaiting them, they will become the cause of a universal destruction!"

When Yudhishthira heard of the attempt on the Lord's life, he was furious. "Did he dare to do that? Then there is no hope for him. I will never forgive him for this. We will fight." Bhima was thrilled when he heard this. He threw his mace into the air, caught it, and shouted in glee, "War! War! Let us fight. The earth is thirsting for the blood of these sinners." Yudhishthira ordered his brothers to muster their army for the coming war. Needless to say, the brothers, as well as Draupadi, were delighted at the turn of events, for the injustice they had suffered at the hands of the Kauravas from childhood had fostered a bitterness in their souls that could never be appeased except in battle.

Krishna then gave Kunti's message to her sons. She had been a constant witness to the humiliations they had had to suffer at Duryodhana's hands from childhood and she also realized that war was inevitable. She had told Krishna before He left, "Remind my son Yudhishthira that the time has now come for my sons to fight for the cause of *dharma* on the battlefield. Tell him the story of the weak-minded Prince Sayana, who had to be goaded to fight a righteous war by his mother, even though she knew that he would perish in the battle."

This was a fitting message for a noble *kshatriya* lady to give her sons and Yudhishthira bowed to the will of fate. The seven *akshauhinis* and many great warriors assembled in the Pandava camp and Yudhishthira picked out the warriors who were to lead the *akshauhinis*. They were

Drupada, Virata, Drishtadyumna, Shikhandin, Satyaki, Chekitana, and Bhima. He then asked his brothers to choose a general from among these to be in overall charge of the army. Sahadeva recommended Virata, Nakula suggested Drupada, while Arjuna recommended his brother-in-law Drishtadyumna, and Bhima, Shikhandin.

Then, turning to Lord Krishna, Yudhishthira said, "The strength and weakness of everything in the universe as well as the intentions of everyone are well known to You, O Krishna! Old or young, skilled or unskilled, let him be the leader of my forces who is indicated by You, for You are at the root of our success or failure. In You are invested our lives, our kingdom, our prosperity and adversity, our happiness, and our misery. You are indeed the Ordainer and Creator. In You is established the fruition of our desires. Do You, therefore, name the leader of our host. Having selected him and worshipped our weapons, we will, under Your orders, march to the field of battle."

Krishna's opinion was that youth should take precedence over experience. Unhesitatingly, He supported Arjuna and chose Drishtadyumna as commander of the Pandava forces.

The battlefield of the Kurus was known as Kurukshetra and was situated eighty miles north of Indraprastha. The mythical river Sarasvati was supposed to have gone underground there. King Kuru, the progenitor of the dynasty, had himself plowed the land during the course of a holy rite that had been conducted there and had prayed that all those who died on the field would attain heaven. In a previous age, Parasurama, the sixth incarnation of Vishnu, had slaughtered twenty-one generations of evil *kshatriya* rulers on that field and made the holy lake of Syamantapanchaka red with their blood. In the morning, the Pandava host started to move toward this field. They pitched their camp beside the river Hiranavathi. The Lord Himself attended to the most minor details of the stationing of the troops.

At the same time, the Kaurava army also reached the field. Seeing this, Yudhishthira was once again struck with remorse and turned to Krishna for comfort. The latter reminded him of what had happened in the Kuru assembly and how even Bhishma, Drona, and Dhritarashtra had acquiesced in Duryodhana's wickedness by keeping silent. Vidura alone had remonstrated and he had been so badly insulted by Duryodhana that he had broken his famous bow, sworn not to participate in the war, and was already on his way to various pilgrimage spots. With a sigh, Yudhishthira realized that he was helpless against the decrees of fate.

In the Kaurava camp, it was decided that age and experience should take precedence over youth in the choice of a general. Moreover, Duryodhana must have realized that the Elders were helping him only because they did not want to betray their salt and not because they believed in his cause. The least he could do was to give them a place of importance, so he requested Bhishma to take charge of the army. Now it was Bhishma's turn to grade the warriors in their respective ranks according to their abilities. *Adhirathas* formed the first category. They were the bravest and most skilled, capable of fighting alone. Then came the *maharathas*, *samarathas*, and *artharathas*, graded according to the number of soldiers who would have to be deputed to help them. Karna received an unpleasant shock when he was degraded to the lowest category. Bhishma's explanation was that without his armor and earrings he was no longer invulnerable and would need to be protected by many soldiers. Duryodhana had to pacify the angry Karna, who swore not to fight as long as Bhishma was in command. "As long as Ganga's son is in command, O King, I shall never fight, but after he falls, I shall fight and kill the wielder of the Gandiva for you, as I promised." His pride had been so badly bruised that not even Duryodhana could make him waver from this strange decision.

Next came the macabre ceremony of offering a human sacrifice to the goddess Kali in order to ensure a victory. This practice was prevalent at that time, though the Pandavas did not seem to have resorted to such atrocities. The person to be offered had to be a perfect specimen of manhood and not just any senseless clod picked up at random.

When approached by Duryodhana, Bhishma said, "The person to be sacrificed must have all the thirty-two physical attributes of a perfect human being. Only two people qualify for this and both of them are in the Pandava camp. They are Lord Krishna and Iravan, the son of Arjuna. If you can persuade Iravan to sacrifice himself for your sake, then you will have accomplished two purposes, for he is a warrior beyond compare and can defeat the Kaurava forces single-handed in one day. As for the choice of an auspicious date for the sacrifice, there is no better astrologer than Sahadeva. Therefore, go and ask these things of him and Iravan. I firmly believe that, though they be most unreasonable requests on your part, yet devoted to righteousness as they are, they will accede."

Duryodhana is said to have gone to the Pandava camp in the middle of the night, so as not to be noticed by anyone, in order to solicit Iravan and Sahadeva for their help. Sahadeva welcomed him and Duryodhana spoke apprehensively, for even though he was steeped in selfishness, he felt rather uncertain as to the former's reaction. "I have come to you, O Sahadeva, for you have the reputation of being an expert in astrology. I want you to give me an auspicious date for offering a human sacrifice to the goddess Kali in order to ensure our victory."

"Certainly," Sahadeva replied unhesitatingly, and after consulting the almanac he said, "Whoever offers a human sacrifice on the new moon day (*Amavasi*) in the month of Margashirsha (November—December) will be victorious."

They were already in the month of December and the new moon was the day after next. This incident throws a great light on the character of the Pandavas. The fact that Duryodhana believed Sahadeva implicitly shows that not even he had any doubts about their inherent nobility. Jubilant at the success of his mission, Duryodhana hurried off to Iravan's tent without wasting time in thanking Sahadeva adequately. The request to Iravan was put with great trepidation, as can be imagined, for it was a request to sacrifice his own life to promote the cause of his enemies. But once again, Bhishma's words proved true, for Iravan showed himself a true son of the Pandavas and promised to present himself at the appointed time at the Kali temple on the night of the new moon. Certain that the war was already won, Duryodhana hurried back, elated with his success.

The happenings of the night were duly reported to Krishna the next morning. The Lord is the Knower of all things, yet he pretended to be surprised and annoyed at the behavior of the two so that the greatness of Yudhishthira's character would be known.

Yudhishthira embraced Sahadeva and Iravan in joy and said, "I am indeed proud of you both for not swerving from *dharma* even though your act may bring about our destruction." Then, turning to Krishna, he very simply and humbly told Him, "O Lord, we are in Your hands. Do with us as You will."

At first Krishna suggested that He Himself would take the place of Iravan, as He had the necessary qualities, but all of them were adamant that this should not be.

After a moment, He said, "Tomorrow is *amavasya*, the night of the new moon, when the sacrifice is to be offered. Get one thousand two hundred Brahmins to worship the sun and the moon today and persuade three hundred sages to observe the rites pertaining to the *Amavasi* today instead of tomorrow."

Without asking any questions, the Pandavas obeyed. It is said that Surya (the sun god) and Chandra (the moon god), noting these blunders being committed in their names, came down to complain to the Lord. Krishna asked them smilingly, "Do you know when *Amavasi* occurs?"

They were surprised at this childish question and answered, "But of course. It is the day of the new moon, when the sun and moon come together and thus the moon cannot be seen at all."

Krishna laughed and said, "Now, since both of you have come here together, today has to be *Amavasi* and not tomorrow! Now you may both return to your respective abodes."

Both of them were nonplussed at this neat definition and departed. Iravan said to Krishna, "I have promised Duryodhana to present myself at the Kali temple on the night of the new moon, so I should go today. It is unlikely that he will appear today, so grant me permission to sacrifice myself on this auspicious night for the sake of the Pandavas. I shall cut my flesh piece by piece and offer it to the goddess to ensure a Pandava victory, but even then, O Lord, please grant me the boon that I shall not die there, but on the battlefield."

Krishna smiled and granted him the boon. That night, Iravan adorned himself in the accepted manner, went to the Kali temple, and offered his flesh to the goddess. Yet, due to the Lord's blessings, he found himself still alive, though hardly anything more than a walking skeleton, and returned to fight for his father.

All these episodes before and during the war constitute the play of the Lord in which He tested His devotees again and again to prove to the world how great was their adherence to *dharma*. Since they passed with flying colors, the Lord Himself stepped in to prove that their *dharma* was capable of protecting them, thus exemplifying the great *Vedic* dictum, "*Dharmo rakshati rakshitaha* (dharma will protect him who upholds it)."

When he went to the Kali temple the next day and discovered his mistake, Duryodhana was furious. He suddenly remembered the words of his mother Gandhari when he had gone to her for her blessings before leaving for Kurukshetra. She had told him quite simply, "Where there is *dharma*, there will be victory!"

Bitterly, he thought how far he had deviated from *dharma* since he had considered sacrificing Arjuna's son in order to bring victory to himself. He gave vent to his venom by sending Shakuni's son Uluka to the Pandava camp in order to taunt them.

Uluka delivered the insulting message, "The time has come, O Cousins, to make good your oaths. Shamelessly you stood by and watched your wife being insulted and then meekly went away and lived like animals in the forest. Is there no manliness in you? Yudhishthira hides his cowardice under the cloak of righteousness. But beware, Bhima will soon be slaughtered by me, Arjuna by Karna, and as for the two little darlings, they are not even fit to wield arms! Your wife Draupadi is a common woman and the cowherd Krishna's sorcery and magic will be of no avail in the field of battle."

Arjuna said, "Only eunuchs fight with words. When the time comes, my Gandiva shall give a fitting answer to your master!"

Yudhishthira replied, "Remind Duryodhana that I made every effort to obtain my just due through peaceful means, not out of fear but because I believe in peace." Bhima roared that he would break Duryodhana's thighs and drink Dusshasana's blood, as he had sworn to do. Nakula swore to kill Uluka himself, and Sahadeva, his father Shakuni.

Krishna alone laughed at hearing these insults and told the gambler's son to tell his cousins that the cowherd's chariot would move like lightning through the ranks of the Kauravas, leaving death and destruction in its wake.

After Uluka's departure, Yudhishthira was sunk in gloom thinking of the senseless sacrifice of lives that would ensue in the coming battle. Krishna, Bhima, and Arjuna consoled him. "You have done your best, O Brother!" they said, "but fate is inevitable and it is our unpleasant duty as *kshatriyas* to fight for the cause of *dharma*."

Next came Balarama, accompanied by Akrura, and he told Yudhishthira, "This fierce and terrible slaughter seems inevitable. It is without doubt a decree of fate. But fear not, O King! Your victory is certain, for it is Krishna's wish. My affection for Duryodhana, however, is equal to that for Bhima, so I shall not participate in the war but shall go on a pilgrimage so that I need not be a witness to the slaughter."

The commanders in chief of the two armies, Bhishma and Drishtadyumna, now met and decided on the rules of battle. It was to be a *dharma yuddha*, or a war of righteousness. The battle was to take place only from sunrise to sunset, after which the opposing soldiers were free to mingle with each other if they so wished. No one was to attack an enemy from the rear. Anyone who surrendered or fled or played the coward should be spared. Battles should take place only between equals. For instance, those in chariots should only fight with their counterparts. Verbal jousts should not be violated with weapons. The battle would consist of indiscriminate fighting between foot soldiers or duels between equals. A single person should not be attacked by many. These and many other such rules were decided upon by the righteous commanders, but needless to say, during the course of the war most of these rules were abandoned.

Thus ends the twenty-fourth chapter of The Play of God,
named "Declaration of War."

Hari Aum Tat Sat

TWENTY-FIVE

SHRIMAD BHAGAVAD GITA

*Jagatgurave
namaha*

Homage to the
preceptor of
the Universe

*Aum. O Mother Bhagavad Gita, consisting of eighteen chapters
and showering the immortal message of nonduality which is the
destroyer of rebirth, composed within the Mahabharata by the
ancient sage Vyasa, by which Arjuna was illumined by Lord
Narayana Himself. On Thee, O Mother, I meditate.*
—BHAGAVAD GITA MEDITATION VERSE

Wars are first fought in the minds of men before
they are fought in actuality. The bitterness and
jealousy that had been festering in the minds of
the cousins for many years culminated in the mighty
Mahabharata war, which was fought in eighteen days.

The ten days following the new moon, on which the
human sacrifice was to have been made, were spent in
ayuddha puja, or the ceremonial worship of the weapons,
by both sides. Winter rains had swept the field. Kurukshetra was wet and slushy when the great war commenced on the eleventh day of the bright fortnight, when
the planet Krittika was in ascendancy in the month of
Margashirsha. It was the auspicious day known as
Vaikunth Ekadashi. Some modern calculators place the
war on Friday, November 22, 3067 B.C. The great message of Lord Krishna to his friend Arjuna, known as the
Shrimad Bhagavad Gita, was given on the morning of the
first day of the battle.

The mighty epic of the *Mahabharata* reached its climax during the eighteen days of battle. The Lord's role in
this war is similar to the role He plays in our lives as the
inner guide and counselor, ever ready and willing to lead
the chariot of our lives through the turbulent battlefield
of Kurukshetra into the haven of a *dharmakshetra*, or

253

divine life, if we, like Arjuna, give over the reins of our chariot into His capable hands and have utter faith and trust in Him. Though the Kauravas had numerical superiority, the Pandavas won, since the Lord Himself was Partha's *sarati* (Arjuna's charioteer). Even this humble role He was willing to take up for the sake of His devotee and friend who had surrendered his all to Him. This is one of the most sublime and elevating episodes in His enthralling life, His *Uttama Lila*, or Supreme Game. At the commencement of the battle, He boosted up Arjuna's flagging spirits with the glorious teaching of the *Bhagavad Gita* and the revelation of His Cosmic Form. In the following days, it was only due to His advice and skillful maneuvering of the chariot that the Pandavas won against insuperable odds. So also, if we have God with us, there is no adversity we cannot overcome.

The night before the war, Yudhishthira could not sleep. He told Krishna, "My Lord, I cannot bear the idea of fighting with our grandfather and the *gurus*. I hate the very idea of this war. How are we to kill these Elders whom we have been worshipping for all these years?"

Krishna said, "Yudhishthira, you have been born as a *kshatriya*. So do your duty as one. Look at your grandfather. He has willingly undertaken to command the Kaurava army. Kripa, Drona, Ashvatthama, all of them could have refused to fight as Vidura did, but all of them agreed to help Duryodhana. So why are you flinching from doing your part?"

Krishna continued, "What sin is there, O Brother, in killing those who have sworn to kill us? These Elders, though knowing everything about us, have opted to side with Duryodhana, so why are you so frightened to fight them? We have to fight. There is no going back. The river, having once left its mountain fastness, is bound to go rushing down to meet the sea. The river of battle had already started on its course. None can stop it except the ocean of death!"

Both armies were now assembled on the plain of Kurukshetra by the side of the river Hiranavathi. The Pandavas were on the western side near the holy lake and the Kauravas on the eastern. The arena of battle extended over fifty-eight square kilometers of territory. The code of warfare had already been decided upon but, as will be seen, one by one in the following days, every rule was thrown overboard. War corrupts and makes man susceptible to every type of *adharma*. In the end, even the Pandavas succumbed.

On the morning of the commencement of the battle, the sage Vyasa went to the blind King Dhritarashtra at Hastinapura. Dhritarashtra was very anxious to have some idea of the happenings on the battlefield and so the sage endowed the king's Prime Minister, Sanjaya, with clairvoyance to enable him to give a firsthand report of the battle to the king. The events of the battle, as reported in the *Mahabharata*, are therefore spoken by Sanjaya.

The song of the Lord, known as the *Bhagavad Gita*, which contains the crux of His teaching to mankind, is placed at the very outset of the great war and comes in the middle portion of the epic, thus denoting its supreme importance in the eyes of its author, Vyasa. In the opening chapter of the *Bhagavad Gita*, Sanjaya gives a swift portrait to the blind king of the various generals stationed on either side and of the activities preparatory to battle. Flags were flying, drums were booming, conchs and trumpets were blaring, men were eager and restive, as were the horses. The two armies had drawn up in battle formation. The stage was set for the final scene in the mighty drama of their lives, the grand climax the cousins had been expecting and preparing for during the major portion of their lives.

Ten *akshauhinis* of the Kauravas were arranged in a formidable phalanx. The eleventh was directly under Bhishma, who was right in front. His horses were white, his chariot was silver, and his armor gleamed like silver in the morning sun. His banner was a golden palm with five stars. His noble mien gave great confidence to the Kaurava troops. Duryodhana was in the middle. His banner of a serpent embroidered on a golden cloth was fluttering gaily in the breeze.

Suddenly, Sanjaya's narrative was arrested by the appearance of the main characters: Arjuna, tall and handsome, standing in the chariot holding the bow Gandiva and Krishna, seated in front holding the reins in His steady hands, controlling the four milk-white steeds, which were straining at the bit and eager to charge into battle. The Lord's face was beautiful to behold. His lotus eyes were filled with compassion as He gazed at the flower of *Aryan* manhood which had assembled on the battlefield. Bhishma, Drona, and Kripa mentally saluted the noble pair, for they knew that they were beholding the *avatars* of Nara and Narayana. Hanuman had taken his place on Arjuna's terrible ape banner, striking terror into the hearts of the soldiers by his fierce gesticulations.

Arjuna told Krishna to take the chariot to the center of the field between the opposing armies so that he could observe both sides and get an overall picture of the situation before the battle commenced. Obedient to his role as a charioteer, Krishna, the Lord of all the worlds, obeyed the command of His friend Arjuna and drove the chariot to this no-man's land between the opposing armies. Arjuna, the mighty hero of the age, surveyed the opposing army and saw, not his enemies, but his cousins, friends, relations, teachers, nephews, and grandsire. A tremendous psychological revulsion welled up in him. The full impact of the terrible destruction that was to take place hit him like a blow in the solar plexus. His whole body trembled with the shock, his mind reeled, his mighty bow Gandiva fell from his nerveless grasp, and he collapsed in a heap at the back of the chariot. Bringing forth many ethical and moral considerations for avoiding such a conflict, this mighty bowman told the Lord that he would not fight. To him who was thus in such a pitiable condition, Lord Krishna, his friend, philosopher, and God, imparted this most marvelous spiritual instruction, the highest spiritual instruction that can be given to humanity, known as the *Shrimad Bhagavad Gita*, or *The Song of God*. The Lord chose to sing His song in the middle of a battlefield with the background of drums and conchs and not in the silence of the forest, the sanctity of a temple, or the peace of an ashram. What was His purpose in choosing such a location? Arjuna and He had been very close. They had often been alone together when the Lord could have advised him, but He had not chosen to do so. Why was this? Why did He pick this peculiar location?

The philosophy of the *Gita* is not for the weak or cowardly person who is afraid to face life as it is. It is for the heroic one, who is ready to face the challenges of life in the effort to evolve into godliness. The *Bhagavad Gita* does not teach an ethical sentimentalism that loves to look on nature as good and beautiful and refuses to face her grim and frightening mask. Unless we have the courage to face existence as it is, we will never be able to arrive at a solution to its conflicting demands. Harmony has to be achieved in and through the disharmony we cannot deny. War and destruction seem to be the principle not only of our material lives, but our mental lives as well. Life is a battlefield of good and evil forces. We are placed in the center of this field, now swayed by the good, now drawn by the evil. As in the Mahabharata war, the latter appears to be far stronger than the former.

Like Arjuna, we stand in this no-man's land between the opposing forces. Every moment we are faced with decisions and controversies. Perplexed and torn between the warring forces within ourselves, we know not which way to turn. The famous pictorial representation of the *Bhagavad Gita*, in which Arjuna is seated in the chariot with Lord Krishna holding a firm rein over the four white prancing horses, is an allegory of our conflicted life. The chariot represents the body, with Arjuna as the *jivatma*, or the embodied soul, seated within. Lord Krishna is the *Paramatma*, or the cosmic Soul, who has ever been his boon companion, but whom he has not so far recognized as the Supreme. The four horses represent the four aspects of the mind, *manas*, *buddhi*, *ahamkara*, and *chitta* (mind, intellect, ego, and superconsciousness). This mental equipment drives us like uncontrollable horses, hither and thither, in its mad quest for enjoyment. Arjuna, the embodied soul, was faced with a violent crisis that seemed quite incompatible with his aspirations for a spiritual life, or even for a moral life. But he had the sense to realize that by himself he was helpless, and therefore he had given over the reins of his life into the capable and willing hands of his divine charioteer, who steered him through this dangerous battle with ease, protected him, and led him to a glorious victory.

In all their years of friendship, Arjuna had never thought of turning to Krishna for advice because he had always considered himself competent to solve his own problems. Now, at that crucial hour when he should have been at the peak of his mental and physical powers, he found himself a wreck, his mind torn and perplexed as to his duty, and his body weak and helpless. Only then did he think of turning to the Lord and, having surrendered his ego, he begged Him to come to his aid.

The Lord within us, who is ever our boon companion, waits patiently for us to play out our game of make-believe as the sole hero of our life's drama. He waits patiently until the day dawns when we stumble and realize that without the director, we are helpless and turn to Him for help. At this point, the Lord rushes to us like a loving mother, points out the clear-cut path of duty, assists us to avoid the forces of evil, and even carries us across the treacherous crosscurrents of life, if necessary. The message of the *Gita* is thus addressed to the fighter, the person of action, for whom life is a battlefield, as it is to all of us. Kurukshetra (field of the Kurus) has to be conquered before reaching the haven of *dharmakshetra* (field of virtue). Life is not merely a battlefield, but also a field where righteousness prevails.

The teaching of the *Gita* is therefore not merely a spiritual philosophy or an ethical doctrine but a *yogashastra*,[1] which gives us a clear idea of the practical application of these doctrines in daily life. The recipient of the message is Arjuna, the prototype of the struggling human soul who is ready to receive the great knowledge through close companionship and increasing nearness to the Divine Self within him, embodied as his charioteer. The teacher of the *Gita* is, therefore, not only the God who is transcendent, but also the God in us who unveils Himself through an increasing knowledge. He is also the God in us who instigates all actions and toward whom all human life proceeds and travels. He is at once the secret guide to our actions, the highest source of all knowledge, and our closest friend, companion, and relation.

That is why the *Gita's* message is still as fresh as when it was first given five thousand years ago, for it is always renewable in the personal experience of every human being. The central idea is to reconcile and effect a unity between the inner, highest spiritual truth in ourselves and the cosmos on the one hand, and the outer actualities of our life and action on the other. Thus, it is a guide for each one of us in our day-to-day lives. Whatever the problem we might face, whether horrifying or sanctifying, it can be solved by the application of the *Gita's* teachings. Its meaning is so deep that the more we read it, the more we learn from it, and the more we live according to its teaching, the more our level of consciousness rises. Its message is of eternity and so it has a timeless significance for all of us. It is not a message conveyed in a mere temporal language to suit a specific occasion. Rather, the occasion was taken to convey to the eternal individual the knowledge of its relationship with the Eternal Absolute. The union of the *jivatma* with the *Paramatma* is the final consummation of the *Bhagavad Gita*. The word *gita* means song and the *Bhagavad Gita* is the song of God and therefore the song of Life—of Existence and Omniscience leading to Bliss—*Sat*, *Chit*, and *Ananda*.

The first chapter is known as Arjuna *vishada yoga*, or the *yoga* of Arjuna's despondency, in which he refuses to fight with his relations. The Lord listens to his arguments quietly and it is only in the second chapter that He begins His beautiful sermon. Krishna explains to Arjuna that each person has a certain duty in life, his *svadharma*, which depends on his station, birth, and position in society as well as on his nature. This duty should be followed regardless of personal prejudices and without attachment to the fruits. The work itself brings its own reward.

---

[1] *yogashastra*—a scripture on the practical application of spiritual knowledge.

The second chapter gives the philosophy of *sankhya yoga*, or the *yoga* of wisdom, in which the Lord declares the immortality of the soul and the mortality of the body. We grieve, for we think we are the body and therefore mortal. This is the root cause of all sorrow. The moment one understands that one is the *Atman* alone and that the body is a mere appendage that the *Atman* takes and uses for its own purpose and then discards like a worn-out garment, then there is an end to all fears, especially the fear of death. Though knowing ourselves to be the immortal soul, yet we have a duty to carry out the work appointed to us in life. This should be done while maintaining a balance of mind in the face of all dualities such as pleasure and pain, gain and loss, treating alike victory and defeat. The grandsire Bhishma was a perfect example of the *sthitaprajna*, or the person of perfection, as portrayed in the second chapter.

In the third, fourth, and fifth chapters, He delineates the glorious path of *karma yoga*, or the *yoga* of action. All of us have been given the organs of action by which we can make our way in the world. The law of the cosmos is to be endlessly active. Therefore, we who are part of this universe cannot remain inactive for even one minute. Yet, there is a mistaken understanding that if a person remains inactive as far as the organs of action are concerned, this can be called inaction. This is a misrepresentation of the law of *karma*, says Krishna. The greatest action is done by the mind and even one who is inactive physically is never inactive mentally. Again, there is a mistaken notion that physical action alone binds us to the law of *karma*. The Lord asserts that it is not action that binds, for if that were true, no creature could ever become liberated since none can be totally actionless. What binds us is the mind, which imposes certain reasons for doing the action, primarily the burning desire for the fruits of the action. Thus it is that the Lord makes His famous statement in the second chapter: "Your right is to the work alone and not to the fruits thereof."

Karma binds only when it is done for purely selfish reasons. The same action, when done selflessly with no attachment to the results and in a spirit of surrender to the divine, becomes converted to *karma yoga*, a purifying process which leads to liberation, or freedom from the cycle of birth and death. When *karma* is blended with the glorious *vikarma*[2] of love, then it is transmuted into worship and can be offered to the divine, just as one would offer a flower or fruit during the course of worship.

---

2 *vikarma*—special action; used here in the sense of mental action.

Whatever the nature of the work that one is called upon to perform in the discharge of one's station and calling in life, it can be considered an act of worship that can take us to *mukti*, or liberation. To renounce the action physically and dwell on it mentally is denounced vehemently by the Lord as the action of a hypocrite. Thus, a *sannyasi* (monk) who has physically renounced his hearth and home and retired to the Himalayas but continues to dwell upon the objects of renunciation with longing is deluding himself.

A householder who continues to discharge his duties in a spirit of detachment and as an offering to the divine is the true renouncer. We have only one right and that is the right to do our duty in a spirit of *yajna*, or sacrifice. The whole of creation works with this spirit of *yajna*. Nothing is done for oneself alone. Human beings alone defy this law and thus suffer, for no one can flout the cosmic laws with impunity. All of creation is a well-knit whole. Each and every thing in the cosmos is irrevocably bound to everything else. Those who refuse to see this and act purely for selfish reasons live in vain. Suffering and rebirth alone will be the fruits of their actions.

The sixth chapter gives a simple and effective method of *dhyana*, or meditation, by which the mind can be trained to achieve union with God. From the seventh chapter onward, the Lord touches on *bhakti yoga*, or the *yoga* of devotion. The Supreme possesses a twofold nature of matter and spirit. Matter is His lower nature. A true devotee is one who learns to see the spirit alone shining through every atom of matter. After many lives of progressive spiritual attainment, one acquires this type of spiritual vision, which sees Vaasudeva (the Lord) alone in everything. Such a soul is rare indeed! "*Vaasudeva sarvamiti sa mahatma sa durlabhaha* (Rare indeed is the noble soul who can see everything as Vaasudeva, as divine)."

The eighth chapter deals with the little-known and thus greatly feared state called death. The Lord tells Arjuna that whatever thought grips the mind at the time of death is the one which will propel it and decide for it the nature of its future birth. Thus, if one wants to attain God after death, one has to think of Him steadfastly at the time of death. But this is not as simple as it sounds, for at the time of death the mind automatically flies to the thought of that object which has possessed it during its sojourn in the world. If money has been the object of our life's pursuit, to money the mind will fly at the time of death. Thus, the Lord tells Arjuna that if he wants to think of God at the moment of death, he will have to habituate the mind to think of Him constantly. "*Mam anusmara yudya cha* (Think of Me constantly and fight)." Thus, the *yoga* of the *Gita* involves a twenty-four hour affair with the Divine Beloved, culminating in a total fusion at the time of death, when the physical body drops away and there is perfect union with the Divine.

Chapter nine gives the mystic secret by which one may attain liberation even in this very life. A devotee should surrender not only all outer actions but all inner thoughts at the lotus feet of the Lord. Even the negative thoughts should be surrendered, for He will slowly bring about a transmutation of the dross into gold. The one who is thus in constant communion with Him has no need to worry about anything more, for the Lord gives a solemn promise that He Himself will take care of his or her material and spiritual welfare. The Lord will supply all the wants, however mundane, leaving the person free to continue spiritual pursuits and He will lead such a one to salvation just as He did the Pandavas. Helpless and downtrodden, buffeted by the faithless winds of fate, they achieved victory and recovered their lost heritage because the Lord was ever with them, making them perform seemingly impossible tasks, almost carrying them through the gory river of battle, as will be seen. The promise He makes to Arjuna is in fact given to all of us. "*Kaunteya pratijanihi na me bhakta pranashyati* (O Arjuna, I pledge to you that My devotee will never perish)."

Chapter ten gives the *vibhuti yoga*, or the *yoga* of divine glories, so that the mind of the devotee may learn to see Him in all things, both glorious and mundane. To begin with, we must train ourselves to see Him in the majestic things like the sun, the ocean, and the Himalayas, but later we must learn to behold Him even in the smallest and most insignificant objects of the world. One must learn to worship Him in both the elephant and the ant, in both the beautiful as well as the ugly, in both the sinner and the saint.

In the eleventh chapter, Krishna shows Arjuna His fearful form as *Kala*, or all-consuming Time, the greatest killer, the destroyer of all beings. This vision was different from the one He showed at the Kuru court. It was at once supremely beautiful and terrifying, for it was a direct answer to Arjuna's request to see His Cosmic Form. The love He bore Arjuna was so great that He was prepared to grant His every wish. The glory that Arjuna saw was that of the entire cosmos resting within the form of the Lord. The vision enabled Arjuna to understand not only that everything emanates from Him but that He Himself is everything.

"Time eternal and all-consuming am I, the Ordainer with faces turned to every side. I am death, which seizes all, as well as the source of life, from which it all emanates. That which is the seed of all things am I. Supporting this universe with but a tiny portion of Myself do I stand."

Arjuna realized that all beings are one in God. But the most important teaching of the chapter, which Arjuna grasped, was that even the actions which he thought of as his own were really not his, but the Lord's, using him as an instrument.

Arjuna was both terrified and enraptured as he gazed on the Lord's Cosmic Form. The countless hosts of both the Kurus and the Pandavas were seen entering into Him. Each arm, each hand, each weapon was an arm, a hand and a weapon of the Divine Charioteer. Like moths rushing to a flame did all these living beings rush toward Him to be consumed in the fierce and terrible energy that was emanating from Him. This fearsome spectacle overwhelmed him. He shrank back and begged Krishna to forgive him for having treated Him in a familiar manner. All these years, Arjuna had considered Krishna to be only an exceptional human being, but now he saw to his consternation that His friend was in reality the one Friend of the whole universe.

"O God of gods! O Refuge of the Universe! Be kind to me!" he cried, appalled at the enormity of his offense. "Whatever disrespect I might have shown to You in the past, pray forgive me for You are possessed of boundless compassion."

Hearing this plea, the Lord once more resumed His previous form, that delectable form which enraptured all those who saw it. The Cosmic Form was shown to Arjuna to make him realize that a human being can neither create nor destroy. All action is, in fact, universal action. So long as we do not realize this, we are bound by the results of our actions, but once we do realize it, then we are no longer bound, for we act as instruments of the Divine. Our duty is only to make ourselves fitting instruments to be used by Him in whatever capacity He may think fit. "*Nimitta matram bhava savyasachin,*" says the Lord. (Do thou be an instrument alone, O Arjuna.)

The final verse of the chapter sums up the entire teaching of the *Gita*. "O Son of Pandu, the one who performs action for my sake, who considers Me as the Supreme goal of life, who is devoted to Me, who is devoid of attachment, and who is without animosity toward any living being, that one alone finds it easy to attain Me."

The twelfth chapter is known as *bhakti yoga*, or the *yoga* of devotion. In reply to Arjuna's question, the Lord points out that devotion to the formless Brahman is very difficult for the human mind to achieve, for it is conditioned to see forms only. Therefore, it is better to meditate on the Lord with form, for God can be in any form in which the devotee likes to picture Him. If this is done with the knowledge that all forms merely point to the formless and supreme *Purushottama* (Supreme Person), then the devotee will easily reach the goal which striving *yogis* attain only after much painful effort. The devotee of the formless Brahman considers the senses to be betrayers, and suppresses and forces them into submission. The devotee of God with form, however, enlists the aid of even the senses in worship. The devotee offers all the activities of the senses, together with the flowers gathered from the garden, at the lotus feet of the Lord. Seeing his or her Beloved in every form, he or she worships the whole of creation. Friendly and compassionate to all, he or she is ever contented with whatever he or she gets, for everything is an image of his or her Beloved. Such devotee are balanced in joy and sorrow, free from envy, fear, and anxiety. They have no disappointments, since they have no expectations. They are perfectly satisfied with whatever comes unasked, for everything is a gift from their Beloved. Their joy emanates from a nontemporal source and their only resolve is to love Him and serve Him to the best of their ability.

In the thirteenth chapter, Shri Krishna declares that this body of ours is the *kshetra*, or field, which the Divine uses as His playground. The Divine Spirit which thus uses this field is known as *kshetrajna*, or the knower of the field. The bodies of all creatures are the individual fields of action and the universe, the universal field. But the knower of all these is one and the same—the Lord Himself, the *kshetrajna*. In the state of ignorance, the *jivatma* thinks that it alone is both the knower and the actor. Thus it keeps sowing the seeds for future births in different fields and has to reap the harvest of births in successive wombs. With the dawn of enlightenment, the *jiva* realizes that the Lord's *Prakriti* is the universal Actor and the Lord Himself the universal Knower, and that the individual as a separate entity does not exist. With this realization, its role as a separate person in the cosmic drama comes to an end.

In the fourteenth chapter, the three modes of *Prakriti*: *sattva*, *rajas*, and *tamas*, are explained. *Sattva* is the principle of harmony or equilibrium, *rajas*; the principle of kinesis or action; and *tamas*, the principle of lethargy or inertia. This is the modus operandi of *Prakriti*, through which She activates the whole of creation. All imaginable things are formed of a combination and permutation of these three modes. The way to liberation lies in overcoming *rajas* and *tamas* and developing *sattvic* qualities like peace, harmony, and tranquility, for this provides a fitting background for the divinity to shine within us. Finally, of course, even *sattva* has to be transcended, for even it is a product of *Prakriti*. The one who has transcended these three *gunas* is thus known as *trigunatita*, and his or her qualifications are similar to those of the *sthitaprajna* of the second chapter and the *karma yogi* of the third.

The fifteenth chapter is known as *Purushottama yoga*, or the *yoga* of the Supreme Person, wherein Lord Krishna declares Himself to be the *Purushottama* who stands above the *kshara* and the *akshara*, matter and spirit, by the interaction of which the entire world process comes into being. The *Purushottama* can be said to be above this inasmuch as He is both transcendent and immanent. Though He permeates each and every atom, yet creation cannot contain Him, since the effect cannot contain the cause.

The world process is compared to a mighty tree with its roots stretching upward to the infinite, its branches spreading downward into the world, and its aerial roots probing into the earth and binding the embodied soul with its strong bonds of attachment. Using the sharp-edged sword of discrimination, one has to cut asunder these clinging roots and thus gain liberation.

The sixteenth and seventeenth chapters are in the nature of corollaries, and the eighteenth chapter is a grand summing-up of the entire teaching. In the sixteenth chapter, the difference between the divine and the demonic qualities is given, so that one can try to shun the demonic and develop the divine. However noble we may think ourselves, there lurks a devil in each of our bosoms, and one has to strive hard to eradicate it.

The seventeenth chapter is known as the *yoga* of the threefold faith and the Lord gives a masterly analysis of how the three modes of nature (*sattva*, *rajas*, and *tamas*) infiltrate even our noblest actions such as worship, charity, austerity, and sacrifice, as well as mundane things like the food we eat. The three modes color every aspect of our actions so that the *rajasic* person's charity is for show and ostentation, the *tamasic* person's worship is a mere mumbling of prayers with no understanding of their meaning or effect, lacking faith and firmness, while the *sattvic* soul performs all actions with firmness, generosity, and no desire for personal gain. Foods that are bland and promote mental as well as physical strength, vitality, and health are known as *yogic* foods and are *sattvic* in nature. *Rajasic* foods are hot and spicy and give rise to disease and passion. *Tamasic* foods are stale and unwholesome and give rise to sloth and sleep. Thus, the Lord analyzes every aspect of man's nature and activity and gives a perfect method for how best we can try to surmount *rajas* and *tamas*, starting from the basic level with the foods we eat, until our entire system is purified and we can transcend the *gunas* of *Prakriti* and reach the state of the *Purushottama*. The great *mantra* "Aum Tat Sat" should be repeated at the beginning and end of every action, for it denotes the Supreme and reminds the doer that all acts are done by His *Prakriti* and that the fruits should be dedicated to Him.

Finally, in the last and eighteenth chapter, known as the *yoga* of liberation through renunciation, the Lord summarizes all that has been said before. He reiterates that the real *sannyasi* is the one who has renounced the sense of being the doer of actions and such a one is also the real *tyagi* (renunciate), for *sannyasa* is not a mere matter of wearing ochre robes and giving up home and family life. It entails a renunciation in the mind of clinging attachment to the things of the world. Such a one can live in the world and play a part in the cosmic drama as an instrument in the hands of the Supreme *Purushottama*. Thus, Arjuna has to play his part, has to renounce his *tamasic* attachment to relatives and take up his mighty bow in the interests of the world at large. As the Gandiva is in his own hands, so also is he in the hands of the Divine Archer. Krishna's final words to his beloved disciple Arjuna and through him to the world are, "Fix your mind on Me, be devoted to Me, sacrifice all unto Me, offer adorations to Me, and you will surely attain Me. This do I promise you, for you are dearly beloved by Me." And once again as a final benediction, "Having renounced all *dharmas*, take refuge in Me alone. Verily I promise you that I shall free you from all sins and lead you to liberation."

We carry the burden of our lives like mindless donkeys, not realizing that the Lord within us is ever ready to bear the brunt of our lives, to laugh and cry with us, to nurse and suckle us, to care for and comfort us. No one is born alone and none needs to die alone, so why should we live alone? Into this Kurukshetra of life we are projected like Arjuna, not alone and helpless as we think, but ever protected by the charioteer within us. He has ever been with us and is ever ready to help us, provided we allow ourselves to be helped. We must take off the armor of our separative egos, with which we think we are protecting ourselves, but with which we are actually barricading ourselves against Him, the *Paramatma* and the *Purushottama*, nearer to us than our nearest, dearer than the dearest, sole friend, sole relation, sole guide for the whole of mankind. Therefore, surrender to Him and live in harmony and peace, devoid of cares, like the fortunate child who cuddles into its mother's arms and is carried by her through the bustle and turbulence of life.

Tenderly, the Lord asked His beloved Arjuna, "Have you listened to my teaching with single-pointed concentration, O Arjuna? Has your delusion born of ignorance been destroyed?"

At these words Arjuna, with his mind clear and his nerves and muscles made as firm as steel, fearlessly replied, "By Your grace, O Lord, my delusion has gone and I have gained my senses. I am now fixed in my resolve and will do as You command."

Saying this, he sprang to his feet and gave a blast on his conch Devadatta, while Krishna blew the *Panchajanya*, sending a thrill of joy through the Pandava ranks and a shock of fear through the Kauravas. At the end of the sermon, Sanjaya declared to the blind king, "Blessed am I, O King, for by the grace of Vyasa I have heard this thrilling discourse by the Master Yogi and I am enraptured. Wherever there is Krishna, the Master of Yoga, and Partha, the wielder of the bow, there will be prosperity, victory, glory, and righteousness. This is my firm conviction."

Krishna and Arjuna stand for the *jivatma* and the *Paramatma*, the embodied being and God seated together in the chariot of the body. When man or woman and God stand united, when the individual works in collaboration with the Divine, when he or she becomes the living conscious instrument of the Divine, then there can never be defeat for such a one. Righteousness and victory are the natural offspring of this blissful union.

Thus ends the twenty-fifth chapter of The Play of God, *named "Shrimad Bhagavad Gita."*

Hari Aum Tat Sat

This Self is never born, nor does It ever perish, nor having been born before will It be born in the future. This Self is unborn, eternal, imperishable, and ageless. Though the body is slain, the Self does not perish.
—*Shrimad Bhagavad Gita*

TWENTY-SIX

THE MAHABHARATA WAR

Parthasarataye namaha

Homage to the charioteer of Arjuna

The gory river of battle whose banks were Bhishma and Drona, whose water was Jayadratha, whose treacherous blue lotus was Shakuni, whose shark was Shalya, whose current was Kripa, whose tidal wave was Karna, whose terrible crocodiles were Ashvatthama and Vikarna, and whose whirlpool was Duryodhana, was crossed over with ease by the Pandavas with Lord Krishna as their ferryman.
—BHAGAVAD GITA MEDITATION VERSE

Now everything was ready and the two armies were set to commence the war. Yudhishthira, over whose head waved the royal insignia of a pure white umbrella, was seated in his chariot gazing at the opposite side with a set and stern face, prepared to submit to the will of the Lord and abide by his duty, however unpalatable it might be. Next came the gigantic Bhima, who had no qualms about the task at hand and whose mighty arms ached for having been held back so long from grappling with the wicked Dusshasana. His face was red and fiery with repressed anger. Then came Arjuna, standing tall and radiant in the jeweled chariot with the four milk-white steeds driven by Lord Krishna, who was shining and resplendent like a thousand suns risen together. His look, filled with compassion, was enough to grant liberation to all those who died gazing at His immaculate form. The reins of the prancing horses were held lightly, yet firmly, in His slender fingers and His unfailing smile swept over the entire host as if in benediction. Next came the twins, Nakula and Sahadeva, slim and handsome, their chariots drawn by two steeds with flowing manes and tails and fiery eyes. Then came Drishtadyumna, general of the Pandava army, Draupadi's brother, born to kill Drona. Over each warrior waved his own special pennon.

On the opposite side, in the center of the army, Duryodhana appeared, riding on an elephant, beneath the umbrella of state. At the head of his forces, under a banner bearing the device of a palm tree, stood Bhishma, the ancient knight clad in white armor in a chariot driven by white horses. Behind him were Drona, with red horses, and the heroic Karna, waiting to succeed to the command at the fall of Bhishma. Duryodhana, who always suspected that Drona's and Bhishma's allegiance lay elsewhere, approached his preceptor and warned him in veiled terms of the consequences of disregarding his duty. "Behold, O Teacher, the mighty army of the Pandavas arrayed for battle under the command of your wise disciple Drishtadyumna, the son of Drupada!"

This was a deliberate jibe at Drona, who had been stupid enough, so Duryodhana thought, to teach the art of warfare to the son of his archenemy Drupada, who had sworn to kill him. Duryodhana, of course, could never understand the high code of chivalry that motivated great souls like Drona, Bhishma, and Yudhishthira. He warned Drona in no uncertain terms that his duty was to protect Bhishma at all costs. The grandsire roared like a lion and blew his mighty conch, which was a sign for the battle to commence. At that signal, Yudhishthira, to the amazement of the onlookers, dismounted and walked unarmed up to Bhishma and Drona. The Kauravas sneered mockingly, for they thought that this was a last cowardly gesture on the part of the Pandava king. Fearlessly, he walked up to the Elders, bowed low, and spoke. "In our desire for the kingdom, we have dared to array ourselves against you, who are worthy of worship. Pray forgive us and bless us and grant us permission to fight against you."

Drona and Bhishma were full of love and admiration for this great pupil of theirs, who had never deviated from the path of *dharma*. Both of them blessed him and gave him permission to fight against them. After Yudhishthira returned, Bhishma warned Duryodhana that he would never kill any of the Pandavas, who were like his grandsons, but that he would destroy ten thousand of their soldiers daily.

Krishna now took Arjuna to get the blessings of the grandsire, who welcomed them and said, "Hail, O Madhava (Krishna). You know the past, present, and future. Everything is a divine sport to you. As long as I carry weapons, I can never be killed by anyone but you, O Krishna.

Therefore, I desire that you might take up arms against me. Let me see if You will grant my wish!" Then, turning to Arjuna, his favorite grandson, the old knight laid his hands lovingly and tenderly on his head and blessed him. With eyes filled with tears, Arjuna saluted the grandsire and returned. Yudhishthira now shouted to the opposing ranks, "Is there anyone among you who is desirous to come over to our side? If so, you are welcome." At this, Yuyutsu, a great chariot warrior and the illegitimate son of Dhritarashtra by a maidservant, walked over to the Pandava camp and was welcomed.

Just then a small bird, a lapwing, who had built her nest on the turf in the middle of the battlefield, drew the attention of the Lord by her cries of anxiety and distress for her young.

"Poor little mother," He said tenderly, "let this be your protection."

So saying, He removed the nest to the side of the field and placed a great elephant bell, which lay on the ground, over the nest. Through the eighteen days of raging battle that followed, the lapwing and its nestlings were kept in safety by the mercy of the Lord, who never failed to give it some food daily and who was the only one who could spare a thought to the smallest of His creations, even at such a crucial time as this. Similar was the care He took over every person on the battlefield, even though their limited vision may not have been able to appreciate this fact fully. Some deserved death and others life, and to each was given his just deserts. But everything was done so unobtrusively that it appeared to be by chance. It was ever His way to look on the world as if it were a play. Sometimes He would remove an obstacle so that the will of the players would have unimpeded scope and sometimes place an obstacle for the same reason. In this way, He allowed events to work themselves out according to the law of *karma*, striving ever to aid the course of destiny, even though this led in the end to the self-destruction of all things. In this battle He guided the fortunes of both sides in an unobtrusive manner, but for the sake of the Pandavas, who had surrendered their all to Him, He often broke His normal code of conduct and actively took a lead, even though His role as a charioteer was apparently that of the uninvolved witness. He thus saved them many times from the consequences of their own folly. If there was any *adharmic* (unrighteous) act to be done, He always did it Himself, for the Lord is always above His own laws, whereas for a human being to transgress these laws would result in infamy and ruin. A devotee may act in a quixotic and sometimes foolhardy way, but the Lord will intervene and save him, even at the risk of getting a bad name. With His wide-angle vision encompassing all the three states of Time—past, present, and future—He is ever able to judge and decide what is best for His creation. By the sheer power of their love for Him and the total surrender of their egos, the Pandavas compelled the Lord to do all things for them, just as Bhishma compelled Him by the power of his love to take up arms against him, as will be seen.

Bhishma sparked off the battle by his clarion call to the ranks. "O *Kshatriyas!* Here is a golden opportunity for you to exhibit your hero-ism. We are now standing on the threshold of heaven. The portals are open to you. To die of old age and disease on a comfortable bed in his own house is a shame for a *kshatriya!* To die on a battlefield fighting for a righteous cause is his supreme fortune. Dying thus, bravely, with your bodies pierced all over with arrows, you will go directly to heaven." So saying, he gave another blast on his conch. The battle cry was echoed by the opposing ranks and the horses and chariots charged forward with bloodcurdling cries.

The first day's battle, however, was fought on a cautious note. Both armies had been arranged in phalanxes which were difficult to penetrate. Arjuna, after humbly paying his respects to the grandsire, proceeded to engage him in a fierce combat. A few of the Kaurava brothers, as well as Shakuni and Shalya, came to his assistance, while Bhima and Arjuna's son Abhimanyu joined Arjuna. Bhishma's banner was felled by Arjuna and his horses killed by Abhimanyu, who then proceeded to rout Shalya, Shakuni, and the Kaurava brothers and went on to intercept Bhishma, who had turned away from Arjuna and was creating havoc among the Pandava ranks.

It was a wonderful sight to see the oldest and the youngest of the Kuru warriors forestalling each other with expertise! Finally, this brilliant lad of sixteen, who was almost his father's equal in warfare, managed to wound not only Bhishma but also Shalya and Kritavarma, who had joined the attack. Drishtadyumna challenged Drona, but was routed. Uttara, the young Prince of Matsya, now challenged Bhishma, cut off his staff, killed his charioteer, and destroyed chariot after chariot. After his training with Arjuna, he had turned out to be a formidable fighter. Bhishma was in a dilemma what to do with the boy, when Shalya aimed a deadly javelin at his heart and killed Uttara instantly. This was the first *adharmic* act of the war. Sveta, his elder brother, was furious at seeing how his young brother had been killed and turned his fury on Bhishma. He possessed an invincible bow from Lord Shiva and Bhishma found himself helpless against his onslaught. Realizing that Sveta was invincible so long as he held the bow, Bhishma taunted him, "Were you taught only archery? Can't you fight with a sword?"

The chivalrous Sveta immediately accepted the challenge and took up his sword. Now Bhishma, too, tarnished his fair name by cutting off Sveta's right arm with an arrow. Sveta continued to fight with his sword in his left hand, but Bhishma severed his other arm as well, and Sveta slowly bled to death. In utter dismay, Yudhishthira tried his best to console King Virata for the loss of both his beloved sons on the very first day of battle. Thus the day ended on a disastrous note for the Pandavas, and Duryodhana was jubilant.

The second day was a stalemate. On the third day, Bhishma arranged his army in the eagle formation and the Pandavas formed a crescent. Arjuna, as usual, engaged Bhishma. Gatotkacha, who was the gigantic son of Bhima by his *rakshasi* wife, created havoc in the Kaurava ranks. The *rakshasas* were capable of using many magical illusions, but Krishna forbade him to do so unless the other party resorted to similar tactics.

The sixth day was marked by great slaughter on both sides. Drona proved irresistible. After killing thirteen of the Kaurava brothers, Bhima fought and defeated Duryodhana, who fell unconscious and had to be carried off the field by his brother-in-law, Jayadratha. That night, Duryodhana went to Bhishma, who consoled him and gave him a potion to relieve his pain. On the seventh day, Bhima's tally of the Kaurava brothers reached twenty-six and Duryodhana, for the first time, wept in front of Bhishma, who told him, "It is too late to grieve now. Warriors should go to battle expecting to die."

Duryodhana could not brook this piece of salutary advice and sent his brother Dusshasana to Bhishma, asking him to step down and let Karna take up the leadership. Karna had boastfully promised his friend that he would slaughter the entire Pandava host if Bhishma would only relinquish his post.

Arjuna's son Iravan, though considerably maimed by the sacrifice of his flesh, was still seen to be creating havoc, until at last he was killed. The Pandavas were sunk in gloom and Arjuna had to be consoled by Krishna.

On the eighth day, the Pandava army arranged itself in a three-pronged formation led by Bhima, Satyaki, and Yudhishthira. Sixteen more of the Kauravas fell under Bhima's mace, making the tally forty-two. That night again, at Karna's suggestion, Duryodhana asked Bhishma to retire. The latter reminded him of his folly in having denied the Pandavas their birthright and having insulted Draupadi. He refused to retire from the battlefield so long as he was alive and promised to do better the next day. The next day Bhishma appeared to be the incarnation of the god of death himself! His fiery *astras* (weapons) burned up the Pandava army and they realized that so long as he was alive they would have no hope of victory. The Lord knew that Arjuna's faint-hearted attempts at fighting with the grandsire were going to prolong the war unnecessarily. At last, on the ninth day, when He saw that Arjuna was still avoiding a serious confrontation, He Himself jumped out of the chariot and rushed toward Bhishma armed with a broken chariot wheel in mock anger, as if to kill him. Bhishma was overjoyed. With folded palms, he welcomed Him and said, "Hail to You, O Lotus-Eyed One! Blessed am I to meet death at Your hands."

Arjuna jumped out of the chariot, caught Krishna's upraised arm, and promised to do better. Thus, the Lord's show of anger had two effects. He was able to fulfill Bhishma's desire to see Him take up arms, even at the cost of transgressing His own word, and He was able to whip up the desired wrath in Arjuna.

Duryodhana, on the other hand, was constantly taunting and deriding the grandsire for his half-hearted attempts against the Pandavas, even though he was keeping his promise of destroying ten thousand Pandava soldiers daily. The old man bore up with the insults and continued to do his duty. Drona had been similarly insulted by Duryodhana for not doing his duty, so he also started to harass the Pandava host.

That night, as suggested by Krishna, when darkness had descended and the soldiers on both sides lay chanting around the fires, the five brothers silently slipped into the tent of their beloved grandsire. Bhishma's heart rejoiced at the sight of these men whom he loved dearly. Tenderly, he asked them why they had come and Yudhishthira spoke.

"Grandfather," he said, "it is impossible for us to attain victory so long as you lead the Kaurava host. We have come, therefore, to ask you to tell us how we can kill you, for we have heard that you cannot be killed without your volition."

Strange question for a grandchild to put and stranger still the answer. The aged knight smiled gently. He knew that the time for release had come at last. He had the power to depart from this life as and when he pleased. That same faithfulness that had for such a long time bid him stay was now beckoning him to leave. He was tired of life, tired of the indiscriminate slaughter of the past few days, tired of listening to Duryodhana's incessant taunts. All these years, he had done his best to keep aloft the banner of the Kuru dynasty, even at the cost of personal happiness. Now he realized that the only way to make his life's mission a success was for the Pandavas to rule. For the accomplishment of this purpose, he would have to make the last and final sacrifice of his own life, for as long as he lived they would never win, and for this also he was totally prepared.

"It is true, my child," he said to Yudhishthira, "that your hope of victory while I am alive is in vain. Neither may you hope to slay me while I am armed. But mark you well, I will not fight against those who are afraid, or those who are weak from wounds or illness, or those who have surrendered to me. Nor will I take up arms against a woman or one who had been a woman before. If you attack me tomorrow from behind such a person, you will accomplish your purpose and achieve my death."

He spoke calmly and happily, as if he were discussing the weather rather than the method of his end, abiding to the last by the high code of *dharma* and chivalry which he had always followed. Then Krishna reminded the brothers that Shikhandin, the brother of Draupadi, was such a warrior, who had been born a woman and had changed his sex.

So it was arranged, in front of Bhishma himself, that Arjuna should fight with Bhishma the next day, keeping Shikhandin in front of him so that Bhishma would not retaliate. A wave of love and remorse swept over Arjuna as the plans were completed. He remembered the days of his childhood when he used to be dandled and caressed by the old man, for he had always been his favorite. How could he, who had been so tenderly loved, aim the fatal arrow at the heart of this beloved warrior? Arjuna wept unashamedly and it was Bhishma himself who had to remind him of his duty as a *kshatriya* and steel him to a stern performance of it. The Lord's compassionate glance swept over Bhishma and blessed him. The brothers departed as silently as they had come, leaving Bhishma with a vast sense of relief that at last the long and weary journey was coming to an end.

It could well be asked why the Lord, who knew all things, did not tell the Pandavas how Bhishma could be killed, but as usual He always preferred to allow the true nature of each character to unfold itself, so that the world would come to realize the greatness of his devotees.

The tenth day dawned and Bhishma knew it to be his last day of fighting in the battlefield of life. Happily, he propitiated the gods before proceeding to battle. The Kauravas noted with dismay the many bad omens that were seen on their side. The sun rose bright and Bhishma plunged into the fray. Wherever he went, Arjuna's chariot pursued him. Shikhandin stood in front beside the Divine Charioteer and Arjuna, from behind the maiden-knight, shot arrow after arrow at his beloved grandsire. Scorning to shoot at one who had once been a woman, Bhishma would laughingly aim an arrow at Arjuna whenever a sudden turn of the wheels gave him a chance. The Kauravas did their best to protect him, but Krishna maneuvered the chariot so brilliantly that Arjuna was able to fight his way right up to the grandsire's chariot. Bhishma laughed with joy, for he knew the end was fast approaching but he was determined to terminate his earthly career in a blaze of glory, doing his duty to the last. He let fly showers of arrows at Arjuna's chariot, carefully avoiding Shikhandin. Many arrows pierced the Lord, who looked resplendent with droplets of blood all over Him from the *puja* (worship) of arrows by His devotee. He continued to smile enchantingly at Bhishma, who rejoiced and felt refreshed at the sight of that splendid form brandishing a whip and maneuvering the horses in front of him. Arjuna's and Shikhandin's arrows, which were clustering thicker and thicker on his body, seemed like mere darts to him, for all he could behold was the Lord's enchanting form. Suddenly, with a swoop, Krishna closed in on him, preventing anyone else from coming in between. Raising His conch, the *Panchajanya*, to His lips, He blew long and loud. The sound was of the primeval word, *Aum*.[1] It filled Bhishma's ears and his mind became fixed on that Infinite Absolute which the sound represented. His eyes pinned themselves on the physical form of that Absolute that he saw standing before him holding the reins of his destroyer's chariot. That Formless One who had taken on a form in order to enchant the whole world now seemed to be calling him to stop the game and go to Him.

Arjuna fought as one possessed, for he had shut his mind to everything but the stern call to duty. Rising above the dualities of love and hate, pain and pleasure, he sent arrow after arrow at his beloved grand-

---

[1] *Aum*—the primal or seed Word, said to be the source of all creation.

sire, piercing him all over. Yudhishthira could not see because of the tears that blinded him, but Bhishma was happy that only Arjuna's arrows could pierce him and not Shikhandin's. There was no sound on the field except that of whizzing arrows. The drums and trumpets were dumb, as were all the warriors. Everyone watched the mighty drama with trepidation. At last, the time for the mortal wound had come. The end of the day and the end of his life: Bhishma received the fatal arrow straight into his heart. With his body torn to shreds by his grandson's arrows, his face lit up with a smile of great beauty, with his eyes clinging lovingly to the face of the Lord, which was resplendent in the last rays of the dying sun, the great Bhishma fell, but he did not touch the ground, for he was entirely covered with arrows and he lay, as it were, on a couch of arrows. The sky sent a shower of rain and a wail rose up from both the ranks that resounded in all the quarters. It was as if Mother Earth were crying out in pain at the death of one of her greatest sons. Even now, death could not approach him, for as he fell he remembered that the year was still in its dark half—*dakshinayana* (June to December)—an inauspicious time for the passing of a soul. He determined to stay alive until the beginning of the summer solstice, *uttarayana*, when the sun would start its northbound journey.

With the fall of Bhishma, a truce was called and warriors from both camps crowded around him. With bare feet and bare chests, the heroes surrounded the fallen grandsire. All of them shared the same grief. They would have carried him away to a more comfortable place since he had expressed his wish to remain alive until *uttarayana*, but he refused to move from the spot where he had fallen impaled on sharp arrows.

"This is a fitting bed for a warrior," he said, "but I would like a support for my head."

His head was the only part of him which was free from arrows. Duryodhana had soft pillows brought for him, but he would have none of these. "Arjuna, my child," he said, looking at him who had provided him with a hero's bed. It is said that only Arjuna's arrows had stuck to him, while Shikhandin's had fallen off. "Get me a pillow to rest my head, as you have given me a bed."

Arjuna was standing dumb with grief, hardly able to look at that beloved face, but he understood his request and shot three arrows down into the earth with such accuracy that they formed a perfect support for the hoary head of the mighty warrior. There was a raging thirst within him and his tongue clung to the roof of his mouth. He asked for water, but

Duryodhana's jar of water failed to quench his thirst. Again, he looked at Arjuna, and an unmistakable message passed from his eyes. Arjuna shot an arrow deep into the womb of the earth and a gush of water sprang forth straight into Bhishma's mouth. It is said that Mother Ganga herself came out of the earth to quench the thirst of her beloved son. Bhishma gave a sigh of relief and looked gratefully at his beloved grandson. Arjuna also felt as if that look, like the cooling waters of the Ganga, helped to assuage in some small measure the burning pain in his heart.

Bhishma ordered Duryodhana to dig a deep trench around him so that wild animals could not approach. He forbade him to erect a tent or anything else over him for he wanted to be left alone to spend his remaining days in solitude and worship. "Those of you who are alive after the war may come and see me at the beginning of *uttarayana*," he said. Then, turning to Duryodhana, he said, "My dear child, please listen to me now, at least. Let this enmity cease with my death. It is impossible for you to defeat the Pandavas. If you do not stop the war now, you will all perish. Please heed my words and put an end to this senseless carnage." Duryodhana hung his head and remained silent. Bhishma closed his eyes sadly and surrendered to the inevitable.

In the Kaurava camp, Karna fully expected that he would be appointed general. But after consulting everyone, it was decided that Drona should take over the command, as he might be displeased otherwise. So the next few days saw Drona at the helm, but his leadership lacked the grandeur of Bhishma's. The eleventh day saw Karna in the midst of the Pandava forces wreaking havoc, as he had promised to do. Among the Pandava army, Abhimanyu was the hero of the day, fighting single-handed against many of the Kaurava heroes. Duryodhana ordered Drona to capture Yudhishthira alive, for that would put an effective end to the war. Drona promised to do his best, but at the end of the day he had to confess failure. Duryodhana taunted him, as usual, and stung him to the quick. Drona retaliated and said, "As long as Bhima, with his mighty mace, and Arjuna, guided by Krishna, are protecting Yudhishthira, there is no hope of capturing him either alive or dead."

The Trigarta brothers now promised to lure Arjuna away from Yudhishthira, and Drona said he would try again the next day. News of Duryodhana's master plan to capture the king alive was brought to them. The Pandavas decided to guard Yudhishthira on all sides, Arjuna and Abhimanyu in front, Bhima behind, and Nakula and Sahadeva on the sides. However, the Trigartas challenged Arjuna to a battle two miles away. He was forced to go, but gave strict instructions to his son and his brothers not to leave the king unprotected at any time. However, despite their best efforts, they could not stop Drona from penetrating their barricade, and at last Yudhishthira was forced to retreat.

On his return after defeating the Trigartas, Arjuna was forestalled by Bhagadatta, the son of Narakasura, mounted on his ferocious elephant. Even Bhima was having a terrible time with him. Seeing Arjuna, he turned the full blast of his fury on him, but was unable to close up with him because of Krishna's skillful maneuvering of the chariot. At last, in fury he charged his goad with the deadly *Vaishnava mantra* and hurled it at Arjuna with all his might. It streaked like lightning toward him, cleaving through the arrows Arjuna discharged in defense. Had it reached its mark, it would surely have been the end of Arjuna, but the Lord cast off His whip and reins and stood up to receive the fatal weapon on His own chest. To the amazement of all, the goad changed into a garland of flowers, a *vanamala*, the emblem of Lord Vishnu, and adorned the neck of the Divine Charioteer, who was none other than the incarnation of Vishnu. He explained to Arjuna that this weapon had been given by Him in a previous incarnation to the earth goddess, who had presented it to her son, Narakasura, who in turn had given it to his son Bhagadatta. It would kill anyone except an unarmed person. Without his goad, Bhagadatta was vulnerable and was easily killed by Arjuna.

The twelfth day ended with Drona still being unable to capture Yudhishthira. In the evening, unable to bear Duryodhana's taunts, Drona took an oath that the next day he would either capture Yudhishthira or kill one of the best warriors on the Pandava side. On the thirteenth day, therefore, he arranged his army in the *padmavyuha*, or lotus formation. He himself remained in the center and stationed all their great warriors in each concentric circle of the formation. The remainder of the Trigartas were known as the Samsaptakas, and they swore to fight to the last man and keep Arjuna away from the main battle. Arjuna was forced to go and Drona began to wreak havoc with his impenetrable formation. It soon became obvious that unless the *vyuha* (formation) was broken, the Pandava army would be exterminated. Only Arjuna knew the method of entering into the heart of the lotus formation and returning the same way after having broken it. His son Abhimanyu knew how to penetrate it, but did not know how to return. It is said that while he was in the womb of his mother Subhadra, the Lord, her brother, had begun to explain to her the method of penetrating the *padmavyuha*. When he came to the end of the first half, he realized that his sister was sleeping, so He stopped his instruction and Abhimanyu never after came to learn how to come out of the formation. Yudhishthira was now at his wits' end. Since Arjuna was nowhere in sight and the formation had to be broken, he was forced to ask Abhimanyu to break open the *vyuha*. The lad readily agreed, but shyly told him that he did not know how to return and Bhima and the others would have to follow closely before the enemies closed the breach. Invoking a *mantra* taught by Krishna, Abhimanyu was able to drive a wedge into the hitherto impenetrable *vyuha*. Expecting Bhima to follow, he drove through this wedge, cutting down the opposing hoards on all sides with unerring arrows. Duryodhana's brother-in-law, Jayadratha, however, quickly closed the gap with his elephant army. To stop Bhima from following, he threw a garland of unfading flowers given to him by Lord Shiva in Bhima's path. Bhima was charging behind Abhimanyu, but when he saw the garland of his chosen deity, he stood rooted to the spot. "Not even for the sake of saving the life of my brother's child will I cross over and desecrate this garland of my Lord," he said and returned to Yudhishthira.

Abhimanyu cleaved his way deep into the formation. Drona, Shalya, Karna, Jayadratha, and a host of Kaurava warriors tried to oppose this brilliant boy, but he defeated them all and threw their entire army into confusion. Both Duryodhana and Dusshasana were defeated and had to beat a hasty retreat. Duryodhana's son, Lakshman, accompanied by ten thousand soldiers, now attacked Abhimanyu, but was killed by his brilliant cousin. Duryodhana could not bear it when he heard the news.

"This lad must be killed at all costs," he said, "by fair means or foul!"

All of them realized that he could never be conquered in a fair fight, since he had defeated all their best warriors individually. So, throwing fair play to the winds, the Kauravas now closed in on Abhimanyu and attacked him from all sides as he stood in the center of the lotus. Karna crept up from behind and broke his bow and Drona killed his charioteer. Abhimanyu was now surrounded by Drona, Karna, Kripa, Ashvatthama, Kritavarma, Dusshasana, Duryodhana, and Jayadratha. Like a lion facing a pack of jackals, he faced his opponents, undaunted by them, fitting son and nephew to Arjuna and Krishna. With amazing brilliance, he kept his attackers at bay, hoping against hope that his uncle would soon come to his rescue. With lightning movements of his sword, he managed to prevent even a single arrow from scratching him. Suddenly, he sprang onto Drona's chariot and smashed it to pieces. Looking at him disdainfully, Abhimanyu said, "You're a Brahmin and the commander of the Kaurava forces and yet you allow this injustice—six *maharathikas* to attack a single warrior like me!" He turned to Karna and said, "I thought at least you were capable of some nobility. Aren't you ashamed to have attacked me from the rear?"

He had no time to talk, for, disregarding the codes of warfare, Drona cut off the lad's right arm, which was brandishing the sword. Undaunted, Abhimanyu took up the sword in his left hand and continued to terrorize his opponents. But Drona cruelly sent another arrow with unerring accuracy and broke his sword. Now he was defenseless, his bow and sword broken, his charioteer killed, and his right arm cut off. Maimed and bleeding, Abhimanyu took up a fallen chariot wheel in his left hand, whirled it around, and thus kept his attackers at bay. Again he said, "I'm giving you a chance to redeem your honor. Come and fight with me one by one and I can still kill you all." Saying this, he rushed at Drona, whirling the chariot wheel and looking like Lord Vishnu Himself. He was a most remarkable sight as he stood there torn and bleeding, yet with a smile on his lips and the wheel held aloft in his left hand. Even before he could fling it at Drona, the six great heroes of the Kaurava army closed in on him and smashed the wheel to a thousand fragments. Abhimanyu now took up a mace. Once again, he said scornfully, "Come to me one by one, O Heroes, and I will still defeat you."

Abhimanyu now turned on Dusshasana's son and the two closed in deadly combat. Weak from loss of blood, the boy fainted for a minute. Before he could rise up, at Duryodhana's instigation, Jayadratha crept up from behind and smashed the weak and bleeding boy's skull with his mace, while Dusshasana's son pounced on his fallen body and hacked him to death. Six great car warriors had dared to commit this most dastardly crime on the holy field of Kurukshetra. Arjuna's noble son was lying dead in the dust and grime of the battlefield and these ghoulish men danced around the corpse in exultation. The common soldiers beheld him as he lay in the mud like a lotus bud trampled by a herd of mad elephants, and they wept unashamedly. Vyasa[2] says that even the vultures that flew

---

[2] Vyasa—Vyasa is said to be the author of the *Mahabbarata*, the great Indian epic in which the story of the Mahabbharata war is told.

around the battleground incessantly seemed to be lamenting and saying, "Not thus! Not thus! We do not want any share of this noble body!"

The massacre of Abhimanyu was such a dastardly act that it is supposed to mark the end of the *Dvapara* Age and to usher in the Iron Age of *Kali*, in which we now live.

Thus ends the twenty-sixth chapter of The Play of God,
named "The Mahabharata War."

Hari Aum Tat Sat

The spirit is not born, neither does it die. Nor does it come into existence at birth. It is birthless, constant, eternal, and ancient. It is not slain when the body is slain.
—BHAGAVAD GITA

TWENTY-SEVEN

THE END OF THE WAR

Kalatmane
namaha

Homage to
the spirit
manifested as
Time

*Salutations to Krishna, who is the wish-fulfilling tree to those
who take refuge in Him. In one hand He holds the whip and
the other is held in the jnanamudra (symbol of knowledge). It is
He who has milked for us the divine ambrosia of the Gita.*
—BHAGAVAD GITA MEDITATION VERSE

Yudhishthira's state of mind on hearing of Abhimanyu's death can well be imagined. He blamed
himself bitterly for his folly in having sent the boy
to his doom. In the meantime, Arjuna, after having
defeated the Samsaptakas, was returning, filled with foreboding for he knew not what. The Lord knew very well
what had happened and invoked the aid of Indra, Arjuna's father, in order to save him. Indra took the form of
an old man, made a huge fire, and was just preparing to
jump into it when Arjuna and Krishna came along. When
Arjuna intervened, the old man said, "You would do the
same if you were in my position, for I have just lost my
only son."

In order to comfort him, Arjuna replied, "Please
refrain from this ignoble act. I swear to you by Lord
Krishna and my Gandiva that were I to lose my son, I
would never stoop to such an act!"

The old man seemed appeased by this pronouncement. Arjuna returned to the chariot and Krishna drove
off, but the Lord took the extra precaution of hiding
Arjuna's weapons. On reaching the camp, Arjuna saw the
silence and the way everyone seemed to be avoiding his
eyes and he asked the Lord, "Tell me, what calamity has
befallen us?" He looked at the Lord's face and saw a
glimmer of tears in those lotus eyes.

"My nephew has been killed," He said.

Unable to bear the shock, Arjuna fainted. There was a deathly silence in the camp. None of the brothers could speak a word. On recovering, Arjuna took up the mangled remains of his beloved son and lamented. "O mighty Hero! You were able to discharge your arrows even before your enemies could string their bows, so how could they have killed you? Have you really gone to the realm of the dead? Why did I leave you and go? What will I say to your poor mother? O Brothers! Knowing how much I loved him, how could you have sent him alone to his doom? Sahadeva, light a fire. I want to join my son!"

Sahadeva obeyed without protest, for he knew that Krishna would save Arjuna. Yudhishthira was too scared to interfere, for he felt wretchedly guilty. All he could do was to look imploringly at Krishna. Arjuna, however, refused even to look at the Lord, for he knew that He could have saved his son had He so wished. Krishna summoned Indra again and the old man whom Arjuna had prevented from suicide now appeared and reminded him of his oath not to take his life.

It might be asked why the Lord had not stopped Abhimanyu's murder. The special message of Lord Krishna to Arjuna in the *Gita* is the message of the divinity in the human soul. By the force of the power generated in the performance of *nishkama karma*, or performance of one's duty without desiring the fruits thereof, it is able to unfold itself from the veil of its own lower nature and reach the full flowering of its divine status. The outcome of such action is our liberation from the limited ego and our elevation to a higher nature that is divine, enabling us to act in the world in the truth of the spirit, for the sake of God in the world and not for the sake of our own limited egos. To call Arjuna to such action, to make him aware of the power that was in him and that acted through him, was the purpose of the embodied Godhead. To this end, the divine Himself had become his charioteer. To this end, the vision of the world *Purusha* and the divine command to action had been given to him.

The sermon of the second chapter had shown him that, though the body is slain, the soul can never die, for one is purely temporal and the other eternal. Treating alike pleasure and pain, joy and sorrow, victory and defeat, his duty was to fight in the battlefield of life as an instrument of the divine. For this, both Arjuna and the rest of the Pandavas had to pass through the fire of sorrow and suffering many times in the course of their lives. The *avatar* of the Lord was not to put an end to the dualities of life, but to provide a firm bedrock of knowledge, faith, and action which would help one to rise above it as a *sthitaprajna*, one established in the highest knowledge.

He reminded Arjuna now of this great message of the second chapter, but Arjuna was sunk in gloom and no dry philosophy, however exalted, could comfort him. Knowing his psychology, the Lord rallied him, "O Arjuna! Why are you mourning like any woman? Instead of shedding tears like this, should you not be asking for the name of his murderer and taking revenge?"

Arjuna was a man of action and this was just the way to deal with him. He jumped up and having learned of Jayadratha's perfidy, he swore, "I swear by my Lord Krishna and my Gandiva that if I do not kill Jayadratha, who was responsible for my son's death, by sunset tomorrow I shall immolate myself in the fire!" The brothers were temporarily relieved and looked gratefully at the Lord.

Arjuna begged Krishna to break the news of her son's death to Subhadra, since he could not face her. Krishna went to His dear sister. She could not control her grief on hearing the dreadful news. After allowing her to weep unchecked for some time, He spoke to her. "Dear Sister, you are the daughter of the clan of the Vrishnis, you are the wife of the greatest archer in the world, and the mother of a hero. Wipe your tears, as befitting the mother of such a son. Abhimanyu was killed by unfair means. He died the death of a hero. He was mercilessly murdered by six of the greatest warriors on the Kaurava side, since they could not tackle him single-handed. Cast away this sorrow and remember that today your son is with the gods. Arjuna has sworn to kill Jayadratha, who manipulated your son's death. Stop this weeping and comfort Uttara, who is bearing Abhimanyu's son in her womb. Guard her carefully, for danger awaits the fetus."

So saying, He took her to Uttara and after comforting both of them and Draupadi, He returned to Arjuna. The latter was waiting to worship Him before retiring to bed, as was his daily custom. After the *puja*, he offered flowers, fruit, and honey to Him. The Lord blessed him and told him to go to bed, for the next day would be the most taxing he had had so far. He would have to plow through the ranks of the Kauravas before reaching Jayadratha. The year was in the second half, *dakshinayana*, when the sun was in the southern solstice and would set early.

That night, Arjuna had a curious dream. He thought that he was taken by the Lord to Kailas, the abode of Lord Shiva. On the way, Arjuna felt weak and hungry, but refused to eat until he had finished his formal worship of the Shiva *linga*. Krishna told him to worship Him instead and Arjuna obeyed, offering the flowers and the garland made for Shiva to Him. The Lord sat in the pose of Dakshinamurti, the meditating Shiva, and accepted Arjuna's offerings. When they reached Kailas, Arjuna was astonished to see the garland he had offered to Krishna adorning the blue neck of Shiva. The latter knew what was passing through his mind and told him, "Know, O Arjuna, Krishna and I are one and the same! We are none other than the impersonal, formless Brahman."

Krishna now spoke, "We have come here so that Arjuna can receive your blessings for killing Jayadratha, who has received some boons from you."

Jayadratha had practiced severe austerities to Lord Shiva to procure boons from him for the annihilation of the Pandavas. Though Shiva had given him the boons, he had also warned him that his evil machinations would have no effect against the Pandavas, who were protected by Krishna. Lord Shiva then demonstrated to Arjuna how the Pashupata weapon he had given him could be used to full effect, since that was the only weapon which could save him against what Jayadratha had.

In the meantime, Yudhishthira, in his obsession to adhere to *dharma* at all costs, ordered Gatotkacha, Bhima's son, to inform the enemy of Arjuna's oath. He was rudely received by Duryodhana, who was far from being grateful for the message and proceeded to abuse the messenger. When Jayadratha heard of his death sentence, he was all set to flee to his own country, but Duryodhana assured him that he would be given every protection. The next morning, he was sent to a hiding place twelve miles away from the Pandava camp.

On the morning of the fourteenth day, Arjuna was again challenged by the remnants of the Samsaptakas. He routed them in no time and pushed forward, but Drona intercepted him.

Arjuna spoke. "Though you played an active part in my son's death, yet you are my preceptor and I will not kill you, but let me pass for I must get to Jayadratha soon."

Drona was already bitterly regretting the part he had played and allowed him to pass unmolested. Arjuna fought his way through the ranks of the Kaurava army, which had been detailed to stop him at all costs from reaching Jayadratha before sunset. Next, he was accosted by Srutayudha, who had a mace that could kill anyone instantly, but if it hit an unarmed person it would ricochet back on him and destroy him. After a fierce interchange with arrows, Srutayudha flung his mace with deadly accuracy at Arjuna's chest, and once more the Lord saved him by changing the direction of the chariot so that the mace fell squarely on His own chest. As expected, it bounced back and killed its owner. Slowly, Arjuna was beginning to realize that he owed his life, every moment, not to his own skill but to the Lord's grace alone.

But the horses were tiring and the Lord, with His usual consideration for all His creatures, told Arjuna that they had to be rested before proceeding further. Arjuna agreed to fight on foot while the horses rested. Then Krishna said, "But Arjuna, they need to quench their thirst and there is no water in sight." Arjuna smilingly took up his bow and, invoking Varuna, god of waters, he shot an arrow into the ground. Water gushed out and formed a pool. The Lord released the tired animals from the chariot and led them to the water. Gently He pulled out the arrows from their flanks and caressed them with a bewitching smile on His face. Without showing any sign of hurry, He spoke gently to them and made them relax with His loving touch. In the meantime, the Kaurava troops were harassing Arjuna, who kept them at bay with ease, as his son Abhimanyu had done the previous day. Calmly, the Lord harnessed the refreshed horses back to the chariot and the two of them cleaved their way through the Kaurava army, weaving in and out of the phalanxes. Subduing the army on either side, they sped forward like a forest conflagration.

As sunset was nearing, Arjuna fought with the fury of a man determined to avenge the death of his beloved son, but still they had not discovered their quarry. The red disc of the sun began to slip fast into the western horizon and once more the Lord intervened to save the life of his beloved devotee. Holding aloft His divine weapon, the *Sudarshana*, He masked the sun so that the Kauravas thought that it had set and Jayadratha crept from his hideout. Arjuna felt desperate and Krishna now expressed a wish to hear the twang of the Gandiva for the last time. Arjuna was past caring for anything and did as he was told. As the twang of the Gandiva reverberated in the air, striking terror into Jayadratha's heart, the Lord removed the *Sudharshana* and to the amazement of all, the setting sun appeared on the western horizon in a positive blaze of glory. Krishna galvanized Arjuna into action by shouting to him, "Look, Arjuna! There is the sun! It has not set and there stands the killer of your son, creeping out of his lair in the dark like a jackal!"

Arjuna was already preparing himself to jump into the fire, but the Lord's words made him spring into action. Using the Pashupata with deadly effect, he neatly severed Jayadratha's head from his body, but Krishna knew that the danger was not yet over. Jayadratha's father had obtained another boon—that whoever felled his son's head to the ground would perish. The father was sitting near the banks of the lake Syamantakapanchaka close to Kurukshetra and, quick as a thought, Krishna told Arjuna to keep shooting arrows so that Jayadratha's head would be relayed to his father's lap. The gruesome object dropped with a thud into the old man's lap as he was meditating at the lakeside. Instinctively, he threw it to the ground and his own head broke into fragments according to his wish.

Once again, Arjuna's life had been spared by the Lord, and all the brothers fell at His feet. As usual, He disclaimed all credit, "A noble man's anger is the most potent weapon," He said. "The gods will not sit idly and watch the good suffer, even though they may give boons to the wicked."

The negative vibrations aroused by the death of Abhimanyu were so great that the rules of *dharmic* warfare were waived aside and fighting continued into the night with the aid of torches. Gatotkacha now resorted to the use of his magic arts, for the opposite side was also using these tactics. He caused havoc in the Kaurava army, for being half *rakshasa*, his strength increased with the falling of night. Arjuna was itching to come to grips with Karna, but Krishna kept detaining him, for the time had not yet come. Karna was busy trying to restrain Gatotkacha, who brushed aside his weapons as if they were toys. A vast portion of the Kaurava army had been annihilated and Duryodhana begged Karna to kill Gatotkacha at all costs. Karna was in a dilemma, for only two of his weapons, the *Shakti* and the *Nagastra*, were capable of killing Gatotkacha and he had been reserving both for Arjuna, since he was allowed to use them only once. Reluctantly, at Duryodhana's repeated pleas, he discharged Indra's weapon, the *Shakti*, up into the sky, from which vantage point Gatotkacha was fighting. It pierced through the veil of illusion woven by the *rakshasa* hero and brought him down lifeless. But even in death, Bhima's son proved to be formidable, for he expanded his mighty form and crushed many Kaurava soldiers as he fell. The Pandavas were plunged in grief, but Krishna consoled them by saying that Arjuna's life had been partly saved, since the *Shakti* could no longer be used against him. This was the reason the Lord had not allowed Arjuna to come to grips with Karna before now.

The fifteenth day dawned and once more Duryodhana accused Drona of partiality for the Pandavas. Drona had been destroying the enemy troops without compassion, throwing overboard all codes of warfare that had been agreed upon. This unjust accusation, as well as his own indiscriminate slaughter of innocents, which was quite against his *svadharma* as a Brahmin, made him feel thoroughly disgusted with life. Yet he fought on and at last killed his childhood enemy Drupada. But this victory brought no joy to him. All the scenes of his boyhood spent with his friend flooded his mind and he felt a bitter disgust at the strange role that fate had forced upon him. Drishtadyumna rushed to avenge his father's death, but Drona routed him easily. Now Arjuna proceeded to engage the aged preceptor, but he proved to be invincible, for on that day he was fighting with utter disregard for his own life and none could approach him. The Lord knew what was passing through Drona's mind, how he was disgusted with life and ready to leave this world. He also knew that Drona could never be killed unless he laid down his weapons. This he would never do unless they could manage to convince Him of the death of his son Ashvatthama. He told Bhima to go and kill an elephant called "Ashvatthama" and prepared Yudhishthira as to what he should say if Drona questioned him. The former refused to tell a lie and had to be cajoled into saying the literal truth. Bhima returned and roared loudly so that Drona could hear, "I have killed Ashvatthama!"

Drona, however, did not trust Bhima and turned to Yudhishthira for confirmation. With great reluctance, Yudhishthira mumbled, "Yes, Bhima has killed Ashvatthama, the elephant."

However, the sound of the Lord's conch drowned the last two words, so that Drona had to infer that his son was dead. He was already disgusted with life and he started to behold celestial beings in the sky beckoning him to leave his mortal body. Then did the great Dronacharya lay down his arms and sit in meditation in his chariot. Drishtadyumna, who had been born to kill him, rushed forward and cut off his head, despite the exclamations of the others.

A temporary truce was now declared to lament over their fallen preceptor. When Ashvatthama heard of his father's death, he was so infuriated that he discharged the deadly *Narayanastra*[1] against the Pandavas. This had been given to him by his father when he was a boy, since he had been jealous of his father's partiality for Arjuna and had begged him to give him some weapon not possessed by his disciple. It was a devastating weapon and Drona had warned him that it should be used only in the case of dire necessity and that it could not be used twice. The *astra* now came in the form of thousands of small missiles, threatening to engulf and destroy the entire Pandava clan. Krishna ordered everyone to throw down their weapons and prostrate in submission before the oncoming missile. Bhima alone stood up defiantly and it zoomed toward him. Krishna pushed him down in the nick of time and stood before him, and once again the *astra* proved to be helpless against the Lord. Ashvatthama was furious with everything and everyone including his father who he thought had cheated him. Just then the sage Vyasa appeared and told him, "Your father did not cheat you, O Ashvatthama! He gave you the *Narayanastra*, which is potent with the power of the Lord Narayana, and you have been foolish enough to use it against those who are being protected by Krishna, who is none other than the Lord Narayana."

Ashvatthama realized his mistake. He and Kripa now begged Duryodhana to stop the senseless slaughter, but the latter was now sure of a miraculous victory, for Karna had been installed as general of the Kaurava forces. Duryodhana ordered the Yadava army, the *Narayana sena*, to fight with Arjuna. Many of Krishna's own sons were in the army and Arjuna was most reluctant to fight with them, but Krishna, the perfect *karma yogi*, encouraged Arjuna to perform his duty unflinchingly. He was forced to fight and kill many of the Lord's sons, while He charioted him without a tremor.

Next, Karna tried to grapple with Arjuna, but had to turn away defeated. He went to Duryodhana and told him that he could kill Arjuna only if he had a charioteer of Krishna's caliber and asked him to request Shalya to take up this role. Shalya was not too happy to drive the chariot of someone lowborn, but consented when Duryodhana pointed out the Lord's example. Since Shalya was noted for his acid tongue, Duryodhana warned Karna to exercise great control over his temper and not to

---

[1] *Narayanastra*—an *astra*, or guided missile, into which the power of Lord Narayana is invoked.

retaliate whatever Shalya might say.

On the way to battle the next day, Shalya was determined to provoke and humiliate Karna and they had a wordy battle that very nearly broke up the union. Strangely enough, a similar scene was being enacted in Arjuna's chariot, with Krishna provoking him with such statements as, "Karna is invincible in a fair fight. You will need all your wits to defeat him."

But while Krishna's provocative words only served to strengthen Arjuna's determination to slay Karna at all costs, Shalya's served to inflame Karna so that he forgot the promise made to Duryodhana and retaliated word for word.

Both Nakula and Yudhishthira were defeated by Karna. He refused to kill them since he had promised his mother to kill no brother but Arjuna. He, in turn, was hurt so badly by Bhima that he fainted, but Bhima desisted from killing him, for he was reserved for Arjuna. Now Sahadeva accosted him, but Karna let him go and pushed forward, until at last the two great protagonists came face to face. A fierce battle ensued in which Karna appeared to be getting the upper hand. When Krishna asked Arjuna what the matter was and why he was fighting in such a half-hearted manner, he replied, "I do not see Karna in front of me, but only my brother Yudhishthira. I don't know what the matter is, but I cannot fight with him now. Please take me away from here!"

So Krishna broke through the network of arrows made by Karna and took Arjuna to Yudhishthira's tent, where the latter was lying in severe pain from wounds inflicted by Karna. Even he reprimanded Arjuna mildly for shirking his duty and Arjuna, for once, became furious with his brother.

On the seventeenth day of battle, Karna prepared his weapons carefully and bade a loving farewell to Duryodhana, for he knew that the day of reckoning had come. In the meantime, Bhima came face to face with Dusshasana. The vivid scene of the disrobing of Draupadi flashed across his mind, so that he threw away the mace which was in his hand and caught hold of Dusshasana's hair. Using his fists and feet, he broke his right arm and wrenched it from its socket—the arm that had dragged Draupadi by her beauteous hair through the streets of Hastinapura into the open assembly of the Kurus—the arm that had done its best to tear her clothes away. With a diabolic cry, Bhima threw Dusshasana down, jumped on his chest, tore open his ribs with his bare hands, scooped out his heart, and proceeded to make good his oath of drinking his blood. Krishna stoped him in time and told him to spit it out, for he had already fulfilled his oath. Though he was still in a violent mood, Bhima complied, while the rest watched horrified. Karna was thoroughly demoralized by this macabre scene, for he also remembered that shameful incident of Draupadi's disrobing, his own comments, and the dreadful oaths taken on that day by the helpless Pandavas. Turning around, he beheld his only surviving son being killed by Arjuna after a brief duel.

Brushing away his tears, he girded himself for the final battle. Both of them realized that it would be a fight to the finish. As they fought on, using more and more potent weapons and tactics, they were each mentally applauding the other for his skill! The rest had stopped fighting and stood watching the duel between these two who had sworn to kill each other. The charioteers were maneuvering with great skill and care.

Finally Karna, realizing that all his best efforts were in vain, decided that the *Nagastra* (the snake missile) was the only weapon that could finish off Arjuna. Fixing it on his bow, he took careful aim at Arjuna's throat. The arrow, in the shape of a hissing cobra with mouth and fangs wide open, darted toward its mark like lightning. For the first time in his life, Arjuna, the great hero, lost his nerve and begged Krishna to save him. The Lord, who had saved him many times all through his life without being asked, now smiled comfortingly and effortlessly pressed the chariot down twelve inches into the mud. The *Nagastra*, which had been aimed at Arjuna's throat, just missed his head and carried away his helmet.

Karna now decided to resort to the *Brahmastra*, the most powerful missile, the *mantra* for which he had learned from his preceptor, Parasurama. To his dismay, he found that he could not remember a single word of the *mantra*, due to his *guru's* curse. To make matters worse, his own chariot had also sunk into the mud and would not move. Shalya refused to get down to dislodge the wheel. Karna rebuked him for deserting him. At this, Shalya angrily flung down his whip, threw the reins into his face and left him to his fate. Karna was forced to jump out of the chariot and try to lift the wheel out of the quagmire, calling to Arjuna to stop the fight for a while. The latter was willing to do so, but Krishna, in His role as Karmaphaladatta (he who gives the fruits of actions), thundered at him, "Where, O Karna, was your talk of fair play when you and the Kauravas surrounded the boy Abhimanyu and slaughtered him?"

Karna remembered his own part in that dreadful episode and knew that the Lord spoke but the truth. With a sigh, he remounted and continued to fight from his stationary chariot but though Arjuna wounded him severely, he was unable to kill him. Krishna explained to Arjuna that Karna could not be killed until his entire stock of merit was exhausted. Taking on the form of a mendicant, the Lord approached Karna for alms, but he had nothing to give Him, so the Lord said, "I have come to seek your *punya*, or spiritual merit. I shall be content with that." Karna knew it was another test for him, so he smiled and unhesitatingly replied, "Gladly will I give You all the merit I have accumulated, am accumulating, and might accumulate in the future, if it will satisfy You."

Thus by surrendering even his spiritual merit to the Lord, who is the giver of all merit, Karna achieved immortality. But the Lord was not done with him as yet. He had come to test him to the utmost and He now said, "A gift to a Brahmin should be solemnized with an oblation of water."

Karna said, "I'm unable to find some water even to quench my thirst, but this I can do if it will satisfy you." So saying, he drew out an arrow embedded in his body and solemnized the gift with a spurt of blood. As he collapsed from loss of blood, the beggar gently supported him against the chariot wheel.

Feeling drops of water falling on him, Karna wearily opened his eyes and was thrilled to behold the glorious vision of the Lord upholding him with one arm and gazing at him with lotus eyes overflowing with love, from which a few drops of compassion had splashed on him.

"Your name and fame will live forever, O Karna!" the Lord said. "You have amply atoned for all your sins. Now ask for any boon and I shall grant it to you."

Karna whispered, "What terrible sins have I committed against my brothers and my sister-in-law! My only comfort is that I feel that I have paid my debt of gratitude in full to Duryodhana, and I have never failed to give to anyone whatever has been asked of me. If I have to take another birth, grant me the boon that once again I will never be able to deny anything to anyone."

The Lord smiled gently and said, "Your sins are insignificant when compared to the merit accrued by your charity and magnanimity. Your present physical suffering is due to those sins but fear not, Karna. By your final act of surrendering even your merit to Me, I Myself shall take on the burden of your sins and will relieve you from your physical pain." So saying, He gently released Himself and went back to Arjuna and told him to shoot the fatal arrow. Arjuna was reluctant to shoot at a fallen enemy, but took it as the command of God and discharged the *Anchari-ka* missile. Thus fell the mighty hero Karna. Though his sins were many, yet his heart was so large that one remembers him only for his love and not for his crimes. A heavenly voice now proclaimed that Karna was not a lowborn, but the son of Kunti and the brother of the Pandavas. Hearing this, Kunti came to the battlefield, where lay the fallen hero in the mud and grime and gore of Kurukshetra. Taking her dead son in her lap, she lamented long and loud over him, as she had promised she would do, and announced to all that he was her firstborn. The Pandavas, however, were not there to hear this.

Duryodhana rushed to the scene. If there was anyone in the world that he was genuinely fond of, it was Karna. When he realized that Karna had already known his parentage and had fought against his brothers only out of gratitude to him, he was inconsolable. Arjuna now realized why he had found a striking resemblance between Karna and his eldest brother and felt terrible at having killed him. Karna's wife Kanchanamala also came to the scene and threw herself on his body and mourned for him. All of them eventually turned on Krishna, for they felt that He had known everything and had not disclosed it at the proper time. They forgot the fact that God has no partiality for persons and that He only saw to it that each one got his just deserts.

The Lord said, "Karna himself requested Me not to reveal his secret until he had died. He sacrificed himself out of gratitude to Duryodhana. I am fully prepared to bear the responsibility for his death, just as I am prepared to assure you that he will never be born again. On two previous occasions I had given you hints about his identity, but you were not prepared to understand. None of you cared to enquire when Draupadi confessed to having a sixth person in her mind, nor when Arjuna retreated, thinking he saw Yudhishthira in him."

Thus ended the seventeenth day of battle. The eighteenth day dawned murky and gloomy, as if the weather gods themselves bemoaned the birth of such a day. The end was a foregone conclusion, but Duryodhana still hoped for a miracle. After consulting Ashvatthama, he chose

Shalya as the new commander. As only a few heroes remained, they decided to avoid individual combats. Shalya now fought with an inspiration born of despair. Krishna suggested that Yudhishthira was the right person to fight with him. Yudhishthira amazed everyone by his dexterity with the javelin. After a long and well-matched battle, Yudhishthira hurled his javelin after invoking the Lord's name and it found its mark on Shalya's chest. The Lord explained that it was only the power of Yudhishthira's accumulated *dharma* that had vanquished Shalya. The Kaurava army was in shambles by now and thoroughly demoralized. Duryodhana tried to rally them and sent his remaining brothers to fight with Bhima, who promptly finished off all of them. Shakuni's son, Uluka, was now singled out by Nakula, who fulfilled his oath by killing him under the very eyes of his father. Now it was Sahadeva's turn to make good his oath to kill the arch villain of the *Mahabharata*—Shakuni, Prince of Gandhara. He cut off his arms and left him to die in mortal agony.

The Pandavas now set out to exterminate the remnants of the opposing army. At the end of the morning, there were only four Kaurava chiefs left, Duryodhana, Ashvatthama, Kripa, and Kritavarma, general of the Yadava forces. Seeing the bloody field of his own making, spattered with the blood and heads of his own brothers and loved ones, the Kuru prince wept like a child. Forlorn and defeated, he decided to beat a hasty retreat and went to the Dvaipayana lake to cool himself. The other three followed him. Some hunters happened to hear their conversation by the lake and reported the matter to the Pandavas, who had been searching for their cousin. They hurried to the lake where Duryodhana, like a coward, had hidden himself in the water, breathing through a reed. The other three had also hidden themselves elsewhere. Seeing the bubbles in the water, the Pandavas discovered Duryodhana's hiding place and taunted him, telling him to come out and face his end like a hero. At this, Duryodhana emerged and magnanimously offered his kingdom to Yudhishthira. The Pandavas laughed at this generous offer from the defeated king and told him, as once before he had told Yudhishthira, that if he wanted to retain his kingdom he would have to fight for it.

Then Yudhishthira, in his usual quixotic fashion that sometimes bordered on foolishness, offered to give over the entire fortunes of the war to the winner of a duel between Duryodhana and one of his own brothers, quite forgetting the fact that Bhima had sworn to kill him. In his anxiety to be fair at all costs, he even told Duryodhana that he could choose one among them to fight with. The rest of the brothers were aghast at this astounding offer, but kept quiet even though they knew that this might well result in the collapse of all their hopes. But the cold war between Duryodhana and Bhima had continued too long for the former to even contemplate fighting with any of the others. His blood boiled when he thought of how Bhima had killed all his brothers and the gory scene of the killing of Dusshasana, his favorite brother, was fresh in his mind. His eyes became bloodshot and he looked scornfully at Yudhishthira, as if despising him for his weakness in having made such an offer. Then he turned his gaze on Bhima and the two glared at each other. They had many a score to settle and they both knew that the moment of reckoning had come. They had been looking forward to it.

They decided to fight this decisive battle on the banks of the Syamantakapanchaka lake. Silently, the seven of them marched toward the spot. Bhima took off his armor, as Duryodhana had none. Just as the battle was about to commence, Balarama returned from his pilgrimage, in time to witness the mighty battle between his two disciples. He warned them to observe the rules of fair play that he had taught them. The others made a circle around the two titans, who were ready to settle their lifelong feud once and for all. They were well matched. Bhima's blows were more powerful, but Duryodhana's body was like adamant as a result of his mother's look. The only time Gandhari had taken off the scarf around her eyes had been to instill strength into her eldest child when he had approached her and begged her to help him. She had told him to come to her naked and she would infuse the strength of a hundred elephants into him by the mere power of her gaze.[2] But he had insisted on wearing a loincloth, and thus his thighs alone had not received the benefit of her powerful rays.

Duryodhana had been practicing on an iron effigy of Bhima for many years, preparing himself for this very day, so he was well acquainted with the length and girth of his opponent's body. For some time, they grappled without either of them being able to get the upper hand. At last, Duryodhana, selfish to the last, asked Bhima for his vulnerable

---

2 "...by the mere power of her gaze"—Hindus believe that a wife's perfect devotion to her husband is a form of great spiritual austerity that bestows power to her. Gandhari, Dhritarashtra's wife, was so perfectly devoted to her blind husband, she tied a cloth around her eyes so she also could not see. Thus she had the gift to grant this protection to her son, Duryodhana.

spot. The latter truthfully pointed to his head and was immediately smitten down. Bhima fell like a log, but somehow he made a tremendous recovery just as Duryodhana pounced on his inert body. When he asked Duryodhana for his weak point, the latter pointed untruthfully at his own head. Bhima pounded on it with little effect, for his head was like iron. Actually, his weak point was his thighs and Bhima had sworn to smash them on that fatal day when Draupadi was humiliated in public. On that day, Duryodhana had bared his thigh to her, slapped it, and beckoned to her with vulgar gestures. In the heat of the fight and perhaps due to the blow on his head, Bhima had forgotten his oath.

The Lord, as usual, came to the rescue and reminded him of this by slapping his own thighs. Bhima saw this and the whole humiliating scene flashed before his eyes. Draupadi's piteous look of appeal to him and his utter helplessness then, filled him with fury now. His eyes became red and bloodshot, and like an infuriated bull he charged at his tormentor. He should have smashed those thighs on that very day, but he had not been able to do so. Now, nothing could stop him, not even the thought that he was committing *adharma*. Is the question of *dharma* or *adharma* a simple one when dealing with one as low and unrighteous as Duryodhana, who had tried every mean and foul trick all through his association with the Pandavas to gain his own way?[3]

Swinging up his mace, he pretended to be aiming another blow at his head. As Duryodhana nimbly jumped aside to avoid the blow, Bhima, summoning all the pent-up feelings of many years, brought the mace down with tremendous force on his adversary's thighs and broke them so that at last the villain fell, mortally wounded. Bhima roared the lion cry of victory. His anger unabated, he pressed his foot on Duryodhana's head, for he said a snake should be stamped on the head, but Yudhishthira intervened and restrained him. Bhima then knelt at his brother's feet and offered him the throne of the Kurus, which had been wrested from him by such unfair means.

At that moment Balarama, who had been a witness to the battle, rushed at Bhima with upraised plow to punish him for his unrighteous act. Krishna stopped him and asked him gently why he had not thought of restraining Duryodhana when he had committed so many atrocities

---

3 There is a recurring theme in the story of the Mahabharata War, of righteous men acting apparently unrighteously in extremely difficult, seemingly impossible, situations out of their own deeply righteous nature. This story does not give simplistic answers to the complex dilemmas of life.

against the Pandavas. Balarama did not say a word and left for Dwaraka without waiting for the end. In spite of his agony, Duryodhana now burst out in a spurt of venom against Krishna.

The Lord calmly replied, "Think of the evil and suffering you have caused, the number of lives that have been lost only because of your refusal to see reason and listen to Me when I came for peace. All creatures get their just deserts. The wheel of Time turns slowly, but in the end it encompasses the destruction of all things."

Leaving Duryodhana to brood over his wrongs, the Pandavas returned to the enemy camp to take over. When they reached the spot, Krishna ordered Arjuna to dismount. Soon, to the amazement of everyone, the chariot burst into flames and was reduced to ashes.

Arjuna turned to Krishna with tears in his eyes, "My Lord," he said, "What is this I see? My chariot, which was given to me by Agni when he burned the Khandava forest, has been burned up before my very eyes. What is the reason for this?"

The Lord replied, "This chariot has withstood the powerful *astras* sent by Drona, Karna, and Ashvatthama only because I was sitting in it. It should have been burned up long ago. I have abandoned it now that you have achieved what you set out to achieve. So it is with everything in this world. Each thing is created for a purpose. The moment that purpose is achieved, it will perish. This is so even with men. Each man sets out on this strange journey called life. Each one has come with a definite purpose and once that is served, the earth has no more need of him and so he has to quit. This is the case even with Me. I have created Myself on this earth for a purpose. It is not yet over. But the moment it is fulfilled, I will also die and so will you and your dear brothers. But come, do not grieve. Let us be on to our next task." He then turned to Yudhishthira and congratulated him in formal terms.

All of them were deathly tired, both physically and mentally, and were ready to go to their camp and drop down on their beds, but Krishna forbade them to do so and insisted that it was customary for the victors to sleep outside. Thus, the five brothers, together with Satyaki, slept far away from their own camp, while the Lord Himself took on the thankless task of going to Hastinapura to comfort the parents of the Kauravas.

Sanjaya, who had been narrating the events of the battle to the blind King Dhritarashtra, had already informed him of the calamities that had overtaken his son. When Krishna came, Vidura was doing his best to console the weeping parents. The Lord's eyes filled with tears when He saw the condition of the old parents. He sat beside them and spoke gently and lovingly to them for a long time. Turning to Gandhari, He said, "Do you remember that on that day when I came to Hastinapura on a mission of peace, you told Duryodhana, 'Where there is righteousness, there will be victory'? Mother, as you have said, so it has come to pass. You must not blame the Pandavas for this calamity. You know how hard Yudhishthira tried to avert the war. If only Duryodhana had listened to all the advice everyone tried to give him, this catastrophe could have been averted. Now it is your duty to be kind to the children of Pandu. They have suffered so much in life. You must not turn your eyes in anger toward them."

Thus the Lord spent some time with them and left only after He had brought some measure of relief to their grief-stricken hearts. Krishna hurried back to Kurukshetra accompanied by Sanjaya, who wanted to pay his last respects to the Kuru king who was now in mortal agony. Even in his last hours, he was burning with thoughts of revenge. He felt no remorse for all he had done. After Sanjaya left, the other three, Ashvatthama, Kripa, and Kritavarma went to him and, in order to ease his pain a little, they offered to make a last attempt to annihilate the Pandavas. Duryodhana was delighted, made Ashvatthama their leader, and sent them off to do their worst.

The shades of night had fallen by now and as they rested under a tree, Ashvatthama noticed an owl silently coming and killing the baby crows while the birds were sleeping. A diabolical plan for revenge began to take shape in his maddened brain. He woke up the other two and detailed the plan to them. They refused to have anything to do with it, but Ashvatthama was determined and managed to persuade them to accompany him. The three planned a cold-blooded massacre of the sleeping Pandavas and their army. In the small hours of the nght, the devilish trio silently slipped into the Pandava camp. Even the sentries were sleeping, since the war was supposedly over. No one dreamed of such a horrifying sequel, except perhaps the Lord Himself and He, for some reason known only to the Cosmic Mind, refrained from saving any except the Pandavas. Perhaps the time had come for the chariots of their bodies to perish, as Arjuna's chariot had perished.

Leaving Kripa and Kritavarma to guard the exits and kill anyone who tried to escape, Ashvatthama slipped as silently as an owl into each of the tents to accomplish his hateful task and show his loyalty and love for Duryodhana. First he entered Drishtadyumna's tent and, despite his pleas to be killed quickly with a sword, he strangled him to death. Then he kicked Shikhandin violently until he died. He then mercilessly chopped off the heads of the five sleeping sons of the Pandavas by Draupadi. To prevent anyone from escaping, Kripa set fire to all the tents.

There was complete pandemonium and the survivors rushed to the exits only to be mowed down by the three devils. Intoxicated with the blood oozing from his hands, Ashvatthama took the five heads of what he thought to be the Pandavas and presented them to the dying Duryodhana so that he could die in peace. The latter lovingly took them into his hands, gloated over them, and crushed them one by one with his dying hands. Suddenly he realized that Bhima's hard head could never be crushed so easily. He asked for a torch to be brought and in the flickering light he realized bitterly that fate had snatched the victory from beneath his nose once again. His gratitude now gave way to anger and he berated Ashvatthama with a stream of invective. The latter was already half demented and at this barrage of abuse he left in fury, not knowing what he should do.

At last, shaking with pain, rage, and frustration, Duryodhana, whose villainy has no parallel, gave up his life, unattended, unmourned, and alone except for the silent vultures that were circling him in the night sky.

News of the midnight massacre was taken to the Pandavas by Drishtadyumna's mortally wounded charioteer. Their grief at their hollow victory can be imagined. As the sun rose on the nineteenth morning, the scene was one of utter desolation and despair. Taking Draupadi with them, the Pandavas went to examine the horrific scene. Seeing the mangled bodies of their children, they fainted. Draupadi was the first to recover and she appealed to Bhima to wreak vengeance on the villain, Ashvatthama. He rushed off with Nakula as his charioteer. Krishna followed with Arjuna, for he well knew the power of Ashvatthama's *Brahmashirshastra*, which he would not hesitate to use if his own life were jeopardized.

Bhima found him hiding on the bank of the river. The last shreds of his sanity seemed to have left him. Not content with the massacre of innocent men and children for the sake of a man who had no gratitude to him and whom he knew to be a devil incarnate, Ashvatthama, the son of the great Dronacharya, who had already tarnished his caste and lineage by his actions, now condemned himself to a dreadful hell by taking up a blade of grass, invoking the *Brahmashirshastra*, and hurling it at Bhima and Arjuna with these words, "May the world be rid of the line of the Pandavas!"

The *Brahmashirshastra* was the most potent missile of that age and none of them had used it so far, since its consequences were far-reaching and devastating. Usually, it was not entrusted to one like Ashvatthama, who was morally incompetent to use it.

From the blade of grass there sprang a terrible flame that threatened to engulf the whole world. Krishna instructed Arjuna to counter it with his own *Brahmashirshastra*. The opposing missiles flashed through the air and, had they collided, there would have been universal destruction, but Vyasa and the celestial sage Narada came at the opportune moment and stopped the fiery onslaught by the power of their *tapasya*. Krishna asked Arjuna to recall his *astra* and he obeyed, but Ashvatthama, having lost his powers by his inhuman acts, was unable to recall the *astra*, which recoiled on him and would have destroyed him. He ran to the sages and begged them to save him. They did so out of consideration for his father and because they knew that it was too easy a death for him. Arjuna now bound the felon hand and foot and took him to Draupadi.

Krishna wanted to test her and said, "You may now pronounce the death sentence. How would you like him killed?"

But when the Lord chose to test His devotees, He generally gave them the strength to excel in the test and Draupadi, to her great glory, replied, "He is the cold-blooded murderer of my five sons as well as of my beloved brothers and so deserves the worst of deaths. But when I remember that he is the son of my husband's *guru* and that his mother, Kripi, is still alive, I do not feel like making another woman experience the pain which I am experiencing now. Moreover, his death will not bring to life my own sons. I do not want him killed."

The Lord was eminently pleased with her answer and said, "Instead of cutting off his head, we can take off his tuft of hair as well as the crest jewel adorning it. This is tantamount to death for a hero."

Draupadi agreed and Bhima cut off his hair in five places and took off his precious crest jewel, which had guarded him against all weapons, diseases, and hunger. But to crush a cobra without killing it is always unwise and the unrepentant villain crept away to nurse his grievance and make further plans. Devoid of mercy and completely deranged, he made a last, desperate attempt to exterminate the line of the Pandavas, for he realized that he could never kill the Pandavas themselves, who were divinely protected. Taking up another blade of grass, he discharged it with the potent *mantra* of the *Brahmashirshastra*, directed against any babies in the wombs of the Pandava wives, so that the line would become extinct. Uttara, the wife of Abhimanyu, was the only widow who was carrying a child in her womb and the missile came rushing at her. Her mother-in-law Subhadra, Lord Krishna's sister, took her to Him and begged Him to protect her. The Lord instantly dispatched his discus to counter the attack and saved her. He then went after the terrified Ashvatthama, who was fleeing for his life. Catching up with him, Krishna proceeded to punish him. The latter pleaded for death, but death at the hands of the Lord was too good for such a wretch.

In dire tones the Lord pronounced these fateful words, "May you live for thousands of years, condemned to wander over the world like a leper, shunned by all, afflicted with all sorts of diseases, your name itself a bane to all!"

Hearing this dreadful pronouncement, Ashvatthama fled from the scene to wander the world forever.

Thus ends the twenty-seventh chapter of The Play of God, *named "The End of the War."*

Hari Aum Tat Sat

TWENTY-EIGHT

THE ADVICE OF BHISHMA

*Bhishmamukti–
pradayakaya
namaha*

Homage to
Him who
granted
liberation
to Bhishma

*Bhishma, on his deathbed, to Yudhishthira: "By concentrating
one's mind on whom with intense devotion and by reciting whose
names and glories with one's lips a dying aspirant is liberated
from the bondage of desire and duty, may Bhagavan Krishna,
with His radiant face beautified by His benevolent smile and
lotus-petal eyes, who is generally realized only in the heart
through meditation, remain before my physical eyes until life
leaves my body."*
—SHRIMAD BHAGAVATA

The sun that rose over the battlefield of Kurukshetra
the day after the war was pale and insipid, as if
loath to light up such a scene of utter desolation
and despair. Vultures and carrion birds cried and circled
over the field before falling on the carcasses of men and
horses below. Though the Pandavas stood uninjured and
victorious, yet around them lay the death of all their
hopes. They had won an empire at the cost of their sons.
The throne of the Kurus was theirs, but their hearts and
homes were empty. Scattered on the bloody field of
Kurukshetra lay the flower of *Aryan* knighthood, silent
forever. Those who had marched to battle with flying
flags, prancing steeds, gaily bedecked chariots, and
conches and trumpets blasting just a month ago now lay
on the cold, cold earth, a prey to kites, vultures, jackals,
and wolves. In the distance was seen the woe-stricken
procession of the royal women of the Kurus, coming to
mourn their dead, as predicted by Krishna to Draupadi.
Their hair was loose, their clothes disheveled, and their
faces smeared with collyrium from the tears that were
streaming down while they beat their breasts in anguish.
The Pandavas trembled when they gazed on them, for

301

they whose forms had never been seen beyond the four walls of their palaces now walked abroad, their faces bared in utter indifference to the public eye, as Draupadi had once been dragged through the streets of Hastinapura. The hundred sons of Dhritarashtra all lay dead and their widows came mourning and weeping, as Draupadi had once wept when their husbands had so callously dragged her, the greatest of them all, into the court of the Kurus fourteen years ago, in the full flower of her youth and beauty. There had been none to shed a tear for her at that time, but today the Pandavas wept when they saw this pathetic procession, for the milk of human kindness still flowed in them, and they mourned as deeply as the women for the deaths in which they had been instrumental.

Unable to witness this sight any longer, they left with Krishna for Hastinapura to meet the bereaved parents, for because of their age and blindness they had not come to the battlefield. Yudhishthira fell like a log at Dhritarashtra's feet and was embraced by him. It was Bhima's turn next and the blind king's rage against him was so great that he would have crushed him to death had not Lord Krishna, with great presence of mind, thrust the iron image of Bhima into his arms. This image was the one on which Duryodhana had been practicing and the king's anger was so great that the iron image shattered like glass with the force of his hug. Though the entire battle was his own fault, he could not hide his chagrin at the fate of his sons. Had he made a push to curb Duryodhana's temper and direct him in the path of righteousness from childhood, all this might never have taken place, as Krishna pointed out to him. He also told him that at least now he should behave like a father to the Pandavas.

Next they turned to Gandhari. From the beginning, she had known that Kurukshetra would see the end of her house. She also knew that it was her husband's weakness, coupled with his greed, that had led to this disaster. But the fact that her husband was being crushed under the doom he had brought upon himself made her burn with rage and sorrow. She had blindfolded herself of her own free will from the day she had been brought to this palace as a beautiful young bride, denying herself the light of day so as not to enjoy that which was not seen by her lord. Such was her fidelity and such the power of her wrath that she feared to gaze at the faces of the Pandavas in case the fire of her anger should burn them, even through the folds of the cloth she tied around her eyes. As Yudhishthira approached to seek her blessing, she bent her eyes down so that her blindfolded gaze fell upon his foot and it was scorched at that very spot. Seeing this, Bhima and Arjuna quailed and hid behind Krishna, and Gandhari's anger passed over their heads.

The Pandavas now met their mother Kunti after fourteen years. Kunti caressed them and ran loving fingers over their wounds. Taking Draupadi in her arms, she did her best to comfort her. At last, they all followed the king and Gandhari to the battlefield, since they insisted on going. Gandhari spoke to Draupadi. "Look at me daughter and comfort yourself. Vidura prophesied this long ago and Krishna gave due warning when He came as ambassador. My dear child, I have lost all my sons, as you have. Who is to comfort whom? The destruction of the entire race is due to me."

They walked toward the battlefield. Gandhari could see it all in her mind's eye. Turning to Krishna, she looked directly at Him, for she knew Him to be indestructible. She showed Him the dead forms of her sons and the women who were mourning for them. Then, going to the spot where Duryodhana lay, she fell down in a faint. Krishna stood by her side and said nothing. She showed Him all the scenes, of Uttara weeping over her dead husband, Abhimanyu. They had been married but six months. Seeing all this, Gandhari's anger flared up once again, but this time it was directed at the Lord.

"Behold, O Lotus-Eyed One!" she said. "Behold the daughters of my house, widowed and bereft, with locks unbound and eyes swollen with weeping! Do You not hear their piteous laments, brooding over the dead bodies of the heroes? Behold them seeking for the faces of their loved ones in the field of Kurukshetra. They search for their husbands, fathers, sons, and brothers. The whole field is covered with these childless mothers and widowed wives. Where are they now, my splendid sons who were like burning meteors? The battlefield is scattered with their costly gems, golden armor, their splendid ornaments and diadems. The weapons handled by those heroic hands lie in confusion on the field, never to be dispatched again upon their dreadful errands. Beholding these pitiful images in my mind, O Krishna, my whole body is afire with grief. The world seems empty and desolate. I feel as if the elements themselves have been destroyed. Like the darkened coals of a dead fire lie the heroes who took part in this mighty battle. They who had slept cradled on the soft bosoms of their wives now sleep on the cold, hard breast of the earth. Jackals alone are there to chant their glory, in lieu of bards. The wailing of the women mingles with the howl of hungry beasts. What was that destiny, O

Krishna, that pursued my sons from the time they were born? Whence came this curse on the house of the Kurus? Why does my heart not break into a thousand fragments at these dreadful happenings? What sin have I and these weeping daughters of mine committed that such a disaster should have befallen us?"

Hearing the sobs of Kunti and Draupadi, it suddenly flashed upon her that the whole battle was like a play in which the armies had destroyed each other. She also realized that the sole director and producer of the drama was standing beside her. Turning to Him, she addressed Him in prophetic tones. From the depths of her sorrow came the courage to curse the Lord Himself. "Two armies, O Janardana, have perished on this field. Where were You while they thus put an end to each other? Were You blind or had You deliberately blindfolded Yourself? Why did You allow this calamity to befall the house of the Kurus? I know well that You could have prevented it if You had so wished. Why did You hold Your hand, O slayer of Kamsa? By the power of my great chastity and fidelity, I pronounce this curse upon You and Your race: You shall become the slayer of Your own kinsmen thirty-six years from now. After having brought about the destruction of Your sons and kinsmen, You Yourself shall perish alone in the wilderness, as my son Duryodhana did, lying alone and helpless beside the lake, even though he was the King of the Kurus. The women of Your race, deprived of their sons, husbands, and friends shall weep and wail in their bereavement, as do the wives of the Kauravas today!"

As her voice died away in sobs, the Lord looked tenderly at her and said, "Blessed are you, O Mother, for you have aided Me in the completion of My task. My people, the Yadavas, are incapable of defeat and therefore they have to die by My own hands. Behold, O Mother! With folded hands I gladly accept your curse!"

Then the Holy One bent down to the aged queen, who had sunk down in sorrow, and lifted her up gently. "Arise, O Gandhari!" He said. "Think of the wrongs inflicted on the virtuous Pandavas by your sons over the years, which they have borne so patiently. At that time it was you who was indifferent, not I, and now you blame Me for indifference. The law of *karma*, though inexorable, is also just. He who sows the wind has perforce to reap the whirlwind. Your sons brought about their fate by their own actions, as did the Pandavas. All must inevitably be mown down by Time—the wielder of the scythe. It is the Lord's power as Time which has contrived the end of your sons, as well as the sons of the Pandavas. Set not your heart on grief, O Queen! By indulging in sorrow, one increases it twofold. The cow brings forth offspring for the bearing of burdens, the Brahmin woman bears children for the practice of austerities, the laboring woman adds to the ranks of the workers; but the *kshatriya* woman bears sons who are destined to die on the battlefield. Why then do you grieve?"

The queen listened in silence to His words. Only too well did she realize their truth. With her inner vision clarified by her great sorrow, she looked at the world and found it all to be unreal. There was nothing further to be said. Then she and Dhritarashtra, together with Yudhishthira and the other heroes, restraining that grief which stems from weakness and leads to weakness, as the Lord had told Arjuna on the battlefield, now proceeded to the banks of the Ganga to perform the last rites for the lost heroes.

When Kunti saw the body of Karna being lamented over by his wife, she could not bear it. The same Ganga who had taken her baby away so many years ago was now carrying away his ashes. The river flowed as placidly as she had on that day, indifferent to the cares and worries of mankind. Karna had no sons to perform his obsequies. They had all been killed. He was as much of an orphan now as he had been when she had abandoned him. Now was the time to make recompense for the great wrong she had done to her firstborn. She walked with firm steps toward Yudhishthira and said, "There is one more person to whom you have to make an offering." The brothers looked enquiringly at her. The Lord alone knew of her dilemma and watched with compassion.

"Who is this person to whom I must make an offering, Mother?" Yudhishthira asked. "I don't understand."

"It is Karna. You must make offerings for him."

"Why should I, a *kshatriya*, perform the funeral rite for a *sutaputra* (the son of a charioteer)?" Yudhishthira asked in surprise.

Kunti was dumb with agony. But at last she burst out, determined to see that Karna died with all the honors of a *kshatriya*, even though she had denied him a life as one, "He was a *kshatriya* and not a *suta*!"

"Not a *sutaputra*!" they all cried out in amazement. "Tell us, Mother, who was his father?"

Kunti said, "Karna was the son of the sun god Surya. He was Suryaputra and not a *sutaputra*! His mother was a *kshatriya* princess who abandoned him as a baby, since she was still a maid, and floated him down the river, where he was found by the *suta* Adhiratha and his wife Radha, who brought him up as their own son. He preferred the name Radheya to all his other names, for she was the only mother he had ever known."

The Pandavas looked in amazement at her. At last, Yudhishthira asked, "Who was his real mother?"

All eyes were fixed on her. She shot a look of desperate appeal at the Lord. His lotus eyes were filled with infinite pity and infused in her the strength to speak the truth. Turning to Yudhishthira, she said firmly, "I am his mother. Karna was my firstborn child." Saying this, she slipped to the ground in a faint. Vidura rushed to her side.

Yudhishthira was too stunned to speak. At last, he whispered, "Karna was my brother!" Arjuna clutched his arm and cried out, "What have I done? I have killed my own brother and gloated over his death."

The Pandavas were prostrate with grief. When Kunti revived, Yudhishthira asked her, "Tell me, did Karna know of this?"

Krishna answered for her and said, "Yes, he knew." The Pandavas hung their heads in shame as they each recalled the times they had taunted him with the name *sutaputra* and he had kept silent. "Mother, how could you do this to us?" they asked Kunti and walked away leaving her alone with her grief. For one month they had to stay in huts built on the banks of the river until the obsequies were over. Yudhishthira was inconsolable. The sages Vyasa and Narada came to him and Narada told him the story of Karna and tried to comfort him.

In the meantime the Lord, with His usual compassion, went to the stricken queen. He realized what she was going through. She had denied her firstborn to save the other five and now they, in turn, were shunning her for the first time. He alone stayed with that brave queen, who had borne with fortitude all the trials and tribulations to which her life had been exposed from the time she was a child.

Addressing the Lord, Kunti said, "Salutations to You, the Supreme Person, Lord of All. As an ignorant spectator cannot recognize the actor in his theatrical robes, so also have we failed to recognize You who have chosen to hide Your true nature under the garb of an ordinary mortal. Yet due to Your grace, I have been able to penetrate the garb and recognize You for what You are. Salutations to You, O Krishna, born of Vasudeva and Devaki. Salutations to You, the Brahman of the *Upanishads*, who has appeared in His sportive manifestation as the foster son of Nanda. Salutations to the lotus-eyed and the lotus-garlanded. Just as you released your sorrow-stricken mother Devaki from the prison cell of the wicked Kamsa, so have you rescued me and my sons from several perilous positions. I can scarcely recount the dangerous situations from which you have saved us—from the murderous attempts on Bhima, from the flaming palace at Varanavata, from the menacing demons of the forest, from the humiliation of the gambling meet, from the perils of our forest life, from the weapons of these great warriors in this mighty battle, and now, finally, you have saved our line from extinction by protecting Uttara's fetus from Ashvatthama's *Brahmashirshastra*."

Then Kunti placed before the Lord, in faultless accents, a unique prayer. "O Preceptor of the Universe, I pray You to give us bad luck all the time. Let dangers surround us always, for it is only when peril threatens us from all sides that we feel Your divine presence. It is only when our minds become single-pointed through extreme sorrow or anxiety that we are able to call to You with the greatest of intensity, and it is only then that You come running to help Your devotees and save them from their dire straits. Therefore, I do not pray for comforts, for when we are surrounded by ease on all sides, the treacherous mind fails to focus itself on You, who alone are responsible for both comforts and discomforts. Therefore do I thank You for not having given me comforts, I thank You for not having given me any wealth, for due to that I have realized that You are my only treasure. You alone are the wealth of those who have no other wealth. I care not for kingdom or glory, but only to have Your blessed vision all my life. I deem You to be the eternal Time Spirit, endless and irresistible, whose steady movement makes no distinction between good and bad, small and great. What Gandhari said is true. It is this quality of Yours that brings about feuds among people, leading to their death and destruction. You have neither friends nor enemies. Even the destruction of Your so-called enemies is only to bless them and give them salvation, for Your *avatar* is only to redeem all *jivas*. The apparent birth and activities of the Unborn and Unchanging Spirit, the Soul of the Universe, in all Your various incarnations is indeed a mystery. O Lord of all, pray do not abandon us, for we are totally dependent on You. We have no refuge except Your lotus feet. My beloved Lord, help me to cut asunder my attachment to my people. Casting off all other attachments, let my mind cling to You alone. Let it, like the Ganga flowing to the ocean, flow toward You, the infinite

Ocean of Mercy, in a never-ending stream of love and delight. O Friend of Arjuna! O Krishna! Leader of the Vrishnis! Lord of Gokula! Protector of the weak and holy! Master of *Yoga*! Sole spiritual guide of all humanity! Salutations again and again to You!"

So saying, Kunti fell like a log at the feet of the Lord, unable to contain her love and emotion, filled with ecstasy when she thought of all the times He had saved her and her sons, overpowered with love for this glorious Being who stood before her in flesh and blood. The Lord cast His bewitching smile on her and blessed her with total and undying devotion for Him, which was what she had prayed for.

After a month of mourning, Yudhishthira agreed to hold his coronation at the suggestion of Krishna, Vyasa, and the *rishis*. Honored by all the Brahmins and sages, extolled by the bards, Yudhishthira was led to the throne by the Lord Himself, who officially placed the sacred crown of the Kurus on his head. It was a unique moment, when man was crowned by God incarnate. How blessed was Yudhishthira!

In the *Ramayana*, it was the opposite. God as Shri Rama was crowned by a man. After this, Bhima was crowned *Yuvaraja*. Vidura was made minister and personal counsellor, Sanjaya was put in charge of finance, Arjuna was commander in chief of the army as well as foreign minister, Nakula was made the head of the army, Sahadeva was made the king's personal protector, Dhaumya was high priest, and Yuyutsu was personal attendant to his blind father and Gandhari, as well as the manager of the outlying provinces. At the end of it Yudhishthira said to Krishna, "My Lord, You have given me back my kingdom. In Your affection for us You have played the role of a man—You who must be worshipped as the Eternal Soul. You are the Lord of Lords, yet You have pretended to be a man, wept with us and laughed with us. You are our guiding star and show us the Truth. The only recompense I can make is to fall at Your feet and wash them with my tears." So saying, he fell at His feet.

In spite of being consoled and instructed by the sages and by the Lord Himself, Yudhishthira's deep remorse for his role in the destruction could not be assuaged. Unaware of the inscrutable power of the Lord, not realizing that everything happened because of the divine will alone, Yudhishthira was overcome by sorrow for what he thought to be his fault.

"What a wicked fellow I am," he said. "For the sake of this body which is going to be food for jackals and vultures, I have caused the destruction of countless men. I will never be liberated from hell even after thousands of years of suffering, slayer as I am of children, Brahmins, friends, relatives, brothers, and teachers. The tremendous suffering I have caused to these women whose husbands have met death because of me cannot be atoned by any sacrifices or charities."

Brooding over his sins, Yudhishthira fell into a mood of great depression, from which everyone failed to shake him. The Lord's sermon to Arjuna had not been imbibed by him. Thinking himself to be the sole slayer, he wept and moaned and could not be comforted. Seeing this, the Lord decided to take him to the spot where the dying Bhishma lay. He had two purposes to fulfill. One was to clear Yudhishthira's doubts and the other was to bless Bhishma before he departed for his heavenly abode. Accordingly, everyone set out for Kurukshetra, where Bhishma lay on his bed of arrows. Krishna laid His healing hands on the dying knight's pain-wracked body. Immediately, he felt calm and at peace and his mind grew clear. With strong accents he proceeded to impart to Yudhishthira the lesson of *dharma*, as the Lord wanted him to do.

First, Bhishma folded his palms to the Lord and then said, "Why should You, who are the epitome of *dharma*, ask me to impart this lesson to Yudhishthira? This is in line with Your mysterious design to bring glory to Your devotees."

The Lord smiled and said, "Your utterances will be on a par with the *Vedas* and will bring undying glory to you. So speak on."

Fixing his eyes on that form which had been residing in his heart all these years, Bhishma's eyes filled with tears and, turning to Yudhishthira, he spoke. "My son, strange indeed are the ways of the divine. Why should dangers stalk the fortunes of your family, which has the son of *dharma* as its head, which is protected by the mighty Bhima, the son of Vayu, the wind god, and Arjuna, with his reputed Gandiva, and above all having Shri Krishna, the Supreme Being, as your guiding star? O King! None can know the will of that Supreme Being. Even the farsighted *rishis*, who have tried their best to fathom the divine mind, have recoiled in utter failure. Therefore, O Leader of the Bharatas, recognizing that all that has happened has been wrought by providence alone, follow the dictates of that divine will and protect the people, who have become like unclaimed orphans. *Dharma* is that which leads to the advancement of evolution. To do one's *svadharma* without coming under the sway of the opposites of like and dislike, hatred and love, is the way of the enlightened person.

You are bound to act, but the action alone is your right and not the fruits, which should be given over to the Lord. That is the way to liberation. The action done with attachment leads to bondage and the same action done with detachment leads to liberation. Renounce this ego, which claims all glories for itself. Neither the credit nor the discredit is yours. The Lord alone is the doer and the instigator.

Strange indeed that you, who have the Lord Narayana Himself as your companion, should have come to me for advice. You have been looking upon Him as your uncle's son, your dear friend, your selfless ally, and your most important well-wisher. You have even utilized His services as an adviser, a messenger, and even a charioteer, taking advantage of His love for you. He in turn has played these various roles for you with perfection, feeling neither elation nor humiliation. He is the Soul of all, even-sighted, devoid of egoism, free from all taints. In His infinite mercy He has now brought you here, for He knows that the time for my departure has come. May that Lord, with His radiant face, who is realized only in the hearts of aspiring *yogis*, be present before my physical eyes until my life leaves my body!"

Yudhishthira's eyes filled with tears when he heard this, for he realized, as Arjuna had at the vision of the Cosmic Form, that He whom they had taken for granted and treated familiarly was none other than the Supreme Lord. He closed his eyes and mentally begged pardon for all the sins of commission and omission they had been guilty of. When he looked at the Lord with tears in his eyes, he found Him looking encouragingly at him, for Shri Krishna knew what was passing through his mind. Feeling immeasurably comforted by that look of compassion, Yudhishthira turned to his grandsire and proceeded to question him on all the aspects of *dharma*, the duties of men in general, their duties according to their caste and birth, the duties of a king, of women, of the seekers of liberation, and so on.

Bhishma gave a lengthy discourse on these and various other matters, covering all details of *dharma* so that Yudhishthira was completely satisfied. His teachings can be summarized in brief: "Destiny is powerful, but self-effort can modify it. Truth is all powerful. The adherence to truth can never fail in life. One should practice self-control, humility, and righteousness. One should be neither too soft nor too stern. One should be able to adjust to the circumstances. Weakness is not a virtue and it breeds many evils. Compassion should be combined with stern discipline. Tolerance of irregularity and *adharma* leads to downfall. Life rusts in indolence; it shines in industry. Hatred is the most terrible poison. Love is the one constructive force and is all-powerful. It can reclaim even a sinner. *Dharma* is one's only friend, for it follows the body that has been abandoned by all."

Then Yudhishthira asked him in what form one should worship the Supreme Being and in what manner. Bhishma smiled and, looking at Krishna standing before him, he said, "The Supreme God, the one object who is the sole refuge of all mankind, is standing before me. The Lord of the universe, the God of gods, by Him is pervaded the entire universe. By meditating on Him and His manifold names, one can transcend all sorrow. He is the greatest source of energy, the highest penance, the Eternal Brahman. Surrender your heart and soul to Him, for He is the Lord of the past, present, and future. He is the Supreme Purushottama."

So saying, Bhishma fixed his eyes on the shining form of the Lord standing before him and chanted the "Vishnu *Sahasranama*," the thousand and one names of Lord Vishnu. He then lay back exhausted, yet exalted. Having blessed Yudhishthira, he told him to come back later when *uttarayana* had commenced, the beginning of the summer solstice when the sun starts its northward journey.

Accordingly, on the first day of *uttarayana*, all of them returned to the same spot. Bhishma turned in adoration to Krishna and said, "You are the Lord of the universe, the Supreme *Purusha*, the Creator, the Eternal Soul. Pray reveal to me Your *Vishvarupa* (Cosmic Form)."

The Lord did as he wished and Bhishma called for flowers and worshipped the Lord with them. He said, "You are the Lord of the universe. You are the Supreme *Purusha* and the Creator. You are the Eternal Soul. Grant me leave to cast off this human body. Permitted by You, I will reach the highest state."

The Holy One spoke, "Devavrata, I grant you leave to return home. Go back to the Vasus. You will never be born again in this world of mortals. Death is waiting at your doorstep, waiting like a servant for your summons. You have My permission to summon him."

Once again, Bhishma exhorted the Pandavas, "Follow the Truth always. Strive for it in thought, word, and deed. Practice self-denial. Be compassionate. Attain knowledge of the Supreme Brahman. This is the *dharma* of all *dharmas*. Know that where Krishna, the Universal Self, dwells, there *dharma* will ever be. And where *dharma* is, victory will inevitably follow."

Then, closing his eyes, he steadily gathered his vital energy to the top of his head and thence passed out in the form of a great light, as he gently willed himself to die. Those around saw a wonderful glow leave his body and rise up to the sky. A gentle breeze blew and heavenly instruments played sweet music as he shuffled off his mortal coil, the stainless knight before whom even death had to wait. The Pandavas performed the last rites for their beloved grandsire.

It is said that on the next day, when Bhishma's ashes were taken to the Ganga for immersion, the river stopped flowing and the goddess Ganga rose up and approached Krishna, weeping for the death of her beloved son.

Krishna consoled her. "O Divine Mother! Why do you weep like an ordinary mortal? Do you not know that your son was one of the immortals known as the Vasus, who had to spend these long years on earth due to a curse? Rejoice that now he has returned to be with the immortals!"

At the Lord's words, Ganga was consoled and resumed her flow, taking with her the ashes of her son.

The Lord now returned with the Pandavas to Hastinapura and stayed with them for some months to advise and console them. At last, He decided to return to His city of Dwaraka. Bidding a fond farewell to the Pandavas, He got into His chariot. Though they had seen their kith and kin slaughtered and their own children murdered, the Pandavas had not felt such a great a sense of loss as they experienced when Krishna left. They felt like rudderless boats tossed in the sea of circumstances. Lapped by the waves of His benign influence, they were secure and protected. Even during the major crises of the war, they had thought themselves invincible, since He was in their midst. Unable to bear the parting, Arjuna escorted Him beyond the city gates. He refused to return until at last Krishna had to ask him gently to go back, for his presence was essential to Yudhishthira. Like a creeper whose sole support had been suddenly snatched away, Arjuna returned with bent head and brimming eyes after having seen the last of the flag with the sign of Garuda (eagle vehicle of Lord Vishnu) gaily fluttering in the wind. Thousands of the citizens of Hastinapura had also followed to have a last glimpse of the Lord. Wearily, they returned home.

On the way, Krishna met an old Brahmin friend of His called Uttanga. The old man had obviously not heard of the stupendous happenings that had been taking place in the land, for he was an inveterate traveler.

Very politely, he enquired about the welfare of the Pandavas and Kauravas. Krishna brought him up to date about the affairs of the country. The old man became very angry when he heard this, for he felt that the Lord could have stopped the battle had He so willed! Krishna pacified him and explained to him that it was in concordance with the cosmic plan that the battle had taken place. For Him to interfere in the governing of the universe according to the impersonal law of *karma*, which He Himself had established, would not be correct. "O Uttanga! Age after age I am born into the world to uphold righteousness. If this can be accomplished only by the destruction of the unrighteous, then I appear in the form of *Kala*, or all-consuming Time, and bring about the destruction of all creatures. Life and death are but two sides of the same coin. One cannot exist without the other. I did My best to bring the sons of Dhritarashtra to the path of righteousness, but those souls, steeped in wickedness, would not listen to the voice of *dharma*, even though I granted them a vision of My Cosmic Form. Thus, the battle became inevitable."

Unrestricted freedom granted to an individual can only lead to downfall, as was proven in the case of Duryodhana, who had never had any restrictions placed on him. Freedom is a universal principle and not the prerogative of any single person. This is why history never seems to care for individuals. Even the strongest of empires and greatest of emperors have been reduced to the dust of the earth. It is not the individual, whether in the form of a person, family, community, or empire, that is of value to the universal justice. What is of value is the fulfillment of the cosmic plan, the necessity to grow by a gradual ascent through various degrees of humanity to the divinity present in each one of us. Hence, the Lord's actions in the Mahabharata war have a cosmic purpose and a universal intention which cannot be completely understood unless we also have reached the shores of that Ocean of Immortality of which He is the essence.

Uttanga accepted the Lord's explanation and begged to have a vision of the Cosmic Form which was shown to the Kauravas. Krishna obliged him. After this, He asked him to choose a boon.

Uttanga being a simple soul, did not have many wishes, but at the Lord's insistence he said, "My Lord, having seen Your Universal Form all my desires have been fulfilled, but since you insist, I have one request. Many times in my travels I have suffered from intense thirst. So if it pleases You, kindly grant me the boon that I shall get water whenever I need it."

"So be it," said the Lord and having blessed him both proceeded on their ways.

Later on, during his travels in the desert, Uttanga was afflicted with a terrible thirst and mentally he reminded the Lord of His boon. Just at that moment, he was approached by an outcaste hunter, clad in filthy rags, carrying a water bag made of animal hide, from which he offered some water to the thirsty man. But parched though he was, the high-caste Brahmin refused to touch the water offered by an outcaste in such unclean conditions. The hunter went on his way and the Lord appeared. Uttanga upbraided Him for having sent this unclean creature to give him water.

Krishna smiled and said, "O Uttanga! For your sake, I had prevailed upon Indra, the king of the gods, to give you *amrita* (the nectar of immortality). He was loathe to do this, since he did not want to grant immortality to a mortal. Since I insisted, he agreed, provided I allowed him to take on the form of a lowborn hunter in order to test the purity of your mind. I accepted the challenge, thinking that you had attained wisdom and the eye of equality, which would enable you to see the same Universal and Divine Spirit shining in each and every creature, whether high caste or outcaste. By your foolish act, you have lost the opportunity to become immortal."

Uttanga realized his mistake and understood the lesson which the Lord was trying to teach him. He resolved to become a *jnani*, a man of wisdom, in action as well as in principle.

Thus ends the twenty-eighth chapter of The Play of God, *named "The Advice of Bhishma."*

Hari Aum Tat Sat

TWENTY-NINE

THE STORY OF SUDAMA

Satchidanandaya namaha

Homage to the One who is pure existence–knowledge–bliss

"May I, who have had this intimate association with the great Lord Krishna, the abode of all auspicious qualities, be blessed with devotion, comradeship, and servitude to Him life after life. May I also have association with His devotees." Thus spoke Kuchela.
—SHRIMAD BHAGAVATA

The Lord now reached Dwaraka, where the Yadavas welcomed Him back with great joy. Unfortunately, He was not able to remain there for more than a few months since Yudhishthira once again urgently summoned Him back to the Kuru capital. Yudhishthira was still tormented by the gruesome events of the past and his unhappiness was made worse after Krishna's departure. Despite all the advice he had had from Bhishma and all the sages, he still found it impossible to reconcile himself with the carnage that had taken place. Vyasa now advised him to conduct the *Ashvamedha yajna*,[1] which would absolve him from all sins. Yudhishthira agreed and sent word to Krishna to come soon and bless the *yajna*, as He had blessed their *Rajasuya yajna* so many years before.

The Lord arrived just in time to save the child in Uttara's womb. Reducing Himself to the size of a thumb, He had entered her womb and safeguarded the fetus from the effects of the missile directed at it by Ashvatthama. Even so, when the infant was born it seemed to be lifeless. His sister Subhadra and Abhimanyu's widow, Uttara, started to weep and begged the Lord to save the child. Krishna said, "If the infant is touched by

---

[1]*Asvamedha yajna*—the Vedic horse sacrifice, usually conducted by a king in order to proclaim himself emperor.

one who is a *nitya brahmachari*[2] it will come to life."

Many sages were standing around, but none dared to touch the babe. Finally the Lord Himself stepped forward and took the lifeless child in His arms. Gently He passed His lotus palms along the inert body from head to toe. At the touch of His blessed hands the infant took a great gulp of air and began to breathe, and the onlookers were filled with amazement and joy.

The palace now became an abode of happiness. Even Yudhishthira shook off his mantle of sorrow, for the baby was a boy. He would be the successor to the throne of the Kurus and he had been born at a most auspicious time.

The sages pronounced many blessings and said, "O King, when this sprout of the Kuru race was about to be destroyed by the *Brahmashirshas-tra*, he was saved by the all-powerful Vishnu and delivered to you as a gift from Him. Therefore, he will become famous as a great devotee and a great king and should be given the name Vishnuratha (the one saved by Vishnu). He will also be popularly known as 'Parikshit' (one who tests), since he will always be testing creatures to find out whether the form he saw in the womb is the same as the one manifesting in all creation as the indweller."

When Parikshit was in his mother's womb, he had noticed a divine person standing close to him. The size of a thumb, lovely to behold, blue as the rain cloud, wearing a yellow robe and a shining diadem, He scattered the power of the *Brahmashirshastra* with His mace. As the ten-month-old fetus watched in wonder, the figure disappeared. He came out of the womb and from thence gazed at all the faces he saw looking for that inner dweller.

Preparations were now made for the Ashvamedha *yajna*. Since the treasury was sadly depleted after the great war, they did not have enough funds to conduct the *yajna*. At the Lord's bidding, the brothers went to the Himalayas and returned with the necessary wealth. The ceremony was then performed with all due pomp and Yudhishthira's mind felt vastly relieved.

The Lord spent some more time with the Pandavas. Arjuna and He visited all the favorite haunts of their youth. Arjuna had by now forgotten most of the glorious teachings of the *Gita*, yet considered himself to be a

---

[2] *nitya brahmachari*—lifetime celibate.

great devotee. The Lord always contrived to bring about situations that would deflate the egos of His devotees. One day, while they were wandering disguised as ordinary travelers, they came across a Brahmin who was ferociously sharpening his sword. Arjuna gazed at him in surprise and enquired, "Why are you resorting to violence, O Brahmana?"

The Brahmin replied, "There is no sin in killing for the sake of my Lord. Three people have treated Him very badly. One is that rascal Sudama, who allowed Him to wash his feet and forced Him to eat his unclean rice flakes, the second is the sage Narada, who is always disturbing my Lord's sleep by his incessant reciting of His names, and the third is that fellow Arjuna, who insisted on making my Lord take on the menial position of his charioteer!"

Krishna looked on in great amusement at Arjuna's discomfiture and whispered to him that discretion was the better part of valor. It would be expedient to quit the scene before the irate Brahmin discovered his identity!

The incident with Sudama referred to by the Brahmin took place soon after the Mahabharata war, when the Lord was residing at Dwaraka. Sudama was a Brahmin who was also known as Kuchela because of the tattered condition of his clothing. He had studied with Krishna and Balarama at Guru Sandipani's *ashrama* at Avanti. Though they had parted with many promises to keep in touch with each other, as is the case with many childhood friends, they lost contact with each other. However, his intimacy with Krishna had evoked a deep and abiding devotion in the poor Brahmin boy. He had lived a life of complete austerity and devotion to the Lord, totally uncaring about his own welfare, wandering about singing the Lord's songs and meditating on His glories. Observing his careless state, some well-meaning friends decided to get him married so that he would have someone to care for his daily needs. They found him a wife who was well suited to his temperament, pious and devoted. With such an improvident husband, she was forced to fend for both of them and eked out a miserable existence by begging. Kuchela hardly ever thought of enquiring how they managed, for he was confident that the Lord would provide, as He had always done. His needs were few and if something was placed before him, he would eat. Otherwise, he would fast. Neither made much difference, for he was ever immersed in some inner vision which sustained him. But his poor wife, who was not so blessed, could not bear to see the plight of her children. Once it came to pass that even the pittance she managed to get was denied, and the hearth had not been lit for many days. Unable to bear the sight of her children starving to death in front of her eyes, she approached her husband and said, "O holy One! I have heard you say that the worshipful Lord Krishna, protector of the Yadavas, the consort of Lakshmi, the goddess of wealth, was your friend and schoolmate at the *gurukula*. He is a lover of pious men and a haven of refuge for all. Could you not approach Him for a small favor for us? It will mean nothing to Him and will be the saving of our family. The condition of our children is pitiful indeed. Pray listen to me and go to Him."

Kuchela was not at all happy at the idea. The thought of begging for material goods from One who was capable of granting immortality was galling to him. The Lord knows the wants of all. The fact that He did not give him wealth meant that he was undeserving of it. What an insult it would be to go and coerce Him into giving it! The lack of material wealth meant nothing to him. He felt no hardship whatsoever. He was the true devotee, asking for nothing but the opportunity to love and worship the Lord every moment of his life, with no expectation of fruits.

After having been entreated by his wife many times, he agreed, more because of the exciting thought that he would be able to meet the Lord of his heart once again. But he was worried at the thought of going empty-handed to meet such a glorious personage. It was considered proper to take a gift, so he asked his wife to get him something. She looked at him in astonishment. Their hut was absolutely bare of even the basic necessities and here was her husband asking her to produce a gift fit for a king! What was she to do? Suddenly Kuchela himself came up with a bright idea.

"I know just the thing He will like," he said. "Krishna was very fond of the little flakes of beaten rice the *guru's* wife used to make for us. You must get some paddy and pound it for me to take to Him."

The poor lady was at her wit's end. Where was she to get anything? They had not cooked in their house for days and they had exhausted the charity of their neighbors. She ran out in despair and saw a man approaching her. Though he was a complete stranger, she ran to him and opened her palms in supplication. He took three fistfuls of grain from the bag he was carrying and gave it to her. It is said that the Lord Himself had appeared to help her! Thankful at having obtained something from such an unexpected quarter, she hurried back, cleaned the paddy, and pounded it into flakes. It looked a pitiful handful indeed. She searched in vain for some cloth in which to tie it, but could find nothing in that poverty-stricken household. Tearing off a piece of her own tattered attire, she lovingly tied up the rice flakes into a very small bundle. This she anxiously presented to her husband when he set out the next morning.

Kuchela went with a joyous heart, for he was going to see the Lord soon. By evening, he reached the precincts of Dwaraka and saw the golden turrets of the palaces glinting in the rays of the setting sun. With every step he took, his heart beat faster in anticipation. He had not eaten for days, yet his feet hastened of their own accord and his tired eyes gleamed at the thought of the bliss in store for him.

"Will He recognize me?" he wondered. "Will He remember me?"

Timidly, he hovered outside the palace gates wondering what to do. The guards looked at him curiously and turned away, for they did not think him worthy of attention.

Inside the palace, Krishna's consort Rukmini wondered at His distraught and restless behavior during the day. He seemed unable to concentrate on anything. He kept going to the balcony to watch the road. At last, she timidly ventured to ask Him what the matter was. "I'm expecting a very dear friend," He replied. "Prepare the best dishes and the best room for him, for there is none so dear to Me!"

Rukmini also watched and waited anxiously for the sight of a royal coach or chariot, but evening came and no one appeared. Suddenly, the Lord got up from the swing bed on which He was resting and rushed to the palace gates. Rukmini followed Him in haste, carrying all the auspicious articles she had kept ready in order to welcome the honored guest. When she reached the gate, she was surprised to find Krishna clasping to His chest an emaciated and wizened morsel of humanity, a mere bundle of skin and bone held together by a few rags! However, at a sign from her Lord, she hurried forward to wash his feet with perfumed water.

Krishna practically carried Kuchela upstairs to His own room, preceded by ladies carrying lamps. He seated him on His own favorite swing bed. He sat Himself down beside Kuchela with His arm flung around his scraggly neck. Rukmini proceeded to fan them both with the royal fan made of a yak's tail. Kuchela was absolutely bewildered. Never in his wildest dreams had he expected a welcome like this. He sat in a daze of happiness while Krishna pelted him with questions to which he could scarcely formulate a reply.

"O dearest Friend! Why have you never come to see Me before? How has life treated you? Are you married? How many children do you have?" and so on. This was Kuchela's cue to have put in his request, but the poor man had completely forgotten the reason for his visit. He could only smile and gaze adoringly at that beloved face so close to his. As soon as he arrived, Kuchela was so overwhelmed by the magnificence of his surroundings that he had felt quite ashamed of his pitiful offering, and had tucked the bundle away under his armpit. Everyone in the palace was astonished to see the Lord worshipping this emaciated Brahmin with such love. A man who would be scorned by the world in general was being treated like His brother by the Lord. What merit had he acquired to deserve such treatment? Soon after, Balarama also came and the two of them sat on either side of the Brahmin and reminisced over the happy days of their youth at the *gurukula*. The Lord spoke of the greatness of the preceptor.

"Those through whom one is born in this world are one's first *gurus*. Thus, the parents should be first worshipped as *gurus*. The one who invests the sacred thread and gives eligibility to study the *Vedas* is the second *guru*, greater even than the first. And finally, the one who imparts the wisdom of the Supreme is the greatest of all *gurus*. Know that one to be none other than Myself. Though I reside in all beings, yet worshipping Me through the *guru* is the worship I like best. It is only by the grace of the *guru* that one can attain the fulfillment of spiritual aspirations."

Kuchela replied, "O Supreme Divinity! O Thou Teacher of all the worlds! What further fulfillment in life can I have, who have had the great good fortune to have spent some days with you at the abode of the *guru*? How can I ever forget those days? My life since then has been spent in contemplation of their blessed memory. Do you remember how we used to go to the forest to collect firewood for the *guru* and how one day we were caught in the heavy rain and could not return? You sheltered me in Your arms then, until our compassionate preceptor came and rescued us in the morning and blessed us. Surely it is through the blessing of that venerable being that I have had the opportunity of being with You like this."

So saying, Kuchela nestled close to his beloved divinity, gazing at Him with adoring eyes. However, he was careful to keep his arm pressed close to his side all the time, for he didn't want the Lord to see his miserable offering.

The Lord knew what was in his mind and looked pointedly at the place where He could see a tiny piece of rag sticking out and waited expectantly for the gift, but in vain. Kuchela only hugged the bundle closer. Though the Lord wants nothing and expects nothing, yet even the humblest gift His devotees offer is accepted with joy, for it is the coin of their love. It is not the magnitude of the gift that matters, but the magnitude of the heart which offers it. In front of the Lord of Lakshmi (goddess of wealth), all of us are Kuchelas. Even so, we can offer Him a fistful of rice flakes moistened with the tears of love that overflow from our eyes. At last, having lost all hopes of being offered the gift, the Lord teasingly said, "O dearest Friend! What gift have you brought for me from your home? Even a trifle offered to me with love is precious to Me. Whatever is offered with love, be it leaf or flower or fruit or grain or even water, I accept with delight!" Despite these broad hints and pointed looks at the hiding place, the bashful Brahmin looked down and did not present the handful of rice.

At last, tired of waiting and not wishing to tease him any further, Krishna stretched forward and pulled out the miserable bundle from its hiding place. "Ah, what is this?" He asked teasingly with a twinkle in His eyes. "O, you sly one! Were you keeping it as a surprise for Me?"

He opened the rag and looked at the contents and continued, "How clever of you to guess what I would like most. Do you remember the rice flakes our *guru's* wife used to make for us? I have never eaten such delicious stuff since then, but I feel sure your wife must have made a similar kind. These royal princesses do not know the art," He said with an amused look in Rukmini's direction.

So saying, He took a fistful of the stuff and ate it with evident relish. Then He took another and was just about to put it in His mouth, when Rukmini caught His hand. "Lord, be not so hasty. Would You give me away as well?" she asked. The moment the Lord ate one fistful of this potent stuff, charged with the entire love of Kuchela's heart, He had already blessed him with all worldly goods. Had He taken another, Rukmini feared that she, the goddess of wealth herself, would have to take up her abode as handmaid to Kuchela's wife! If we were to offer our gifts to Him with the love and humility of a Kuchela, there is no doubt that we would also be showered with all fortune. But we know only the language of the market. Our gifts are bribes and hence, we get what we deserve.

Kuchela spent a blissful night with the Lord. During the whole time, not once did he even remember the reason for his visit and the condition of his wife and children. Even though Krishna prompted him many times in order to test him, Kuchela's mind did not waver from its contemplation of the Lord. At last, when morning dawned, he rose up reluctantly, hoping that the Lord might urge him to stay, but He made no such attempt, neither did He offer him anything. All He did was to urge him to make frequent trips in the future. They parted with the utmost affection. Krishna hugged him, personally escorted him to the gate, and bade him a fond farewell. Kuchela was filled with sorrow, not because he had not received anything, but because he had to part from his beloved Master.

As he trudged his weary way back, he suddenly remembered the reason for his visit and wondered what he was going to say to his wife. But he put the matter out of his mind as of no consequence, for his mind was filled with the bliss of the hours he had spent with the Lord. "Though I am the poorest of the poor, yet He has hugged me to His bosom, which is the abode of Lakshmi. Like a brother, he made me sit on His own couch, which He shares with His consort. My tired body was fanned by His queen! He Himself performed every form of service for me, including washing my feet with His blessed hands and applying *sandal* paste. Thus, I was honored like a king by Him who is the God of all gods. In His mercy, He did not tempt me with wealth, for He knows that a sudden acquisition of wealth may go to a poor man's head, make him vain, and eventually lead to his downfall."

Ruminating in this manner, that noble one reached the spot where his hovel had stood. In its place he saw the towers of a mansion as luminous as the one he had just left. He stopped short, wondering whether in his bemused state of mind he had retraced his steps back to Dwaraka. The mansion was surrounded with numerous parks and gardens and by lakes filled with lotuses and swans. While the poor man stood hesitating outside the gates, he saw a vision clothed in silks and jewels gliding toward him, escorted by many beautiful maids carrying auspicious articles. To his bewildered gaze, she appeared like the goddess Lakshmi herself and he felt sure that he was seeing an illusion. When the beautiful lady came closer and addressed him as her lord, he realized that she was none other than his own wife, whom people used to call Kukshama because of her emaciated condition. Gently, she led him inside the mansion and bade him take a bath and clothe himself in the costly garments that had been laid out for him. His beautiful children now came and danced all round him. Disturbed by this display of wealth, Kuchela closed his eyes and remained rapt in contemplation.

"The reason for the attainment of such heavenly prosperity by a poverty-stricken man like me must be my meeting with that embodiment of grace and plenty. He showers His blessings on His devotees as the clouds their rain, without any announcement and as if they were a trifle. Yet He ate my insignificant gift of beaten rice with such delight. But, O Lord, the fact that I have been blessed with such wealth is a great trial for me. All I want is to be blessed with undying devotion and service to You, life after life. This is my only prayer."

Thinking thus, the Brahmin wanted to renounce those objects of worldly enjoyment, but to please his wife, he continued to live in that mansion as if he were only a guest and completely detached from it all.

"Let not the change in my material state affect my spiritual state," was his continuous prayer. "Let me ever rejoice in You alone and not in the baubles of a worldly existence."

He had not minded when he went about in tatters and did not care now that he was clad in silks. He was as unaffected by his affluence as he had been by his poverty. He was the true *sthitaprajna*, or the man of enlightenment, of the *Gita*. Actually, the Lord had conferred all worldly goods on him not for his sake, but for the sake of his wife, who was also a devotee and who had not been able to bear the pitiful state and hungry cries of her children. Because of her great love and fidelity, this poor woman had conquered the Lord, who cannot be conquered with swords. She continued to do her duty to her husband and children until the end of her life, while the Brahmin spent his time in continuous meditation on the Lord until the knot of his body's bondage was cut asunder and he attained the deathless realm.

Thus ends the twenty-ninth chapter of The Play of God, *named "The Story of Sudama."*

Hari Aum Tat Sat

The highest charity is the relinquishing of the idea of violence toward all beings. Penance is the giving up of desires. Valor is the conquest of one's nature. Honesty is looking upon everything with an equal eye.
—LORD KRISHNA, ADVICE TO UDDHAVA IN THE SHRIMAD BHAGAVATA

THIRTY

DHARMA RULES SUPREME

Dharmakrite namaha

Homage to Him who is the foundation of all righteousness

O Son of Kunti (Arjuna), I give you my solemn word that My devotee will never fall.
—*SHRIMAD BHAGAVAD GITA*

The years following the battle of Kurukshetra were peaceful. Yudhishthira proved to be an ideal monarch, reminding one of the days of *Ramarajya.*[1] He ruled wisely and well and the interests of his subjects were always closest to his heart. *Dharma* flourished once more in Bharatavarsha, as the Lord had predicted it would after the purifying effects of the Mahabharata war.

Once, Lord Krishna, accompanied by His friends Uddhava and Satyaki and a retinue of sages, went to the city of Mithila in the country of Videha, famed since the time of Janaka for its philosopher kings. The present ruler was also a great saint and devotee of the Lord. It so happened that in that city there was a poor Brahmin called Srutadeva, who found his life's fulfillment in devotion to Lord Krishna. He met the limited wants of his life with what chance brought him, without much effort on his part. Daily he got just enough for his upkeep, neither more nor less, and he was well content with it. The hallmark of a noble soul, according to the Lord in the *Gita*, is that he should be satisfied with whatever comes unasked, secure in the knowledge that the Lord would see to even his material wants. The Lord's visit to Mithila was prompted by the desire of both these devotees, the king of the land as well as the poor Brahmin, that He

---

[1]*Ramarajya*—The rule of Lord Rama, a divine incarnation who lived earlier than Krishna, a model king according to Hindu belief. His reign was marked by peace, prosperity, and righteousness The Ramayana tells the story of his life.

325

should visit their residences. The whole route from Dwaraka to Mithila was crowded with the populace, who thronged to have a glimpse of Him whose fame had reached the far-flung corners of Bharatavarsha. At the sight of the Lord's wondrous face and charming smile, all felt as if they had attained the bliss of enlightenment. The streets of Mithila were beautifully decorated and packed with people eager to have a vision of the Holy One. Both Bahulasva, the King of Videha, and Srutideva, the Brahmin, fell at His feet and invited Him to come to their residences at the same time on the same day. He accepted both their invitations, for they had chosen an auspicious time and He did not want to hurt either of them or to show preference for the king.

When the Lord and His retinue arrived at the palace, they were royally welcomed, entertained, and served a magnificent repast of the choicest viands on golden platters. The king washed the feet of the Blessed One and sprinkled the holy water on all those assembled there. He personally attended to all the Lord's wants, not allowing anyone else to do even the humblest task. Having worshipped Him in this way, the king begged Him to stay on in their city for some days and thus bless everyone. The Lord agreed.

In the meantime, the poor Brahmin had also arranged a modest reception for the Lord of his heart at his humble dwelling place on the same day. The hut had been swept clean and bright and the mud floor covered with straw mats and sprinkled with tender shoots and all the auspicious articles he could afford. When the Lord arrived, accompanied by the sages and a few of His close friends, the Brahmin's joy knew no bounds. He danced about in an ecstasy of devotion and, seating them on the mats, he washed the holy feet of the Lord and sprinkled the water reverently on himself and his family. Then he worshipped Him with fruit, *tulsi* leaves, and lotus petals, all gathered from the forest. He placed before his holy guests some herbal water and some fresh gooseberries. This water, when drunk after eating the gooseberries, became sweet and delicious. Of the many mud bowls kept before his guests, the Lord picked out an imperfect one and drank from it. When Srutideva saw this, tears sprang to his eyes and, falling at the feet of the Lord, he said, "O Holy One! It is fitting indeed that of all these cups You should have picked this faulty one, for similar is the way in which You deal with human beings— picking out the frail and imperfect ones like me in order to shower Your blessings. Your behavior will appear strange to those whose vision is clouded with conceit. Only the mind saturated with devotion can grasp Your mysterious ways. May You be pleased to instruct us who are helplessly floating in the ocean of *samsara* (mortal existence). How can we serve You, in what forms worship You?"

Holding Srutideva's hand in His own, the Lord gave a discourse on the greatness of the sages. "O noble One, know that I am ever present in the holy ones, the sages. They are My reflections and therefore they should be adored with the same faith with which you adore Me. That indeed is My true worship, not the worship of images with costly offerings. Holy men are the embodiment of all the *Vedas* and those who worship images in temples and slight these sages, who are My very Self, are guilty of great error. Know that they have come here now to bless you. They travel over the world sanctifying all regions with the dust of their feet." When he had thus been blessed by both the Lord and the sages, Srutideva's cup of bliss was overflowing.

By these two episodes, Lord Krishna demonstrated that He Himself is a devotee of His devotees. By accepting both invitations at the same time, He showed that neither poverty nor affluence need be a bar to His worship. It is the attitude of the mind that matters. One person may offer a gooseberry and another a costly fruit, but in the eyes of the Lord the value is the same if it is offered with love.

Most religions stress the fact that riches are a hindrance to realization. This is because wealth is accompanied by pride and this is the barrier that blocks the path to God. The poor, on the other hand, find it fairly easy to turn to God for they have no one else to turn to and no bank balance to depend on. The rich, surrounded by sycophants, flatterers, and coffers filled with gold, feel themselves to be secure, with no need to worship God.

Bahulasva shows us that even riches need not be a barrier to devotion, for though he was a king he considered himself merely the custodian of the wealth given to him by the grace of the Lord. He spent his wealth in helping the poor and needy and attending to the wants of the sages, mentally surrendering all his wealth to Him by whose grace alone he had procured it. The lesson to be learned from Srutideva is that the poor need not lament over the fact that they cannot offer anything of value to the Lord. In His eyes the greatest value lies in a humble and devoted heart and not in any physical object.

Fifteen years of Yudhishthira's rule had passed when Vidura

approached Dhritarashtra one night and told him that it was time for him to quit this worldly life, for which he should have had a distaste by now, retire to the forest, and remain there in contemplation for the rest of his earthly sojourn. The blind king realized the truth of his wise brother's counsel. He decided to leave the very next day and declared his intention to his nephews. Gandhari, Sanjaya, and Kunti also determined to follow him, for they felt that Vidura's advice was intended for them as well. All attempts to dissuade them proved futile. The Pandavas tried their best to stop at least their mother from following them, but Kunti took it on herself to serve the blind couple until the end of her life. Perhaps it was to atone for what her sons had been forced to do to theirs.

Her parting words to Yudhishthira were, "Do not try to dissuade me, for I know I must die in service. Look after Sahadeva, for he is the youngest, Madri's beloved son. Never swerve from *dharma*." Thus, till the end, Kunti proved an exemplary character. The next day, they departed to the forests in the foothills of the Himalayas, accompanied by Vidura.

The Pandavas had been told not to go after them for a year at least. At the end of the stipulated period, they visited them and were most pained to see their self-imposed deprivations. During their stay of a few days, Vidura, their beloved uncle and savior, passed away after having given all his spiritual wealth to his favorite nephew, Yudhishthira. A year or two later, Dhritarashtra, Gandhari, and Kunti exposed themselves to a forest fire and allowed their mortal bodies to be consumed. Sanjaya spent the remainder of his life meditating in the Himalayas.

Soon after this, Arjuna came to stay with Krishna at Dwaraka and the Lord realized that His friend had completely forgotten the glorious message of the *Gita*, delivered to him at Kurukshetra. An opportunity was provided to remind him of it. There was a Brahmin who lived in the city who found that all his babies died the moment they were born. Each time this happened, he would carry the little corpse to the gates of the Lord's palace and cry out, "My child has died because of the misdeeds of the *kshatriyas*, who persecute holy men and who are evil-minded. Poverty and misery are the fate of those subjects who are ruled by oppressive kings, devoid of control of their senses."

On the occasion of the death of the ninth infant, when he went for his routine visit to the assembly hall of the Yadavas, Arjuna happened to be there and he was quite upset to hear this lament. "O learned One!" he said. "What is the use of wailing like this? Is there no *kshatriya* who wields a bow in this land of yours?" After the Brahmin left, he questioned Krishna about these occurrences. The latter merely smiled and said, "Who can avert the effects of one's past *karmas*? They have to be experienced by him alone."

Arjuna was not satisfied with this answer. Thinking himself the great hero of the Mahabharata war and forgetting to whom he owed his victory, he hurried after the Brahmin to offer his services. "Do not grieve, O blessed One," he told the unhappy father. "Let me know when your wife conceives again and I promise to deliver the baby, safe and sound."

The Brahmin was not impressed by Arjuna's claims to be an expert in midwifery and asked scornfully, "Who are you that you can boast of achieving what not even Balarama, Krishna, Pradyumna, nor Aniruddha could do?"

Arjuna proudly proclaimed his lineage. "True, I am not one of them, but I am Arjuna, the middle one among the Pandavas, wielder of the Gandiva. Do not belittle my prowess, which evoked the wonder and admiration of the Three-eyed Lord (Shiva) Himself! I shall restore your next issue to you even if I have to conquer the lord of death himself. If I fail to fulfill this vow of mine, I shall enter into the fire as an expiation for breaking my word!"

The Brahmin, who had nothing to lose, was ready to clutch at any straw and readily agreed to let him know as soon as his wife conceived. This yearly event took place shortly after and he came at intervals to apprise Arjuna of the progress of the infant in the womb. Each time he came, Arjuna would have a secret parlance with him. Krishna would ask him what it was all about, but Arjuna refused to avail himself of the opportunity to confide in Him and always gave an evasive answer. Such was his arrogance that he never once thought of asking for the Lord's help. At last, the great day dawned. The Brahmin rushed to Arjuna with the momentous news that his wife was in labor. Armed with his Gandiva and his inexhaustible quiver, he stepped out, confident of success. Hardly had he put one foot out when Krishna, whom he had thought to be sleeping, called after him, "O Arjuna! Where are you off to, so early in the morning?"

The Lord was giving him a last chance, but the overconfident Arjuna replied, "I'm just going for a stroll!"

"Going for a stroll? Armed with the Gandiva? Whom are you expecting to meet, my dear friend? Are there wild animals in the vicinity of

Dwaraka? You look as if you are expecting some trouble. Would you like Me to accompany you?" "No, no, no," said Arjuna hastily. "Don't trouble yourself so early in the morning!"

"No trouble at all, my dear friend," said the Lord with a twinkle in His eyes. "Anyway, be sure to call Me if you need Me. You know I will always come to your aid."

But even after these hints, Arjuna did not think of confiding in Him. Proud of his prowess as the victor of a mighty war, he quite forgot that without Krishna's aid, he would have been reduced to pulp a thousand times during the war. So also, the Lord whispers in each one's heart to go to Him for aid in all troubles, whether big or small, for there is no burden, however heavy, that He will not bear for the sake of His devotee, no problem, however petty, that He will not solve. But, steeped in our own conceit, we fail to make use of His offer. "Surrender your ego to Me, O beloved Arjuna. Place your trust in Me. Invest your heart in Me and I will surely lead you to victory in this life and liberation hereafter."

This was the sweet path of *bhakti* (devotion) and *prapati* (self-surrender) which He had taught Arjuna on the field of the Kurus, but the latter had forgotten it. However, he was soon to have his pride humbled and to realize that without divine aid, he was totally helpless, as we all are.

Arjuna marched up to the Brahmin's house and was met with the latest bulletin by the anxious father. Arjuna allayed his fears and proceeded to cover the entire labor room with a cage of arrows, in a very precise and methodical manner, as he had covered the Khandava forest a long time ago. He then placed himself at the entrance so that none could pass either in or out without his knowledge. Within a few minutes, he heard a dreadful wail and the distraught father rushed out crying, "Monster! What have you done with my baby? Nine times this has happened, but at least I used to be left with the corpse. But now, thanks to your meddling, even the body has vanished. I should never have listened to you. When neither Krishna nor Balarama could protect me, how could I have expected you to do so?"

The Brahmin was not one to mince words. His temper was always precariously balanced and this was the last straw. Pointing scornfully at the woodshed, he continued, "There lies the woodshed. Help yourself to what you need. At least let me have the satisfaction of seeing you roast alive!"

Poor Arjuna had gone quite pale and silent as the harangue continued. "Give me a little time," he begged. "I'll search the whole world. If your baby is anywhere in all the three worlds, I'll surely discover him and bring him back to you!"

The Brahmin gave him a skeptical look and reluctantly agreed to let him go. Calling on his favorite deity, Lord Shiva, to help him, Arjuna proceeded to Yama's abode as well as to Indra's heaven, but he could not find the infant anywhere. After a vain and frustrating search, he returned empty-handed to the Brahmin, who had thoughtfully prepared the pyre for him, so sure had he been of the outcome of Arjuna's search! Arjuna was pale but unafraid. He lit the fire, prayed to Lord Shiva, and then took three steps backward to get the momentum to jump into the middle of the flames. Even at this last moment, he never thought of invoking Krishna. But the Lord never forsakes a devotee who has once entrusted himself to Him. Even if the devotee forgets, the Lord never forgets! As Arjuna took the third step backward, he found himself clasped firmly from the back by two loving arms. Without looking around, he tried to shake off the restraining hold and said, "Leave me. I've made up my mind to give up my life!"

"What temper!" Krishna chided softly, turning the distraught Arjuna around. "Why could you not have approached Me, O Friend? Don't you know that there is nothing I wouldn't do for your sake? You're My friend, My devotee, My dearly beloved. You are in Me and I am in you. How can I desert you? Come with Me and I will show you something."

So saying, He took Arjuna with Him in His chariot and they started in a westerly direction, passing over the seven continents and seas. Arjuna felt as if the chariot was being lifted above the earth and they penetrated the intense darkness of outer space. The Lord sent His divine discus, having the brilliance of a thousand suns, to illumine their path. At last they reached Vaikuntha, the abode of Lord Vishnu. Arjuna beheld an expanse of milky-white water crowned by huge waves stirred up by powerful winds. There he saw Adishesha, the huge and awe-inspiring serpent, luminous with the countless gems set on his thousand hoods, looking like a mountain of sparkling crystal, and gleaming with blue necks and tongues. Seated on the body of that mighty serpent he saw the Supreme Lord, Mahavishnu (the great Vishnu), blue as the infinite, clad in yellow garments, with a wondrously serene face and lustrous eyes. He had the *Shrivatsa* mark on His chest, like Krishna, and He was adorned with the jewel *Kaustubha* and the garland, the *vanamala*. He was surrounded by sages, attendants, and His accouterments, which had assumed forms.

Lord Krishna made obeisance to Him as part of His divine play and Arjuna prostrated with great excitement. The Supreme One spoke in a sonorous voice. "I brought the sons of the Brahmin to My realm so that I might meet you both. You are the incarnations of the great sages Nara and Narayana, who are My own Selves. Though you have no desires of your own, you have to perform your duties for the good of the world and for the maintenance of *dharma*."

To his astonishment, Arjuna saw that the Brahmin's children were all playing around that divine Being. They were most reluctant to leave the abode of bliss and return to the earth, which seemed to them like a dark planet. Krishna and Arjuna took leave of this mighty Being and returned to the earth, where they presented the bewildered Brahmin with ten offspring in the place of the one promised by Arjuna.

Once again, Arjuna realized his own folly and he also saw that all the successful enterprises a person appears to achieve through self-effort are only the operation of the Lord's grace. He prostrated full length at Lord Krishna's feet and begged for forgiveness, as he had done on the battlefield when he saw the Cosmic Form.

Krishna smiled tenderly at him and said, "Remember, Arjuna, we are both linked together as the Lord Vishnu said. I will never desert you, even if you forget Me. The moment a person surrenders to Me, I will set his steps in the right direction. In fact, My friend, I shall carry him safely through the jungle of this earthly existence as the mother cat carries its kitten."

The last years of the Lord's sojourn on earth were spent in giving advice to those nearest to Him and those who approached Him for help. Herein lies the greatness of His teachings. He insisted that each individual could and should find the path best suited to his own nature.

The qualities of *Prakriti* are three in number—*sattva*, *rajas*, and *tamas*. Human nature can also be categorized into these three. *Sattvic* people are characterized by their goodness, love of contemplation, nonviolence, and so on. *Rajasic* individuals are ever engrossed in acquiring, losing, and spending, filled with anger, lust, and greed. *Tamasic* people are full of sloth and ignorance, interested in nothing but sleeping and eating, content to lead an animal existence, uninterested in any form of knowledge, dull and inactive. Actually, we can never find these three in their pristine forms. All of us are a mixture of the three, with a predominance of one or the other. The *sattvic* individual is a being of light and goodness; the *raja-*

sic man, on the other hand, is constantly worrying and scheming and unable to sit still. To such men of action as Arjuna, the Lord's advice was to go ahead and act, but to dedicate the fruits of all action to Him, the Lord, who is the controller of the action as well as the giver of the fruits. This may sound difficult, but it can be done with practice. It is only a question of training the mind in a different channel. No one can remain entirely without action, as the Lord says. Hence, it is imperative to know how to act so that the action does not create bondage. Every action done with desire opens the door to another desire, which forges a link in the iron fetters of *karma* leading to repeated births. This is called *samsara chakra* (the wheel of the cycle of birth and death).

Thus, it is not the action which causes bondage, as is commonly misunderstood, but the desire that prompts it. If it is prompted by selfish motives, then however good it may appear externally, the Lord, who sees into the hearts of all, will find it worthless. If the motive is pure, even if the action fails to bring about the expected results, it will cause no bondage and will lead to evolution. Hence, His admonition to do our duty regardless of success or failure. What the world considers a failure may well be a glorious success in the eyes of the All-Seeing Divinity.

The moment we get rid of our anxiety over the results, we experience a sense of freedom that is felt only by the sages. Another step forward is to act with the thought that one is not the doer, but only an instrument of the divine. Repeatedly thinking thus, we will be able to control our passionate nature and bring it under the pure and calm influence of the Divine Will. This is a better path for the *rajasic* man than trying to follow the path of the *sattvic* nature, forcing himself to sit and contemplate when his whole being longs to find fulfillment in some form of activity. Those whose predominating quality is *tamas* (ignorance) should sit and practice *japa*[2] whenever possible. This needs no exertion or effort, which is foreign to their nature. The Lord's name, even if repeated without much understanding and in a mechanical fashion, will eventually bring about a change in the psyche, just as medicine taken even without knowledge of its benefits will cure the patient. The main thing is that one should resolve rightly and force oneself to sit and practice, however lazy one might feel. Even a person devoid of understanding, if he or she decides that he or she must

---

2 *japa*—a practice intended to attain constant remembrance of God by repeating at all times a name of God, often accompanied by counting on a *japa mala*, a Hindu rosary.

improve and starts practicing *japa yoga* (disciplined practice of japa), will certainly improve. We are all potentially divine, children of infinity, and it is possible for each one of us to work out our own salvation at our own pace. In the beginningless and endless school of mortal existence, no one is ever expelled. We may have to repeat a class, not once, but many times, perhaps take ten births or ten thousand, but no soul is damned forever, for every soul is divine. Whether he or she is high or low on the scale of evolution is immaterial. What matters is that each one should try to perfect himself or herself and in this very affirmation and sincerity lies the victory. This is the beautiful philosophy of Lord Krishna, which promises fulfillment to every individual whatever his or her temperament or weakness by pointing out to each the path best suited to his or her nature. There is no dictatorial affirmation that one path alone is the only truth and way. There may be as many paths as there are people, for each individual is unique.

He created us in this way and He accepts us as we are. He allows us to proceed from where we stand, not requiring that we jump to some impossible peak of purity beyond the capacity of most of us. He points out that even those who worship other gods, worship Him, the *Purushottama*, for the entire creation is nothing but He and the worship of "another" is impossible. He who sees the One in the many and the many as coming from the One is the seer, the man of true knowledge. This alone is supreme knowledge. All else is secondary. Like the delicate web coming out of the spider, the intricate web of creation comes out of Him. Instead of struggling in the web like the poor fly, if we only surrender our little egos to Him, He will guide us and take us to our final destiny of union with Him, the source of all. The major block in our path is our ego and this was the question raised by His father, Vasudeva.

His parents had seen His divine form at birth, but as is usual with the human mind, familiarity and increasing intimacy had made them forget that glorious vision and they considered their son to be human like themselves. But as they neared the end of their lives, they remembered the advice of the sages at Syamantakapanchaka and decided to approach Him for advice.

Vasudeva came to Him and said, "Considering this perishable body as the Self, I have been thinking of You, the Supreme Self, as my son alone. Human birth, with all the faculties of the mind intact, is very difficult to get. Having it, I have wasted it without bestowing attention on its real purpose, which is to seek union with You, the Supreme Self. You have bound this whole world with the cord of self-centered attachment. At Your very birth, You had declared to us the reason for Your incarnation. Yet, bound as I have been to this bodily existence, I have forgotten those words. Pray instruct me how best I can get rid of my feelings of being the doer, the strong pull of my ego, which is what blocks the path to liberation. You have given liberation to so many, my son, will You not tell me, Your father, how best I can attain it?"

The Lord bowed to His father and said with a smile, "O noblest of Yadus, all beings, you and I and everything moving and unmoving, should be looked upon as manifestations of the divine, not merely Me, your son. There is nothing wrong in thinking, 'This is mine.' The difficulty comes when you limit your outlook to your family and relations alone. Expand your vision so that it embraces the whole world. If you see the divinity in Me, your son, then look upon all men and women as your sons and daughters and thus recognize that they are also divine. I am *Vishvatma*, the Soul of all. Therefore, you should consider the whole world as your own and every creature in it as Myself. See the unity underlying the diversity and you will come to recognize the entire universe as nothing but an extension of your own self. The spark of divinity that glows in the core of your being blazes in the heart of all creation. Do not limit your ego to the narrow confines of your own body and family, but let it expand to embrace the whole of creation. There lies your path to liberation!" Thus instructed by that Preceptor of the Universe, in such a simple manner suited to his personality, Vasudeva gave up his narrow vision and attained wisdom.

The next one to approach Him was His mother Devaki. Her desires were different but, in fulfilling them, He led her also to liberation. "Krishna, my most beloved son, I know You to be that Supreme Being who for some mysterious purpose of His own has taken birth in my womb. I have been glorified by that contact, but weak as I am, I cannot get over my maternal instincts. I long to be able to have a glimpse of my six sons who were born to me before Your advent. I have heard it said that You brought back the son of Your *guru*, Sandipani, at the request of his wife. Will You not accede to my request and show me my other sons, Your brothers who were murdered by my brother Kamsa?"

Krishna smiled His assent and immediately it seemed to Devaki that her six children were dancing about before her eyes. She picked them up and satisfied the unfulfilled longing in her heart to nurse them. Deluded by the veil of *maya*, the illusionary power of the Lord, she seated them in her lap and embraced and kissed them. Imbibing the nectar-like remains in Devaki's breasts, the *prasad* (that which was left after offering to Krishna), they attained liberation instantly. They prostrated to her and to Krishna and vanished to the divine spheres. Devaki was filled with wonder at these strange happenings and asked Krishna, "O Son! I know You to be a Master *Yogi*. Tell me, did you conjure up these infants by magic? Were they real or were they only an illusion?"

Krishna laughed and replied, "O Mother! This whole world is only an illusion. It has no permanence. Everything we experience with the five senses is transitory. Some things last for a few seconds, some for a few hours, some for a few years, and others for a few centuries. But they will all have to come to an end some time or other. Everything is subject to change. Birth, growth, decay, and death are the inherent qualities of all things. The only true everlasting and immutable entity is God Himself. So put not your desires on ephemeral things like husband, house, and children, which can at best yield only a passing joy, but place it at the lotus feet of Him who is full of unending bliss and who is the only Reality. Surrender to Him with love and He will guide you to the life eternal. Why clutch at a straw when there is a boat close by, ready to rescue you from the ocean of *samsara*? Attach yourself to Him and He will steer you to the shore of infinite bliss."

Following this beautiful advice given in the form best suited to her mentality, she also attained liberation. Unfortunately, His sons did not think of approaching Him. The Lord never thrust His advice on those who were not receptive. Knowledge is not to be bartered in the marketplace nor shouted from the rooftops. One who seeks knowledge should approach a teacher in all humility and only then will one be able to benefit from the instruction. Thus, He never tried to thrust unwanted advice on His sons, neither did He criticize them nor try to dissuade them from their chosen path. It was ever His way to be the witness, detached and uncritical, unless called upon to exert His will.

Thus ends the thirtieth chapter of The Play of God,
named "Dharma Rules Supreme."

Hari Aum Tat Sat

THIRTY-ONE

THE CURSE OF THE SAGES

Sarveshvaraya namaha

Homage to the Lord of lords

Placing his head at My feet and holding them with both hands he should pray, "Deign to give shelter to this Thy servitor, who seeks refuge at Thy feet through dread of the crocodile called death, which infests this ocean of samsara."
—SHRIMAD BHAGAVATA

The end of the era was fast approaching. Many years had fled since the great battle of Kurukshetra and men had almost forgotten about it. In fact, thirty-six years had gone by, the period stipulated by Gandhari before the fulfillment of her curse. Under the reign of Yudhishthira, the land had reposed in peace and plenty. The people living in different parts of Bharatavarsha looked up to their wise and noble emperor and were content. All the wicked rulers had been wiped out and the great powers subdued during the war. None remained to challenge the might of the Kuru dynasty except perhaps the Yadavas themselves.

Their country, stretching from the city of Mathura on the river Yamuna to Dwaraka on the western seacoast, was filled with abundance and plenty. They were invincible warriors and there were none who dared attack them. As citizens, they had become habituated to a life of luxury. Under the noble leadership of their hero and God, Lord Krishna, they had come to enjoy a prosperity and status hitherto unheard of. Their cities were fantastic, their mode of living was splendid, they possessed great treasures. The men were healthy and strong, the women beautiful and charming. They were blessed in all ways. But slowly, like a canker growing within a perfect rose, affluence was taking its inevitable toll. The high principles of physical fitness and spiritual brilliance which had characterized the previous generation were giving way to moral laxity and physical weakness. Krishna's own sons were no exception to this. No leniency would the Lord show to any just because they happened to have blood relationship with Him. The whole of creation was related to Him. The Lord knew that the Yadavas could not be checked by any other power and that He Himself would have to amputate the putrid arm. The time was ripe for the fruition of Gandhari's curse.

In order to fulfill the conditions of the curse, the Lord invited certain sages to visit Dwaraka. Some members of the Yadava families, including Samba, Krishna's own son by His wife Jambavati, approached the sages in mock humility and questioned them about an imaginary problem. They had dressed Samba as a pregnant woman and thrusting him forward, they mockingly asked the sages, "O Sages of unerring insight, here is a young and beautiful woman who is expecting to be a mother soon. She is too bashful to question you directly and wants us to do so. She is anxious to know the sex of the child to be born to her. She is keen to have a boy. With your great powers, perhaps you could grant her wish!"

All this was said in the most sarcastic fashion, since they had completely forgotten the Lord's repeated advice to venerate and honor all holy men, who were repositories of divine wisdom. The holy ones turned a scornful eye on them and pronounced a dire curse, "O fools! It will be neither a girl nor a boy but an iron pestle, which will be the instrumental cause of the destruction of your entire race."

The men burst into loud guffaws at this improbable pronouncement, but their mirth was short-lived. Hardly had the sages gone than Samba began writhing in the throes of some mortal agony and very soon an iron pestle came out of his stomach, as foretold by the *rishis*. Everyone was terrified and ran to King Ugrasena with the pestle and made a clean breast of the whole story. The king was in a panic when he heard the story. He gave the pestle to a blacksmith and made him powder it to fine dust. But one small bit was left that defied all efforts to pulverize it. This was thrown, together with the filings, into the sea that lapped the shores of Dwaraka. These iron filings were all washed by the sea to the farther shore, to the mainland of Prabhasa, where they grew into a kind of grass called *erata*, strong and sharp like swords. The small piece of iron was swallowed by a fish, which was caught by a fisherman. He took the iron piece from the stomach of the fish and forged it into an arrowhead, which he gave to a hunter called Jara. Though nobody told the Lord about these details, yet He knew everything. Though He was capable of counteracting the evil effects of the curse, He did not care to do so. He Himself was the spirit of Time, which mows down all creatures, and all these things had come to pass with His full approval.

Rumors of these happenings began to be circulated among the people, and a nameless terror was felt by them. At the very moment when their pride was at its height, it seemed as if the shadow of disaster was looming over them. Ugrasena knew well that if only they maintained their self-control, they need not fear anything, for they had no external enemies. Their foes were all within themselves. These antagonists were greed, lust, and anger, against which Krishna had warned Arjuna long ago on the battlefield. Ugrasena knew this and sternly forbade the sale of intoxicating liquor within his dominions on pain of death. His subjects, appreciating the wisdom of this command, obeyed implicitly.

Knowing that the time was approaching for the Lord to depart from this mortal world, all the gods, with Brahma and Shiva, came to Dwaraka to have a glimpse of Him before the ascension. In that city of Dwaraka, famed for its beauty, resplendent with riches of every kind, they saw the wondrous form of Krishna, upon which they looked with unwinking eyes. Covering that Noble One with myriads of celestial garlands, they extolled Him.

Brahma said "O Gracious Lord! In times gone by, I came to You and prayed that the earth may be relieved of her burden of evil. O Soul of all the worlds, You have accomplished all this and more. You have established *dharma* in the minds of men. Your fame has spread all over the world. Born in the line of Yadu, You engaged Yourself in various sportive activities for the good of the world. O Lord, by hearing or repeating these accounts of Your *lilas*, men in the Age of *Kali*, which is about to come, will be purified and will be able to overcome the darkness of ignorance. O Supreme Being! It is now one hundred and twenty-five years since You incarnated Yourself in the line of the Yadus. O Support of the universe, You have now accomplished the purpose of the gods. There is nothing left for You to perform. By the curse of the holy men, even the clan of the Yadus is on the verge of extinction. So if You think fit, may You be pleased to return to Your transcendental abode. Protect us, Your servants appointed by You as guardians of the world."

The Lord gave His assent to this prayer and set about making final preparations for His departure.

Witnessing all these terrifying portents and watching the Lord's grave mien, Uddhava, His constant companion, prime minister, and supreme devotee, approached Him while He was sitting alone in silent contemplation. Making due prostrations, he spoke to Him in all humility. "O Master *Yogi*, Your holy life blesses all those who hear about it. Yet I fear that You are making ready to quit the world after bringing about the destruction of Your own clan. Though You are capable of warding off the curse of the holy men, I see that You have done nothing about it, which makes me fear the worst. O Krishna, my beloved Lord and Master! I cannot dream of remaining on this earth even for a second without being able to see Your divine form. Even those who have only heard about You cannot bear to continue leading a mundane existence. How then can I, who have been serving You for the whole of my life, bear to be separated from You? Sitting and lying, waking and sleeping, walking and talking, eating and playing, I have been with you. I have worn Your cast-off clothes, eaten only the remnants of Your food, and adorned myself with the *sandal* paste and flower garlands discarded by You. Thus have I lived in Your shadow, O Master. How can I bear to be parted from You? O Lord of Lords, Friend of the helpless, do not leave me behind. Take me with You when You go to Your divine abode."

The Holy One smiled tenderly at Uddhava, for he was very dear to Him, having been with Him from the time that He had come to Mathura from Gokula. Uddhava was the perfect example of the *jnana-bhakta*, the man of wisdom who also has intense love for God, a rare combination, and it was to him that the Lord gave His final message.

Gently lifting up His devotee, who was lying like a fallen log at His feet, the Blessed Lord said, "O Uddhava, it is true that I am going to leave the world, for My work here is over, but for you there is still much to be done. You shall be the bearer of My message to the world. Having surrendered your ego at My feet, you have sailed through life with ease. But, O Uddhava, those who come after us will not know this method of surrender and the sweetness of this path of love you have learned. You shall therefore be their teacher. Love for family, friends, and for one's own body is what binds the *jiva* to the world and makes it repeat innumerable births. Therefore, abandon all attachment to your own relations, resign yourself to Me, and wander over the world recognizing My presence in everything. Know that this world, as it is grasped by the mind and senses, is but a magic show. It is transitory. For the one with uncontrolled senses, there is an erroneous perception of multiplicity. Such a person is subject to the notion of good and evil and to the differences between ordinary action, inaction, and prohibited action. But the one who sees the whole world as nothing but the Supreme Lord is filled with joy and sees no differences and meets with no obstruction from any source. Such people have transcended the distinction between good and evil. They neither avoid the bad because of compulsion nor promote the good because it is advantageous. Their responses are spontaneous and unmotivated, like those of a child. Ever established in the truth of the Spirit, they see the Lord as the essence of this passing show and roam about, free from the bondage of *karma*."

Uddhava replied, "O Lord of lords, this wondrous state of detachment is difficult for people like me to achieve. Pray instruct me in the method of achieving it, for You are the Supreme Teacher!"

The Lord replied, "All people are endowed with the capacity to investigate the truth of things and lift themselves from the evils of a life of instinct, such as the animals live. They need no teacher for this. Human beings are endowed with intelligence and discriminative power, and can surely be their own teachers. By observation and inference, they will be able to understand what constitutes ultimate good. The senses by themselves will not be able to discover that which is pure Spirit. But through presumption and inference and by using the faculties of the mind and intellect for that which they are meant to be used, the intelligent person can come to know of the existence of the Spirit. The world itself is full of illustrations pointing to the existence of the Supreme. I will repeat to you the conversation between the great sage Dattatreya and our own ancestor, Yadu. King Yadu once met this sage during the course of his wanderings and questioned him thus:

'O Holy One, kindly tell me what it is that fills your heart with joy though you possess none of the objects of enjoyment'.

"Being thus questioned by our ancestor, the sage replied, 'Hear from me, O King, of the twenty-four *gurus*, from whom I have learned much during my travels. These are the earth itself, the air, the sky, water, fire, the sun, the moon, doves, a python, the ocean, a river, a moth, honeybees (two types), an elephant, a deer, a fish, Pingala (a courtesan), an osprey, a maiden, the arrowsmith, a snake, a spider, and a wasp. From the earth I learned patience and nonretaliation. From the trees I learned to strive unselfishly for the good of others and find the meaning of existence from this very striving. Like the air, the sage should remain untouched by the good and bad effects of contacts with sense objects. The air passes over many types of places but is unaffected by their contact. As the sky is not tainted by the clouds that pass over it, so also the *Atman* is not affected by the body it inhabits. Like water, the sage is pure and holy and sweet. Like fire, he is unpolluted by anything, yet purifies everything that comes in contact with him. As fire resides unrecognized in the heart of fuel, so the Supreme Lord resides in the heart of everything. Though the moon appears to be waxing and waning, yet it never alters. So also, the changes of the body do not affect the *Atman*. As the one sun is seen reflected in different types of water, so also the one Spirit is seen reflected in all things.

From observation of a family of doves, I learned that one should not have intense love or attachment to anything, for that will only lead to one's downfall, like that of the dove which committed suicide when it saw that its wife and nestlings had been caught by a fowler. From the python I learned not to be swayed by the sense of taste. The python does not hunt for its prey, but swallows whatever creature comes near it, driven there by its own destiny. So also, the saint should eat whatever is offered to him regardless of taste. Like the ocean, he should be still and calm, deep and profound. Ever absorbed in the contemplation of the divine, he should not be exhilarated by a plentiful supply of the good things of life nor dejected by their absence, like the ocean that keeps its boundaries irrespective of the amount of water that flows into it. Objects of the world will attract us, but if we fall under their sway, we will perish like the moth in the flame that entices it. Like the honey-gatherer that collects just a little nectar from each flower, the sage may accept small quantities of food from just a few houses. But he should not hoard anything, for if he does, he will perish like the bee that gets burned with the honey it has hoarded when a man sets fire to the hive to collect the honey. A sage should never have physical contact with a woman, for the sense of touch may betray him, just as even the mighty elephant is caught by being enticed by the touch of a she-elephant. The deer, on the other hand, is trapped by the hunter who imitates the call of its mate and thus lures it to the trap. So the sage should not listen to sensuous music, for the sense of hearing can also betray us. The fish perishes due to its attachment to the sense of taste, so the wise should be abstemious in eating and thus conquer the sense of taste, which is the most powerful of all the senses. Each animal has a special sense organ that is extra sharp and that leads to its downfall, but in a human being all the five senses are equally powerful, so he should be on his guard on all fronts. From the courtesan Pingala, I learned that desire is the source of all sorrows, and desirelessness leads to the most intense delight. The osprey taught me that a sage should avoid all objects prized by others, for, if he possesses such a desirable object, everyone will be after him like the poor little bird chased by all the big birds because it happened to be carrying a tiny morsel of meat in its beak. Like the child, a sage should roam about having no worries and immersed in the bliss of the Self alone. Only the child and the sage can be said to be totally free of cares.

From watching the actions of a maiden who was wearing a number of bangles, I learned that a sage should travel alone. Even two bangles on the maiden's wrist made a noise and attracted the attention she wished to avoid, so she was forced to take off all her bangles one by one until only one was left. Then there was no more noise. From the arrowsmith, I learned how to concentrate the mind without allowing it to be distracted by anything else, however grand. His attention did not waver from the arrow tip he was sharpening, even though a royal procession passed by him. Like the snake that never makes a hole for itself, but always occupies one made by rats, the sage should never possess a home of his own. The Supreme Being creates, manifests, and withdraws the universe from Himself and into Himself, just as the spider does with its web. From the wasp I learned that on whatever object a person concentrates his mind, whether it be through love, fear, or hate, he attains the state of that object.

Finally, my own body has been my teacher, from which I learned dispassion and discrimination. Yet I am unattached to it, for I know that it belongs to others, to the dogs, vultures, and jackals that may feast on it after death. The human body is attained only after countless births in the bodies of different creatures and, while it lasts, the wise person should strive for the attainment of the ultimate good and use it only for the purpose for which it was given.' Thus the sage, having instructed King Yadu in this fashion, went on his way free and unattached, with no cares."

The Lord enumerated the qualities of the true sage to Uddhava because he was ready for a life of renunciation, and *karma yoga* to Arjuna, who was a man of action. To all persons He outlined the mode of action best suited to their temperaments, thus facilitating their spiritual progress.

Next, He gave a discourse to Uddhava on the *Bhagavata Dharma*, the great doctrine of *bhakti* and surrender, which was His unique contribution to the history of the *Sanatana Dharma*.

Those who follow the *Bhagavata Dharma* should not shun action, but should continue to follow their *svadharma*, giving up all rites, rituals, and works aimed at fulfilling their own selfish interests. They should observe those rules of internal and external purification known as *yamas* and *niyamas*.[1] After having thus purified their minds and bodies, they should seek an enlightened *guru*, whom they should serve faithfully. The *Atman* being the same in all, it is meaningless to think of any particular person or object as one's own, like wife, children, or property. The *jiva's* involvement in *samsara* arises from its identification with bodies generated by the *gunas* of *Prakriti*.[2] Knowledge of its real nature alone will put an end to its entanglements. So long as there is perception of multiplicity, there will be no freedom for the *jiva* and the Lord's power as Time will terrorize it.

Uddhava then asked the Lord how the same *Atman* can be called free yet bound at the same time.

The Lord replied, "All talk of bondage and liberation is only in respect to the body and mind, which are products of the *gunas* and not of the *Atman*, which is one with Me. The *jiva* and the *Atman* are like two birds sitting on the same tree. The former pecks at the fruits of the tree, enjoys the sweet ones, discards the sour ones, and is continually swayed by its likes and dislikes. It knows nothing and is bound by its strong desire for these fruits. The other bird, the *Atman*, though not eating the fruits, yet thrives splendidly on the same tree. The illumined person, though tenanting a body, will have no identification with it. The ignorant person, on the other hand, equates himself with the body and thus has to suffer the pangs and pleasures of it. The sage is not affected by the contact of the senses with their objects. Though his senses function at peak level, yet he remains a witness, like the sky or the sun or the wind. Though he has a body, he is free from the domination of its urges. He remains unaffected whether his body is persecuted or adored. He does not view experiences as being either favorable or unfavorable. A person may be an adept in scriptural knowledge but if his mind is not absorbed in Me through spiritual disciplines, his liter-

---

[1] *yamas*—practices of moral virtue—nonviolence, truthfulness, nonstealing, continence, and freedom from greed.
niyamas—cultivation of the qualities of contentment, practice of spiritual disciplines, study and self-inquiry, and surrender to God.
[2] *gunas of Prakriti*—see footnote 2 on page 64.

ary efforts will be in vain, like one who keeps a barren cow in the hope that it might yield milk."

Then Uddhava asked who was the best type of *sadhu* (renunciant) and what was the best type of devotion.

The Lord replied, "A *sadhu* is one who is kind, forbearing, and truthful. He is unperturbed in joy and sorrow, ever helpful to all, with perfect mastery over his senses. He is calm and nonattached, eats sparingly, and is vigilant and courageous. Though he expects no respect from others, yet he shows respect to all. Abandoning all other duties that might contribute to his material welfare, he concentrates his entire energies on the practice of wholehearted devotion to Me. Even if one worships Me with no knowledge of My infinity and majesty, with the feeling that I am his own and that he has no other support, know him to be the greatest of all devotees. By this type of devotion, generated through contact with holy men, many ignorant beings in Vrindavan, like the cows, trees, animals, and *gopis* attained Me. Of these, the *gopis* are the supreme example. Just as the differentiation of name and form ceases to exist in the minds of great sages in *samadhi* (superconscious state), just as rivers lose their individuality when their waters mingle with the ocean, so also the *gopikas* (*gopis*) of Vrindavan lost their separate existence in Me, lost the awareness of their kith and kin, and even the awareness of their own bodies. Though ignorant of My real nature as the Supreme Brahman, yet through the intensity of their love they attained Me.

Therefore, O Uddhava, abandoning all reliance on scriptural injunctions and prohibitions, the ways of work and renunciation, surrender your entire being, body, mind, and soul to Me, the all-comprehending and all-comprehensive Being, the essence within all embodied beings. By that alone shall you attain liberation. My true devotees desire nothing, O Uddhava. Not even the state of an emperor, nor that of Brahma, nor heaven, nor for the attainment of *yogic* powers, nor even for liberation. Their only hope, their only goal is to attain Me. Such devotees are supremely dear to Me, O Uddhava. They are dearer to Me than My own self. I am always following the footsteps of such sages so that all the worlds within Me may get purified by the dust of their holy feet. With universal love filling their hearts, they have no wealth other than Me, O Uddhava. Though My devotees may be under the domination of the senses at the start of their spiritual life, yet with the growth of devotion they will be able to overcome them. Just as the flaming fire reduces any type of fuel to ashes, so devotion to Me destroys all the sins that might prove an obstruction to growth. Not *Yoga*, nor philosophy, nor *karma*, nor *Vedic* study, nor austerity, nor renunciation have the power to attract Me as does intense *bhakti*.

Those whose words falter with excessive joy when they speak of Me, whose hearts melt due to the overflowing tenderness of love for all beings, who laugh at the thought of the mysterious workings of My *maya*, who weep at the agony of separation from Me, who care for nothing and nobody but Me, who have renounced their separate existence and are ever submerged in thoughts of Me, such people, O Uddhava, purify the three worlds just by their existence. Rare indeed are such souls, O Friend. If you see such a one, worship him, for he is equivalent to Me. The way to attain such an exalted state is to think of Me constantly, O Uddhava. Just as the mind of a person who always dwells on sense objects becomes attached to them, so also the mind of one who thinks of Me constantly dissolves in Me. Therefore, whatever task you might be engaged in, mundane or sacred, let your mind be constantly absorbed in Me, as the lover's mind on his beloved. Thus will you become absorbed into Me. This is the supreme secret I am imparting to you, for you are supremely dear to Me."

Thus ends the thirty-first chapter of The Play of God, *named "The Curse of the Sages."*

Hari Aum Tat Sat

Fortune is the attainment of My divine state. The greatest profit comes from devotion to Me. Wisdom lies in the destruction of the idea of the multiplicity of the Self. Shame is the abhorrence of evil deeds.
—LORD KRISHNA, IN THE ADVICE TO UDDHAVA IN THE SHRIMAD BHAGAVATA

THIRTY-TWO

ADVICE TO UDDHAVA

Bhagavataye namaha

Homage to the Blessed One

Salutations to Thee, O Master Yogi! Thou art the One who confers the fruits of striving on all yogis. Bless me, Thy servitor who has no other refuge, that I may have constant and unswerving attachment for Thy lotus feet.
—SHRIMAD BHAGAVATA

Uddhava's next question was on meditation and the Lord answered him fully. At the end of it, He warned Uddhava to beware of the *siddhis*, or miraculous powers, which might accrue to the *yogi*. Deliberate cultivation of such powers would act as obstacles and might well lead to the *yogi's* downfall, for the mind gets distracted by them and deflected from its main purpose of attaining the Supreme. Uddhava then questioned Him about the *vibhutis*, or divine manifestations, just as Arjuna had done on the battlefield. The Lord gave him a similar answer and said that it would be easier to count atoms than give a complete list of His glories since they were inexhaustible.

Uddhava then questioned Him about *Varnashrama dharma*, or the duties pertaining to one's birth and station. After giving him a comprehensive answer, the Lord concluded by saying that the common *dharma* of all persons irrespective of caste and creed was to be free from cruelty, dishonesty, lust, anger, and greed, and to do what was good and beneficial to all creatures.

Once again, Uddhava asked Him to briefly describe the nature of *jnana* and *bhakti*.

The Lord replied, "*Jnana*, or knowledge, is that which sees the One Supreme Consciousness alone impregnating all creation from Brahma, the creator, down to the smallest of his creations. When that permeating substance is seen to the exclusion of all changing modes, then that understanding is known as *jnana*. I have already taught you what *bhakti* is, but because of My love for you, I shall repeat it and also tell you how that *bhakti* is generated. Recital of My names, steadiness in My worship, diligence in the service of My devotees, remembrance of My presence at all times, and utilization of all the senses in My service are the methods of generating *bhakti*, O Uddhava. The senses have been given with a special objective and that is to worship Me, the Divine in all things. The hands are to be used to offer worship to Me in the form of service to all creatures, the eyes to discover My beauty in all creation, the nose to smell My perfume in all things, the ears to hear the sanctifying accounts of My glories, and the tongue to taste the divinity in all food and to extol Me through speech, song, and hymn. All of creation provides both the method and the means for My glorification, leading to self-fulfillment. By constantly practicing such disciplines, one can reach the state of complete self-surrender and obtain deep-rooted and motiveless devotion."

Uddhava then asked Him to explain the true meaning of the different virtues such as charity, truth, valor, and so on. The Lord replied, "The highest charity is to refrain from thinking ill of others and to refrain from harming them and not the mere doling out of alms. Truth is to see God in everything and *dharma* is the greatest wealth. Heroism lies in the conquest of one's own mind and lower nature and not in the killing of enemies. The greatest profit is the attainment of devotion and not of wealth. True beauty comes out of desirelessness and austerity and not through decoration of the body. Hell is not a region but the dominance of the quality of *tamas*. The greatest relation is the *guru* and he is none other than the Lord. The wealthy person is one who is rich in virtue and the pauper is the greedy one who is never satisfied whatever he might have. The house is the human body and its master is the one who is free from attachment to it. The slave is the opposite. This, in brief, O Uddhava, is the description of the good and bad, but know that real virtue lies in transcending these two opposites."

Immediately, Uddhava took Him up on this statement. "The scriptures teach us to distinguish between the two, so when You say that there is no distinction, I am confused. Pray enlighten me."

The Blessed Lord replied, "Virtue and vice are determined by their relevance to the spiritual advancement of humanity and not by anything inherent in them. The system of determining actions and objects as good or bad has been laid down in the scriptures in order to check humanity from the pursuit of the animal instincts. Some of these rules are meant to help in spiritual progress and some are relevant for practical reasons. What is described as good consists in adhering to the action and ways of living within one's spiritual and moral competency. The object of these rules is to make one more introspective.

"They can apply only to certain situations dictated by time and place. What is right in one context can be wrong in another. For instance, not to care for the home and family is wrong for the householder but right for the *sannyasi*. An act that is a sin for a person of moral elevation need not be so for a fallen person or for one in a low state of evolution who is ignorant of rules. The person who is already in the mud cannot have a further fall. The fall is for one who is high up. The lesson to be learned from this nonrigid nature of *dharma* and *adharma* is that people should come to realize the impermanent nature of the external world, slowly try to retire from the pursuit of material desires, and fix their minds on the Supreme Reality. To the extent that one is able to do this, to that extent one will be free. If a person practicing *sadhana* (spiritual practice) happens to commit something of a sinful nature, that sin should be burned by the power of spiritual communion and not by the accepted code of penances.

O Uddhava, this body is given for the purpose of attaining Me. By practicing the three *yogas* prescribed by Me—*jnana*, *karma*, and *bhakti*—one will be able to attain the highest through this body alone. But one should bear in mind that this body is mortal, so a person of discrimination should strive constantly to realize the goal before being overtaken by death. Birds may perch on a tree, but when they see that the tree is being felled, they quickly change to another that is safe and unshakable.

"So also, the tree of life is ever being chopped down by that master chopper Time. Before it is completely felled, those with wisdom will take at My feet a seat that is firm and unshakeable. The frail barque of your body may get wrecked by the mighty whales of anger, greed, and passion. Attach yourself to Me, therefore, and I shall take you across to the farther shore. In the form of your *guru*, I shall come and be your captain, mark your course, and set your compass in the right direction."

Then Uddhava questioned Him about the phenomenon of death, and the Lord answered, "The mind, the five senses, and the tendencies derived from *karma* constitute the *linga sharira* or *karana sharira*, or the subtle body. This is what transmigrates from body to body. The mind of the dying man, swayed by his own actions and their impressions, thinks intensely of the outstanding experiences and attachments of his life. Consequently, he feels that he has entered a new body that has manifested itself by the very intensity of his thought. With the coming of the consciousness of the new body, there is complete oblivion of the old one and its history. On account of the intensity of attraction for the new body, the memory of the old one is completely effaced.

"Death is the complete forgetfulness of the old body and birth is the complete identification with the next body. How this happens can be understood from the study of the dream state. In the dream state, the *jiva* becomes completely oblivious of its waking body and gets identified with its dream body. The flames rising from a fire and the water flowing down the stream are all being subjected to change, though we may not be aware of it. So also, Time is subjecting the bodies of all creatures to the aging process. The *Atman* is the witness to these changes of birth and death of the body but is not subject to these processes.

A man may observe a plant and note all its changes from sprout to sapling to tree and eventually its decay and degeneration, but he is totally different from the tree. So also, the *Atman* is the knower of the body and its transformations and not a partner to them. The one who is ignorant, incapable of distinguishing the *Atman* from the body, identifies with it and is swept into the cycle of births and deaths. If *sattva* is the predominating quality at the time of death, the *jiva* gets the body of a sage or a god. If *rajas* is the dominant element, it gets the body of an *asura*[1] or a human being, and if *tamas* is predominating, of a brute or a disembodied spirit. Just as a person who witnesses a dance or a drama dances or sings or laughs or weeps with the characters on the stage by identifying intellectually with them, so also the *jiva*, though by nature actionless, is drawn by the intellect to behave as if it were the body. Just as the obsession with dream experiences will remain with the sleeper so long as the dream lasts, so also the experiences of *samsara* will continue until one is awakened to the truth. Know well that it is only ignorance of the *Atman* that is the cause of the delusion of the mind. So, however you might be subjected to abuse, insult, ridicule, or calumny, do not allow yourself to be shaken from your convictions. Remain calm within yourself and look on all these as being only a product of your past *karmas*."

---

[1] *asura*—a kind of demonic being.

As an example of this, the Lord told Uddhava the story of the mendicant who suffered all types of ridicule and insults with an equal mind, for he realized that it was but the result of the way he had treated people in the past, when he had been young and rich.

Thus goes the song of the mendicant: "The mind alone is the sole cause of turning this mighty wheel of *samsara*. It is more powerful than all the senses. The one who conquers it is the true hero. Without conquering or making an effort to conquer this almost invincible enemy who works with unimaginable speed, the foolish person enters into vain quarrels with others, regarding them as friends, enemies, or neutrals. The *Atman* alone is the sole reality and the appearance of 'another' is merely a figment of the mind's imagination. People blame the stars for their misfortunes. But how can the stars affect the *Atman*? They can only affect the body and so only the one who identifies with the body can be affected by the stars and planets. The *Atman* is beyond all dualities. With whom, then, can one be angry? Does one knock out one's teeth because they happen to bite one's tongue? It is only the one who has not awakened to this truth who lives in fear of others."

The Lord then continued. "This *samsara*, which produces happiness and misery and distinguishes among friend, foe, and neutral, is entirely a product of the mind. Therefore, O Uddhava, equipped with a mind that is totally dedicated to Me, put your best efforts into controlling the mind. This is the sum and substance of all *yoga*."

The Lord then spoke of the philosophy of creation and dissolution. "The One Pure Consciousness, unmodified and beyond the comprehension of thought and speech, becomes divided into two as the seer and the seen, the subject and the object, as a consequence of the operation of my mysterious power called *maya*. Of these two, one is *Prakriti*, the object, with its two states of manifest and unmanifest and the other is the *Purusha*, the center of consciousness, the supreme subject. The *jivas*, lying submerged in *Prakriti*, come into existence with their three aspects of *sattva*, *rajas*, and *tamas* due to the urge of their karmic tendencies. All objects, big or small, are permeated by their cause, the *Purusha* and *Prakriti*, from whom they have sprung. This reality is the causal substance, which forms the very stuff of these objects. The effects have no substantiality apart from their cause. Brahman is the ultimate causal substance and therefore the ultimate reality. Time is the factor which manifests this universe of effects out of its causal condition. All these three,

Purusha, *Prakriti*, and Time, are Myself, the Supreme Brahman. As long as the creative will of the Lord operates, this continuous flow of material energy is sustained, providing scope for the *jivas* to enjoy or suffer, depending on their previous *karma*. When the creative will subsides, then the process of dissolution, or *pralaya*, sets in and this cosmic shell in which innumerable universes arise and decay is invaded by Myself in My aspect as Time, bringing about the dissolution of all things into their causal condition. Reflect over these processes, O Uddhava, and the delusion of your mind will vanish."

The Lord next discussed the *gunas* and their effect on the mind. "All things are constituted of the three *gunas*. The *jiva* goes round and round in its transmigratory existence according to the *gunas* it has been associated with and the *karma* springing from them. The one who overcomes the influence of these *gunas* and becomes securely established in Me through devotion becomes fit for My state. So let a person who has attained this human body, which is the means for spiritual enlightenment, abandon attachments to the objects of material life and adore Me and Me alone."

The Lord then warned Uddhava of the dangers of associating with those whose minds are given over to sensual pleasures. He narrated the story of King Pururavas, who was led to his downfall by his dalliance with the heavenly nymph Urvashi and who eventually attained liberation by associating with saints. The mind is easily swayed, and the company of holy men leads it naturally to a holy life. "Just as food is the life of all living beings, so the holy person is the only relief for those who are sinking in the sea of *samsara*. The sun can only give you objective vision to see external objects, but the saints can give you spiritual insight."

Uddhava then begged Him to briefly outline once more the three paths of *jnana*, *karma*, and *bhakti*, as well as the method of ritualistic worship.

The blessed Lord replied, "Gold made into diverse ornaments or lying in a lump by itself is still gold. Though the form changes, there is no change in its essential nature. So also, know Me to be the beginning, middle, and end of all creation if you would find Me through *jnana*; then you will not have to seek far. From the highest Brahmin to the lowest *chandala* (casteless person), from the creator Brahma to the smallest of his creations, it is I and I alone. Discover Me in everything and everybody. This is *jnana*. This is wisdom. Realize the unity in the midst of the diversity. The ability to find out the essence of everything is true intelligence. I alone shine in the heart of the raindrop as well as in the mighty ocean.

That one is the *jnani* who knows this and acts accordingly. Know him to be the *pandit* (learned person) who perceives and honors all beings as My manifestations, be they holy men or outcastes, persecutors or protectors, the sun or a spark of fire, a calm or a cruel person. Overlooking the ridicule of friends and relatives, casting aside the sense of high and low on mere physical considerations, throwing away all sense of pride based on such ideas, one should prostrate before all beings, whether they be dogs, outcastes, cattle, or donkeys, seeing all of them as manifestations of the Supreme Being. This is true *jnana.*"

Uddhava answered, "That is too difficult for me, O Lord. I see that what you say is true, but the mind is weak and I may not be able to put this *jnana* into practice. Knowledge alone is not enough without the wisdom to practice it. Teach me a simpler path."

The Blessed Lord replied, "Until the consciousness that all beings are My manifestations has been assimilated by the mind, one should commune with Me through external worship and action. By doing this, a devotee gains that knowledge by which he perceives everything as Brahman. Of all methods of spiritual discipline, the best according to Me is to practice seeing My presence in everything through the functioning of the three instruments of the mind, speech, and action. This is the essence of the *Bhagavata Dharma*, in which all actions are done as a dedication to Me without expectation of their fruits. In this, there is no waste of effort. Unlike rites performed with desire for their fruits, which would end in total failure if done improperly, in this path every act serves to help one's spiritual evolution, if not in this birth then in another. The basis of these actions being spiritual, their effects are imperishable. Even mundane actions like crying or running away, if done as a dedication to Me, come to have spiritual potency. What need then to speak of those high spiritual actions practiced consciously? To reach Me, the Immortal, with the help of this mortal body, is the wisdom of the wise and the skill of the skillful. Thus, O Uddhava, do your work after having dedicated the fruits of it to Me, regardless of success or failure, for when you have dedicated it to Me, it is My duty to see that you get the true results. The best advocate does not care whether his case is right or wrong. His duty is only to place the facts before the judge. It is for the judge to pass judgement. Therefore, let Me be the judge of your actions."

Then, in answer to Uddhava's question about devotional methods, the Lord gave him an elaborate account of those practices which are open to all. At the end He concluded, "These are the many ways in which I may be worshipped, O Uddhava, but the safe rule is to offer everything to Me, as I have already told you. But if you still wish to offer something particular, remember that whatever is offered with love I will gladly accept. Be it a leaf, a flower, some fruit, or even water, if it is offered with love I will be immensely pleased. The best *puja* is that done without any desires, for then I Myself will decide what is best for the devotee. At the end of the *puja*, you should renounce the sense of personal action and offer your very soul or *Atman* to Me, and then the *puja* will purify you."

Uddhava then asked, "What should I do if I am in the desert and not even water is available? With what should I worship You then?"

The Lord smiled and said, "So long as the water in your eyes has not dried up, My friend, do not fear. One drop from My devotee's eyes is more precious to Me than the costliest diamond."

Uddhava was overwhelmed when he heard this, and his eyes brimmed with tears. For a few minutes he could not utter a word. At last, he rallied himself and asked still another question, not for himself but for the sake of posterity.

"Even these things about which You have spoken may be too difficult for Me, O Master!" he whispered. "I may not be able to go on a pilgrimage, I may not be able to offer daily worship to You. The Age of *Kali* is at hand and people have short memories and short lives and no time to accomplish anything. Give me, then, a shortcut that will lead me to You."

Krishna smiled tenderly at him and replied, "Until My advent, O Uddhava, an immersion in the Ganga was supposed to eradicate all sins, but now an immersion in the holy story of My life is enough to cleanse the sins of a thousand lifetimes. The ones who listen to the story of My life, who narrate it or explain it to others, will sanctify themselves as well as their listeners. If even this is too difficult, O Uddhava, take a dip in the flowing river of My names. The chanting of My name alone is enough to attain liberation. My names are not difficult to learn like the *Vedic mantras*, which are reserved for the favored few. They can be enjoyed and repeated by anyone regardless of birth or sex. Sweeter than honey is My name, giving bliss to those who utter it as well as to those who hear it. It is the ripe, juicy fruit of the *Vedas*. Like a calf following its mother, I Myself will follow the ones who call on My name in order to see that no harm comes to them. Thus listening to the tales about My life and chanting My names, you will definitely be victorious over death itself. After studying this discourse, there is nothing more for a spiritual aspirant to enquire about and understand, just as after drinking honey, there is nothing sweeter for one to drink."

Being thus instructed by the Lord, Uddhava stood speechless for a while, conscious of the great blessing that the Holy One had bestowed on him. With great effort, he controlled his mind, which had been overpowered by emotion. His voice choking with surging waves of love and his eyes overflowing with tears, he said, "When You have departed from these mortal coils, O Lord, where will I find You? Where will I seek for You?"

The Holy One replied, "Go to My temples, O Uddhava! I will be residing there. And if you are in any doubt as to where My temples are situated, I will tell you. My temples are in the hearts of My devotees. Therefore, go where My devotees congregate. Wherever you hear My names chanted and My stories recited, there will I also be. Therefore, seek Me among My devotees, for through them will I ever manifest Myself in this world."

Uddhava remained silent and speechless with grief at the thought of the imminent parting. The Lord looked at him with infinite tenderness and asked, "My beloved one, have I convinced you? Have you heard enough? Are your doubts cleared?"

With sobs choking his voice and eyes brimming with tears, Uddhava spoke. "O Supreme Preceptor! Your very proximity has removed my delusion born of ignorance, just as a burning fire dispels the darkness, cold, and fear of those who sit next to it. You have lighted the lamp of knowledge in the dark recesses of my mind. You have ignited the unquenchable flame of Your divine name in my heart. You have broken asunder my strong bond of attachment to my kinsmen. You have permeated my entire being so that nothing other than You exists for me anymore. What can I offer You who have given me my all? What gift can I place before You who are the giver of all gifts? Therefore do I place myself as an offering at Your lotus feet, O Lord. I have nothing else to give you." So saying, he prostrated full length before that soul of compassion and catching hold of His lotus feet, he cried out, "Prostrations to You, O Master *Yogi*. I have surrendered at Your lotus feet. I have no other refuge but You. Bless me with deep and undying devotion to these, Your feet. Wherever I may wander, whatever I may do, let my mind run to You every second, every minute, and feel for You that love which is eternal and indestructible."

Uddhava lay on the ground like a fallen log, unable to rise up, unable to do anything but bathe the Lord's feet with his tears. The Holy One laid His hands firmly on the bowed head and blessed him. He then gently helped him to rise up and gave his final instruction to him. "O Uddhava, I direct you to go to the famous place of pilgrimage in the Himalayas known as Badrikashrama, which is especially sanctified by My presence. There flows the river Alakananda, the very sight of which is purifying. Wearing clothes made of bark, subsisting on roots and fruits, free from all desire for worldly enjoyments, live without caring for the extremes of climate, putting up patiently with all the adverse situations that might confront you. Ponder deeply in solitude over that which I have taught you. With speech and thought ever absorbed in Me, live according to the dictates of the *Bhagavata Dharma* I have taught you and you will quickly pass through these material realms and attain to My transcendental state."

Instructed thus by that Holy One, Uddhava circumambulated his dearest Master and placed his head once more at His feet. Though his mind had transcended the three *gunas*, the thought of leaving his beloved Master and going to Badrinath produced such waves of agony in his heart that it expressed itself in torrential tears which flowed down his cheeks and washed the Lord's holy feet. With his mind stricken at the thought of the imminent separation from his dearest Lord, he found it impossible to move from that place and stood rooted to the spot, gazing piteously at that well-loved face as if he could not bear to tear his eyes from it.

The Lord, understanding his predicament, spoke. "Dearer to Me than My sons, dearer to Me than My wives are you, O Uddhava. For you are the shining example of the *jnana-bhakta*. You have fettered Me to yourself with the bonds of your intense love; yet the time has now come for our bodies to part, for they are made of the five elements and must return to them. So go, My faithful friend, and do as I have instructed you."

Seeing Uddhava still reluctant, He continued, "In my previous incarnation as Rama, when I had to part from My beloved brother, Bharata, I had given him My footwear. Like you, he could not bear to be parted from Me. Now I will give them to you, My dear friend, for they have been attached to My feet, the ultimate goal of all devotees. Take them, therefore, and proceed to Badrikashrama, for I have no further use for them."

Reverently, Uddhava accepted the precious gift. With tears streaming from his eyes, he addressed them. "O divine *padukas* (sandals), do not think too harshly of me for being the cause by which you have been forced to separate from His lotus feet. Forgive me. Taste once more of the perfume of those tender feet and then let us depart."

So saying, he placed them once more tenderly beneath the Lord's blessed feet and then, holding them with great reverence on his head, he circumambulated that Divine Presence once more. With eyes blinded with tears, he tore himself away with many a backward glance. Only now did he experience the bitter anguish suffered by the gopis of Vrindavan so many years ago. When he turned around for the last time, he saw Krishna's eyes following him and for the first time he saw a glimmer of tears in those lustrous orbs. He ran back and fell at His feet once more. The Lord said nothing, but gently placed His foot on Uddhava's bent head and thus passed to him the Supreme Wisdom. Then tenderly, He lifted up his face, placed His lips on his forehead, and gently turned him around toward the direction in which he had to go. Uddhava was filled with an inexpressible joy and he felt replete. At the end of the path, he turned around and saw the Lord, shining from afar, and heard gentle music playing in the air. Up in the sky, he saw celestial beings folding their palms in adoration. An ineffable peace stole into his heart as the beatific vision so filled his being that he felt as if there were no difference between him and Krishna. The divine beings were singing hymns in praise of him as well. Without any conscious volition, and without feeling the heavy burden of his body, Uddhava, the great *bhakta*, proceeded northward and reached the holy shrine of Badrikashrama in the Himalayas. There he spent the rest of his days in the manner prescribed by his dear Master and thus attained to the eternal abode.

Thus ends the thirty-second chapter of The Play of God, *named "Advice to Uddhava."*

Hari Aum Tat Sat

THIRTY-THREE

THE DEATH OF THE DEATHLESS

Visvasmai namaha

Homage to the One in whom the entire universe is established

O Thou Lord and master of our souls! Ordain that, however many births we might have, we shall be endowed with devotion to Your feet. Salutations to that Supreme Hari, by chanting whose name alone we are freed from all sins and by prostrating to whom alone we are saved from all misery.
—*Shrimad Bhagavata*

Having given His final advice to His dearest devotee Uddhava, and through him to all posterity, the Lord had accomplished all He had set out to do. He waited calmly for the curtain to rise on the final act of the mighty drama of His Life Divine.

Dwaraka seemed to be in the throes of some mortal cancer that was gnawing at its vitals and depleting its strength slowly but surely. The citizens had trembled with fear ever since the sages had been insulted and a nameless dread held them in thrall. The once joyous and prosperous city seemed to have sunk into gloom.

Day after day, the strong winds blew from the ocean and many were the evil portents that were seen. The streets swarmed with rats, pots showed cracks, cranes were heard to hoot like owls and goats to howl like wolves. Asses were born out of cows and donkeys out of elephants. Kittens were fathered by dogs and mice by mongooses. The sun, as it rose and set over the doomed city, seemed to be encircled with the headless bodies of men. Then the Yadavas, in their dread of the destiny that seemed to be inexorably approaching them, went to the Lord. Krishna was waiting for them and knew that the time had come for the words of Gandhari, uttered when she was burning with grief at the death of her hundred sons, to be fulfilled. He did not attempt to turn aside the course of destiny, but rather set Himself calmly and cheerfully to make the path of events easy. He sent heralds through the city to command the people to make a pilgrimage to the opposite seacoast to the holy spot of Prabhasa, where the river Sarasvati is supposed to flow west. "Taking a purifying bath at Prabhasa and observing a fast there, we shall adore the gods and sages and perhaps avert the danger," He said.

All of them agreed to this proposal. They crossed the ocean in their boats and traveled to Prabhasa in their chariots. They took all their provisions with them, including a large store of wine and spirits. These had been illicitly brewed, since the king had placed a ban on the making or drinking of intoxicants. All types of costly viands and wines were carried by the vast contingent of all the men of the city. Little did they realize as they set out that they would never return. Only the Lord knew the character of the hour and watched unmoved.

Having reached the coast, they went to the place of encampment in their chariots and pitched their tents for a prolonged stay. As destiny had ordained, the site chosen was close to the vast clump of *erata* grass, which flourished like swords on the shore. For some weeks they followed the advice of the Lord and engaged themselves in many holy rites and in worship of the gods and sages, but soon, impelled by fate, as it were, they stopped their worship and fasting and started their feasting and carousing. Surreptitiously at first, and later with abandon, wine started to make its appearance at the feasts and soon flowed like water at all the banquets. The reason for their pilgrimage was forgotten in the exuberance of the hour and the shores echoed and reechoed with the strains of revelry and music and laughter. Plays, tournaments, and feasts took the place of worship, devotion, and prayers.

Deprived of discrimination, they started to imbibe heavier and heavier doses of the heady, sweet wine called *maireya*. A fierce quarrel soon rose among those proud and haughty Yadava heroes under the influence of the powerful drink, augmented by the deluding effect of the Lord's resolve. A spark will cause a conflagration when the timber is dry. It began with a word said in a drunken jest, some indiscreet reminiscence of the war that had been fought long hence. Satyaki and Kritavarma had been on opposing sides, since the main Yadava army had been given to Duryodhana, while a few of Krishna's close friends, like Satyaki, had chosen to fight with the Pandavas. Deluded by the liquor, Satyaki taunted

Kritavarma, "Will any *kshatriya* attack and kill sleeping soldiers?" This was a reference to Kritavarma's blind following of Ashvatthama's insane orders to destroy the remaining Pandava army.

"How dare you taunt me, when you slaughtered the great Bhurisravas when he was seated in *yoga!*" shouted the enraged Kritavarma.

Soon the other Yadavas joined the fray, taking sides with one or the other and it was but a matter of time before they proceeded from words to blows. In a few moments, the scene of revelry had turned into a field of slaughter. Kith and kin stood ranged against each other. Son killed sire and sire killed son. The Yadavas, having reached the day of their doom, rushed upon death like moths to the flame. Not one of them thought of flight.

"Here's the end of the coward who kills sleeping children," said Satyaki and fell upon Kritavarma and cut off his head.

Kritavarma's supporters immediately fell upon Satyaki. Pradyumna rushed to his defense, and in the ensuing fray both were killed. Maddened by liquor and driven by destiny, they were intent on killing one another and fought with bows and arrows, swords and maces, spears and javelins. With the banners of chariots, cavalry, and infantry fluttering, and seated on various kinds of mounts like bulls, buffaloes, and donkeys, they confronted one another like maddened elephants in the forest, causing mutual destruction.

A prey to delusion, the great Yadava heroes fought with each other, totally oblivious of their kinship. Sons with fathers, brothers with brothers, uncles with nephews, grandfathers with grandsons, friends with friends, and relatives with relatives, all intent on self-destruction. When their weapons and arrows were exhausted, their bows broken and maces shattered, they plucked the erata reeds with their bare fists. These became hard as adamant in their hands and they charged at each other's throats armed with these swords of destiny. The Lord alone stood calmly in the midst of the fray and watched in silence as His deluded kinsmen destroyed one another. The maddened men now charged at Him and Balarama too, so the two of them also picked up the sword-like reeds and used them to deadly effect. Cursed by the holy men and deluded by the Lord's *maya,* the flames of their anger, ignited by a spark said in jest, were enough to burn up the entire race of the Yadavas. It was like a fire generated by the mutual friction of bamboo trees that consumes the entire grove.

The sound of the strife died away in silence as one by one the mighty heroes fell, victims of their own wrath. The scene of revelry had changed to a ghastly slaughterhouse. The strong and bright and beautiful Yadava clan had come to an end. Balarama now sat on the shore lapped by the white waves. He went into a trance, and a stream of light issued from his forehead like a silver serpent and coiled its way up to the skies.

At Hastinapura, Arjuna suddenly felt as if Krishna was calling him. Lying down, he saw the beauteous form of the Lord gently smiling at him. The Lord said tenderly, "Arjuna, do you remember my telling you that everything in this world is born to serve a purpose? This is the case even with Me. Arjuna, I have come to tell you that the purpose of My life has been fulfilled. I am going. Soon you will follow me." So saying, the vision vanished from his sight. Arjuna jumped up, pale and trembling, filled with dread.

The Lord could easily have given up His breath in a *yogic* trance, as Balarama had done, but He was playing the role of a man and He had to act in accordance with the rules of the game.

The Lord, knowing that the time for His own exit had come, returned to the city and called upon His father to assume the direction of affairs and hold the women of the Vrishnis under his protection until the arrival of Arjuna from Hastinapura. Krishna prostrated at His father's feet and turned to leave his presence. A loud wail of sorrow broke out from the women of His household. Hearing this the merciful Lord retraced His steps and, smiling on them for the last time, He said gently, "Arjuna will come and take you to Hastinapura. All your needs will be met by him."

Saying this, He departed from the palace and made His way to the forest. Never again was His form as Krishna seen in the world He had left behind. Reaching the hidden depths of that wild place, he sat silently beneath an *ashvattha* tree and established Himself on a superconscious plane. Restraining all His senses He drew in His perceptions and steadied His mind on the Supreme Brahman, His own Self! Wrapped in the impenetrable mantle of self-communion, His form was wonderful to behold, illumining all the surroundings with His lustre, like a fire without heat or smoke. Blue like a rain cloud, shining like molten gold, sporting the *Shrivatsa*, adorned with shining fish-marked earrings, girdle, diadem, bracelets, anklets, and necklaces, His neck encircled by the *vanamala*, He sat in *yogic* trance, resting His lotus-pink left foot on His right thigh, waiting for the last part of the prophecy to be fulfilled.

A hunter called Jara had the remaining piece of the iron pestle from the fisherman and had made it into an arrowhead. In the gloom of the forest, he mistook the holy foot of the Lord for the face of a deer and shot the fateful arrow at it. Running up to retrieve his prey, he beheld the glowing visage and knew Him to be divine. Filled with remorse, he threw himself at the Lord's feet and burst into sobs. The Lord opened His lotus-petal eyes for the last time, smiled upon His slayer, and blessed and comforted him. The first liberation He had given in His *avatar* as Krishna had been given to Putana, the wicked witch who had come to kill the baby Krishna with her poison-tipped breasts, and the last one was given to the poor hunter-boy who had shot Him with a poison-tipped arrow.

Jara cried, "O Lord of Vaikuntha! Deign to pardon this misbegotten wretch who has done this crime in ignorance. Kill me soon, hunter of wild animals that I am, so that I may never more commit such terrible crimes! Even the gods fail to understand the mystery of Your creation. How then can a most ignorant and humble hunter like me understand the purpose of Your divine *lila*?"

The blessed Lord said, "O Jara! Do not entertain any fear. Arise and be blessed, for it is only due to my own resolve that you have acted thus, and you shall precede me to My divine abode of Vaikuntha. You shall go to that world where men go who have done great and good deeds."

Commanded by the Lord, Jara ascended the divine vehicle that had come to fetch Him, and he, too, attained to the celestial abode.

The last one to see the Lord in His body as Krishna was Daruka, His charioteer. By following the fragrance of His *vanamala* made of *tulsi* leaves, he had traced Him to the place where He was seated. He beheld his Lord and Master beneath the *ashvattha* tree surrounded by His luminous weapons, glowing with a divine radiance. At this sight, Daruka rushed toward Him, overflowing with love. Falling at His feet he said, "Having lost track of You, O Master, I have been wandering in the wilderness like a lost soul, like one caught in the darkness of the night after the moon has set. I have lost all sense of direction. I know not where to go or what to do."

The Lord said to him, "O Daruka! Proceed to Dwaraka and inform all those that remain there that I have abandoned My earthly body. Tell everyone to evacuate the city immediately, for seven days from now it will submerge in the ocean. All of them with their families, as well as My parents and wives, should go to Hastinapura under the protection of Arjuna, who will come for them. Then proceed to Hastinapura and tell Arjuna everything. Ask him to accompany you back to Dwaraka and escort the women and children back to Hastinapura. As for you, O charioteer, remember that I am the Divine Charioteer seated in the heart of every human being. Follow the *Bhagavata Dharma* which I have expounded. Knowing the whole universe to be but an expression of My *maya*, leave the reins of your life in My hands and remain at peace."

Instructed thus by the Lord, Daruka circumambulated Him again and again and prostrated before Him, placing his head under the lotus feet. He returned sorrowfully to Dwaraka, as bid by his dear Master. Then the sky became filled with the celestials who had come to see the final act of the drama of the Lord's life in this world. Just as mysterious as the divine birth is the divine death. Inexplicable is His *maya*, which brings into existence that which is ever existent and once again gives an appearance of having ceased to exist. Birth and death are but the two sides of the coin of creation. They can have no meaning when applied to the Creator.

As at the time of the Advent, the sky was covered with a pearly light, the air was filled with music, and the gods thronged to witness this unique event. Beholding them who were but manifestations of His own power, Shri Krishna's wondrous eyes, filled with the knowledge of eternity, glowing with a love that was boundless, overflowing with compassion for all creation, closed gently, like a lotus closing its petals for the night. His world-enthralling form, the most auspicious object for meditation, glowed with an unearthly light and disintegrated into the elements before the wondering eyes of the celestials.

Just as one beholding a flash of lightning speeding beyond the expanse of clouds cannot trace its course, so the divinities failed to trace the Lord's path as He disappeared from the earthly scene. Kettledrums boomed and showers of flowers fell on the place where He had been sitting. As the gods made salutations, the sages came and worshipped the place where He had sat. They wondered at the fact that He, who had the power to create, preserve, and dissolve this world, did not choose to allow His own body to remain after the destruction of His clan. Perhaps He wanted to demonstrate that this mortal body has no ultimate value, and the way of those established in Brahman is to let it fall without regret after it has served its purpose.

Thus was the last scene enacted of that unique life. But though the bottle might be broken, the perfume of the essence within can never be

destroyed. It lingers on for all eternity in the hearts of His devotees, for it
is the perfume of a life that was divine, the life of the Infinite, Eternal,
Unborn One, the Lord Narayana Himself, who took on the burden of this
mortal life in order to bring joy and liberation to the countless generations that have come after Him. *Aum namo Narayanaya!*

Having parted from Krishna, Daruka repaired to Dwaraka, prostrated
before Vasudeva and Ugrasena, and drenched their feet with his tears. He
then gave a full account of the total destruction of the Vrishnis. All of
them were stunned. Weeping and beating their breasts at the thought of
the Lord's demise, they went to the place where their kith and kin were
all lying dead. Unable to bear the separation from their beloved sons,
Devaki, Rohini, and Vasudeva gave up their lives. Rukmini and several of
the other wives of Krishna entered into the flames of the funeral pyre,
concentrating their minds on Him alone.

Daruka hurried to Hastinapura and gave the news to Arjuna. He
returned with Arjuna, who was grief-stricken when he heard the news and
witnessed the scene of devastation. He attended to the proper obsequies
of all. After this, he sorrowfully started his journey back to Hastinapura
with the remaining women and children. Seven days after the Lord's
departure, the ocean swept away the last vestiges of that once prosperous
city of Dwaraka. Only a few people remained to tell the tale. Under the
gaze of the watching people the ocean broke its boundaries and coursed
through the streets of that beautiful city. One by one the gleaming
palaces were swallowed up. Within minutes it was all over. The ocean was
now as placid as a lake.

In Hastinapura, Yudhishthira was already full of forboding as he waited for his brother to return, and when he saw Arjuna's face his deepest
fears were confirmed. With a trembling voice, he asked after the welfare
of their dear ones at Dwaraka.

For a few minutes Arjuna was unable to speak a word. At last, revolving in his mind the Lord's various acts of love and compassion toward
him, he began to speak in a voice choked with emotion. Recalling all his
great acts of skill, he came to the conclusion that none of them would
have been possible had it not been for the guiding hand of his dear Lord
beside him.

"O King," he said, "all those about whom you have made kind
enquiries are no longer in the land of the living. Only four or five of our
friends are surviving. Just as the body, even if it be of a dear person,

becomes repulsive when life has flown out of it, so also this world has become repulsive to me because my Beloved Friend has left it. My prowess, which was once the wonder of even the gods, has vanished and my heart is spiritless and weak because of the absence of that great one, my dearest friend and well-wisher. You will not be able to believe this, but I have met with defeat at the hands of a few wretched herdsmen as I was bringing the women from Dwaraka, as He had wanted me to do. The same bow, the same arrows, and I the same warrior before whom even heroes bowed in submission. But today, alas, lacking the presence of the Lord behind me, all of them have been reduced to utter futility, like sacrificial offerings poured into ashes or seeds sown in a desert. Now I understand that it was by His grace alone that I was able to do everything—to defeat the kings at Draupadi's *svayamvara* and to cross the limitless ocean of the Kaurava armies. Sitting beside me as the charioteer and moving skilfully in front of the enemy army made up of great warriors like Bhishma, Drona, and Karna, He took away their lives by a mere look. It was by His protection alone that I was not even scratched by the mighty weapons hurled at me by Karna, Salya, Jayadratha, and others. O King! My heart burns when I recall how He used to joke with me, bathing me in His brilliant and charming smile, how he gave me His immortal teaching on the battlefield, and how He showed me His mighty Cosmic Form, which has so rarely been shown to others. How patiently He bore with my sarcastic and stupid remarks! My only solace now is to remember that glorious advice He has given me and try to follow it, but my heart is heavy indeed within me, and I would fain depart from this world, which has lost all savor for me."

Hearing this, Yudhishthira and the other Pandavas were also sunk in gloom. They lost all interest in life and decided to prepare for their final journey. It is said that the *Kali Yuga*, or the Iron Age, began from the day that the Lord departed from this earth. Yudhishthira made arrangements for the continuation of the Yadava and Kuru dynasties and the well-being of his people. At Mathura, he enthroned Vajra, the only surviving grandson of Krishna, as King of the Surasenas. Parikshit, the only surviving son of the Pandavas, was now crowned emperor at Hastinapura, and Subhadra and Yuyutsu were left to look after his interests, with Kripa as his preceptor. Then the Pandavas, together with Draupadi, discarded their royal insignia and clad themselves in deerskin and bark and left the city without any regrets.

They proceeded first to Dwaraka and saw the city completely submerged in water. It appeared to them as if the spirits of their friends were beckoning to them from the water. Suddenly Agni, the god of fire, appeared before them and said to Arjuna, "I obtained the Gandiva and the quivers of arrows from Varuna, the lord of the waters. Return them, therefore, to him, as their purpose has been served."

Arjuna came forward and, standing on the shore, hurled into the ocean his priceless bow, the Gandiva, and the two inexhaustible quivers. The ocean rose up with a roar and swallowed them up.

The Pandavas now decided to do a circumambulation of the holy land of Bharatavarsha before retiring to the Himalayas to practice austerities in the mountains, and perhaps to meet Uddhava at Badrikashrama. So they went to the extreme east, then traveled to the southern tip, then proceeded northward along the western coast, thus circumambulating the entire holy land, the birthplace of that Holy One.

At last they reached the mighty Himalayas, the home of meditating souls. There they saw the majestic snow peaks and beyond that, Meru, the mountain of the gods. At this stage, a wild-looking dog and a noble buffalo joined the party. The buffalo was a form taken by Lord Shiva and they gave chase to Him and eventually He allowed Himself to be caught. The animal came apart into five pieces in their hands. They threw the pieces in different spots and the places where they fell came to be known as the *pancha Kedars*, the five important Shiva temples in the Himalayas. Then they proceeded to climb up toward Badrikashrama, where the Lord had told Uddhava that He could be found. They walked in single file, with Draupadi bringing up the rear and the dog behind. As they journeyed on, with faces set toward their goal beyond Badrikashrama, all the errors of their lives began to bear fruit and one by one they fell. The first to collapse was Draupadi. Yudhishthira kept walking without faltering. The others stood rooted and Bhima asked his older brother why the faultless Draupadi had to fall before they reached heaven. Yudhishthira replied that it was because she had always had a definite partiality for Arjuna. A little later, Sahadeva collapsed and Yudhishthira explained to Bhima that he was too vain of his wisdom. Then Nakula fell and Yudhishthira said that he had been too proud of his physical beauty. Then came Arjuna's turn, and Yudhishthira's explanation was that he had been too conceited about his valor. With his last ounce of waning strength, Bhima tried to keep pace with his brother, but soon even he staggered and fell. Yudhishthira explained that his weakness lay in his boasting about his physical strength and his glaring fault had been gluttony. Hardly looking back, Yudhishthira continued his painful steps forward, followed by the dog. Suddenly, there was a deafening peal of thunder and Indra appeared in His chariot. He asked Yudhishthira why he had not stopped to render aid to his fallen wife and brothers.

Yudhishthira replied, "One progressing toward perfection should not look back with attachment at what is being naturally relinquished. This mortal body is to be shed. The immortal Self alone is to be realized. I am in search of that Self and can no longer be detained by these mortal bodies."

Indra spoke, "The immortal Self of your brothers and your wife have preceded you to heaven. But it is ordained that you shall have the unique privilege of entering heaven in your physical form. Therefore, do you ascend this chariot."

As Yudhishthira got into the chariot, the faithful dog ran after him, but Indra forbade it from entering the chariot and told Yudhishthira that there was no place in heaven for a dog.

Yudhishthira replied, "If there is no place for it, there is no place for me, either. Never in this life will I desert one who has shown me devotion, nor one who has sought my protection, nor one who is too weak to protect himself. Therefore, I would rather abandon heaven than abandon this poor creature."

Indra cajoled, "Wherefore, O King, are you so foolish? You have renounced Draupadi and your brothers. Why should you not renounce this dog?"

The king replied, "I did not abandon my brothers and my wife as long as they were alive. I renounced only their corpses, which could not be revived. It is against the code of *dharma* to abandon a dependent. Therefore do I reject your heaven!"

As he finished speaking, the dog vanished and in his place appeared the radiant god of righteousness—Yamadharma, who was his father! "Hail, O Yudhishthira," he said, "you who have renounced the very abode of the celestials on behalf of a dog! Verily there is none equal to you in heaven."

Flowers rained from above on the head of this greatest of all mortals, Yudhishthira the Just, Yudhishthira the Great, as he got into the car of Glory surrounded by the chariots of the gods, and ascended to heaven in his mortal form. Looking around him, he could see neither his brothers nor his wife. Instead he saw Duryodhana and his brothers looking resplendent like suns. Turning to Indra he said, "I will not stay in this place, however happy it may be. I must go where Draupadi and my brothers reside."

He was now escorted to a dark and polluted region, infested with stinging insects and beasts of prey. It was a place filled with dread. The attendants of Indra who were escorting him now spoke, "Thus far and no farther, O King, can we come with you. We have to go back, but you may also return with us if you so wish."

His mind stupefied with the noxious vapors and sunk in gloom, the king stood not knowing what to do. Just then, he heard the moaning voices of his brothers and his wife, begging him to stay since the very sight of his blessed form brought relief to their tortured spirits.

The king pondered for a minute. "Duryodhana and the Kauravas in heaven and my poor brothers in hell! What justice is there in the universe? For this crime I shall abandon the very gods themselves! Go!" he said to the guide. "Go to the gods who sent you and tell them that Yudhishthira will not return to that place of felicity. I shall abide here where my brothers suffer and where my presence brings some measure of comfort to them."

The messenger bowed his head and swiftly passed out of sight. The king stood alone in that vast and dreadful gloom, brooding over this strange inversion of justice. Not more than a moment passed when a cool and fragrant breeze began to blow and the repulsive sights vanished. Yudhishthira, raising his head, found himself surrounded by the radiant beings of heaven.

"These tortuous experiences, O King," they said, "have ended. Now ascend to your own place. Hell must indeed be glimpsed by every king, however noble he might be. Happy are they whose good deeds overpower their bad, for then they suffer first for a short time and then afterwards enjoy. It is the reverse for the wicked, who enjoy the benefits of their few good deeds first and then are cast into hell for the duration of their stay in these regions. The Kauravas will experience heaven for a short while, for the Lord had promised Karna that all those who fell on the battlefield of Kurukshetra would go to heaven. After this, they will have to suffer in hell for their sins before attaining another birth. To you and your brothers, O Yudhishthira, hell has been shown for only a short time. Come then, O Royal Sage! Here is the heavenly Ganga. Take a plunge in its purifying waters and cast off your human body, together with your grief. O One of never-ending glory! Rise up and join the rest of your kinsmen and Draupadi in those blessed regions where they already dwell."

Thus ends the story of the Pandavas, who were so greatly loved by the Lord that He was prepared to sacrifice His own integrity to save them from infamy, Himself shouldering the blame for all the *adharmic* acts of the Mahabharata war so as to safeguard them, who had surrendered their all to Him. Though tested to the utmost both in heaven and on earth, the Pandavas transcended the frailties of their humanity and rose to the heights of their divinity due to His grace alone, thus providing a unique lesson, inspiring the generations to follow in times to come.

Thus ends the thirty-third chapter of The Play of God, *named "The Death of the Deathless."*

Hari Aum Tat Sat

LILA—
THE COSMIC PLAY

*Lila
manushavigrahaya
namaha*

Homage to
Him who has
taken on a form
for sport alone

I bow to the playful form of that child who has Incarnated Himself to fulfill the cosmic purpose and who, though completely uninvolved, gives the appearance of being totally involved in the dance-drama of His own creation.
—POPULAR VERSE

W hy does the Brahman, the immutable, the eternal, the ineffable, manifest Himself? Why and how does the nondual become dual? *Advaita* (nondualism) proclaims that duality is only an illusion. All is *maya*. Brahman alone exists. That alone is *nitya* (eternal). All else in *mithya* (transitory). Once That is realized, the world of dualities will cease to exist.

The Puranas, however, give a sweeter explanation. Lord Narayana is the Supreme Person, equivalent to Brahman, and this creation is His *lila*, His play, the cosmic game. He is pictured as lying on His serpent couch, with His consort Lakshmi sitting at His feet, with eyes half closed, immersed in bliss. From this abode of peace, He decides to incarnate Himself in order to enjoy His own creation. He takes on many incarnations, but His incarnation as Krishna is the exciting climax—a burst of joyful laughter, as it were, exploring the frailties and beauties of His own creation, admiring its grandeur, plumbing the heights and depths of its meaning, sometimes flouting His own laws and sometimes obeying, for He is the *Purushottama*, the Supreme Being, who possesses both the immutable unity and the mobile multiplicity. Lord Narayana is *sat-chid-ananda*, existence, knowledge, and bliss, and His incarnation as Krishna is the expression of His *ananda*, or bliss. Because of it, all

371

creation is possible—because of His play, His delight, and His sweetness. Krishna is the incarnate divinity of Love. He is the essence of the love of the divine for the divine, for the *jiva* is also divine and only the divine is capable of loving the divine with a love that is also divine. Krishna is the Supreme's eternal, infinite, immortal self-play, self-issuing, self-manifesting, and self-finding. The blue boy of Vrindavan is the Lord descended into the world-play from the divine *Ananda*. The call of His flute seeks to transform the lower ignorant drama of mortal life into this divine *Ananda*. Those who are deaf to this enchanting call of love may be forced to listen to the crack of the whip at Kurukshetra, but to the seer, that is only another aspect of His love. If He appears to break the established human molds, it is only in order to create new molds from the higher planes, and for this He has to shock the sleeping mind of humanity in order to change, liberate, and divinize it. He is perfect Love and perfect Beauty, giving rise to perfect Delight—the complete revelation of *Sat-chid-ananda* in a mortal frame.

If this is Krishna, then what about the *jivas*? Why and how did they manifest? Are they not divine and therefore part of the game? Why, then, do they not realize that it is a game? Why do they have to suffer and sin and laugh and cry? Why does the beggar not realize that he is in truth the divinity clothed in tatters? The Puranas declare that the whole of life is indeed the *lila* of the Lord, in which He Himself is the hero and the villain, the actor and the audience, the director and the producer, the song and the silence, and even the very stage on which the drama is enacted. It is by a large mobilization of His *Prakriti*, His energy, His will and power, that He manifests Himself in all this multiplicity. But then the question arises as to why He allows Himself to get caught in the web of His own creation? Can the spider be trapped in its own web? The explanation is simple. The best actors are those who can completely immerse their private lives in the personality of the character they are portraying. So also in the cosmic drama, the Supreme Actor has to forget His true nature and allow Himself to be caught in the web of His own *maya* if He is to completely and satisfyingly enact the different roles. He becomes the king on the throne and the beggar in the street, the murderer about to be hung and the victim lying in a pool of blood, as well as the judge pronouncing judgment in the court. He the solo actor, the sole enjoyer, the only experiencer, oblivious of His divine origin, submerged in the role He is playing—laughing, crying, dancing, singing, living, and dying.

The *avatar* comes in order to free the *jiva* from this complicated web of divine origin and enable it to realize its own nature. Fortunate are they who happen to catch the lilting strains of His sweet music, emanating from His magic flute. For them the mundane world ceases to charm and, like the *gopis* of Vrindavan, they run in rapture to that enchanter in the forest, forgetting everything, spellbound by the form of that Lord of Love and Beauty—Shyamasundara-Manamohana-Vanamali! *Advaita* seeks for that indefinable existence beyond personalities, but the devotee of Krishna sees in Him that indefinable personality. By adoring Him and by union with Him the *jiva* can come to enjoy its own divine status. This is the promise made by Him to Uddhava and Arjuna. Only then does the beggar realize that he was, in truth, the king who had taken on the role of the mendicant. Then, the cosmic drama comes to a close, the curtain falls, and the actor-director-audience remains in blissful, enraptured consciousness of Himself as *sat*, *chid*, and *ananda*.

This is the cosmic play—The Play of God—inexplicable, tantalizing, adorable.

Samarpanam at the Lotus Feet of Vanamali—the producer and director of the whole drama.

Thus ends the last and final chapter in this particular game
of Lord Krishna known as The Play of God.

At the beginning, I am the omniscient One,
I am the moving and the unmoving,
All this creation comes into being
by the unfoldment of My power supreme.
I play with My own maya, My power divine.
—SWAMI VIVEKANANDA

Hari Aum Tat Sat

O Lord of Lords! This work is devoid of knowledge, devotion, or literary skill, yet I beg of Thee to make it perfect.

Consider me to be Thy servitor and pray forgive me for the countless mistakes committed on every page.

LIST OF
CHARACTERS

ॐ

*Aravindakshaya
namaha*

Homage to the
lotus–eyed One

Abhimanyu—Arjuna's son by Subhadra

Achyuta—Name of Krishna/Vishnu

Adhiratha—Karna's foster father

Adishesha—Name of serpent on which Lord Vishnu reclines

Aditi—Indra's mother, mother of the gods

Aditya—Name of the sun

Agha—Demon in the form of a python

Ajatashatru—Appellation of Yudhishthira

Akrura—Krishna's uncle

Amba—Princess of Kashi, who reincarnated as Shikhandin

Ambalika—Princess of Kashi, married to Vichitravirya

Ambika—Princess of Kashi, mother of Dhritarashtra

Aniruddha—Krishna's grandson

Anuvinda—Brother of Krishna's wife Mitrabinda

Arishta—Demon in the form of an ox

Arjuna—Third of the Pandava brothers

Ashvatthama—Son of Drona

Asti—One of the wives of Kamsa

Ashvini Kumaras—The divine physicians

Bahulashva—King of Mithila

Baka—Demon in the form of a crane

Balarama—Brother of Krishna Incarnation of Adishesha

Bana—Demon king, father of Usha

Banu—One of Krishna's sons

Bhadra—One of Krishna's wives

Bhagadatta—Son of Narakasura

Bhanumati—Duryodhana's wife

Bhauma—Narakasura

Bhima—Second of the Pandava brothers

Bhishma—Son of Shantanu and Ganga, great grandsire of the
   Pandavas and Kauravas

Bhojas—A clan of the Yadavas

Bhumidevi—The earth goddess
Bhurishravas—Son of Somadatta, who fought for the Kauravas
Brahannala—Arjuna's name at the court of Virata in his disguise as a eunuch
Brahma—God as creator
Brahma loka—The celestial abode of Brahma
Brahman—The Supreme consciousness
Brihadratha—Jarasandha's father
Brihaspati—Preceptor of the gods

Chandakaushika—A sage
Chanura—Wrestler in the court of Kamsa
Charu—One of Krishna's sons
Chekitana—Yadava warrior who fought for the Pandavas
Chitralekha—Artist friend of Usha, possessing supernormal powers
Chitrangada—Son of Santanu

Dakshinamurti—Name of the meditating Shiva
Damaghosha—King of Chedi, father of Shishupala
Damagranthi—Name of Nakula during the thirteenth year of exile
Damodara—A name of Krishna
Dantavakra—A king who was killed by Krishna
Daruka—Krishna's charioteer
Dattatreya—A highly evolved sage
Devakan—Krishna's maternal grandfather
Devaki—Krishna's mother
Devi—Goddess
Dhaumya—Spiritual guide of the Pandavas
Dhenuka—Demon in the form of a donkey
Dhritarashtra—Father of the Kauravas
Draupadi—Wife of the Pandavas, daughter of Drupada
Drishtadyumna—Son of Drupada, brother of Draupadi
Drona—Preceptor of the Kauravas and Pandavas
Dronacharya—Honorific title for the preceptor Drona
Drupaga—King of Panchala; father of Draupadi, Shikhandin, and
  Dristadyumna
Durvasa—Sage noted for his short temper
Duryodhana—Eldest of the hundred Kaurava brothers
Dusshasana—Second of the Kaurava brothers

Gandhari—Wife of Dhritarashtra, mother of the Kauravas
Ganga—Personification of the Ganges River

Ganesha—Elephant-headed son of Shiva
Garga—Preceptor of the Yadavas
Garuda—Eagle vehicle of Lord Vishnu
Gatotkacha—Bhima's son by his *rakshasi* wife Hidimbi
Gopalakrishna—A name of Krishna
Govinda—A name of Krishna

Hari—A name of Lord Vishnu/Krishna
Hidimba—A *rakshasa*, Hidimbi's brother
Hiranyaksha—A demon killed by Lord Vishnu in His incarnation as the boar
Hiranyakashipu—Hiranyaksha's brother, killed by Lord Vishnu in His
    incarnation as the Man-lion

Indra—King of the gods; god of thunder, lightning, and rain
Iravan—Son of Arjuna by the Naga princess Ulupi

Jambavan—A devotee of Lord Rama, father of Krishna's wife Jambavati
Jambavati—A wife of Krishna
Janardana—Name of Vishnu/Krishna
Jara (1)—Hunter-boy who shot the fatal arrow at Krishna
Jara (2)—Rakshasi who put together the two halves of King Jarasandha
Jarasandha—King of Magdha, who was killed by Bhima
Jaya—Sentry at Vaikuntha, Lord Vishnu's abode
Jayadratha—Duryodhana's brother-in-law

Kalanemi—Kamsa's name in his previous birth as a demon
Kalayavana—A foreign king who was killed by King Muchukunda
Kalindi—Name of a river, as well as one of Krishna's wives
Kaliya—Snake vanquished by Krishna
Kamsa—Tyrant king of Mathura, Krishna's uncle
Kanchanamala—Karna's wife
Kanka—Name taken by Yudhishthira in the thirteenth year of exile
Karna—Kunti's illegitimate son by the Sun God
Karthyayani—Name of a goddess
Kaunteya—A son of Kunti, applicable to any of the Pandavas
Kauravas—Collective name for the hundred sons of Dhritarashtra
Keshava—A name of Krishna
Keshi—Demon in the form of a horse
Kichaka—Brother-in-law of King Virata
Kripa—Drona's brother-in-law, tutor at the court of Hastinapura
Krishna—The eighth and supreme incarnation of Lord Vishnu

Kritavarma—General of the Yadava forces, who fought on the side of the Kauravas

Kubera—King of the *yakshas* and the god of wealth

Kuchela—Poverty-stricken friend of Krishna

Kukshama—Kuchela's wife

Kumbhakarna—Brother of the demon Ravana

Kunti—Mother of the Pandavas

Kuntibhoja—Foster father of Kunti

Kuru—Founder of the Kuru dynasty

Lakshman—Duryodhana's son

Lakshmana (1)—One of Krishna's wives

Lakshmana (2)—Durodhana's daughter, who married Krishna's son Samba

Lakshmi or *Lakshmi Devi*—Consort of Lord Vishnu Goddess of wealth

Madhava—A name of Vishnu/Krishna

Madri—Wife of Pandu, mother of Nakula and Sahadeva

Mahabali—A demon king, killed by Lord Vishnu in His incarnation as Vamana, the dwarf

Mahadeva—A name of Shiva

Manamohana—"One who bewilders the mind," a name of Krishna

Manigriva—Son of Kubera, the Lord of Wealth

Manmatha—God of love

Maya Devi (1)—Cook to Sambasura, incarnation of Rathi, the wife of Manmatha

Maya Devi (2)—Goddess who incarnated as Yashoda's daughter and was exchanged for Krishna

Mayan—Divine architect

Meghapushpa—One of Krishna's horses

Mirabai—Great medieval woman devotee of Lord Krishna

Mitrabinda—One of Krishna's wives

Muchukunda—An ancient king

Muka—A demon who took on the form of a boar

Murasura—Demon who lived in the moat in Narakasura's capital

Mushtika—Wrestler in the court of Kamsa

Nagnajit—King of Kosala, father of Krishna's wife Satya

Nakula—Fourth of the Pandava brothers

Nalakubera—Son of Kubera

Nanda—Krishna's foster father, chieftain of Gokula

Narada—Celestial sage

Narakasura—Demon king who was killed by Krishna

Narasimha—Fourth incarnation of Lord Vishnu, as the Man-lion

Narayana—The Supreme Godhead dwelling in His abode at Vaikuntha; a sage of that name

Nriga—King who took on the form of a garden lizard due to a curse

Panchajana—Demon from whom Lord Krishna procured His conch

Panchali—"Woman from Panchala"; another name for Draupadi

Pandavas—Collective name for the five sons of Pandu

Pandu—Father of the Pandavas, son of Ambalika

Parashara—A great sage, father of Vyasa

Parashurama—Sixth incarnation of Lord Vishnu

Parikshit—Son of Abhimanyu and Uttara, sole heir of the Pandavas

Parjanya—A name of Indra

Parvati—Consort of Lord Shiva

Paundraka—Foolish king who claimed to be the eighth incarnation

Pradyumna—Krishna's son by Rukmini

Prapati—A wife of Kamsa

Prasena—Brother of Satrajit, a Yadava chief

Pritha—Kunti's former name

Punardatta—Son of Guru Sandipani

Pundarikaksha—"The lotus-eyed one," a name of Krishna

Purochana—Man who had been ordered by Duryodhana to burn the Pandavas alive at Varanavata

Pururavas—Ancestor of the Pandavas

Purusha—Male aspect of God, formless ground of being, as opposed to Prakriti or the manifest universe, the creation; also used to denote masculinity.

Putana—Demoness sent by Kamsa to kill infants

Radha (1)—Krishna's favorite playmate in Vrindavan, said to be an incarnation of God in the aspect of the Divine Mother

Radha (2)—Karna's foster mother

Raivata—Father of Revati, the wife of Balarama

Rama (1)—Seventh incarnation of Lord Vishnu, whose story is told in the *Ramayana*

Rama (2)—Short form for Balarama

Ravana—Demon king of Lanka, who was killed by Shri Rama

Revati—Wife of Balarama

Rohini—Wife of Vasudeva, mother of Balarama

Rudra—A name of Lord Shiva

Rukmi—Brother of Rukmini

Rukmini—Princess of Vidarbha, first wife of Lord Krishna

Sahadeva—Youngest of the Pandava brothers
Shaibya—Name of one of Krishna's horses
Sairandhri—Draupadi's name in the thirteenth year of exile
Salva—King who owned the aerial car Saubha
Shalya—Uncle of Nakula and Sahadeva
Samba—Krishna's son by Jambavati
Sanatkumara—Son of Brahma (the creator), a sage.
Sandipani—Krishna's preceptor at Avanti
Sanjaya—Dhritarashtra's Prime Minister
Shantanu—Bhishma's father
Satyabhama—One of Krishna's wives
Satyavathi—Wife of King Shantanu
Satrajit—Father of Satyabhama
Satyavati—Yadava chieftain Krishna's close friend
Shakata—Demon in the form of a cart
Shakuni—Duryodhana's uncle and evil counselor
Shankachuda—Servant of Kubera
Shatadhanva—Former suitor of Satyabhama
Shesha—Adishesha, the celestial serpent
Shikhandin—Son of Drupada, first born as a girl
Shikhandini—Daughter of Drupada who later changed her sex
Shishupala—Prince of Chedi, Krishna's cousin
Shiva—Embodiment of the aspect of God associated with destruction, as opposed to Brahma and Vishnu, which see
Sita—Wife of Lord Rama
Skanda—General of the gods, son of Shiva
Shri—Name of Lakshmi, consort of Lord Vishnu
Shrutayudha—Son of Varuna, fought for the Kauravas
Shrutideva—Devotee of Krishna in the city of Mithila
Subhadra—Krishna's younger sister, wife of Arjuna
Sudama (1)—Garland maker at Mathura
Sudama (2)—Krishna's friend at Guru Sandipani's ashrama
Sudarshana—Name of Krishna's discus
Sugriva—Name of one of Krishna's horses
Sura—Ancestor of the Yadavas
Surabhi—Celestial, wish-yielding cow
Surya—Sun god
Surya Narayana—Lord Narayana in the form of the sun
Suyodhana—Another name for Duryodhana
Shveta—Son of Virata

Tantripala—Name of Sahadeva in the thirteenth year of exile
Trinavarta—Demon in the form of a cyclone
Trivakra—Name of the hunchback in Mathura whom Krishna straightened

Uddhava—Krishna's cousin and close friend as well as prime minister
Ugrasena—Father of Kamsa king of the Yadavas
Uluka (1)—Son of Shakuni
Uluka (2)—Brahmin who was sent as ambassador to the Kuru court
Upananda—An old herdsman at Gokula
Urvashi—The celestial nymph
Usha—Wife of Krishna's grandson Aniruddha
Uttama Purusha—The Supreme Person
Uttanga—An old Brahmin devotee of Krishna
Uttara—Virata's daughter, wife of Abhimanyu
Uttara Kumara—Virata's son

Vaasudeva—A name of Krishna, meaning son of Vasudeva
Vasudeva—Krishna's father
Valahaka—Name of one of Krishna's horses
Valala—Bhima's name during the thirteenth year of exile
Vamana—Fifth incarnation of Lord Vishnu, in the form of a dwarf
Vanamali—A name of Lord Vishnu/Krishna, meaning "wearer of
    the wild flower garland"
Varuna—Lord of the waters
Vasishtha—A great sage, great grandfather of Vyasa
Vayu—Lord of the winds
Vichitravirya—Father of Dhritarashtra
Vidura—Dhritarashtra's half brother, renowned for his wisdom
Vijaya—Sentry at Vaikuntha, Lord Vishnu's abode
Vinda—Prince of Avanti, Mitrabinda's brother
Virata—King of Matsya, at whose court the Pandavas spent their
    thirteenth year of exile
Vishnu—God in aspect of sustainer of the universe, the harmonizing aspect
    of the Supreme among the Trinity
Vishnuratha—Name of Parikshit, the son of Abhimanyu
Vishvakarma—Architect of the gods
Vraja—The area where Krishna spent his childhood, including
    Gokula and Vrindavan
Vyasa—Sage who composed the *Mahabharata* as well as many other epics
Vyoma—A demon

Yadava—Name of Krishna or anyone belonging to the Yadava clan

Yadu—Ancestor of the Yadavas from whom the clan got its name

Yashoda—Foster mother of Krishna

Yogamaya—The goddess of illusion

Yuyutsu—Illegitimate son of Dhritarashtra who fought on the side of the Pandavas

Yudhishthira—Eldest of the Pandava brothers

ॐ

*Bharthaya
namaha*

Homage to
the One who
governs all
beings

GLOSSARY

Abhisheka—Coronation or consecration ceremony in
  which water or milk is poured over the head

Adharma—Unrighteousness

Advaita—The teaching that all of the creation is the
  projection of the One; that only God exists

Agni—Fire; the god of fire

Agnihotra—Fire sacrifice

Agnihotri—Priest who makes offerings to the fire

Ahamkara—Ego

Akola—A type of tree

Akrura—Not cruel

Akshara—Nonperishable, immobile, immutable

Akshahridaya—A style of dice playing

Akshauhini—Battalion in an army

Akshaya patra—The bowl of plenty

Amavasya or *amavasi*—New moon night

Amrita—Nectar of the gods, which confers immortality

Ananda—Bliss

Ancharika—The missile which Arjuna used to kill Karna

Arghyapuja—Worship of the foremost person

Arupa—Without form

Artha—Wealth, worldly prosperity, self-interest

Artharathi—A chariot warrior who needs the help
  of many foot soldiers

Aryan—Pertaining to the Aryans, a people from
  central Asia that came to India; noble

Ashrama—A retreat for spiritual aspirants

Ashvamedha yajna—The Vedic horse sacrifice, usually
  conducted by a king in order to proclaim himself emperor

Astra—Weapon; missile

385

Asura—A hostile and demonic being

Atma or **Atman**—Individual soul, not of the ego or lower self aspect but the divine spark within

Atmavidya—The science of the Self

Atmic—Pertaining to the soul or Self

Aum—The mystic sound denoting the Supreme

Avabhritha-snana—The ceremonial bath taken after the conclusion of a holy rite

Avadhuta—An enlightened ascetic, usually noted for eccentric habits expressive of total freedom

Avatar—Descent or incarnation of God

Ayuddhapuja—Worship of weapons

Bethua—Type of spinach

Bhakta—Devotee

Bhakti—Love for God, devotion

Bharatavarsha—Ancient name for India

Bhava—A mood or attitude; a mode or manner of relating to God

Bhavana—Subjective state or feeling, often used in sense of one or other flavors of devotion to God

Brahmachari—One who is celibate in thought, word and deed

Brahmamuhurta—An auspicious time of the day, between 3:00 and 6:00 a.m.

Brahmastra—The missile of Brahma

Brahmin—A member of the priestly caste, regarded as the highest of the four Hindu castes, traditionally assigned the occupations of priest, scholar, and teacher

Buddhi—Intellect

Champaka—A type of flower

Chandala—An outcaste, a person at the bottom of the social order

Chid or **chit**—Consciousness

Chitta—Superconscious part of the mind

Dakshina—Gift to a holy person

Dakshinayana—The six months of the year from July to December

Deva—A god

Devi—A goddess

Dharma—Righteousness, duty; cosmic law

Dharmayuddha—A "just" war

Dhyana—Meditation

Digvijaya—Ceremony in which an emperor proves his suzerainty over all other kings by sending his warriors through their territories

Dvadasi—Twelfth day of the lunar fortnight

Dvapara—The third of the four ages that according toHindu cosmology, the earth cycles through. Krishna is said to have lived in this epoch, which ended at his death, at which time the fourth age, the Kali Yuga, began, in which we are said to be living today

Ekadashi—The eleventh day of the lunar fortnight, a day of partial fasting for many Hindus

Gandharva—A celestial singer, said to have a very beautiful voice

Gayatri—Hymn or mantra, repeated daily by many Hindus, to the sun as emblematic of God

Gita—Song

Gokula—Name of cowherd settlement where Krishna grew up

Gopa—Herdsman

Gopala—Cowherd boy

Gopi or *Gopika*—Milkmaid; usually refers to the milkmaids of Vraja, who are said to have been the purest devotees of Krishna

Guna—The three qualities that are said, in various combinations, to be the building blocks of the entire creation and all of its objects: *sattva* (harmony, peace, stillness), *rajas* (dynamism, stimulating activity, motion, desire) and *tamas* (dullness, lethargy, inertia, stupidity).

Guru—Spiritual guide and preceptor

Guru dakshina—Fee given to the guru at the end of the course of study

Gurukula—Hermitage of the guru

Ishvara—God.

Japa—Repetition of the Lord's name, as a yoga or spiritual disipline

Japa yoga—Repetition of the Lord's name

Jiva or *Jivatma*—The individual, embodied soul

Jnana—Spiritual insight or knowledge

Jnana-bhakta—A devotee of God who has realized with spiritual knowledge

Jnana mudra—The symbol of knowledge made by joining the thumb and forefinger

Jnani—A sage who has realized the highest wisdom

Kadamba—Type of tree

Kala—Time

Kali (Yuga)—The Dark Age, in which we are living at present, the forth of four cosmic ages of Hindu lore, the first being the Golden Age

Kali—Ferocious aspect of the Divine Mother, the female aspect of God

Kama—Desire or passion

Karana sharira—Subtle body

Karma—The law of moral cause and effect as it applies to an individual's thoughts, words and deeds

Karma phaladatta—He who gives the fruits of action

Karma yoga—The yoga of acting without desire for fruits, offering all results to God

Karnikara—Small red berry

Kaumodaki—Name of Krishna's mace

Kaustubha—Ruby on Lord Vishnu/Krishna's chest

Kavacha—Armor

Krishna maya—Filled with Krishna's love

Krishnavatar—Incarnation as Krishna

Kshara—Perishable, changeable, impermanent

Kshatriya—Second highest caste; the ruling and warrior class

Kshetra—Field; the manifest universe

Kshetrajna—Knower of the field, consciousness

Kundala—Earrings

Lila—Creation as the play of God; the actions of God, seen by Hindus as his play or lila

Linga—Stone symbol of Shiva

Linga sharira—Subtle body

Madhura (or *Madhurya*) *bhava*—Literally "sweet mood"; a mode of relating to God in which God is felt to be one's lover, as with the Gopis.

Maharatha—First category of chariot warriors

Mahayogi—Great yogi

Malati—Jasmine creeper

Mallika—Jasmine flower

Manas—Mind

Mantra—A name of God or sacred verbal formula that is repeated with reverence for its spiritually uplifting and purifying effect

Mantric—Pertaining to the *mantra*

Maya—The divine power of illusion that projects the world of multiplicity and conceals the transcendent unity

Moksha—Spiritual liberation

Mithya—Unreal, false

Mukti—Spiritual liberation

Muni—A silent sage; often a recluse

Nagastra—The cobra missile

Narayanastra—The missile of Lord Narayana

Nishkama—Without worldly desire
Nitya—Eternal
Nitya brahmachari—One celibate from birth
Niyamas—Observances which cultivate positive qualities;
    contentment, practice of spiritual disciplines, study and self-enquiry,
    and surrender to God

Padma-vyuha—Lotus formation in an army
Paduka—Footwear
Panchajanya—Krishna's conch
Pandit—Learned person
Paramatman—The Supreme Soul
Pitambara—Yellow garment, of kind Krishna is said to wear
Prakriti—Nature
pralaya—Deluge, dissolution; refers to destruction of the world at the
    end of the creation cycle
prapatti—Surrender
prasad—Remainder of food offered to God or a saint, eaten by devotees
    as consecrated food
puja—Ritualistic worship
punya—Spiritual merit
purnavatar—The supreme or complete incarnation
Purusha—God in formless, unmanifested aspect, as opposed to *prakriti* or
    nature, the creation or manifest universe
Purushottama—The Supreme Person

rajas—Quality of activity, passion, motion or desire, the *guna* (which see)
    that instigates action
rajasic—Passionate, full of action, dynamic
Rajasuya or *Rajasuya yajna*—A Vedic ceremony conducted by kings
rakshasa—Member of a cannibalistic tribe existing in ancient India, a demon
rakshasi—Female *rakshasa*
Ram rajya—The reign of Shri Rama, filled with prosperity and happiness The
    story is told in the *Ramayana*.
rasalila—The blissful dance of love, by which Krishna entertained the gopis
rishi—Seer, sage
rudraksha—Type of berry used in a rosary, considered sacred to Shiva

sabha—Hall, assembly
sadhana—Spiritual self-training and exercise
sadhu—Holy man
sahasranama—"Thousand names," a hymn containing a thousand names of God
sakhya bhava—A feeling of friendship; the mood in which the devotee relates to

God as a friend

samadhi—Superconscious state achieved in meditation

samarathi—Lesser type of chariot warrior

samsara—Life and worldly existence, the manifest universe in which reincarnation takes place

samsara chakra—The wheel of births and deaths

Sanatana Dharma—The Eternal Religion; correct name for Hinduism

sandal—Sandalwood

sandhya vandana—Worship of the sun in the morning and evening with the famous Gayatri hymn

sankhya yoga —Yoga of wisdom; yoga of discrimination between Self and non-Self

sannyasi—One who has renounced worldly life, a monk

Saranga—Name of Krishna's bow

sarati—Charioteer

sat—Existence, being, goodness, truth

sat-chid-ananda—Existence-knowledge-bliss, said to be a description of the essential nature of God

sattva—The *guna* (which see) of harmony, intelligence, and clarity; peace, stillness

sattvic—Pertaining to *sattva*; pure, spiritual, light

sena—Army

shakti—Power, force, energy, the divine or cosmic energy, usually thought of as feminine

siddhi—Supernormal power, attained through spiritual disciplines and austerites, said to be best avoided by many saints

soma—Medicinal plant used in *Vedic* ceremonies

Shrivatsa—An imprint on the chest of Lord Vishnu/Krishna

sthita prajna—One firmly established in wisdom, as described in the second chapter of the *Bhagavad Gita*

Sudarshana—Name of Krishna's discus

suta—A charioteer

svadharma—One's own law of action, one's own sacred duty, particular to each individual

svayam prakasha—Self-effulgent

svayamvara—Marriage by the personal choice of the bride

tamas—The *guna* (which see) that hides or darkens, giving rise to inertia, sloth, and ignorance

tamasic—Pertaining to *tamas*

tapasya—Spiritual discipline or austerity, such as meditation; concentration of spiritual force

tandava—The cosmic dance of Lord Shiva

tilaka—Auspicious mark on the forehead

trigunatita—One who is beyond the control of the three *gunas*

tulsi—A type of basil plant, beloved by Krishna

tyagi—A renouncer, one untouched by worldly desires

Upanishads—Certain portions of the Vedas dealing with the Supreme

uttama—Highest.

Uttama Lila—The Supreme Game

Uttama Purusha—The Supreme Person

uttarayana—The six months of the year from January to June

Vaishnava—A devotee of God in the form of Lord Vishnu

vanamala—Garland made of wildflowers and tulsi, worn by Lord Vishnu/Krishna

varnashrama dharma—Duties pertaining to one's caste and state in life

vatsalya bhava—A feeling of love toward children; the mood in whch the devotee
     assumes the attitude of a loving parent towards God, who is experienced
     as a Divine Child, such as Mary and Joseph towards Jesus or Yashoda and
     Nanda towards Krishna.

Vedanta—General term for the Upanishads; the nondualistic philosophy
     based on the Upanishads

Vedantin—One who practices or expounds Vedantic philosophy

Vedas—The most ancient scriptures of Hindism, four in number

Vedic—Pertaining to the Vedas

vibhutis—Extraordinary manifestations or powers of the Lord

vibhuti yoga—Chapters in the *Bhagavad Gita* and the *Uddhava Gita* dealing
     with the manifestations of the Lord

vijaya dasami—Literally the "victorious tenth," the tenth day of a worship
     ceremony of Durga, the so called wrathful aspect of the Divine Mother, Kali,
     who is God as the manifest universe

vina—A stringed instrument with a very sweet sound

vishada—Sorrow, despondency

Vishvarupa—Literally "universal form"; refers to form of God, which Krishna
     showed to Arjuna in the *Bhagavad Gita*, that is the entire manifest universe

Vishvatman—The Cosmic Soul

Vraja—The area where Krishna spent his childhood as a cowherd boy,
     including Gokul and Vrindavan

vrittis—Mental modifications, thoughts

yajna—Sacrificial ceremony, usually involving fire

yaksha—A kind of spirit being.

yamas—Practices of moral virtues: nonviolence, truthfulness, nonstealing, continence, and freedom from greed

yoga—Union or achieving oneness with the Supreme; spiritual disciplines

yogamaya—The Lord's power of illusion

yogashastra—The science of achieving union with God; treatises in which both the theory and practice of yoga are combined

yogi—One who is striving to achieve union with the Supreme

Yuvaraja—Heir apparent to a throne

Hari Aum Tat Sat

Blue Dove Press will be offering a number of audio cassettes by Devi Vanamali, including *Nitya Yoga*, a twelve cassette program on the Bhagavad Gita. They will be available in November, 1995.

The name Blue Dove signifies peace and spirituality. Blue Dove Press publishes books by and about saints and sages of all of the religions of the world as well as on other spiritually and inspirationally oriented topics. To receive our free catalog of books available at your bookstore or directly from the publisher or for the catalog of audio cassette programs by Devi Vanamali, contact:

Blue Dove Press
Post Office Box 261611
San Diego, CA 92196
phone: 800–691–1008
FAX: 619-271-5695